URSULA K. LE GUIN

Recent & forthcoming *Paradoxa* titles

All *Paradoxa* titles are available for $24, postage included to destinations within the U.S. For destinations in Canada or Mexico, add $10 per title, for all other destinations, add $20.

URSULA K. LE GUIN

Published by *Paradoxa*
Vashon Island, Washington 98070

ISBN: 1-929512-20-1
ISSN: 1079-8072

First published in 2008

Address all orders, queries and changes of address to *Paradoxa*, P.O. Box 2237, Vashon Island, WA 98070, USA. Fax: (206) 567-5711. Email: Info@Paradoxa.com.

Authorization to photocopy items for internal or personal use, the internal or personal use of specific clients (excluding the article author), and for educational classroom use, is granted by *Paradoxa*, provided that the appropriate fee is paid directly to Copyright Clearance Center, 222 Rosewood Drive, Danvers MA 01923, USA. Telephone: (508) 750-8400, Fax: (508) 750-4470.

Visit our Web Site: http://www.paradoxa.com

Paradoxa no. 21
Ursula K. Le Guin

Table of Contents

Boldly to Re-Venture:
New Writing on the Works of
Ursula K. Le Guin

Sylvia A. Kelso
James Cook University, Townsville, North Queensland, Australia

Introducing a critical volume on Ursula K. Le Guin in 2008 is a task that, to outrageously misappropriate a famous Australian poem, well might make the boldest hold "his" breath. Given the current accumulation of journal articles, essay collections, and full-length books on Le Guin's work, bold indeed must be the soul who dares assume the usual omniscient, omnipotent editorial voice, implying that he or she has not only read all the original texts, but all the secondary work, and now knows better enough to pontificate upon it all.

It hardly seems necessary to supply the obligatory career sketch with an author like Le Guin: especially since said author is currently garnering starred reviews for *Lavinia*, a return to the historical novel, last seen from her with *Malafrena* (1979), which, we usually assume, grew out of the Orsinian tales composed in her oldest imagined country of all. Nevertheless, between There and Here intervenes a writing span of more than half a century, if we include those early unpublished inventions, not only studded with notable works, but in my view, growing stronger as it goes. The nearest parallel I can find is W. B. Yeats, whose fruitful span is also astonishing, and whose work "improves," from the melopoeia of the "Celtic Twilight" and classics like "The Sally Gardens," to the bareboned landmarks of final poems like "Under Ben Bulben." Nor is it difficult to apply to Le Guin, as is so often done with Yeats, the adjective "great."

It's personally heartening to me, a late starter in publication, that over ten years of that writing span lie before Cele Goldsmith published "April in Paris" in 1962. Any writer would hope to emulate the ensuing progress: five, six short stories appearing in the mid '60s, along with three novels, before the quantum leap in 1969. The short story "Winter's King," the prelude, in so many senses, to *The Left Hand of Darkness*.

Nor does it seem necessary to labour *Left Hand*'s import. Le Guin's first Hugo and Nebula awards—so affirming to a young writer, as she noted in a recent interview (Chee, "Breaking")—the visibility the novel brought to SF as a whole, when a literary luminary like Harold Bloom edited the first collection of critical essays; most importantly, perhaps, to

Le Guin as well as to others, her first public engagement with feminism, and her first visibility to feminists.

More gallons of ink must have been expended on *Left Hand of Darkness* than any other Le Guin opus, except perhaps *The Dispossessed* (1974). The blaze of attention has tended to mask her other remarkable achievements of the '70s. Stories that have become SF classics, like "Vaster than Empires and more Slow (1971), "The Day before the Revolution"(1974), and of course, "The Ones Who Walk Away from Omelas"(1973). Cheek by jowl with *Left Hand*, the first Earthsea trilogy—I shall use editorial force majeure here to apply Darko Suvin's suggestion that the later Earthsea books form a second series—then *The Lathe of Heaven* (1971), *The Word for World is Forest* (1972), and in the middle, *The Dispossessed* itself. Beyond that, *The Language of the Night* (1979) establishing Le Guin's lyrical, unruly, and individual critical voice with essays like "From Elfland to Poughkeepsie," "Science Fiction and Mrs. Brown," and "Why Americans Are Afraid of Dragons." Also *Orsinian Tales* (1976), and a book of poetry, *Wild Angels* (1974)... does the woman ever eat or sleep?

Not, apparently, in the '80s, which produced another critical collection, *Dancing at the Edge of the World* (1989) with such pieces as "The Carrier Bag Theory of Fiction." Short stories are assembled in *The Compass Rose* (1982), with such memorable inclusions as "The New Atlantis" and "The Author of the Acacia Seeds," then the further collection, *Buffalo Gals* (1987), which to stories of "Animal Presences" added the viewpoint of rocks, or in "View of the Road," trees.

Along with these come two further poetry books, and the novels *The Eye of the Heron* (1983), when Le Guin herself judges she first made the full transition to a female-centred novel (Chee, "Breaking"), and the major achievement of the decade, *Always Coming Home* (1985), a work where Utopian social thoughts unite, at last, with a Utopic experiment in form.

At this point most writers would be resting on their laurels. Not Le Guin. The '90s open with the first of the two new Earthsea novels, *Tehanu* (1990), in itself a major achievement, topped by *The Other Wind* (2001), which rewrites not merely Earthsea's gender politics but its cosmology, as the series moves into its most powerful resistance to Le Guin's longtime model, the binary oppositions of Jung and the Tao. These traditional hierarchies of light/dark, male/female, white/black, good/bad, now turn emphatically on their archetypal heads.

Along the way, we have five story collections, including *Tales from Earthsea* (2001), the "back-stories" of both Earthsea trilogies, *Searoad* (1991) Le Guin's "realist" variations on Living in Oregon, *Four Ways to Forgiveness* (1995), with its notable novellas, and two more. Oh, yes, did I mention the three books of poetry, the book of criticism, *Steering the Craft* (1998), and the translations, one from Spanish, the other of that proverbial mind-cracker in both Chinese and European critical milieux, the *Tao Te Ching* …?

Nor is the hard-pressed critical commentator allowed to relax in the 21st Century. So far we have another book of poetry, *Incredible Good Fortune* (2006), two more Spanish translations, the critical collection *The Wave in the Mind* (2004), with Le Guin's thoughts on the importance of rhythm, in particular; and two story collections, *The Birthday of the World* (2002) and the suite of post-modern parables, *Changing Planes* (2003). To open the millennium on the novel front, we have *The Telling*, in 2000, followed by the Annals of the Western Shore. *Gifts* (2004), *Voices* (2006) and *Powers* (2007)—categorized as YA, but as unlike most of the works scrambling to slipstream behind Harry Potter as any text could be. And in 2008, *Lavinia*, which tells the second woman's story running beside *The Aeneid*—not unhappy Dido's, but that of the woman Aeneas did marry.

The critical commentary is beginning to rival that on the *Tao Te Ching*. From here I discern some three critical generations, and three distinguishable though not mutually inaccessible faces, to use a geographical metaphor, by which critics and theorists most often approach the *oeuvre* that comprises Mt. Le Guin.

Notable from the beginning has been the Taoist face, first mapped, perhaps, by Douglas Barbour in 1973. Unearthing evidence of the Tao's presence and function in Le Guin's oeuvre is an ongoing critical enterprise, as in Dena C. Bain's and Elizabeth Cummins' (then Cogell) 1970s work, soon supplemented by critiquing uses of the Tao in Le Guin. At this point the Taoist face may also be traversed by feminist critics.

As second-wave feminist thought has worked on the philosophical underpinnings of women's oppression, the question of binaries and superior/inferior oppositions has been a lasting focus. And since Taoism is so apparently thoroughly binary, Le Guin's long fidelity to its imagery and its paradigms has collected some serious flak along with simple explorations and explanations. An article by Jewell Parker Rhodes in the late '80s, which actually targeted the use of the androgyne in *Left Hand of Darkness*, also pointed out the problems with a binary that can simplify and essentialize a man/woman opposition that '80s feminists were eagerly, angrily, or desperately finding had already fractured into Women. As Audre Lord asked Mary Daly at the end of the '70s, Who you calling Woman, white girl?

The feminist face of Mt. Le Guin is one of the most frequently traversed, from the early strictures of Joanna Russ on that male/female hero in *Left Hand of Darkness* (90-91) to the pointed remarks of Sarah Le Fanu in the '80s on the dead weight of the liberal humanist hero at the centre of the great '70s novels (137). Despite Le Guin's own public espousal of feminism, and its often militant infiltration of her work from *Left Hand* on, as feminism has diversified, among the praise, so have the critiques.

Most frequently, such critiques centre on Le Guin's enduring heterosexuality, her determination that love, usually heterosexual, can bridge even galaxies, and what she herself has called the central topic of her work: marriage ("Introduction to *Planet of Exile*," 143). Outliers such as Elyce Helford, using post-colonial as well as feminist theory, have complained about what appears appropriation of non-white cultures, as Le Guin herself attempts to redress the not always repressed racial bias in, particularly, SF.

Among these critiques, essentialism is not infrequently mentioned, especially from the '90s on. First Woman had to become Women, then, in the burgeoning field of masculinity studies, Man almost at once became Men. I myself find that some of Le Guin's more exhilarating essays produce a certain draft of second thoughts up the back of the neck. "The Carrier Bag Theory of Fiction" is a good case. It's very righteously valorizing to think that WE, by virtue of our mere sex, don't produce those tales "starting *here* and going straight *there* and THOK!" (169) as heroes', and by implication men's stories do. That we, out "wrest[ing] a wild-oat seed from its husk, and then another" (165) could produce the novel like a "medicine bundle" (169) that Le Guin herself sewed so brilliantly in *Always Coming Home*.

But, memory ripostes, is all men's work so linear? What, for instance, about Laurence Sterne? The last thing *Tristram Shandy* does is go from here to there.... Even more uncomfortably, there's Homer, and after him, Vergil. "In medias res" was coined for Greek and Roman epics, the template of "heroic" tales. Those loops may not be a carrier bag, but a (human) appendix, perhaps? And there's always the grand-daddy of modern novels, with those wanderings of Don Quixote; not to even begin mentioning modern novelists like Robbe-Grillet.

There has been rather less critique on the third face of Mt Le Guin, which the Utopists map. Here too, there was much early unearthing of sources, as with the anarchism of Kropotkin (Smith), and siting, particularly of *The Dispossessed*, among the famous '70s SF heterotopias and "critical" Utopias (Moylan, Somay) The second generation, following very short upon if not overlapping the first, began to critique aspects of *The Dispossessed*, in particular its heterosexuality, as with Samuel Delany's pioneering "To Read *The Dispossessed*" (1977). Numerous commentators have followed, whose debates frequently spill over onto the mountain's feminist face. An entire recent collection, reviewed by Mike Cadden in this volume, debates the possibly bourgeois nature of *The Dispossessed*.

As these expeditions continue, a variety of new climbing tools—I am unable to resist this slightly passé extension of the metaphor—have appeared, from post-colonialism to queer theory as well as masculinity studies, and eco-feminist or other environmentally based approaches. Le Guin specialists, such as Elizabeth Cummins, Mike Cadden, and Warren Rochelle, have emerged, whose scholarly focus has been largely on her texts. Indeed, Mt. Le Guin is beginning to resemble *Beowulf* in Tolkien's essay, "The Monsters and the Critics": a massive site—not, in this case, a ruin—that provides an inexhaustible source of academic building material (8).

Reading for this volume, I also began to discern the three critical generations adumbrated above. Though these blend and overlap, the first includes pioneering approaches and source identification, among which should also be counted Le Guin's entry in the first anthology of feminist SF criticism, Marleen Barr's *Future Females* (1981). The second generation, who began to debate and critique earlier with Russ and Delany, is now extending into the third, who, just as *Beowulf* is being re read against post-modern theories, are coming to scale the faces and re-view the famous prospects of Mt. Le Guin with new voices, and sometimes, different tools.

Le Guin's international standing appears in the history of this volume. The first call for papers brought responses from academics and non-academics across three continents. Beyond the US, abstracts and proposals came from the UK, from Sweden, Germany, Hungary, Italy, Hong Kong, and Australia. At least two of the essays here use English as a second or even third language, and some of their authors have read or are studying Le Guin in second language programs in non-English universities.

Deliberately, the scope of the volume also exceeds the purely academic. At its heart, we have a new essay from Le Guin herself, "Living in a Work of Art," an aesthetic/philosophical pondering on beauty, and whether beauty might instill moral awareness, especially if encountered in youth. These thoughts spring from a memoir that opens a door—yes, the metaphor is also deliberate—on Le Guin's own youth: the experience of growing up in a Maybeck house in San Francisco, a house where early and continuous experience of aesthetic beauty may foster an expectation of order and harmony that might in turn lead to an active desire for moral clarity.

As a direct foil to Le Guin's essay comes April Kendra's memoir, "On Almost Meeting Le Guin." Kendra speaks for all those readers who have discovered, cherished, lived with and loved Le Guin's work, but will never reach—or want to reach—the public forum of an academic article to convey what she means to them. Kendra expresses the compelling urges, on the one hand to pass that feeling back to the writer, and on the other, the sheer overpowering terror—it's not too strong a word—of meeting such a writer in the flesh.

At the other end of the spectrum, a Le Guin specialist lifts the mask of academic anonymity to tell how her work has shaped his life. Warren Rochelle's "fan-letter" is an exemplary mix of the personal, the academic, and the political, and a fitting closure, I feel, to this volume's essays.

The properly academic essays form two sections bracketing the personal "Interludes." It's notable that of our original proposals, four wanted to work on *The Lathe of Heaven*, more than on any other single work, while three had in mind a mixture of *Lathe* and *Left Hand of Darkness*. The section on Earlier Work opens with a Marxist/Utopian reading of *The Dispossessed*, as the culmination of a theoretical essay from a founder of SF theory, Darko Suvin. There can be very few academics working on SF who have not, at some point, used some of Darko's ideas, from "cognitive estrangement" to "the novum" and on. This essay is a notable addition to his oeuvre.

As a foil to Suvin's "Cognition," we have Beth Snowberger's essay on *The Lathe of Heaven* and *The Dispossessed*, reaching a very different position on Mt. Le Guin after traversing much the same ground, applying not merely new theoretical tools, but new tools drawn direct from science. In this case, superstring theory. This essay made one referee, a quantum physicist, actually go out and read *The Dispossessed*.

Amy Clarke supplies another new voice with her third generation feminist reading of the entire Earthsea series, a succinct and also up-to-date handling of cruces that feminist critics have discussed for years. Then Vera Benczik re-visits *The Left Hand of Darkness*, where, using no particularly new theoretical tools, she nevertheless achieves a fresh vista on that much traced journey over the ice. The third generation in all these essays is particularly evident in the references. Clarke, Keating and Snowberger all cite Suvin on Le Guin; Benczik and Keating cite Barbour and Bain; Suvin himself cites a current female professor of philosophy, Katherine Z. Elgin.

The fourth new voice in the group also ascends a very familiar face, but with an approach of unusual depth. Kathy Keating re-views *The Lathe of Heaven* via a discussion of Taoist thought that first contextualizes and then engages the *I Ching*, the "oracular" older work behind the *Tao te*

Ching and *Chuang Tzu*. The consequent reading of *Lathe*, especially in its relation of narrative movement and structure to the *I Ching*'s sense of "change" and the method of reading its hexagrams, breaks genuinely new ground in Le Guin criticism.

After the "Interlude" comes a section on Newer Work, where well-known SF critic Rich Erlich examines the satirical elements in *Always Coming Home*, with particular interest in attacks on monotheism. To Le Guin, it appears, as to Donna Haraway, "One is too few, and two is only one possibility" (180). Such possibilities appear in the work of other third-generation critics, firstly as Linda Wight sites the suite of stories in "The Matter of Seggri" (1993) against previous feminist SF texts using the trope of separatism. She does not completely endorse Le Guin's attempt to show how gender inequity can oppress men as well as women, but the essay sites "Seggri" discerningly in the ongoing field of both masculinity studies and feminist SF.

Howard Sklar, in contrast, bases a study of Le Guin's writing skills upon reader-response theory. He discusses the concepts of and differences between empathy and sympathy, and then provides an illuminating reading of the novella "Betrayals" (1994) from *Four Ways to Forgiveness*. Kasi Jackson, in contrast, examines Le Guin's animal stories against a history of feminist debates over the praxis and theory of science, which moves from animal behaviour in specific to science in general, with the work of Karen Barad and Donna Haraway, casting light on a theoretical field along with the stories to which it is applied.

Donna Haraway makes a differently inflected appearance in Jenny Gal-Or's performative reading of "Newton's Sleep"(1991). Here the essay takes on the diffractive, fracturing, boundary-blurring nature of Haraway's style as well as her agenda, as Gal-Or demonstrates Le Guin's fictional fulfillment of Haraway's ideas. Equally feminist, but working from detailed comparisons of Le Guin's texts and Robert Scott's account of the *Discovery* voyage, Traci Thomas-Card shows precisely how, in the frequently anthologized "Sur"(1983), Le Guin critiqued, undercut and deconstructed the archetype of the Polar explorer, and at least one concept of heroism.

In the process Thomas-Card often cites Marleen Barr's study of "Sur." And with a combination of new Le Guin text and first-generation critical voice, Marleen Barr herself reads *Changing Planes* against the changing planes, in both senses, of New York, the US, and the world in general after 9/11. Barr's knowledge of fiction both inside and outside SF, her enthusiasm for Le Guin's work, and her very pertinent comparison to another pattern-maker, needle-worker Ita Aber, provide a fitting finale for the purely academic sections.

There are gaps not unnaturally left in (re)viewing such a prolific author. We have no essay, due to illness and other problems, on Le Guin's poetry, or/and her translation, as the two converge in her work with Gabriela Mistral's poems. We have nothing on her children's books, or the position of her essays in the now formidable fields of SF or feminist SF criticism. We have nothing on later work such as *The Telling*, or the Annals of the Western Shore. Limited by space and time from tackling these projects, I found my own thoughts turning to the importance of rhythm to and in Le Guin's work as a whole.

Rhythm, as opposed to scansion, eludes most contemporary critical frames. It is not susceptible to ideological analysis, cultural or gender theory, and attempts to relate it to race can produce alarming stereotypes. One theoretical foothold is Julia Kristeva's post-Lacanian formulation of language as two "dispositions" (133): the "symbolic" or "attribute of meaning" (134), which is continually invaded by the "semiotic." For Kristeva this springs from pre-Oedipal drives (136-7) which perpetually disrupt the symbolic, particularly with rhythm: poetic language produces a "pulsation of sign and rhythm," (139), a fracturing, like Celine's ellipses (141) that "impose a music, a rhythm," which can "wipe out sense" (142. Nevertheless, the symbolic can never be completely erased (134). Purely semiotic utterances are literal non-sense.

Two essays from *The Wave in the Mind* indicate Le Guin's longstanding interest in this difficult and nebulous topic. The first uses rhythm to define the central structural unit in *The Lord of the Rings*, reading the finished text at the level of part, chapter and incident (98-107). Most critical discussion of rhythm operates either at this level, or by close reading sentences and paragraphs, which I soon found sliding toward aesthetic judgements and discussion of vocabulary, rhythm's Siamese twin.

Despite these tendencies, such analysis finds a rich field in Le Guin's work. But in this example, rhythm at sentence level foreshadows the tenor of the work as a whole:

> Current-borne, wave-flung, tugged hugely by the whole might of ocean, the jellyfish drifts in the tidal abyss. (*Lathe of Heaven*, 7)

The sentence's four opposing blocks, two compound adjectives, two clauses, echo the rhythm of ocean on beach: Here—and-back. Here—and-back. But this continued change within continuity, of dynamic alternations and oppositions, is also the pattern of the yin/yang dynamic as Kathy Keating reads it in the *I Ching*. And her reading argues that this is the overall structure of *Lathe of Heaven*, where change occurs, and re-occurs, and re-occurs again, fluidly, unexpectedly, in the "same" places, yet never entirely the same.

At the same time, the two compound adjectives and "tidal abyss," "tugged hugely," lean to the more "embroidered," to use Yeats' term, side of vocabulary. Elsewhere *Lathe* reaches a contrasting simplicity:

> ... they made love. Love doesn't just sit there, like a stone, it has to be made, like bread; re-made all the time, made new. (136)

Here too the rephrased repetition echoes the central motif. But the closing clauses, rhythmically necessary, actually detract slightly from the antithesis of bread and stone, and the entirely homely simile.

Words and rhythm blend more perfectly later, this time in a literal vision:

> I can stand here in the old pasture where there's nothing but sun and rain, wild oats and thistles and crazy salsify, no cattle grazing, only deer, stand here and shut my eyes and see: the dancing place, the stepped pyramid roofs, a moon of beaten copper on a high pole over the Obsidian. If I listen, can I hear voices with the inner ear? Could you hear voices, Schliemann, in the streets of Troy? If you did, you were crazy too. The Trojans had all been dead three thousand years. Which is farther from us, farther out of reach, more silent—the dead, or the unborn? Those whose bones lie under the thistles and the dirt and the tombstones of the Past, or those who slip weightless among molecules, dwelling where a century passes in a day, among the fair folk, under the great, bell-curved Hill of Possibility? (*Always Coming Home* 4)

Here there are no rhythmic superfluities. The long opening clause checks into the shortening phrases that throw up first the whole section's motif, the wild oats, then brake to a heavy pause with the colon at "see." Then the actual vision appears, returning through a triple of lengthening syntactic units to the run that ends with a singing polysyllable "on a high pole over the Obsidian."

A series of shorter sentences bring a turn of aspect, from Here to There, to Troy and the past, and the central, unpunctuated statements that end with the roll, reminiscent of *Urn Burial*, of "three thousand years." After which the paragraph moves into its final rhetoric, another mix of simple and polysyllabic words, "thistles," "dirt" "tombstones," and the rhythm begins to lift with "slip weightless among molecules" to the small sections bringing the polysyllable that closes both paragraph and image in an echo of "Obsidian," as it underlines the bravura flourish of "bell-curved," on the Hill of "Possibility."

Like Yeats, Le Guin does seem to move toward simplicity, or at least austerity, in both the rhythm and content of her later work. As *Always Coming Home* opens among wild oats and thistles, *A Wizard of Earthsea* starts among village goats. But such is a beginning is traditional for fantasy heroes, as is Ged's prompt move to higher things. Magic. Palaces. Wizard schools. *Tehanu*, on the other hand, starts in farm-life, descending at times to the edge of poverty, and the austerity of a few goats, and a patch of bean vines (251-52), is where it ends.

At the same time, *Tehanu* can show the skill of experience making less do more, rather than more do more, as in the previous quote. Here is a key "data dump" between Tenar and Moss:

> 'Dearie,' she said, 'a man, you mean, a wizardly man? What's a man of power to do with us?'
> 'But Ogion –'
> 'Lord Ogion was kind,' Moss said without irony.
> They split rushes for a while in silence.
> 'Don't cut your thumb on 'em, dearie,' Moss said. After which 'Ogion taught me. As if I weren't a girl. As if I'd been his prentice, like Sparrowhawk. He taught me the Language of the Making, Moss. What I asked him, he told me.'
> 'There wasn't no other like him.'
> 'It was I who wouldn't be taught. I left him. What did I want with his books? … I wanted to live, I wanted a man, I wanted my children, I wanted my life.'
> She split reeds neatly, quickly, with her nail.
> 'And I got it,' she said.
> 'Take with the right hand, throw away with the left,' the witch said. 'Well, dearie mistress, who's to say? Wanting a man got me into awful troubles more than once. But wanting to get married, never! No, no. None of that for me.'
> 'Why not?' Tenar demanded.
> Taken aback, Moss said simply, 'Why dear, what man'd marry a witch?' And then, with a sidelong chewing motion of her jaw, like a sheep shifting its cud. 'And what witch'd marry a man?'
> They split rushes. (*Tehanu*, 55-56.)

Where playwrights can score dialogue with significant silences, writers have to rely on "business" — more words. So here the apparently trivial "women's" occupation of splitting rushes for baskets operates as a suite of variations to indicate pause and emphasis, which the rhythm underscores. The first leisurely, "They split rushes for a while in silence," quickens to the snaps, echoing Tenar's emotion, of "neatly, quickly, with her nail." Then, "They split rushes," cuts this phase of the scene with a brevity only foreshadowed in the "simple" quote from *Lathe*.

In contrast is Kalessin's first arrival, emerging from Tenar's reverie on the cliff:

> She watched the slow beat of the wings, far out in the dazzling air. Then she got to her feet, retreating a little from the cliff's edge, and stood motionless, her heart going hard and her breath caught in her throat, watching the sinuous, iron-dark body borne by long, webbed wings as red as fire, the out-reaching claws, the coils of smoke fading behind it in the air.
>
> Straight to Gont it flew, straight to the Overfell, straight to her. (41)

The rhythm here is almost somnambulistically smooth, the second sentence extraordinarily long, commas again weighting the critical words: "sinuous," "claws," "fire." The next paragraph opens with a classic triple repetition whose final word links by assonance to the previous paragraph: "her" with "air," and again, "air." The sound device suggests how closely this approaches actual poetry. But the type of rhythm here also moves us past the felicities of skill and experience in a finished text, to adumbrate rhythm's earliest and perhaps most vital role in the work.

This role is substantiated in the second essay from *The Wave in the Mind*, where Le Guin cites Woolf's own full quote: this implies that without the right rhythm, words themselves will not assemble. The inchoate idea will not "unlock." Then Le Guin describes writing *Tehanu*:

> ... the story came in flights—durations of intense perception ... which most often occurred while I was waking, early in the morning.... Then I had to get up, and go sit outdoors, and try to catch that flight in words. If I could hold to the rhythms of the dragon's flight, the very large, long wingbeats, then the story told itself. ("Collectors, Rhymesters and Drummers," 183-84)

Though Le Guin probably means the pattern of the narrative overall, "very large, long wingbeats" describes precisely the rhythms of the quote above. And where Woolf indicates that writing cannot begin without the right rhythm, Le Guin tells the consequences of its loss.

> ... When I lost the beat, I fell off, and had to wait ... until the dragon picked me up again. (184)

A famous anecdote preserves a perhaps similar but less happy experience. The person from Porlock is generally credited with breaking Coleridge's "dream" from which "Kubla Khan" reputedly began. I think it as likely the person broke the rhythm that runs swift, unerring and dream-sure through the surviving piece of the poem: the relic of a dragon flight that Coleridge, unlike Le Guin, could never reclaim.

These instances present rhythm as more than a part or product of writing: it is also writing's enabler, or even its source. For Kristeva, rhythm, like all semiotic elements, springs from the *chora*, the female body that the Symbolic Order must repress to allow language (137). But many writers derive inspiration from some other sub-terrain. In "The Fisherwoman's Daughter," Le Guin repeats Woolf's description of the writer, "letting her imagination down into the depths of her consciousness" (227). Narrating the progress of a novel in *Misery* (1990), Stephen King refers repeatedly to ideas produced by the guys down "in the sweatshop" (132,173, 180). And R.L. Stevenson divided writing between "the part done when I am sleeping," by "the Brownies," and the editing and marketing, "done when I am up and about" (207).

Consequently, inspiration is often sourced in the unconscious, the sub-conscious, or even, as I have heard some SF and F writers call it, the "lizard brain." But the true lizard brain is in the cerebellum or pons, concerned with breathing and heartbeat and "automatic function." And the "unconscious" and "sub-conscious," like the "*chora*," are metaphorical constructs. A more likely biological source is supported by empirical research.

The human right brain was long read as the weaker twin, even as a "vestige" of the dominant left (Edwards, 31). Then Roger Sperry's work showed the right brain possesses an equally massive form of processing, but parallel rather than sequential (32): where the left brain is verbal and analytical, the right is "global, rapid, complex, whole-pattern, and spatial" (33). Betty Edwards, author of a classic work on teaching art, considers either "brain" can actually lead, or they can work together, or even keep knowledge from each other (34). In fact, the double function has long been intuited, but in the usual hierarchical binary, the right brain has been identified with the literally sinister, supposedly weaker hand in the left/right opposition (35-37).

Scientific evidence now shows that the right brain lets us "understand metaphors ... dream ... create new combinations of ideas" (38.) All crucial to the basis of writing, as for thought itself. Edwards teaches art students to "see" differently (50-53), and the results are spectacular (18-19). As she herself puts it, the students must learn to silence the left brain: to overthrow their acquired symbol system (81-82.) Which is precisely how Kristeva theorises "poetic language" (re)-invades symbolic sense with unruly semiotic elements, a process in which rhythm plays a major part. The tie of rhythm and creative inspiration is then explicable in both Kristevan and empirical terms. Rhythm comes from the pre-Symbolic *chora*. Rhythm, like metaphor, springs from the nonverbal right brain. But how does this help writers, if language is a left-brain mode?

Edwards points out that in fact, "L-mode" and "R-mode" thinking are not physically limited. Two percent of right-handers mediate language in the right brain, eight percent in both, while 15% of left-handers do the same, and 15% use the right brain alone (42). Being left-handed, it seems I actually have a better chance of writing with L and R-mode combined. But the statistics indicate some right-handers do too. Perhaps we can all learn to draw on the right brain, like Edwards' students. Or perhaps, supremely gifted writers like Le Guin and Coleridge, who acknowledge or imply their reliance on rhythm for impact but also for inspiration, have already learned to do so. To reclaim Le Guin's own metaphor, they do not merely ride the dragon: they know how to set the dragon loose.

Acknowledgements and Gratitudes

First in chronology, Dave Willingham and I would wish to acknowledge Alleen Nilsen, the original proposed editor of this volume, for setting up the "seed" seminar which produced the first collection of possible papers, and for retaining and passing them on. Without Alleen's energy and generosity, this volume would not exist.

I myself owe a huge debt to Dave, who first conceived the project, later asked if I'd co-edit, and has been a fount of knowledge and a tower of strength (often both at once), through the process of drafting a call for papers, collecting submissions, and the more intensive work of actually editing/revising contributions. Apart from his critical perception and editorial expertise, his meticulous type-setting is a boon, but valued above all has been his encouragement.

Thanks must go next to everyone who submitted to this volume. Winnowing out the final inclusions proved one of the most difficult, at times painful, processes of my academic life. I would particularly like to recall and thank those whose complete or near-complete contributions we were unable to include, through illness, duplication of essays, pressure of other work or family problems. Whether or not your work appears here, your generosity of thought, energy and time was essential to the whole.

Sincerest thanks are due to the referees, most extremely busy academics, who, for no recompense, read and perceptively critiqued submissions. Almost everyone I asked, usually completely out of the blue, was able to do so, some almost at once, and sometimes more than one essay. Your kindness, help, and actual reports were indispensable.

I owe a last and special thanks to the published contributors, who both astonished and delighted me with their patient responses to my often detailed, sometimes radical, and at times very difficult requests for revision, and who in almost every case surpassed not merely their previous work but the best of my expectations. It has been a real pleasure as well as matter for vicarious pride to oversee your work as it reached its final form.

Works Cited

1. Barbour, Douglas. "*The Lathe of Heaven*: Taoist Dream." *Algol: A Magazine about Science Fiction* 11.21 (1973): 22-24.

2. Bain, Dena C. "The 'Tao Te Ching' as Background to the Novels of Ursula K. Le Guin." In *Ursula K. Le Guin*, ed. by Harold Bloom. 1980. New York: Chelsea House, 1986. 211-33.

3. Chee, Alexander. "Breaking Into the Spell. An Interview with Ursula K. Le Guin." http://www.guernicamag.com/interviews/505/breaking_into_the_spell/ Accessed 26.4.08.

4. Cogell, Elizabeth Cummins. "Taoist Configurations in *The Dispossessed*." In *Ursula K. Le Guin: Voyager to Inner Lands and to Outer Space*, ed. by Joe De Bolt. Port Washington: Kennikat Press, 1979. 153-79.

5. Delany, Samuel R. "To Read *The Dispossessed*." In *The Jewel-Hinged Jaw*. New York: Berkley, 1977. 218-83.

6. Edwards, Betty. *The New Drawing on the Right Side of the Brain*. 1979. New York: Jeremy P. Tarcher/Putnam, 1999.

7. Haraway, Donna. "A Cyborg Manifesto: Science, Technology, and Socialist-Feminism in the Late Twentieth Century." *Simians, Cyborgs, and Women: The Reinvention of Nature*. London: Free Association, 1991. 149-81

8. Helford, Elyce Rae. "Going 'Native': Le Guin, Misha, and the Politics of Speculative Literature." *Foundation* 71 (1997): 77-86.

9. Kristeva, Julia. "From One Identity to an Other." In *Desire in Language: A Semiotic Approach to Literature and Art*, ed. by Leon Roudiez. Oxford: Basil Blackwell, 1981. 124-47.

10. Lefanu, Sarah. *In the Chinks of the World Machine: Feminism and Science Fiction*. London: Women's Press, 1988.

11. Le Guin, Ursula K. *Always Coming Home*. 1985. New York: Bantam, 1986.

12. —. "The Carrier Bag Theory of Fiction." 1986. In *Dancing at the Edge of the World: Thoughts On Words, Women, Places*. 1989. New York: Harper and Row, 1990. 165-170.

13. —. "Collectors, Rhymesters and Drummers." In *The Wave in the Mind*. Boston: Shambhala, 2004. 171-84.

14. —. "The Fisherwoman's Daughter." In *Dancing at the Edge of the World: Thoughts On Words, Women, Places*. 1989. New York: Harper and Row, 1990. 212-37.

15. —. "Introduction to *Planet of Exile*." In *The Language of the Night: Essays on Fantasy and Science Fiction by Ursula K. Le Guin*, ed. by Susan Wood. New York: Perigee, 1979. 139-43.

16. —. *The Lathe of Heaven*. 1972. London: Panther, 1972.

17. — "Living in a Work of Art." *Paradoxa* no. 21.

18. —. "Rhythmic Pattern in *The Lord of the Rings*." In *The Wave in the Mind*. Boston: Shambhala, 2004. 95-107.

19. —. *Tehanu*.1990. New York: Bantam, 1991.

20. Lorde, Audre. "An Open Letter To Mary Daly." Extract. In *Feminisms: A Reader*, ed. by Maggie Humm. New York: Harvester Wheatsheaf, 1992. 138-39.

21. Moylan, Tom. *Demand The Impossible: Science Fiction and the Utopian Imagination*. New York: Methuen, 1986.

22. Rhodes, Jewell Parker. "Ursula Le Guin's *The Left Hand of Darkness*: Androgyny And The Feminist Utopia." In *Women and Utopia: Critical Interpretations*, ed. by Marleen S. Barr and Nicholas D. Smith New York: UP of America, 1983. 108-20.

23. Russ, Joanna. "The Image of Women In Science Fiction." In *Images of Women in Fiction: Feminist Perspectives*, ed. by Susan Koppelman Cornillon. Bowling Green: Bowling Green University Popular Press, 1972. 79-94.

24. Smith II, Philip E. "Unbuilding Walls: Human Nature and the Nature of Evolutionary and Political Theory in *The Dispossessed*." In *Ursula K. Le Guin*, ed. by Joseph D. Olander and Martin Harry Greenbergs. York: Taplinger, 1979. 77-96.

25. Somay, Bulent. "Towards an Open-Ended Utopia." *Science-Fiction Studies* 11. (1984): 25-38 Tolkien J.R.R. "Beowulf: The Monsters and the Critics." 1937. In *The Monsters and the Critics and Other Essays*. 1983. Ed. by Christopher Tolkien. London: HarperCollins, 1993. 5-48.

Sylvia Kelso is an adjunct lecturer at James Cook University of North Queensland, Australia. Her PhD. was on the interactions of feminism and the modern Gothic and SF, 1968-89. She has published on SF, fantasy, the Gothic, (horror), and the creative writing process, in *Science Fiction Studies*, *Journal for the Fantastic in the Arts*, *Foundation*, *Paradoxa: Studies in World Literary Genres* and *The New York Review of Science Fiction*. She is a member of the Editorial Board for *Femspec* and *Paradoxa*. Her novel *The Moving Water* was short-listed for best fantasy novel in the 2007 Aurealis Australian genre fiction awards.

Cognition, Freedom,
The Dispossessed as a Classic

Darko Suvin
Lucca, Italy

To Don Theall, who hired me to teach within our common
humanist horizon.

PART 1. On Ursula Le Guin's *The Dispossessed* and its
Liberating Librations: A Commentary[1]

1.1. A Pointer to Fictional Articulation, Poetry, Freedom

I have argued elsewhere at length three points about narrative in
general.

First, that fictional narrative can be understood as based on *thought
experiments and models* (cf. Suvin, "Can People"). Re-presentation in
fiction takes model images of people and spacetimes from non-fictional
ways of understanding and reconstructing social reality into a process
which, in works that can be taken as good or significant cases, develops
roughly as follows: the new schemes of how people live together
glimpsed by the writer go about subverting the heretofore received
fictional norms of agential and chronotope structuring; but as this is
happening, the schemes themselves are in turn modified in and by some
autonomous principles of fictional articulation. All of this together
enables the resulting views of relationships among people, elaborated

---

[1] My thanks for help with materials go to Johan Anglemark and the Carolina
Library in Uppsala, Sweden, and to Rich Erlich for comments and editing assistance
much beyond normal collegiality. James Bittner was the first to broach thoroughly
and interestingly in his 1979 U of Wisconsin dissertation. many central problems
of TD, and I think with pleasure of our discussions at that time, from which much
must have continued to work in me subconsciously.

Where useful, I adopt the abbreviation: TD = *The Dispossessed*. The citations
are identified by chapter number: page number, keyed to the Avon 1975 paperback
edition of TD. Unacknowledged translations are all mine.

Fairness in advertising: I have read an interview by Ursula Le Guin, the source
of which escapes me, in which she credits me for pointing out there should be a
separate thirteenth chapter. I remember well reading the MS. of TD and two small
textual changes I gingerly proposed (she accepted one and firmly rejected the other)
but I don't remember at all this proposal. I don't doubt I committed it, and I'll gladly
take whatever small credit thus accrues to me, though I much doubt Le Guin's highly
colourful dramatization of our dialogue.

by the restructured piece of fiction, to return into our understanding represented and reformulated *with a cognitive increment* that can range from zero through very partial to very large. This better understanding permits what Brecht called intervenient, effective or engaged thinking (in the technical sense of meshing or being engaged in gear). It allows the reader to pleasurably verify old and dream up new, alternative relationships: to *re-articulate*, in both senses of the word, human relationships to the world of people and things. As Aristotle argued in *Politics* (I.2), humans necessarily live in political communities. Thus, all central human relations are, in this widest sense, communal or communitarian, what we humans have or are in common: significant fictional re-presentation of relations among people presents the reader with the possibility of rearticulating our political relationships.

Second, that any text unfolds a *thematic-cum-attitudinal field*, and that fiction does so by necessarily presenting relationships between fictional agents in a spacetime. While my argument in "Metaphoricity and Narrativity" is more complex, my contention is that all texts are based on a certain kind of metaphoricity, but that narrative texts add a concrete presentation in terms of space and time, the *chronotope*. The argument ends with the definition of narrative as a finite and coherent sequence of actions, located in the spacetime of *a possible world* proceeding from an initial to a final state of affairs, and *signifying possible human relationships*: the agential signifiers or vehicles can, of course, be gods, Martians, Virtues, talking animals or Bauhaus machines, and the chronotopic ones any spacetime allowing for coherent events. All fictional texts are in this view "analogical mappings" (Gentner 109) of one semantic domain upon another. Among the great virtues of Le Guin's *The Dispossessed* is the fact that such a mapping is discreetly foregrounded in it by means of Odo's Analogies.

Third but not least, my essay "The Science-Fiction Novel as Epic Narration," argued that there is a central distinction to be made between what I called *the epic and mythological horizons* and their ways to articulate fiction. In principle, the epic events are presented as contingent and not fully foreseeable, and thus historical and as a rule reversible, while the mythological events are cyclical and predetermined, foreseeable descents from the timeless into the temporal realm. The verse or prose epic therefore foregrounds the plot, which was a foregone conclusion in mythology. Thus, an epic text will be meaningful only if each significant event is the result of a value *choice*, as opposed to a pre-established or automatic sequence reposing on unquestionable fixed values of the mythological text. That choice constitutes the poetry of post-mythological prose, opposed to the myth's incantatory repetitions of always already given names and patterns. Choice shapes the agential relationships within the narration in unforeseeable and therefore potentially new and better ways. It is the narrative equivalent and rendering of freedom.

I could easily document how much of the above is consonant with Le Guin's views about fiction. But I think it is better if I do so on the material of TD, and restrict myself here only to one essay, her thoughts on narrative ("Some"). She focusses, in Odo's "ethical mode," on the fact that all actions imply choices and entail consequences: "[Narrative] asserts, affirms, participates in directional time, time experienced, time as meaningful" (39). In what I would call the syntactic or epistemological mode, she cheers George Steiner's suggestion "that statements about what does not exist and may never exist are central to the use of language," which often means a "refusal to accept the world as it is"—though she rightly notes that celebrating some choice aspects of a world is often as significant (43-44). The "scientific" focus on statements of fact is ably swatted as a noxious fly:

> Surely the primary, survival-effective uses of language involve stating alternatives and hypotheses. We don't, we never did, go about making statements of fact to other people, or in our internal discourse with ourselves. We talk about what may be, or what we'd like to do, or what you ought to do, or what might have happened: warnings, suppositions, propositions, invitations, ambiguities, analogies, hints, lists, anxieties, hearsay, old wives' tales, leaps and crosslinks and spiderwebs. (44)

Le Guin's conclusion speaks to what I also want to come to as a main horizon of TD--a kind of freedom:

> The historian manipulates, arranges, and connects, and the storyteller does all that as well as intervening and inventing. Fiction connects possibilities, using the aesthetic sense of time's directionality defined by Aristotle as plot; and by doing so it is useful to us. If we cannot see our acts and being under the aspect of fiction, as "making sense," we cannot act as if we were free.
> Only the imagination can get us out of the bind of the eternal present, inventing or hypothesizing or pretending or discovering a way that reason can then follow into the infinity of options, a clue through the labyrinths of choice, a golden string, the story, leading us to the freedom that is properly human, the freedom open to those whose minds can accept unreality. (45)

****

I should note here that my essay has three further sections in this Part 1 constituting an extended commentary on TD, and called "1.2. A Hypothesis on *The Dispossessed*"; "1.3. Some Buttressing"; and "1.4. Simulsequentiality, or Preaching by Example." They have been omitted here due to the essay's length, but will resurface in a planned book of mine.

PART 2. Some Propositions about Cognition in Science and Fiction

2.0.

Le Guin's TD is that actually rather rare thing, a real *science fiction* novel: a work of fiction seriously exploring science—both as a human way of knowing and as human social activity. To understand this better, I proceed here with a discussion of cognition. In the process I wish to deal with two varieties of science: one, the positive older sister ("S1"); the other, the troublesome younger brother, let's say for now, problematic ("S2"). But first I need to consider science as a way of asking how to understand the universe, that is, science in terms of epistemology. I shall then come to fiction as cognition.

2.1. Central Orientation Points for Epistemology

I am not aware of a systematic basis for epistemology we could today use, but I postulate that our interpretations of what is knowledge or not, and how can we know that we know, are largely shaped by the "framework of commitments" we bring to them. Catherine Z. Elgin usefully formulated in 1982 a strategic "soft" skepticism that still allows such commitments:

> Philosophy once aspired to set all knowledge on a firm foundation. Genuine knowledge claims were to be derived from indubitable truths by means of infallible rules. The terms that make up such truths were held to denote the individuals and kinds that constitute reality, and the rules for combining them ... were thought to reflect the real order of things. — This philosophical enterprise has foundered. Indubitable truths and infallible rules are not to be had. (Elgin, 183)

Instead, thinking always begins with working approximations based on "our best presystematic judgments on the matter at hand" (Elgin 183). As we advance toward understanding, we often discover these approximations are untenable or insufficient—but there is no other ensemble to be had.

Scientists of a positivist inclination will discourse on evidence, in the sense of proof. Evidence is important, but it is always "theory-laden," determined by "our conception of the domain and ... our goals in systematizing it ..." (184-85). The *New York Times* claims it brings "All the news that's fit to print," but who determines what is fit news? Alternatively, a tradition from the more radical Skeptics through the Post-Modernists and extreme constructionists has questioned whether there is a reality to be known and whether, if it is there, we could know it or talk about it. Neither tradition is satisfactory. The horizon I am sketching is characterized by Elgin and Nelson Goodman in 1988 as "reject[ing] both absolutism and nihilism, both unique truth and the indistinguishability of truth from falsity" (3). A univocal world—*the* fixed reality out there—has been well lost, together with the Unique Final Truth, divine or asymptotically scientific, and other Onenesses of the monotheist family. A sense of panic at the loss of this clear world, at the loss of theological certitude, not only permeates dogmatists of all religious and lay kinds, but has also engendered its symmetrical obverse in an absolutist relativism. How is a third way possible beyond this bind?

It can begin by recognizing that right and wrong persist, but that rightness can no longer be identified with correspondence to a ready-made, monotheistic Creation, but must be created by us, with skill and responsibility. Goodman and Elgin think that truth as usually conceived is too solidly embedded in faiths and certitudes of monotheistic allegiance to be safe and useful; categories and argument forms that are products of continual human cognition are better instruments for practical use, testable for situational rightness. Truth is strictly subordinate to rightness in this approach, and this rightness is dependent on our various symbol systems (cf. Aronowitz vii-xi and passim). One consequence is that science loses its epistemic primacy: like art and everyday perception, "[it] does not passively inform upon but actively informs a world" (Elgin 52-53). The arts and sciences overtly repose on intuitions, which are for science buried in their axioms as indubitable certainties. Whether you prefer Marx's or Balzac's description of 19th-Century France will depend on your general or even momentary interests, but they're in no way either incompatible or subsumed under one another: and both are cognitive.

Sketching an operative epistemological way can further proceed by recognizing that there are still some logical ways if not of defining truth then at least of defining untruth (Goodman and Elgin 136). As Orwell might have put it, all opinions are constructed and relatively wrong or limited, but some are more wrong than others. This holds pre-eminently for those I would call *monoalethist* (from **alethe**, truth): all those—from monotheists to lay dogmatists (Fascists, Stalinists, and believers in the Invisible Hand of the Market)—who hold they have the Absolute Truth, including the belief that relativism is absolute. Only belief in the absolute right—Haraway's "God-trick" ("Situated" 589)—is absolutely wrong.

2.2. Cognition Is Constituted by and as History: Multiple Sources and Methods

In a remarkable passage right at the beginning of *Works and Days*, Hesiod invents the myth, or allegory, of the two Erises, the benign and the malign one (I: 11-26). The bad Strife favours wars and civil discords. But the firstborn is the good Strife, whom Zeus has placed at the roots of the earth, for she generates emulation: one vase-maker or poem-singer envies the other, the lazy and poor peasant imitates the industrious and richer one. This *polar splitting of concepts* seems to me a central procedure of critical reason, dissatisfied with the present categorizations and trying to insinuate opposed meanings under the same term. I shall adopt this Hesiodean procedure for knowledge and then science.

The principal ancestors to this endeavour may be found in Marx and to a minor, but still significant degree in Nietzsche. I take from Nietzsche that belief in the correspondence of intellect to thing/s—an Aristotelian correspondence of knowledge to reality—is an ideal impossible to fulfil and leads to faking and skepticism. This Truth is a lie, and whenever erected into a system, as in religion and in Galileian science, compels lying. Any cognition developed against this fixed horizon partakes for Nietzsche of a huge, finally deadly "illusion" (*Zur Genealogie* 128). The constructivist account, on the other hand, is a creative transference of carrying across, in Greek **meta-phorein**, whence his famous hyperbolic statements that knowing is "Nothing but working with the favourite metaphors" (*Philosophy* xxxiii). For Nietzsche wisdom arises out of the knowledge of nescience: "And only on this by now solid and granite basis of nescience may science have arisen, the will for knowing on the basis of a much more powerful will, the will for *unknowing*, for the uncertain, the untrue! Not as its opposite, but—as its improvement!" (*Jenseits* 24). Nietzsche is not necessarily a source for Le Guin, she rightly prefers the Dao, but nescience and non-being are important ideas for her. Yet take care: in terms of Le Guin's worlds and ours, Nietzsche's "untrue" is the opposite of the illusionistic, and rules out angels, UFOs, Mickey Mice, and the Invisible Hand of the Market. Nescience demolishes The Monolithic Truth but retains verifiability for any given situation, and denies the illusions that so often lead to fanatical belief.

More useful still is Marx, whose relevant views I discuss at length elsewhere ("Living" and "On the Horizons"; cf. also Aronowitz, esp. ch.s 2 and 3). Suffice it here to say that Marx had a dual view: on the one hand he rejected positivistic approaches, pouring his scorn on the falsities of bourgeois political economy, but simultaneously he chastised all attempts to subject science or cognition to "a point of view from the outside, stemming from interests outside science" (MEW 26.2: 112). *Capital* itself is presented as a project of "free scientific research," which assumes the task of clarifying the inner relationships of the phenomena it deals with without imposition from the outside, and in particular against "the Furies of private interest" (MEW 23:16). His two major, consubstantial cognitive insights are first, that societal injustices are based on exploitation of other people's living labour; but second, the insight that the proper way to talk about the capitalist exploitation which rules our lives is not in the **a priori** form of dogma, a closed system, but in the **a posteriori** form of *critique*. Legitimate cognition is epistemically grounded in the process it describes, and strategically developed by articulating a radically deviant stance against a dominant in a given historical situation (cf. Marcuse). After Marx, it should be clear that "All modes of knowing presuppose a point of view.... Therefore, the appropriate response to [this is]... the responsible acknowledgement of our own viewpoints and the use of that knowledge to look critically at our own and each others' opinions" (Levins 182). The rightness of a theoretical assertion depends on evidence as interpreted by the assertor's always socio-historical needs, interests, and values.

Approaching science from this epistemological basis, I suggest the Hesiodean procedure of splitting the institutionalized horizons of science-as-is fully off from those of a potentially humanized science-as-wisdom, which would count its casualties as precisely as the US armed forces do for their own (but not for those they bomb). I wish I could call the latter "science" and the former something else, perhaps technoscience, but I do not want to give up either on science or on technology. I shall provisionally call the firstborn, good science "Science 1" (S1) and the present one, whose results are mixed but seem to be increasingly steeped in the blood and misery of millions of people, "Science 2" (S2). The medieval theologians would have called them **sapientia** vs. **scientia**, though in those days they optimistically believed **scientia** could be tamed.

These are ideal types only, intermixed in any actual effort in most varied proportions: also, the beginnings of S2 are in S1, and amid its corruption it retains certain of its liberatory birthmarks to the present day. Nonetheless, the fixation on *domination* and the consubstantial *occultation of the knowing subject* in S2 "is a particular moment in the division of labor" (Levins 180). The avoidance of capricious errors "does [not] protect the scientific enterprise as a whole from the shared biases of its practitioners." In sum, "The pattern of knowledge in science is ... structured by interest and belief.... Theories, supported by megalibraries of data, often are systematically and dogmatically obfuscating." It is not by chance that "major technical efforts based on science have [led] to disastrous outcomes: pesticides increase pests; hospitals are foci of infection; antibiotics give rise to new pathogens; flood control increases flood damage; and economic development increases poverty" (Levins 183 and 181).

Bourgeois civilization's main way of coping with the unknown is aberrant, said Nietzsche, because it transmutes nature into concepts with the aim of mastering it as a more or less closed system of concepts. It is not that the means get out of hand but that the mastery—the wrong end—*requires* wrong means of aggressive manipulation. S2 is not only a cultural revolution but also a latent or patent *political* upheaval. The scientific, finally, is the political.

There are strong analogies and probably causal relations between the "search for truth, proclaimed as the cornerstone of progress" and "the maintenance of a hierarchical, unequal social structure," within which capitalist rationalization has created the large stratum of "administrators, technicians, scientists, educators" it needed (Wallerstein, *Historical* 82-83). In particular, it created the whole new class of *managers*. As Braverman's *Labor and Monopoly Capital* pointed out, "to manage" originally meant to train a horse in his paces, in the manège (67). F.W. Taylor did exactly this—he broke "the men," calling in his *Shop Management* for "a planning department to do the thinking for the men" (Braverman 128). Later, since "machinery faces workers as *capitalized* domination over work, and the same happens for science" (Marx, *Theorien* 355), control was built into the new technologies. During the 19th Century, "science, as a generalized social property" (S1) was replaced by "science as a capitalist property at the very center of production." This is "the scientifico-technical revolution" (Braverman 156), while technoscientific ideology becomes, as Jameson notes, "a blind behind which the more embarrassing logic of the commodity form and the market can operate" (*Singular* 154). Already by the early 1960s, 3/4 of scientific R&D in the USA was corporate, financed directly or through tax write-offs by the Federal government, that is, by money taken from tax-payers, while profits went to corporations (164-66). It is almost a century by now that scientific research is mainly determined by expected profits to the detriment of S1 (cf. Kapp 208ff.), where such research is not neglected for purely financial speculation.

The supposition that science does not deal in values, which began to be widely doubted only after the Second World War, had as "its actual function to protect two systems of values: the professional values of the scientists, and the predominant [status quo] values of society as they existed at that moment...." (Graham 9, and cf. 28-29). The stances of "objectivity" and erasure of the subject actively fostered a treatment of people (workers, women, patients, consumers) as objects to be manipulated as a part of nature. As a hierarchical institution devoted to manipulation, S2 was easily applied to "human resources" too: the Nazi doctors' experiments were only an extremely overt and acute form of such **Herrschaftswissen,** knowledge used for domination.

We must ruefully accept, with due updating, Gandhi's harsh verdict about science: "Your laboratories are diabolic unless you put them at the service of the rural poor" (Gandhigram). S2 is Power (over people), S1 is Creativity (within people). In this view science is a usable and misusable ensemble of cognitions, not an absolute truth we can approach asymptotically. It is principally a "by whom" and "for what" — an "impure" productive relationship between, for example, workers, scientists, financiers, and other power-holders, as well as an institutional network with different effects upon all such different societal groups, which can and must become less death-oriented. S1 must be based on holistic *understanding*, which would englobe and steer analytical knowledge (Goodman and Elgin 161-64). This would not at all diminish its impressive status as institution; on the contrary, S1 would finally be as truly liberating, both for its creators and its users, as its best announcers have, from Bacon to Wiener and Gould, claimed it should be. It could at last embark not only on the highly important damage control of its capitalist misuse, but also on a full incorporation of aims that would justify Nietzsche's rhapsodic expectation: "An experimenting would then become proper that would find place for every kind of heroism, a centuries-long experimenting, which could put to shame all the great works and sacrifices of past history" (*Fröhliche* 39) — truly, a joyous science. It would have to ask: what questions have not been asked in the last 400 years, and for whose profit have we ignored them?

In 1932, sensing the worse to come, Brecht asked:

> Faced with all these machines and technical arts, with
> which humanity could be at the beginning of a long, rich day,
> shouldn't it feel the rosy dawn and the fresh wind which signify
> the beginning of blessed centuries? Why is it so grey all around,
> and why blows first that uncanny dusk wind at the coming of
> which, as they say, the dying ones die? (GBFA 21: 588)

He went on for the rest of his life to worry at this image of false dawn
through the example of Galileo. His final judgment was that Galileo,
representing reason, science, and the intellectuals, failed, and helped the
night along, by not allying himself with a political dawn-bringer. But
then, we might ask today, where was he to find a revolutionary class
who wanted such an ally, and where indeed was Brecht to find it after
1932? In his poem "1940" Brecht matter-of-factly noted:

> From halls of learning
> Emerge the butchers.
>
> Hugging their children tightly,
> Mothers scan with horror the skies
> For the inventions of the scientists.

So, what would an updated, sophisticated S1 mean—how can we
really get a science for (the) people, science wedded to easing human
life and to a humane quality of life? This is a question dealt with by
fictional cognition in TD.

2.3. Narrations in Science and Fiction

Kant had a major difficulty in the *Critique of Judgment:* judgments deal
with particulars, but how is one to account for any particular, notoriously
contingent and as it were anarchic, for which the general concept has still
to be found? He sometimes finessed this by using examples, which hide
a generalized allegory: the particular Achilles is the example of Courage
in general. This welcome subterfuge pointed already to the untenability
of claims for science as *the* best or only knowledge, since an example
partakes both of image and of an implied story, as Achilles before Troy.
Kant's example reintroduced history as a story, enabling us to understand
why the *Iliad* was an unsurpassed cognitive fount for the Hellenes. It
follows that science and other ways of cognition (say art) do not relate

as "objective" vs. "subjective" or strong male vs. weak female, but as human constructions guided by different constraints for coherence and different conventions of anchoring or "entrenchment."As Bruner argues, the arts are differently entrenched from sciences: they implicitly cultivate hypotheses, each set of which requires a Possible World but not the widest possible extension for applying that set in our World Zero, that is, testability in the scientists' sense; rather, they must be recognizable as "true to conceivable experience" or verisimilar (52 and passim). For one thing, in science it may be a "long duration" additiveness, until the paradigm and the powerful institution supporting it changes. Yet this is not unknown in art: think of Athenian or Renaissance performance, supported, like science, by institutions. This is also the ideal horizon of the more decentralized institutionalization of publishing in periodicals and books, in the case of poetry or the novel, operating with statistical projections. Institutionalization then turns out to be necessary for both, but it goes from top down in strict proportion to domination, in this case by capital: from bottom up is the tradition of S1 and most art, created by independent artisans or workshops.

What are then a few of the relevant differences and similarities between the cognitive horizon and route of science (S1) and of creative writing, poetry in the wider sense? The horizon, source, and finally the aim (the Supreme Good) of both is to my mind the same: making life, that precious and rare cosmic accident, richer and more pleasurable; fighting against entropy by making sense, in different ways, of different segments of nature, very much including human relationships. In brief, both are cognitive tools and pursuits.

More particularly, both deal with *situations* against a horizon of human interest and evaluation. The formalizations of S2 try to taboo this horizon and to erect the very specialized, fenced-in lab as *the* exemplary situation-matrix extrapolatable to reality, though this matrix fails immediately and obviously in all social and biological studies, say primate research. The chronotope of an S2 experiment is manipulated so as to be mathematically explainable, the human agents must be kept out. Yet both the situations of fiction and today's science are constructed or taken up, for different but converging purposes, co-defined by the interests of the subject constructors. Each has necessarily a formal closure—involving among other matters a beginning, middle, and end, as Aristotle phrased it for plays—but they are often open-ended, and their multiplicity is always such. Further, a longer work such as a theory or a novel, is articulated like a chain or a tapeworm, in a series of delimited events which stand together as segments to result in a final unity. When, in several branches of quantum mechanics, and similarly in catastrophe theory, a whole battery of models is regularly used, and "no one thinks that one of these is the whole truth, and they may be mutually inconsistent" (Hacking 37), the differences to Balzac's *Comédie humaine* series or the set (the macrotext) constituted by the poetry of — say — Byron, Shelley, and Keats remain obvious, but the overall formal similarities as cognitive pursuits do not deserve to be slighted either (cf. Spivak on poetry as cognition 115ff.).

Formally speaking, "atom" is the name of an agent in a story about "chemistry," just as "Mr Pickwick" is the name of an agent in a story about "the Pickwick Club" (Harré 89), though there are different rules of storytelling in the two cases. "[Theoretical f]ictions must have some degree of plausibility, which they gain by being constructed in the likeness of real things," concludes the middle-of-the-road historian of science Harré (98). If we take the example of literary and scientific "realism," we find they are consubstantial products of the same attitude or bearing, the quantifying thisworldliness of bourgeois society. This is a contradictory stance, with great strengths, obvious from Cervantes and Fielding on, based on looking steadily at this world as a whole, and with increasingly great dangers based on possessive reification of bourgeois atomized individualism. The dangers surface when institutionally sanctified science stakes out a claim to being the pursuit of the *whole truth* in the form of *certainty*, while the apparently weaker and certainly more modest Dickens escapes them. S2 science likes to think of itself as deductive. However, as a planet's map is regulated and shaped by the grid of cartographic projection, so is any system based on a deductive principle, for example the Aristotelian excluded middle or the Hegelian necessarily resolved dialectical contradiction. And this principle is also a kind of meta-reflection about, or methodic key to, the system that is, in its obviously circular turn, founded on and deduced from it. When a philosophical or scientific system is developed as a finite series of propositions *culminating* in a rounded-off certainty, its form is finally not too different from the 19th-Century "well-made," illusionistic stage play; no wonder, for they both flow out of the Positivist orientation, where decay of value leads to despair. The Lady with the Camellias and the Laws of Thermodynamics are sisters under the skin: both show a beautifully necessary death.

2.4. The Poet's Politics as Semantics, or Thinking as Experience

It was the accepted norm not only for ancient Greece but also for Leibniz or Kant that poetry or fiction convey some transmittable understanding of human relationships, so that Baumgarten called his foundational *Aesthetica* of 1750 the "science of sensual cognition." For many poets it then became logical and ethical to think of translating such cognition into politics as concrete human relationships of power.

How may artistic creators *professionally* participate in politics? This was no problem for poets in the era of Homer, Alcman or Solon, but became complicated when political units grew larger as well as more obviously based on divergent class interests and the attendant oppression of a major part of the body politic. Plato clearly felt poets were worrisome competitors to his philosopher-king and advocated banning all those who didn't fit his norms. After many painful experiences, including the splendid but today not often applicable attempts of the Romantics to either participate directly as bards of revolt or turn away totally from politics—which means leaving it to the status quo—we may today follow the lead given by Rancière and posit something like the following:

The poet-creator can (in fact, cannot but) participate in politics but only paradoxically. This means, literally, that s/he is one who swerves from reigning commonplace opinions by infringing old usages and meanings and, implicitly or explicitly, creating new ones. Epicure's ruling principle of the atoms *swerving* from the automatically straight path may stand as the great ancestor of all creative methods and possibilities (cf. Suvin,"Living"); from Epicure's interpreter Lucretius it passed on—via Cyrano—to Swift, Wells, and thence bedded down into the foundations of SF. As a place of truthful thinking not sundered from feeling, verse and prose poetry—and SF—have often filled in the voids left by institutionalized science and institutionalized philosophy, and of course by most institutionalized politics. Poetic creation did this by combining generalization, irremediably wedded to concepts, to justification from immediate sensual, bodily experience which is (thus far) much more difficult to falsify or disbelieve. What I am getting at may be approached through Caeiro/Pessoa's verse—with a demurral against his identifying thinking with sterile conceptuality—in *The Guardian of Flocks* (poem 46):

> I try to say what I feel
> Without thinking of what I feel.
> I try to lean the words against the idea
> And to avoid the corridor
> Of thought to lead me to the word.

This creative attitude, however, immediately leads to an intimately personal paradox of living in politics as an anti-politics. All that is

commonly taken for politics—for us, say, since the effects of the
antifascist wars, such as peace and the Welfare State, have been largely
or fully expunged—is alien and inimical, where not actively threatening
and deadly. Our immediate major poetic ancestor, Rimbaud, was led to
exasperation at having to reconcile his deep hatred of the bourgeoisie
and existing society with the irrefragable fact of having to breathe and
experience within it:

> ....industrialists, rulers, senates:
> Die quick! Power, justice, history: down with you!
> This is owed to us. Blood! Blood! Golden flame!
> All to war, to vengeance, to terror.... Enough!
>
> -   -   -   -   -   -
>
> ...I'm there, I'm still there. ("Qu'est-ce pour nous...,"
> 113)

The obverse of this "assez vs. j'y suis toujours" aporia is Thomas
More's great coinage of utopia: the radically different good place which
in our sensual experience is not here, but must be cognized—today, on
pain of extinction. What is not here, Bloch's Yet Unknown, is almost
always first adumbrated in fiction, most economically in verse poetry.
From many constituents of the good place, I shall here focus, as does
Rancière (92-93), on *freedom*—Wordsworth's "Dear Liberty" (*Prelude* l.
3) which translates the French revolutionary term of *liberté chérie*—that
then enables security, order, creativity, and so on. The strategic insight
here seems to be that the method or *epistemic principle* of great modern
poetry from Rimbaud on (and prose too, in somewhat differing ways),
is freedom seen as the possibility of things being otherwise. This is to
be understood as interaction between what is being said and how it is
being said. Poetic freedom is a historically situated, political experience
of the sensual, which is necessarily also a polemical swerve from and
against the doxa, in favour of fresh cognition. The common, brainwashed
understanding includes much of what has in the past truly been liberating
politics but has retained only a few impoverished slogans from its heroic
ages (the liberal, communist, and antifascist ones) when it directly
flowed out of human senses. Therefore, "creators have to retrace the
line of passage that unites words and things" (Rancière). And in prose,
I would add, the line that unites human figures and spacetimes by means
of plot and of metaphoric clusters (see Suvin, "On Metaphoricity" and
"Heavenly"). As we see in Le Guin's novel, with the desire, personified in
Shevek, for "a landscape inhabitable by human beings" (TD 10: 268).

To give one example: what is at least one focus around which *The Dispossessed* turns or librates? It might be found in one of its richest semantic clusters, that of *possession*, melding as it does the meanings of ownership and of something stronger than obsession: a subjection to demoniacal powers. The possessors possess equally things, on Urras, and power over others—on Urras and, more rarely but crucially, in the power center of Anarres. Yet the coin has another side: things, that is, reified human relationships, are in the saddle and ride mankind—or manunkind, as e.e. cummings would phrase it:

> You the possessors are possessed. You are all in jail. Each alone, solitary, with a heap of what he owns. You live in prison, die in prison. It is all I can see in your eyes—the wall, the wall. (TD 7: 184)

The terminological family of "possessed" is a set of brilliant portmanteau words, but it has a not unimportant drawback. The sense of possession on Urras as capitalist alienation of and from central characteristics of humanity calls forth on Anarres a dispossession that is simultaneously a) lack of property ownership, b) lack of demonic possession (class power), and c) lack of things. The last term of the triad is on the whole negative—as testified by the permanent siege mentality on Anarres enforced by the drought and culminating in the near-famine of ch. 8. Politico-economically speaking, the last term of the triad muddles up the positive meanings of dispossession.[2] Le Guin's equally wondrous neologism "propertarian" (noun and adjective) has an analogous drawback: it is a mixture of legal and ethical language, without political economy, so that it might be mistaken for ascetic refusal of worldliness. I'm not sure the word capitalism is ever used in *The Dispossessed*: only its consumer effects are shown in Shevek's astonishment at money, the shopping mall, etc.

The question that then arises is, in theological language, why do the wicked prosper? It is not a minor question, for no monotheism has so far been able to answer it—from Job through the Parable of the Tares to the Dr. Faust(us) legend—without inventing Satan. In anthropological terms, the questions in *The Dispossessed* would be: is there a necessary or only an accidental connection, first, between anarchist bareness as

---

[2]There are at least two further semantic variations to be mentioned here: a) a further positive meaning of possession, arising in and from shamanic possession of or by the goal (Radin 132); but it would scarcely fit Shevek to say he was possessed by the Time Theory; and b) the ironic danger, materializing on Anarres, of its becoming again possessed by propertarianism and domination.

well as the immediate readability of direct human relationships on
Anarres and its meager, largely desert ecology (cf. Jameson's pioneering
meditation on the novel, *Archaeologies* 155-59, and many passages in
The Dispossessed itself, perhaps most explicitly in the Shevek-Bedap
discussion of ch. 6: 131-39); second, between the lush fertility and the
manifold propertarian wraps and traps of Urras; and third, between the
two planetary situations, encompassed in the image of twins circling
about each other? Surely William Morris was right when he called for a
radical diminution of unnecessary, usually kitsch things accompanied by
useless toil ("Useful"); yet, must capitalism be always associated with
abundance, however unjustly gotten and distributed, and communism
with scarcity, however puritanically useful as stimulus in adversity and
heroically battled against by a united collective?

PART 3. *The Dispossessed* seen as Fictional Cognition—
Laudation with a Cavil

3.0.

I have long been proposing that we treat SF as loose modern parables
or exempla. If this is the privileged way for understanding SF texts, is
Shevek the parable's vehicle, on the order of Jesus's Mustard Seed? And
what is then the tenor, the worldly and therefore imperfect Kingdom of
Heaven? What is Shevek more precisely an example of or exemplary
for? I shall first focus on him as the central signifying figure of TD and
then on what his course signifies.

3.1. Shevek's Situations and the Binary Librations

Critics of the novel have often accounted for its plot by following the
education and struggle for freedom of Shevek. But as always in Le Guin,
and in all proper anthropology, he is "A person seen... in a landscape"
("Science Fiction" 87). He is obviously *en situation*, an instance of
what Haraway was to recommend as "situated knowledge." Shevek is
centrally an interactor with and interpreter of his twin worlds. He is that
in relation to what we—but not *The Dispossessed*—wrongly separate
into the categories of *freedom* and *cognition*; discussing Enlightenment,
Kant quite unambiguously defines political freedom as "to make public
use of one's reason at every point" (4). Perhaps the central duality or
binary of this novel is: how does the individual person's urge for these
Siamese twins, which in this novel means for unbuilding walls, fare on

both worlds, the anarchist and the capitalist one; how is it both modifying and being modified by them?

I shall therefore neglect here the interesting characteristics balancing Shevek's exemplariness, making him humanly fallible and believable even while he is outgrowing them, such as a self-reliance bordering on egocentrism even though it is done in the service of the Cause (physics as freedom), a puritanic narrowness making for loneliness in the first 2 chapters on Anarres, and so on. The exception is the Shevek-Takver binary, of which I shall mainly consider its wondrous lyrical inception (6: 145-154). There would be much to infer from it about TD as focussed not only on clarity and knowledge but also, consubstantially, on passion and dark suffering. However, I shall approach Takver through her two Tinguelyan mobiles—airy sculptures of wire suspended from the ceiling, the "Occupations of Uninhabited Space," contrasting Shevek's pre-Takver void, and later the "Inhabitations of Time," complementary to his theoretical inhabitation of it. They show how the couple's binary unity is one of separate and complementary equals, Takver the biologist bringing in the immediate life-oriented presentness as the convex of Shevek's concave long-range abstractions in physics. She is Shevek's other illumination beside cosmology: the whole final third of ch. 6 is suffused by an unearthly radiance, rising in the dark as the silvery Moon does and piercing it, like the joy between them, to propagate as well as celebrate clarity. This relationship comes to a head in the pillow-talk coda on being in the middle of life vs. looking at it "from the vantage point of death" (154). True, a separatist sectarian might note that the two characterizations are based on a variant of the hegemonic ascription of male and female qualities, say female concreteness vs. male abstraction. But first, the basis is not the whole beautiful edifice, there is much more in the text to contradict any banal polarization. And second, hegemony also means "a lived system of meanings and values" (Williams 110), in tension between ideology and utopia. The Takver-Shevek pair is a mini-utopia, an ethical harmony quite analogous to the final Simulsequentiality Theory. No ambiguities in either.[3]

---

[3] My original plan for a commentary to TD included a section demolishing S.R. Delany's "To Read *The Dispossessed*." I believe he has not only failed to read most of what is there, but that the few elements he focusses on and blames, such as heterosexuality and ongoing identities, are those which diverged from his own writerly practice and ideology, so that it is (to put it mildly) very ungenerous to imply everybody should write like himself.

I now regretfully pass over the thickly populated world of Anarres to focus on Shevek. He is, centrally, of the family of Sun Heroes, bringers of the light and slayers of pestilential dragons. Light is of course the opposite of blindness, as in *Oedipus* and *King Lear*. It is knowledge of oneself as part and parcel of the world as society and as universe. The very first situation of the book, the baby in the sun ray, begins to establish the strong imagery of light as the physical and cognitive clarity and "difficult to arrive at simplicity"[4] which recurs often—sometimes as light reflected in Shevek's face or eyes (see 2: 45 and 11: 280) or ideas that crave light (3: 58) or his transparent moral personality (6: 146). Yet suns and light are not quite the same after Relativity Theory: light dare not forget, nor does Shevek, that it is the left hand of darkness, as life is of death. And heroes are not the same after socialism and feminism: they are no more given by mythological decree but have to struggle through epic choices, they are Light *Seekers*, a two-legged permanent revolution incompatible with a macho killer role. In this I agree with Milner's observation that *The Dispossessed* is "unambiguously feminist" [209].

Nonetheless, Shevek is also a founding hero, renewer of Odo's correct but corrupted message (cf. 4: 88), inaugurator of communist freedom in physical theory and perhaps, in social practice. Like many heroes, he has to pass through a desert exile, first on Anarres, in the physical desert in ch. 8 and the moral desert of corrupt power in ch. 10, then amid the lush city jungle and fleshpots as well as the underground hideouts of Urras. We leave him—a wise cut-off—before he enters the Promised Land of Anarres, openly named in 1: 7, returning from afar with a new physical Law which does not mean power for one chosen people, caste or gender, but breaking down the walls between people in the whole universe, no less. A dissident and unbuilding builder, the opposite of the channel-digging King Utopus; Remus more than Romulus.

Shevek is presented as having a strong self. But that is to be understood in terms of the novel's all-pervasive librations. It is perhaps best shown a propos the first piece of Shevek's world we see: "There was a wall." Yet immediately after that proposition we are led to see, in a first swing of the pendulum of meaning, that it is also not a wall, for it does not bar the road. It is "an idea of boundary." Yet again "the idea was real," it is a wall—second swing of the pendulum. Wall 1, the physical one, was not important; Wall 2, the notional one, is the most important thing/ notion on Anarres. The method here is not a hesitation from Yes through No to Yes, it is rather a movement that returns by way of depth analysis

---

[4] This is one of Brecht's definitions of communism in the poem "Praise of Communism" (GBFA 11: 234). I hope and trust he would in the 1970s not have withheld the appellative from the equally anti-authoritarian TD.

from notion 1, the mere physical wall, to a changed notion 2, the wall as all-important idea of boundary that bars passage, where both notions use the same term yet destabilize and dynamicize it. Analogously, Shevek's Self is continually shifting, encountering inner and outer walls and working to unbuild them, infiltrating and being infiltrated by the two worlds of Anarres and Urras, by the possessed situations, characters, spaces, relationships of Urras, and by the dispossessed—but sometimes repossessed—ones on Anarres. Very roughly, this shift may be thought of as spirally progressing from the isolated individual, through dispossession from egotism by select interaction with his community, to creator. Shevek's rich libration is the incarnation of Odo's tombstone inscription: "To be whole is to be part; true voyage is return" (3: 68); this is signalled in his encounter with her a dozen pages later.

Of a piece with this is Shevek's delving into or affinity with pain (e.g. his speech on 2: 48-50) and death. The very method of librating between Being 1→Unbeing→Being 2 is a sequence of little deaths and joyful rebirths, as his first step onto Urras shows: "[H]e stumbled and nearly fell. He thought of death, in that gap between the beginning of a step and its completion, and at the end of the step he stood on a new earth" (1: 16). Surely this is a conscious subverting of the PR trumpets and cymbals anent the US colonel's landing on our Moon, just a few years before *The Dispossessed*. The small step for Shevek is not necessarily a giant leap for anything; it is certainly not a step on the upward arrow of progress towards the excelsior of bigger and better military technology, like, say, the giant match-cut leap at the beginning of *2001*... I cannot make here a thorough survey, but only give two more small instances. First is the little death of sexual orgasm, that letting go of the self (2: 41, and then both death and renewal with Takver, from 6: 148 on). Second is the violent death, such as that of the Urrasti demonstrator (9: 243-46), which is horridly different because unnecessary, but possibly part of the same cycle. However, this indispensable theme is pervasive: parting is, as in the French proverb, also a little death, and travel is in Le Guin usually accompanied by loss of consciousness and a more or less useful and successful rebirth into a new one, as in Shevek's spaceship experience of ch. 1.

3.2. The Exemplary Reach for Integrality, and a Limit

Thus, what does Shevek's parable ideally stand for? I think for a double unity-in-duality. The first or thematic one is that of *physics and politics*, in our poor terms: of natural vs. human/social science. Shevek stands for their integrality in the sense of the Pre-Socratics' **physis** or of our ambiguous "physical," usable alike for Einstein and Olivia Newton-John. To unbuild propertarian possession of human nature cannot be divided from the same effort about the world, and vice versa, as we realize today in the capitalist destruction of climate and other eco-systems. We cannot fully imagine any of this, since history has both insufficiently and often wrongly developed our sense(s) — so that Jameson is right to insist throughout *Archaeologies* that utopia/nism relates to the present and not to the future. But perhaps what all of us intellectuals have the greatest difficulty to imagine even feebly is the unbuilding of the division of labour between mental and bodily work, though Le Guin exceptionally attempts to envisage this. Now Shevek, as in/with all major poetry, also stands for the second, attitudinal or methodological integrality of *the thematic What with the relational How*. The metaphors and analogies of the How, steeped in relationships between people and their products, unbuild obsolete categories, as in Rimbaud: "Blood! Blood! Golden flame!/ All to war, to vengeance, to terror.... Enough!/ ..../ ...I'm there, I'm still there." The plot arrow may then, in the best of cases, begin to show, to make visible and understandable, the coming into being of better categories. Only together can the two result in the fully disalienating melding of sense (meaning) with the sensual evidence of poetry fitting words to the world.

The Dispossessed brings this off superbly up to Shevek's encounter with the Urras revolt. But measured by the very high level that far, at that point I grow uneasy. I shall approach this by factoring in Jameson's characterization of Le Guin's SF as world reduction or ontological excision.

The most salient example Jameson gives is the reduction of human sexuality to the periods of "heat" (kemmer) in *The Left Hand of Darkness*, though the lack of animals there and even more so on Anarres could be added. He notes that the method is one of "'thought experiment' in the tradition of great physicists," citing Le Guin's pointers to Einstein and Schrödinger in "Is Gender"—it is "the experimental production of an imaginary situation by excision of the real..." (274). Returning to *The Dispossessed*, he characterizes the Anarresti utopia as a place "in which [humanity] is released from the multiple determinisms (economic, political, social) of history itself..., precisely in order to be free to do whatever it wants with its interpersonal relationships..." (275). As with *The Left Hand*, it is thus "[an] attempt to rethink Western history without capitalism" (277). This rich, anthropological vein—validated by the excision of unlimited sex or most animals—attains a persuasiveness much higher than exclusive Morean or Bellamyan focussing on sociopolitics would.

Let me try to rephrase this as an ambiguous polarity, inherent in the Anarres landscape or nature, between *bareness* as facilitator of understanding by poetic analogy—Anarres as truth, discussed in 1.4— and *barrenness* as Cold War stigmatizing of all revolutionary politics by identifying them with inescapable stagnation in poverty (and the attendant rise of a new privileged class). In the Anarres chapters the stark poetry clearly prevails. The lushness of Urras in chapters 3, 5, and 7 is itself a corrupt denial of bareness when observed by Shevek's sarcastic utopian eye. But in the middle of ch. 9 the stance shifts. Where Shevek encounters the protesters and repression, he is merely our camera eye justifying scattered glimpses about a major social movement of which we know little. His usual overview, coupled with the authorial generalizations, is lacking. We do not know the context in any way even faintly similar to the richness of details about Anarres and the propertarian wraps in Urras; we are restricted to Shevek's fugitive glances. There is a generic kinship to the city revolutions of *News from Nowhere* (William Morris, 1881) or *The Iron Heel* (Jack London, 1908), but the Urras revolt resembles perhaps more something out of *The Sleeper Wakes* (H. G. Wells, 1899), or, in terms of Le Guin's opus, maybe out of Orsinia, than any later depiction. But compared to Morris or London, we do not know much about the Urrasti oppositional movement. It is an alliance of non-violent syndicalists [?] and centralizing communists (9: 239), and seems largely followed by the lower classes, but was it really insurrectionary in intent? It seems to have been suppressed, but it is not clear how permanently. However, the political revolt finds no further place in the novel; I'm not sure it's even mentioned during the return to Anarres.

Correction: there is one movement, nearest in time and political alignment to the author, which *The Dispossessed* melds with the pre-WW1 template: this is the mainly non-violent anti-Vietnam protests, violently put down in Chicago 1968 and in the shootings at Kent State and Jackson State Universities in 1970. In the Urras demonstration, the Vietnam War helicopters shoot people at home. It is after all sparked by a war abroad, in Benbili—the Third World of Urras. Le Guin's view of it shares the 60s protesters' generosity of spirit, radical swerve, and political limitation.

My sense of something lacking here, of a major failure of interest, is rendered more acute by contrast to the splendid beginning of ch. 9, Shevek's breakthrough to his time theory, which is a culmination of this novel, in particular of the wall vs. light imagery:

> The wall was down. The vision was both clear and whole. What he saw was simple...: and contained in it all complexity, all promise. It was revelation. It was the way clear, the way home, the light.
> The spirit in him was like a child running out into the sunlight. There was no end, no end.... (9: 225)

These are also among the best pages of speculation on the creative, here specifically scientific, process of discovery that I know. If SF is to be examined in its relationship to science and creativity, TD will stand out as a beacon with a very few matching examples, one of them being Lem's more systematic tour de force on the history of Solaristics.

It is not fair to demand that the incandescent intensity of such passages be sustained everywhere. But in the whole account of the Urras revolt, only Shevek's speech at the demonstration comes near to it. Even there, I either don't understand or disagree with the final dichotomy: "You cannot make the Revolution. You can only be the Revolution." The rest is seen in an accelerated blur. Workable enough, but predicated on exclusive focus through and on Shevek. Chapter 9 culminates in the Time Theory, and the rest is anti-climactic. The wall is down for the time theoretician but not for the Urrasti insurgents. The splendid analogy between physics and politics seems confined to Anarres. It resurrects forcefully in Shevek's speech to the Terran ambassador (11: 280-81), but restricted to the general philosophy of time. It is not clear whether much hope is left for Urras: this is not left in the balance, it is dropped. Of course, historians may argue Le Guin has been prophetic in this too. When has a revolution ever succeeded at the centre of an empire unless the empire was already in bad disarray?

Yet since utopia is about the present, and ours is in 2007 different from the present of the early 1970s, we have to judge this writing in our world. In ours, the heaviest artillery of capitalism, whose persuasiveness eventually brought down State pseudo-communism, was that capitalism delivers the goods while communism does not. Capitalism claimed and claims what is in TD the lush and teeming beauty of Urras with its ecologically full or overcrowded niches of plant, animal, and city life. Le Guin probably tried to weaken such a claim with the contrast between Urras and ruined Terra in Keng's speech. While an effective bit of ecocriticism on its own, this does not erase the impact of the union, indeed consubstantiality, between communism, however morally admirable, and poverty as shown on Anarres.

We thus get to an imbalance between the morally admirable and the corporeally easy or even feasible, dispossession as lack of ownership with its demons and as lack of things—back to an opposition between purity and—as final horizon denied by poverty—survival. It is politically of a piece with the Odonians' accepting exodus from their society instead of revolution inside it, and Shevek's following this pattern by forgetting his Urrasti brothers. He had, after all, identified the basement where he and other defeated insurgents had to hide as Hell (9: 244); but even this hero was not up to a Harrowing of Hell.[5] By this I do not, of course, mean to indicate psychological or moral stains in a fictional character, and even less to "blame" the poet-author who had discovered for us more than anybody else: it is a matter of the novel as a whole arriving at its own boundary or wall. The properly economico-political critique—that capitalism proceeds by finally ruining the forces of production (people, earth, air, water) at least as thoroughly as it had developed them at its beginnings, that it increasingly delivers destruction—is missing in the Urras story. It is a void as significant as the absence of industrial production at the heart of *News from Nowhere*, the concave that defines its convexities. I do not at all believe this nullifies the great insights and delights of the novel. But while the ambiguity between authoritarian and libertarian utopia is a very fertile one, the ambiguity between capitalism and fertility, however corrupt, is simply misleading.

[5] In sum, "The Odonians on Anarres have created a good society, but even they might have done better to have stayed home on Urras and ensured the Revolution on Urras" (Erlich , chapter 8). Odo's plans were based on "the generous ground of Urras," not on "arid Anarres" (4: 77), quite parallel to Marx's expectation of revolution starting in the most developed countries of France and perhaps England.

The aridity of Anarres is analogous to the Odonians opting for separation rather than permeation, for a revolution only for a vanguard and then exile group instead of for all the Urrasti people. Another analogy is the separation of the "Soviet experiment" from the rest of the world, first imposed from the outside by a capitalist **cordon sanitaire**, then assumed by Stalin, as well as the sectarianism of the parties and people oriented mainly to the defence of the USSR rather than change in their own spaces. Certainly the corruption of the revolution by a rising bureaucracy comes from there, as well as from subsidiary separatisms such as the one to and in Zionist kibbutzes in Palestine. But in the background of everything Le Guin does is her rootedness in the USA, so the fact *The Dispossessed* was written a few years before the US 200th anniversary (roughly as long as the existence of Anarres) and that many on the Left hold the promise of American Revolution was betrayed is another factor.

Still, the overriding story in much the greater part of *The Dispossessed* is one of rare imaginative sympathy by a writer in full command of rich narrative shaping against an explicitly cognitive horizon. I hope I have suggested in this article some of the main admirable facets of the novel, which are very rare in and beyond SF, or utopian fiction if you wish. But in a final abstraction, beyond the great and not to be underrated delights of its micro- and meso-levels, what might be identified as its, so to speak, transportable insight and horizon for us readers today? What I was getting to at the beginning of this sub-section is, put in an allegorical way, that Shevek brings about the marriage of Freedom and Knowledge—or Cognition, including S1 and poetry. It is the vision of *freedom as critical cognition*—which in our epoch means two things: first, solidarity with others of the same horizon, a defence of civil society; second, a radical orientation by contraries to the hegemony stifling us. With warts and all, *The Dispossessed* establishes a horizon of thisworldly justice centered on people and their knowledge. This is where my cavil at the separation of freedom and knowledge in Shevek's final relationship with the Urrasti people comes from: it is a fall back into our "pure," S2 science. Nonetheless, the overall vision is one where freedom and poetico-scientific cognition embrace. I do not believe this can grow obsolete as long as injustice obtains—and it has been steadily deepening. Truth shall make ye free (if you organize).

Works Cited

1. Aronowitz, Stanley. *Science as Power.* Minneapolis: U of Minnesota P, 1988.
2. Beck, Ulrich. *Risk Society.* Transl. M. Ritter. London: Sage, 1992.
3. Boulding, Kenneth E. "Truth or Power." *Science* 190 (1975): 423.
4. Braverman, Harry. *Labor and Monopoly Capital: The Degradation of Work in the Twentieth Century.* New York & London: Monthly RP, 1974.
5. Brecht, Bertolt. *Werke.* Grosse Kommentierte Berliner und Frankfurter Ausgabe. Frankfurt & Berlin: Suhrkamp & Aufbau V., 1988-98. (GBFA)
6. Bruner, Jerome. *Actual Minds, Possible Worlds.* Cambridge MA: Harvard UP, 1986.
7. Collingridge, David. *Social Control of Technology.* London: Pinter, & New York: St. Martin's P, 1980.

8. Elgin, Catherine Z. *With Reference to Reference.* Indianapolis: Hackett, 1982.
9. Erlich, Richard D. *Coyote's Song: The Teaching Stories of Ursula K. Le Guin.* A Science Fiction Research Association Digital Book. www.sfra.org/Coyote/CoyoteHome.htm, accessed Sept. 5, 2007.
10. [Gandhigram Rural University]. www.gandhigram.org.
11. Gentner, Dedre. "Are Scientific Analogies Metaphors?" In *Metaphor: Problems and Perspectives,* ed. by David S. Miall. Brighton: Harvester Press, 1982, 106-32.
12. Goodman, Nelson, and Catherine Z. Elgin. *Reconceptions in Philosophy and Other Arts and Sciences.* Indianapolis: Hackett, 1988.
13. Graham, Loren R. *Between Science and Values.* NY: Columbia UP, 1981.
14. Hacking, Ian. *Representing and Intervening.* Cambridge: Cambridge UP, 1983.
15. Haraway, Donna. *Modest_Witness@Second_Millennium.* New York & London: Routledge, 1997.
16. —. "Situated Knowledge." *Feminist Studies* 14.3 (1988): 575-99.
17. Harding, Sandra. *Whose Science? Whose Knowledge?* Ithaca: Cornell UP, & Milton Keynes, Open UP, 1991.
18. Harré, R[om]. *The Philosophies of Science.* London: Oxford UP, 1972.
19. Jameson, Fredric. *Archaeologies of the Future.* London & New York: Verso, 2005.
20. —. *A Singular Modernity.* London & New York: Verso, 2002.
21. Kant, Immanuel. *On History.* Ed. L.W. Beck, transl. idem et al. Indianapolis: Bobbs-Merrill, 1963.
22. Kapp, K. William. *The Social Costs of Private Enterprise.* Cambridge MA: Harvard UP, 1950.
23. Le Guin, Ursula K. *The Dispossessed: An Ambiguous Utopia.* New York: Avon, 1975.
24. —. "Is Gender Necessary? Redux." In *Dancing at the Edge of the World,* Ursula K. Le Guin. New York: Grove P, 2002, 7-16.
25. —. "Science Fiction and Mrs Brown." In *The Language of the Night,* Ursula K. Le Guin. New York: Berkley, 1978-94.
26. —. "Some Thoughts on Narrative." In *Dancing...* [see above], 37-45.

27. Levins, Richard. "Ten Propositions on Science and Antiscience." In *Science Wars,* ed. by Andrew Ross. London & Durham: Duke UP, 1996, 180-91.

28. Marcuse, Herbert. *Reason and Revolution.* Boston: Beacon P, 1960.

29. Marx, Karl. *Theorien über den Mehrwert I.* Berlin [DDR]: Dietz V., 1956.

30. —. [and Friedrich Engels.] *Werke* (MEW). Berlin: Dietz, 1962ff.

31. Milner, Andrew. "Utopia and SF in Raymond Williams." *Science-Fiction Studies* 30.2 (2003): 199-216.

32. [Morris, William.] "Useful Work versus Useless Toil." In *William Morris.* Centenary Edn. London: Nonesuch P, 1948, 603-23.

33. Nietzsche, Friedrich. *Die fröhliche Wissenschaft.* München: Goldmann, s.d.

34. —. *Philosophy and Truth: Selections from Nietzsche's Notebooks of the Early 1870's.* Transl., ed., and introduced by D. Breazeale. S.l.: Humanities P, 1979.

35. —.. *Werke.* Leipzig: Naumann, 1900-13.

36. —. *Zur Genealogie der Moral.* Ed. W.D. Williams. Oxford: Blackwell, 1972.

37. Radin, Paul. *Primitive Religion.* London : Hamilton, 1938.

38. Rancière, Jacques. "Transports de la liberté." In idem ed. *La politique des poètes.* Paris : Michel, 1992, 87-130.

39. Rimbaud, Arthur. *Oeuvres complètes.* Éd. L. Forrestier. Paris: Laffont, 1992.

40. Spivak, Gayatri Chakravorty. *In Other Worlds.* New York & London: Routledge, 1988.

41. Suvin, Darko. "Can People Be (Re)Presented in Fiction?" In *Marxism and the Interpretation of Culture,* ed. by C. Nelson and L. Grossberg. Urbana: U of Illinois P, 1988, 663-96.

42. —.. "Heavenly Food Denied: Life of Galileo." In *The Cambridge Companion to Brecht,* ed. by Peter Thomson and Glendyr Sacks. Cambridge: Cambridge UP, 1994, 139-52.

43. —. "On the Horizons of Epistemology and Science." (circulating)

44. —. "Living Labour and the Labour of Living." *Critical Quarterly* 46.1 (2004): 1-35, available at www.blackwell-synergy.com/

45. —. "On Metaphoricity and Narrativity in Fiction." *SubStance* no. 48 (1986): 51-67.

46. —. "The Science-Fiction Novel as Epic Narration." In *Positions and Presuppositions in Science Fiction.* London: Macmillan, & Kent OH: Kent State UP, 1988, 74-85.

47. Wallerstein, Immanuel. *The End of the World as We Know It.* Minneapolis: U of Minnesota P, 1999.

48. —. *Historical Capitalism [, with] Capitalist Civilization.* London: Verso, 1996.

49. Williams, Raymond. *Marxism and Literature.* New York: Oxford UP, 1981.

Darko Suvin, born in Zagreb, Yugoslavia, has taught in Europe and North America. Now retired, he is Professor Emeritus of McGill University and a Fellow of The Royal Society of Canada. He has written 14 books of essays, including 8 on Science Fiction and utopianism, three books of poetry, and many articles. His awards and grants include the Pilgrim Award of SFRA 1979. His latest book is forthcoming at P. Lang, London, in the Ralahine Utopian series, working title *Defined by a Hollow*, and consists of 14 essays and five batches of poems.

The Utopian Imagination:
Ursula K. Le Guin and
Superstring Theorists

Beth Snowberger
National Sun Yat-sen University

As scholars of literature, we read, understand, and perhaps create metaphors every day. The world of metaphor is our bread and butter (this sentence being a case in point, created off the cuff and without conscious desire for metaphorical writing). The foundation of metaphor is the physical world, the phenomena of the empirical universe with which we clothe abstract concepts to give them a more easily communicable form. Even further, as Northrop Frye explains, we use metaphor to fulfill "a desire to associate, and finally to identify, the human mind with what goes on outside it" (Frye 33). It is, therefore, only natural for the hard sciences and maths, which investigate and describe the outside world, to prove fertile grounds from which metaphors can arise.

As a hard science amenable to metaphor-making, physics may perhaps be the most fertile ground of all. P.C.W. Davies, a professor of theoretical physics, writes,

> No science is more pretentious than physics, for the physicist lays claim to the whole universe as his subject matter. Whereas biologists are restricted to living organisms, chemists to atoms and molecules, psychologists to man and his fellow creatures, and so on, physicists, like theologians, are wont to deny that any system is in principle beyond the scope of their subject.... [T]he "arrows of explanation" always point downwards to the deepest layers of reality until, ultimately, everything can be explained in terms of the fundamental constituents of matter. (Davies and Brown 1)

At present, even a tiny biological organism such as a bacterium cannot be described comprehensively using the known laws of physics, and something as complex as a human society would be beyond impossible. If direct description is currently impossible, however, we still have our powerful tool of trade, the metaphor. We can reverse the steps of reductionism—those downward-pointing arrows of explanation—in a single bound by extrapolating metaphorically.

Scientific metaphors, and particularly the metaphors of physics, saturate many of the fictional works of American writer Ursula K. Le Guin. Two of the works in which this characteristic is most explicit and visible, the short story "Schrödinger's Cat" and the novel *The Dispossessed*, were written in the same year, 1974. In the former, as the title implies, Le Guin explores the metaphorical implications of Austrian physicist Erwin Schrödinger's 1935 "thought experiment" regarding the randomness of the quantum field, which the scientist describes as such:

> One can even set up quite ridiculous cases. A cat is penned up in a steel chamber, along with the following device (which must be secured against direct interference by the cat): in a Geiger counter there is a tiny bit of radioactive substance, so small, that perhaps in the course of the hour one of the atoms decays, but also, with equal probability, perhaps none; if it happens, the counter tube discharges and through a relay releases a hammer which shatters a small flask of hydrocyanic acid. If one has left this entire system to itself for an hour, one would say that the cat still lives if meanwhile no atom has decayed. The psi-function of the entire system would express this by having in it the living and dead cat (pardon the expression) mixed or smeared out in equal parts. (Schrödinger, n. pag.)

The status of the cat (living or dead) is undetermined until the observer opens the chamber. Of course, one might argue—and some have—that the observer then becomes part of the system, rendering the thought experiment even more paradoxical than Schrödinger originally intended.

In her surreal short story, Le Guin adapts the metaphor fractally, so to speak (a fractal being, in simple terms, a non-Euclidian structure that is self-similar on different scales), expressing it as identically true on the human scale as on the cat scale as on the quantum scale. The cat itself is a figure in the story, but its function in Le Guin's thought experiment is transferred to a pair of humans within an isolated house. Who is the observer who can lift off the roof and determine their fate? The empirical phenomenon of unpredictability of quantum states underlies Schrödinger's metaphor of the cat in a box, which he created for purposes of communication; it in turn underlies Le Guin's metaphor of humans in a house, which she created for purposes of philosophical questioning.

Le Guin later develops a feather-light touch with this particular line of metaphorical thinking in a short story from 1996, "Half Past Four." Rather than overtly linking her metaphor to quantum physics and Schrödinger's cat, she applies the metaphor covertly in her fictive characters and plot. For example, in one of the story's several alternate realities, a young, single mother, Ann, meets with her estranged father, who expresses regret over his abandonment of her twelve years earlier when he divorced Ann's mother. They have the following exchange:

> "Yeah, well," she said. "I guess it worked out OK, anyhow, you know, Mom and me, and anyhow Penny didn't want some teen-age stepdaughter around all the time."
>
> "If I'd fought for you and won custody—and if I'd fought I'd have won—what Penny wanted or didn't want would have been a matter of supreme indifference. I probably wouldn't have married her. One mistake leads to the next one. You'd have lived here. All your summers here. Gone to a good school. And a four-year college, maybe an Eastern school, Smith or Vassar. And you wouldn't be living with a lesbian in San Pablo, working nights for a phone company. I'm not blaming you, I'm blaming myself."
>
> ...But I was really lucky to get the job, Ann thought, but what's neat is that for a while things aren't changing all the time, but you haven't even seen Mom for ten years so how do you know? All these thoughts were mere shadows and underbrush, among which her mind hopped like a rabbit.
>
> "Well," she said, "things are really OK the way they worked out." (Le Guin, "Half Past Four" 28)

On the human scale, an individual is the smallest unit; metaphorically speaking, we might call it the quantum level. Ann's father confidently asserts a lengthy series of predictions based on changing one variable on the quantum level: "if I'd fought for you." Le Guin knows, as we have seen, that quantum outcomes can only be observed after the fact, not predicted based on variables. The father's need to predict an alternate outcome is a self-deception, a lack of understanding of how the world works. Ann, then, being content to accept what she has observed and carry on from there, is more in tune with the true nature of the world than her father is. In contrast with Le Guin's story "Schrödinger's Cat," however, there is no need for the reader to have any prior knowledge of the famous thought experiment and what it represents in quantum physics. The science informs Le Guin's fiction invisibly, in theme rather than language, in this case.

There is more to physics than quantum mechanics, however, and there is more to Le Guin's fiction than stories of individuals. She writes of whole societies and whole worlds as well. When expanding our scale of vision, we find a glitch in our metaphor: the universe cannot automatically be assumed to accommodate "fractal thinking." The known physics of the large scale (general relativity) and of the small scale (quantum mechanics) are not self-similar. In fact, they seem to be entirely incompatible. The mathematics involved in quantum theory—while very successful on the quantum scale—issues nonsense answers on the gravitational scale, for which general relativity is the only reliable theory to employ at present, and vice versa. They cannot operate together.

Returning to our metaphorical identification of the empirical world with the human self, if the quantum and gravitational scales have not been reconciled, can the small (quantum) scale of the individual human be reconciled with the overarching (gravitational) scale of a society? This is a key question, is it not, in utopian thought? Some theoretical physicists search for the unified theory, the TOE—theory of everything. Some social philosophers try to imagine a utopia in which the interests of the individual and the interests of the society are one. None has yet succeeded. The search, however, informs the thematic content of Le Guin's utopian novel *The Dispossessed*.

Le Guin utilizes in *The Dispossessed* both the overt and covert strategies of scientific metaphor we have already examined in "Schrödinger's Cat" and "Half Past Four," respectively. Overtly, she portrays the pursuit and realization of a unified theory of physics via the thoughts and speech of her protagonist, Shevek, who—handily enough—is a genius-caliber theoretical physicist. As in "Schrödinger's Cat," a basic understanding of the state of real-life physics is an assumed quality of the ideal reader of Le Guin's imaginary events.

Shevek's professional goal is the theoretical synthesis of linear and cyclical time. Just before his breakthrough, the reader is privy to his thoughts on the earlier work of a Terran physicist named Ainsetain—a practically undisguised Einstein. The narrator treats us to a relevant summary of Terran physics:

> Having explained the force of gravity as a function of the geometry of spacetime, he [Ainsetain] had sought to extend the synthesis to include electromagnetic forces. He had not succeeded. Even during his lifetime, and for many decades after his death, the physicists of his own world had turned away from his effort and its failure, pursuing the magnificent incoherences of quantum theory with its high technological yields, at last concentrating on the technological mode so exclusively as to arrive at a dead end, a catastrophic failure of imagination. Yet

> their original intuition had been sound: at the point where they
> had been, progress had lain in the indeterminacy which old
> Aisentain had refused to accept. And his refusal had been equally
> correct—in the long run. Only he had lacked the tools to provide
> it... (Le Guin, *Dispossessed* 279)

If we simply change the spelling of the scientist's name and remove a
phrase or two of editorializing, we have a perfectly accurate history of
twentieth-century Earth physics suitable for the general reader.

Shevek's next step—to forget about the "unprovability of the hypothesis
of real coexistence" and to embrace that which is unprovable as "the only
real chance for breaking out of the circle and going ahead"—is what
finally enables him, after ten years of labor, to make the imaginative
leap that Ainsetain and the other Terran physicists could not. "By simply
assuming the validity of real coexistence he was left free" to move
forward and unify the points of view of sequency and simultaneity with
the mathematics already at hand (*Dispossessed* 280). The unproven faith
that unity already existed finally brought down "the wall" that had been
blocking him and gave Shevek the gift of "revelation...the way clear,
the way home, the light" (*Dispossessed* 280). Einstein utilized this form
of lateral thinking in his formulation of the special theory of relativity
by accepting the speed of light as a constant, sidestepping the problem
of whether it is a wave or a particle and allowing him to move forward.
At present the same strategy of lateral thinking, with the ultimate goal
of a TOE, is apparent within the field of superstring theory.

How does this relate to the utopian theme of the novel? The social
discussion mirrors the scientific discussion; the covert metaphor echoes
the overt. First, the idea of inclusion is important. One may not, in physics
or social theory, simply erase or ignore what one wishes were not there.
Shevek understands this on not only the physical but also social level.
For instance, when Shevek finally learns about the lower-class living
conditions on Urras from his servant, Efor, he is impressed: "This was
the human suffering in which the ideals of his society were rooted,
the ground from which they sprang" (*Dispossessed* 284). And yet, he
realizes that lower-class life "was not 'the real Urras.' The dignity and
beauty of the room he and Efor were in was as real as the squalor to
which Efor was native. To him a thinking man's job was not to deny
one reality at the expense of the other, but to include and connect. It
was not an easy job" (*Dispossessed* 284-85). All one observes, even
seeming opposites, must be included in a successful theory—whether
those opposites be the lower and upper classes of a society, linear and
cyclical time, or micro and macro cosmos. A bit later in the narrative, at

a rally in the city center, Shevek also sees the coexistence of micro and macro behaviors on the human level that has proven such a challenge to imagine in physics. The narrator notes:

> There might have been a hundred thousand human beings in Capitol Square, or twice that many. The individuals, like the particles of atomic physics, could not be counted, nor their positions ascertained, nor their behavior predicted. And yet, as a mass, that enormous mass did what it had been expected to do by the organizers of the strike: it gathered, marched in order, sang... (*Dispossessed* 299)

The workings of this paradoxical unity may not be fully understood, but it nonetheless exists in the world of the novel. If we consider, as it is irresistible to do, that Le Guin is "making a point" in writing a utopian novel, and if we take her at her word that she writes fiction to "describe reality, the present world" metaphorically (Le Guin, Introduction, n. pag., 2nd page), we must conclude that she is convinced that this paradoxical unity exists in the real world as well.

Is this conviction of its existence enough? Does it have power? Later in the novel, Le Guin appears to argue (again via Shevek), that it is and does. First, speaking with regard to the "ansible," the new interstellar communications device that his unified theory will make possible, Shevek tells the Terran ambassador, "Men cannot leap the great gaps, but ideas can" (*Dispossessed* 344). He further tells her, "My society is also an idea. I was made by it. An idea of freedom, of change, of human solidarity, an important idea" (*Dispossessed* 345). Speaking (in my opinion) of both his scientific and societal idea, he says, "You would rather destroy us rather than admit our reality, rather than admit that there is hope!" (*Dispossessed* 350). This last sentence indicates that the idea itself is already a feasible reality, and that this fact justifies hope in it becoming an actuality. As with Shevek's physics problem, the assumption of the underlying truth of the idea of unity provides the ability—an ability not provided by step-by-step logical progression—to "leap the great gaps" and solve the paradox of the seeming opposition of micro and macro scales. Shevek's actual society on his home planet Anarres does not operate in full accord with the utopian idea on which it was founded. But the truth of the idea itself—the truth of an underlying unity between micro and macro, self and society—gives Shevek hope, and it is armed with this hope that he returns to Anarres to continue to work toward the idea's realization.

It is this aspect of the novel that is truly utopian, rather than either of the described societies, which are seemingly at odds with each other and which contain domestic elements that are also seemingly at odds. According to Shevek, "realism" is nothing of the sort "if you don't know what hope is" (*Dispossessed* 351). In other words, to deny hope is to embrace the experiential and fractured *seems* rather than the underlying *is*. For Le Guin, utopia is not in fact an impossible genre. For her, Utopia already exists. It is a reality—as an idea—and therefore we, like Shevek, can assume experimental actualization to be theoretically possible and proceed according to that assumption. This is a wholly optimistic view of the universe and one based on an identification of our observed reality as ironic, at odds with an intrinsic truth. The presumption of an intrinsic truth ("truthiness," as George W. Bush would call it) sets her in opposition to the most influential contemporary philosophers and cultural theorists but aligns her with the hard scientists. As physicist Timothy Ferris states it most simply, "There are…an infinite number of logically consistent universes; science asks in which of these universes we actually live" (Ferris 156). For the scientist, the answer exists, and the answer is findable.

Le Guin is, of course, not the only fiction writer to make use of scientific metaphor. All science fiction writers do. She explains this common tie: "All fiction is metaphor. Science fiction is metaphor. What sets it apart from older forms of fiction seems to be its use of new metaphors, drawn from certain great dominants of our contemporary life—science, all the sciences, and technology" (Le Guin, Introduction, n. pag., 6th page). Even some nonfiction writers share in this kinship. For instance, physicist Alan Lightman describes some of his popular science essays as "dealing with science but in an oblique way. Science as metaphor. Science as a way to view the world" (Lightman 172). Also Sarah Voss, a professor of world religions at the University of Nebraska–Omaha, is notable as an academician in the humanities intent on reclaiming the quantitative nature of mathematics in contemporary thought. She considers mathematical and scientific metaphors (which she terms *mathaphors*) to be meaningful tools for illuminating the nature of human consciousness. I find Le Guin a unique case, however, in that she makes such rich use of the potential of a unified theory of physics as an analogy for societal utopia, which so naturally follows from her interest in quantum mechanics as an analogy for individual human behavior.

It is a mark of Le Guin's imaginative power that she wrote *The Dispossessed* after the failure of Einstein to realize his dream of a unified field theory but before the heyday of string theories and during a near-fatal lull in their popularity among theorists. Since that time, there have been significant developments in superstring theory, which has been reborn as one of the leading fields of research in theoretical physics. (When I refer to "superstring theory," I am actually referring to a body of several superstring theories that exist in publication at present, with no one clear winner having yet emerged. Nonetheless, all of these theories have their most metaphorically potent qualities in common, so for grammatical ease I will refer to them in the singular.) Although the mathematical tools necessary for a thorough understanding and testing of superstring theory are still decades in the future, the conceptual framework itself—supported by approximated mathematics—is the closest scientists have yet come toward attaining a TOE. Its metaphorical potential is far greater now than it was in 1974.

Le Guin, of course, tapped into its most resonant feature—the unification of quantum mechanics with general relativity—that Einstein had been searching for. As we have seen, in *The Dispossessed* she exploits its potential as a metaphor for expressing the possibility of coexistence of individual and society, the seeming conflicts between which have long been fuel for dystopian or anti-utopian writers.

Another aspect of superstring theory that is metaphorically pregnant is the conception that there is no such thing as a minimally small particle; particles in fact are not basic. Rather, the most basic things are vibrating strings, resonances. This wreaks havoc with our received conception of perfection and infinity. The spatially extended and vibrating shape of a string leaves a bit of space beyond which there is nothing smaller, yet it is not itself infinitely small. Metaphorically, I find this intriguing and hopeful. We quail in the face of a quest for perfection and infinity. Darko Suvin and others have already revised the definition of utopia away from absolute perfection, and it seems they are not mistaken to do so. "Close enough" may turn out to be all that nature asks of itself and we should be no different. It also may suggest metaphorically that society need not be parsed into its smallest particle, the individual, but rather that a vibration—an action, not an entity—should be the basic unit we consider.

Additionally, superstring theory exemplifies a particularly utopian type of endeavor in that it was launched wholly through imagination; it is truly a leap into the Other. It describes a universe that contains at least nine dimensions of space, plus one of time. It is highly unlikely we will ever have the means to observe more than three spatial dimensions, and one can just barely imagine a fourth spatial dimension when a good science writer explains it. The remaining dimensions must simply remain a matter of faith and mathematics for a person of average imagination.

Nonetheless, some of the top physicists of our age are indeed taking it on faith and mathematics that we have nine or more spatial dimensions, because their existence makes possible the unification of physics in very simple and elegant ways. The simplicity and elegance of this unification reassures these scientists of its underlying truth, which gives them hope and motivation to try to figure out how to reverse-engineer it from theory to experimental evidence. Truth is beauty; beauty truth? String theorists may well be artists as well as scientists. Shevek, I believe, would approve. (He is their fictional and metaphorical counterpart by the end of *The Dispossessed*, as I interpret it, with hopes of eventually reverse-engineering Odonian theory into a real-world experience.)

It is this latter aspect of superstring theory that causes me to consider it the current frontier of utopian imagining. The enormity and beauty of its underlying "truthiness" makes a normally staid bunch of scientists practically giddy. The word *quest* arose in practically every publication on the subject I consulted. (Poor Einstein's three-decade quest was described as "quixotic," however, as he was well before his time and thus was denied the proper technology and mathematics (Greene 15).) Another term commonly appropriated to discuss a TOE is *Holy Grail*. The most shocking term of all to read in a work regarding science, however, is *faith*. Impeccably pedigreed physicist Brian Greene is explicit on this point: "With solid faith that laws of the large and the small should fit together into a coherent whole, physicists are relentlessly hunting down the elusive unified theory" (Greene 386). The faith that a truthful resolution exists, even if it involves bizarrenesses such as nine or ten spatial dimensions, is a powerful motivation to find it.

The absence of faith in the existence of a true idea has weakened post-Soviet utopian imagination among social thinkers, in my opinion. The difference in motivation is illustrated by Alan Lightman, who describes his dual life as a fiction writer and theoretical physicist as follows:

> As a writer, even when I am writing well, I cannot write more than six hours at a time. After that I am exhausted, and my vision has become clouded by the inherent subtleties and uncertainties of the work. Then I must wait for…my own strength to return.
>
> But as a scientist, I could be gripped for days at a time, days without stopping, because I wanted to know the answer….When in the throes of a new problem, I was compelled because I knew there was a definite answer. I knew that the equations inexorably led to an answer, an answer that had never been known before, an answer waiting for me. (Lightman 178-79)

In light of this description, it is interesting to compare an example of a utopian "believer" such as Ernst Bloch with one who considers it an impossible genre, such as Fredric Jameson. Bloch's very title, *The Principle of Hope*, calls to mind the faith I have been discussing. His description of the final stages of utopian development echoes Lightman's scientific compulsion: "the agonizing, blissful work of *explication*." He continues, "Genius is hard work, but of a kind which never wants to allow the elaboration to grow stale or to be anything less than a constant obsession. There must be no break here, either between vision and work or between work and vision" (Bloch 125). The energy behind Bloch's utopian impulse leaps off the pages and we can see that he was dedicated to the realization of what he considered a truthful idea.

When the Marxist experiments failed to produce a successful actualization, however, the faith in the possibility of a true idea seems to have failed as well, disparaged by Jameson as belonging only to "a few belated idealisms" (Jameson 170). Whether Jameson is correct in his jaded view I do not know. I tend to be a believer in a few essential truths myself, but perhaps I am simply more naïve than he is. I do feel, though, that this jaded outlook does no good for one's motivation toward utopian imagining. What we see happening in superstring theory—that is, the unification of disparate poles—Jameson views as Irony, toward which he is hostile, seeing it not as an aspect of deeper truth but as having one's cake and eating it too. He embraces, rather, Louis Marin's "neutral term," a "neither/nor" rather than a "both/and" (Jameson 177-78).

When one is interested in utopian thought, as Jameson is, and then is left simply saying "no, no, no, not that one, nor that one either," it is no wonder it becomes an impossible genre. As Jameson says, it is only Irony that "still believes in content" (Jameson 179). Utopia in the contentless, neutral sense, then, seems little more than a black hole, a curiosity of sorts, wholly lacking in the desire that gave the genre birth. It is, he admits, a bit of an "impasse" and "unpromising place" (Jameson 179-80).

As I say, I do not know whether or not Jameson is right concerning the nature of reality, but I fail to see that he is, in fact, a proponent of the utopian imagination. I will go out on a limb at this point and declare that belief in the possibility of essential truth is the foundation of utopian imagination. Without it, there can be utopia-related theory but not utopian imagining itself. Bloch, Le Guin's Shevek, and superstring theorists all share this faith and hope.

There are some pitfalls and drawbacks to utopian imagining, to be sure. On the purely scientific level, superstring theorists open themselves to the disdain of non-utopian physicists. Celebrated experimental physicist

Sheldon Glashow, for example, refers to his string theorist colleagues as "medieval theologists" for their faith in the "uniqueness and beauty" of their theory even absent experimental evidence (qtd. in Davies and Brown 182). In addition, for nonscientists such as Le Guin, Voss, or myself, the drawing of metaphorical implications from hard sciences contains the ever-present risk of an incorrect or overly simplistic understanding of scientific sources. While Le Guin's understanding of physics seems sound to me, Voss's strikes me as facile at times. In turn, a physicist reading this article may find my own understanding of physics laughable, which would necessarily render my metaphorical musings the same. Finally, in utopian action, the danger exists of ignoring an experimental failure because of overzealous faith in the theory. In the societal laboratory as in the scientific one, if the findings do not support the theory, the experiment must stop and the theory must be revised; the findings must not be swept under the rug or tampered with. As our history books show, ignoring the evidence of a failed utopian experiment can result in massive numbers of deaths. The stakes in utopian experimentation are high.

Despite these risks, however, there is one undeniable benefit of utopian imagining. Bloch referred to it as the "making conscious of the Not-Yet-Conscious, the forming of the Not-Yet-Become" (Bloch 127). A related idea in different terms, those of interruption and presence (Prickett 261-62), can be read into Kierkegaard's metaphor regarding a print of *The Tomb of Napoleon*: "Between the two trees there is an empty space; as the eye follows the outline, suddenly Napoleon himself emerges from this nothing, and now it is impossible to have him disappear again. Once the eye has seen him, it goes on seeing him with almost alarming regularity" (qtd. in Prickett 263). Once a new idea is present in one's consciousness, the presence lingers thereafter, like Napoleon in Kierkegaard's print. The ideas at the heart of cutting-edge science are sometimes absent from or slow to enter the consciousness of the general public and scholars in the humanities, particularly since the relative scarcity of good popular science writing limits our ease of access. Nonetheless, as Ferris notes and Le Guin seems well aware, "science is a great story—the greatest story," one that can "open up vistas onto everything else" (Ferris 158). Superstring theory, as one of the vanguard disciplines in our quest to understand the nature of the universe, can thus extend the horizons of metaphor available to us and thereby expand the limits of utopian thought.

Works Cited

1. Bloch, Ernst. *The Principle of Hope*. 1959. Cambridge, Mass.: MIT Press, 1986.
2. Davies, P.C.W., and Julian Brown. *Superstrings: A Theory of Everything?* Cambridge, Eng.: Cambridge UP, 1988.
3. Ferris, Timothy. "On the Popularization of Science." In *The Future of Spacetime*, ed. by E. Barber. 2002. New York: Norton, 2003. 153-70.
4. Frye, Northrop. *The Educated Imagination*. Bloomington: Indiana UP, 1964.
5. Greene, Brian. *The Elegant Universe: Superstrings, Hidden Dimensions, and the Quest for the Ultimate Theory*. New York: Vintage Books, 1999.
6. Jameson, Fredric. *Archaeologies of the Future: The Desire Called Utopia and Other Science Fictions*. London: Verso, 2005.
7. Le Guin, Ursula K. *The Dispossessed*. New York: HarperPrism, 1974.
8. —. "Half Past Four." *Unlocking the Air and Other Stories*. 1996. New York: HarperPerennial, 1997. 1-37.
9. —. Introduction. *The Left Hand of Darkness*. By Le Guin. 1969. New York: Ace, 1976. n. pag.
10. —. "Schrödinger's Cat." In *Norton Anthology of American Literature*, ed. by Nina Baym et al. 6th ed. Vol. E. New York: Norton, 2002. 2226-31.
11. Lightman, Alan. "The Physicist as Novelist." In *The Future of Spacetime*, ed. by E. Barber. 2002. New York: Norton, 2003. 171-90.
12. Prickett, Stephen. *Narrative, Religion and Science: Fundamentalism versus Irony, 1700-1999*. Cambridge, Eng.: Cambridge UP, 2002. Questia Online Library. Questia Media America, Inc. 2 Jan. 2007 <http://www.questia.com/>.
13. Schrödinger, Erwin. "The Present Situation in Quantum Mechanics: A Translation of Schrödinger's 'Cat Paradox Paper.'" Trans. John D. Trimmer. *Amer. Philos. Soc. Proc.* 124 (1980): 323-38. Technische Universität Hamburg-Harburg. Hamburg, Germany. 31 Dec. 2006 <http://www.tu-harburg.de/rzt/rzt/it/QM/cat.html#sect5>.

14. Voss, Sarah. Mathaphors and Faith Understandings of Consciousness. *Journal of Interdisciplinary Studies* 17.1/2 (2005): 88-104. Wilson Web. National Sun Yat-sen Univ. Lib. Kaohsiung, Taiwan. 2 Jan. 2007 <http://vnweb.hwwilsonweb.com.ezproxy.lib.nsysu.edu.tw:8080/hww/>.

Beth Snowberger is a doctoral student at the National Sun Yat-sen University in Kaohsiung, Taiwan, and an Instructor of English at Ming Chuan University in Taipei. She has published on Taiwanese film and martial arts, and in the U.S. she was a contributing writer for the *American National Biography*. Her research currently focuses on contemporary fairy stories.

Tales from the Distaff:
The Parallax View of Earthsea

Amy Clarke
University of California, Davis

For those of us who long ago accepted the story of Ursula K. Le Guin's Earthsea as fully told, her return to that place was an unlooked for gift. Le Guin provides us a bridge by overlapping the timeframe of the fourth book (1990's *Tehanu)* with that of the third (1972's *The Farthest Shore*). Even so, we might think we are not in Earthsea anymore.[1] Some of the things we would have wished for have transpired. Ged and Tenar finally consummate their relationship, and Lebannen has grown into a fine young king. But other changes are decidedly unpleasant. The peace promised by the reunification of the ring of Erreth Akbe and the return of a king to Havnor has not materialized. The damage to Earthsea's balance brought about by the wizard Cob should have been healed by Ged and Lebannen's journey to the Dry Lands. But it has not. When *Tehanu* opens, Earthsea is dangerous, threatened by dragons and hoodlums, a place where women are unsafe and children are brutalized. The reader is impelled through these new books by an uneasy question: what is wrong with Earthsea?

That the resolution of the trilogy should dissolve in book four into chaos and loss of faith is attributable to a paradigm shift Le Guin experienced, her much-discussed feminist awakening.[2] Her compass points shifted, Le Guin returned to her earlier work with an altered perspective, a parallax view. She questioned the assumptions underlying her earlier work, for example why men were mages and women were not, and "where were the women in Earthsea" (*Earthsea Revisioned* 9). How completely Le Guin favored the male is debatable; there is more

---

[1] The Earthsea books are *A Wizard of Earthsea* (1968), *The Tombs of Atuan* (1970), *The Farthest Shore* (1972), *Tehanu* (1990), *Tales from Earthsea* (2001), and *The Other Wind* (2002). Le Guin also published two precursor stories, "The Rule of Names" and "The Word of Unbinding," both of which originally appeared in *Fantastic* in 1964. I also use the following abbreviations: *A Wizard of Earthsea* (WOE), *The Tombs of Atuan* (TOA), *The Farthest Shore* (TFS), *Tehanu* (TEH), *Tales from Earthsea* (TFE), and *The Other Wind* (TOW).

[2] Le Guin's feminism and its effect on her writing has been the subject of many studies. Donna R. White's *Dancing with Dragons* presents an overview of these. Le Guin's essays in *Dancing at the Edge of the World* are also a source of insight into her feminist theory.

female strength in the early books than critiques suggest. Indeed, rather than rewrite or revise the trilogy, the author now writes the stories that went untold or were suppressed, Earthsea as seen from the distaff point of view. Following the mandate of feminist scholars like Adrienne Rich and Gilbert and Gubar, she dives deep into the original trilogy, bringing to the surface the hidden stories. Her widened Earthsea canon includes stories of women, witches, dragons and ordinary men.

To tell the other side of the Earthsea story, Le Guin has to deal with vestiges of her own pre-feminist thinking, especially as evidenced in aphorisms like "Weak as woman's magic ... Wicked as woman's magic" (*A Wizard of Earthsea* 5). She recasts these as projections of male fear of female power, in particular procreative power. Mages deny this fear by both vilifying and abstaining from women, shielding themselves from sexual contact and hiding behind their ironically phallic staffs. Their celibacy cuts mages off from more than sex. In Le Guin's essentialist conception, women are linked to the "Old Powers," a primeval force far stronger than the power of mages. The Old Powers, deeply rooted in the earth, are consistently portrayed using female sexual imagery; a mage's abstinence from women thus becomes a metaphor for his denial of the life force. Abstaining from a full experience of life, he denies its necessary end, death.

Another question arises: Why do the dead not die? *The Other Wind* (2001), chronologically the last book of Earthsea, appropriates the romance quest to answer this question, although the hero-centric quest is mitigated by the novel's collective point of view. Nominally led by Lebannen, the effort to repair Earthsea depends on the shared knowledge of women, dragons, lay men, and mages. Together they discover a link between the lack of peace and the mages' fear of death. The imbalance in Earthsea results from a breach by mages of the *Vedurnan (verw nadan)*, an ancient agreement between humans and dragons. Long ago one people, they split into two races: humans chose material goods and mortality and dragons chose the freedom of "the other wind" and seeming immortality. Afraid of death, mages broke this agreement, stealing dragon territory and walling it off to create a place of afterlife. The disquiet of the newer books results from dragon anger about this theft and the voices of the dead clamoring to be allowed to truly die. The Earthsea series ends with the harrowing of the Dry Lands and the release of its souls into oblivion. The dragons, their lands restored, leave Earthsea for good. The mages, their core beliefs in tatters, must reexamine their exclusionary practices. Far from her noble depiction of wizards in the original trilogy, Le Guin here places full blame for Earthsea's problems on the masters of Roke. More radically, Le Guin's dismantling of the Dry Lands is akin to refuting the Christian heaven. The history of Roke becomes a cognitive parallel to Western history, with mages standing in for the leaders of the early Christian church who, in some accounts, closed ranks around a male prerogative, writing women out of church history, vowing celibacy and vilifying women.[3]

There is a further question: What kind of peace will reign in a kingdom ruled by a bachelor (if hardly celibate) king, a man as unschooled in the fullness of life as any mage? The chastising element of the new books, where wizardly celibacy misleads and endangers, is counterbalanced by the serio-comic romance of Lebannen and the Kargish princess Seserakh. Forced upon each other, they slowly arrive at a détente and eventually a passion. Their sexual congress is the final step in a return to fertility and hence the full healing of the land. While we never see what it will become, their marriage is also meant to symbolize not just the unity of Archipelago and Kargad but also the co-equal rule of male and female. That they charge the air with sexual longing is so much the better. A marriage plot seems conservative in comparison with the radical inversion of the afterlife paradigm; however, Le Guin paints Seserakh as more than a match for the king. Assuming they are equals, their marriage will unite Havnor and Kargad, promising peace for all Earthsea.

Real Wizards Do It with Their Staffs

Celibacy appears elsewhere in Le Guin's work. In *The Left Hand of Darkness*, indwellers of the Handdara vow celibacy as a discipline, a form of self-concentration and a step toward full awareness (63). We see the same concept in *Always Coming Home*, where young people "live on the coast," willingly forgoing physical contact as they learn to control their sexual energies (488-492). In both cases, celibacy is treated gently, with respect for the discipline and self-sacrifice of those on a spiritual path. In the early Earthsea books, celibacy is unquestioned and even unmentioned. The closest we get to sexual content in the trilogy is Ged, staff in hand, wandering the obviously symbolic maze of Atuan (incidentally a place where women have power but like mages don't

---

[3] In "What Became of God the Mother?" and *Beyond Belief*, Elaine Pagels describes a systematic undermining of women's authority by the leaders of the early Christian church. See also *The River of God* by Gregory Riley, Bart Ehrman's *Lost Christianities*, and the Frontline series, *From Jesus to Christ* http://www.pbs.org/wgbh/pages/frontline/shows/religion/first/women.html. Comoletti and Drout argue that Le Guin's depictions of wizards, their power and their celibacy, draw from a medieval model of the Christian priesthood.

have sex). Le Guin first calls celibacy to our attention in *Tehanu*. When
we left Ged at the end of book three, he had sacrificed his magic powers
to close the doorway from death back to life. Having lost his power,
he leaves his useless staff behind. When we find him again early in
book four, he has lost everything: his powers, his home on Roke, and
his profession. Of him, the witch Moss says, "It's a queer thing for an
old man to be a boy of fifteen, no doubt!" (TEH 97). Tenar realizes for
the first time that Ged is a virgin. Wondering why, despite an almost
life-long friendship, she never felt attracted to him sexually, Tenar
asks, "is it a spell?" Moss tells her a theory which she has heard, but
which she, too practical for abstinence, does not believe: "They witch
'emselves. Some'll tell you they make a trade-off, like a marriage turned
backward, with vows and all, and so get their power then" (TEH 97).
Le Guin's specific attention to celibacy is thus a major shift away from
the first three books. She forces the question of where the belief that
mages must be celibate to have power originates. Celibacy protects the
non-magical from a mage's abuse of power for sexual ends, but must a
mage exchange sex for power?

That wizards do hoard their power by insulating themselves from sex
is shown in *Tales from Earthsea*. A young mage in training is told "to
make love is to unmake power" (TFE 64). In "Darkrose and Diamond,"
Hemlock puts a protective spell on his apprentice Diamond. Like a dose
of saltpeter, the spell dampens sexual longing. It also protects the boy
from sexual advances. When Diamond objects, Hemlock, says, "The
bargain, boy. The power we give for our power. The lesser state of being
we forgo. Surely you know that every true man of power is celibate"
(TFE 125). In the back matter of TFE, Le Guin connects the origins of
celibacy among wizards to the Dark Time, a period in Earthsea history
when the throne of Havnor sat empty and the school on Roke had yet to
be formed. "Women, witchery, and the Old Powers had all come to be
considered unclean, the belief was already widespread that men must
prepare themselves to work 'high magic' by scrupulously avoiding 'base
spells,' 'Earthlore,' and women" (TFE 295).

"The Finder," about the mage Medra, tells the history of the founding
of Roke. It locates the origins of wizardly celibacy in a fear of female
power. In the Dark Time women and men were equally capable of
magic, but magic itself was feared. Roke Island was a haven for witches
and some mages who hid from persecution and who coexisted with no
restrictions on sexual activity. They founded a school on Roke to teach
those gifted in magic. From within their own ranks came a separatist
movement of mages who vilified women, casting them as carnal and
as users of dark magic. Even though Roke Knoll is a center of the Old

Powers, these separatists feared the powers of the Earth. As Medra's partner, the witch Elehal, describes them:

> ... they *are* men, and they make that important beyond anything else. To them, the Old Powers are abominable. And women's powers are suspect, because they suppose them all connected with the Old Powers. As if these Powers were to be controlled or used by any mortal soul! But they put men where we put the world. And so they hold that a true wizard must be a man. And celibate. (TFE 81)

Equating women with these powers enabled the separatists to control them; meanwhile, historical revisionism and a smear campaign worked to subjugate women all over Earthsea.

Yet Medra shows that a mage can be powerful, sexually active, and even partnered. As a finder, his gift is sensing water and minerals in the earth under his feet; his power arises from his connection to the earth, which he calls "mother." At one point he escapes capture by asking the earth to open up and take him in. After some coaxing of "open to me," the ground parts and he enters a huge cavern that leads onto a long passage to safety (TFE 93). As in *The Tombs of Atuan*, the earth is rendered as womb-like and immensely powerful. Medra's willingness to take refuge in the earth mirrors his comfort in sharing his life with Elehal. They are both people of great power, yet their sexual relationship strengthens them. His use name, Otter, further associates him with women's magic. Medra is a model of possibility, an alternative to the story of mage as celibate. Despite the founders' intention that Roke school males and females equally, the separatist movement won the day, and wizardry became the domain only of celibate males.

At least these mages had their staffs to keep them warm at night. Although we don't need much prompting to see the staff as a symbolic penis, its phallic nature is evident in a monologue directed by the mage Dulse to his staff in "The Bones of the Earth:"

> "Stand!" He said to it in its language, and let go of it. It stood as if he had driven it into a socket.
> "To the root," he said impatiently, in the Language of the Making. "To the root!"
> He watched the staff that stood on the shining floor. In a little while he saw it quiver very slightly, a shiver, a tremble.... The staff swayed, was still, shivered again.
> "Enough of that my dear," Dulse said, laying his hand on it. (TFE 152)

As another of Le Guin's good wizards, a man whose power does not
depend on female subjugation, Dulse is perhaps the wrong example
to use here. Like Medra, he operates by merger and empathy, quelling
an earthquake by "getting in with it...Inside" (TFE 159). Again like
Medra, Dulse's teacher was a woman, the witch Ard, who taught him
"old" magic, scorned by Roke and aligned with the dirt and rocks of
the place itself. Yet Dulse hides the gender of his teacher, even from his
own apprentice Ogion, because it is not the way of Roke. And, like any
wizard, Dulse lives a celibate, nearly monastic life. His relationship to
his staff hints at sexual narcissism, or at least sexual immaturity. That a
boy becomes a mage only when given his staff by his teacher suggests
a homogametic quality, a kind of asexual reproduction. Further, since
the staff amplifies and directs the magic words of the wizard, it might
remind us of Gilbert and Gubar's famous question about the penis and
the pen. Illustrating the concept of phallogocentrism, they argue that men
have equated pen and penis, thereby implying that only a man can write.
Here, we might extend the equation: is a staff a metaphorical penis **and**
pen? Is that why only men do magic?

They Might Be Dragons

This leads us on to the question of women, whose knowledge and
bravery will ultimately save these mages from themselves. As noted, in
the years between writing the third and fourth Earthsea books, Le Guin
underwent a feminist awakening. In particular, she describes wondering
why she never wrote about women: "all my early books are about men,
and women are very secondary. In the first and third *Earthsea* books
there really aren't any women to speak of. That's very strange. I'm a
woman. Why was I writing that way?" (*At the Field's End* 37). Starting
with *Tehanu*, women are more central, more powerful, and much wiser
than in the early books. If anything, women and the powers associated
with them—the Old Powers of the Earth and, as we shall see, those of
the dragons—are privileged above the male powers associated with
Roke. In truth, what emerges is a feminist essentialist perspective, one
that argues for nature over nurture and which here elevates female nature
over male. As Ged, Dulse, and Medra illustrate, however, this is not a
separatist paradigm. Some men are more "female" than others, are able
to submerge their egos in the stream of life rather than try to control its
flow. There are good men and bad here, though it must be admitted that
there are no bad women.

Even in the first trilogy, we saw the Old Powers equated repeatedly with the female body. Le Guin herself has described *The Tombs of Atuan* as about sex ("Dreams" 55). Indeed, the underground mazes, the hidden treasury, the virgin priestess, and the violation of the tombs by a man, staff in hand, are almost too symbolic. As Tenar and Ged escape the labyrinth, Ged holds back the tunnel's spasms. The book even ends in an orgiastic collapse of the tombs, underscoring the might of the dark powers residing there:

> The earth of the valley rippled and bucked; a kind of wave ran up the hillside, and a huge crack opened among the Tombstones, gaping on the blackness underneath...then with a crash that seemed to echo off the sky itself, the raw black lips of the crack closed together and the hills shook once, and grew still. (TOA 123)

The femaleness of the earth is even more overt in the recent books, where its powers are far stronger and much older than those of the Roke mages. At the same time, these powers are accorded little reverence. In *The Other Wind*, a cave called the "Lips of Paor" is described as "a sacred place, full of power" (170). Its powers as an oracle long-forgotten, it is used as a dump: "all around it was a litter of rancid scraps of half-cured leather and a stink of rot and urine" (171).

Then there are the dragons. In the early trilogy, they are essentially run-of-the-mill: impressive but not imperative to the story. They know the Old Speech, the Speech of the Making, and being so old they remember things lost to human knowledge. But as characters they are flat. In the new books, the difference is immediate and immense. In *Tehanu*, we hear early on the story of the Woman of Kemay—a woman who is also a dragon. She tells of an ancient time when dragons and humans were all one race. Eventually, some chose the dragon's path—a wild life, free of material possessions, spent flying on "the other wind" (TEH 9). The others chose the human path, of material possessions, flightless and protected. Some people, it emerges, are both. Le Guin has said the dragon "rejects gender" (*Earthsea Revisioned* 24). Of course, both people we meet who cross the boundary from human to dragon are female, the burned child Tehanu and Dragonfly, a young woman turned away by the masters of Roke. Both have suffered sexually at the hands of men, including their own fathers. Clearly, the catalyst that arouses dragon-nature is human rage, in particular female rage. In *Earthsea Revisioned*, Le Guin writes:

The dragon…is wildness seen not only as dangerous beauty but
as dangerous anger…. It meets the fire of human rage, the cruel
anger of the weak, which wreaks itself on the weaker in the endless
circle of human violence. It meets that fire and consumes it, for "a
wrong that cannot be repaired must be transcended." (23)

This wildness and righteous anger are akin to what Susan Griffin
describes in *Woman and Nature: the Roaring Inside Her* (1978), the
influential feminist text which warns of the anger of the oppressed
female. In *Tehanu*, when Tenar and Ged are being tortured, the dragon
Kalessin saves them by burning their captors to death (TEH 222).
Kalessin, also called Segoy (creator of Earthsea), is depicted as awesome,
immense, and ancient. Kalessin calls Tehanu "child" and indicates that
Tehanu will join the dragons one day, when her work among the humans
is done (TEH 223).

Particularly as embodied in Tehanu herself, woman/dragon should
remind us of Medusa, whose punishment for being raped is to be turned
into a monster, one that men cannot look directly upon. Hélène Cixous'
"Laugh of the Medusa" reclaims the myth, seeing it as an imposition of
male fear of castration arising, as Freud would put it, from the snakes
adorning Medusa's monstrous head like so many severed penises.
Though she doesn't fully explain her meaning, Cixous says that the
Medusa, if actually looked upon, is beautiful, even laughing. These
images accord with Le Guin's description of Kalessin, on whom Tenar
is not afraid to look: "She had been told that men must not look into a
dragon's eyes, but that was nothing to her" (TEH 37). Like the women
who are also dragons, Medusa has double identity; she is both the
young woman raped and "punished" and the feared/fearful Gorgon. In
her landmark essay, Cixous also claims for women the power of flight
"Flying is woman's gesture—flying in language and making it fly…
women take after birds" ("Laugh" 291). Further, Cixous argues

Unlike man, who holds so dearly to his title and his titles, his
pouches of value…woman couldn't care less about the fear of
decapitation (or castration), adventuring, without the masculine
temerity, into anonymity, which she can merge with without
annihilating herself. (292)

This sounds much like the territorial differences between human and
dragon—the division of materiality and immateriality. Importantly
Cixous, like Le Guin, leaves room here for men; she says, "there are some
men (all too few) who aren't afraid of femininity ("Laugh" 289).

"All changed..."

Lebannen follows the mode of Le Guin's men who distinguish themselves by considering women (and dragons) his equals. In Arthurian style, he takes council with a Palnish sorcerer, the poor mender Alder, middle-aged Tenar, the maimed Tehanu, and the dragon Orm Irian, who is also the woman Dragonfly. Reluctantly he includes Seserakh, the Kargish princess forced upon him by her father. Along with those few Roke mages capable of self-evaluation, these are his quest companions. As we have seen, Le Guin revises the chauvinism of the earlier books that present the Archipelago (Roke and the associated islands) as the geological and ethical center of Earthsea. Instead, we find that the warrior Kargs and the dark sorcerers of Paln have retained essential knowledge long forgotten in Roke. In fact, the story of the *Vedurnan* comes from Seserakh, who herself is Kargish.

In sharp contrast to the Archipelagans, the Kargs neither practice magic nor believe in an afterlife. When Seserakh learns she is to marry Lebannen, she is terrified that "I won't be able to die. I'll have to live forever without my body, a bird that can't fly, and never be reborn" (TOW 126). Kargs do not fear death. They believe in rebirth in the strictly biological sense, return to the earth and thus to the cycles of nature. In contrast, Orm Irian says of the Archipelagans, "Men fear death as dragons do not. Men want to own life, possess it, as if it were a jewel in a box. Those ancient mages craved everlasting life. They learned to use true names to keep men from dying. But those who cannot die can never be reborn" (TOW 225-226). The wizards who broke the ancient bargain dreamed of something akin to the Christian heaven: "a great land of rivers and mountains and beautiful cities, where there is no suffering or pain, and where the self endures, unchanged, unchanging, forever" (TOW 226). Their mistake was in thinking that they had created a paradise. Instead, walling off the land also walled off water, wind, and sunlight. The dead there clamor to be let free. "It is not life they yearn for. It is death. To be one with the earth again. To rejoin it" (TOW 227). In the pivotal scene of *The Other Wind*, men, mages, and dragons together tear down the wall that keeps the dead from death (236-239). The Dry Lands are returned to the dragons and the dead go free. The price paid is immortality. As Peter Hollindale has argued, the Earthsea series' great theme is "the use and abuse of death" (186).

The final element to restoring Earthsea's balance is the shared rule of male and female, the reunification of nations, and the promise of fertility. Male/female balance was suggested but never fully realized in *The Tombs of Atuan*. The symbolically female labyrinth is penetrated by the staff-carrying Ged. And while this seems a Taoist balance, the dark Ged and the white Tenar, the ring of Erreth-Akbe and the sword of Havnor, Ged's celibacy denies fertility and thus rejuvenation. The true resolution of this element comes only in *The Other Wind*. In a plot pulled straight out of *Henry the V*, the long-promised peace comes through the marriage of Lebannen and Seserakh. They overcome cultural and linguistic misunderstandings to unify the lands. Again, the imagery is almost too obviously symbolic: their coupling, he dark skinned, she light, forms a perfect Taoist circle. This heterosexual marriage plot may seem reactionary. Seserakh, raised in purdah then forced to marry a stranger, initially strikes the reader as a victim; yet her red veils not only suggest fertility, they warn of the hidden dragon. Of Lebannen, Tenar says, "'he's met his match'" (245). This pairing of equals who will clearly share a passionate sex life counterbalances *Tombs'* unconsummated relationship and inequality of the mage Ged and the girl Tenar.

Here the newer books come closest to illustrating Darko Suvin's argument that *Tehanu, Tales from Earthsea* and *The Other Wind* constitute a second Earthsea trilogy. They also seem to illustrate Comoletti and Drout's suggestion that the newer books are a "feminist intervention." Without disagreeing, I would suggest that Le Guin did not intend to negate or deny the original trilogy. She is not rewriting it. Instead, the new books speak in the "other voice" present but to a degree hidden in the trilogy. They form a companion set, albeit one whose values are presented as superior to those of the first. In fact, the newer books are as female essentialist as the first three are male essentialist. Any essentialist perspective, however, is problematic. What good (or perhaps what harm) does it do to equate women to wild nature given the contempt with which nature itself is regarded? To suggest that women are at heart dragons and ought to be feared? Or that the damaged girl can achieve wholeness only as a dragon, flying wild on an immaterial "other wind?"

Imagine There's no Heaven

C. N. Manlove describes the first three Earthsea novels as "profoundly conservative," in as much as they strive to preserve "balance, moderation, and the celebration of the way things are" (287). This balance is achieved in part by acceptance of death. On their way to the Dark Lands, Ged tells Lebannen that "nothing is immortal. But only to us is it given to know that we must die. And that is a great gift" (TFS 122). Yet, as Le Guin parses out in the later books, these "mortals" are not truly relinquishing life. They go to the Dry Lands, where they are shades of themselves, not to the Earth, where they would become part of nature's great recycling program. This, I think, lies at the heart of Le Guin's disquiet with her own trilogy: it insists on mortality but provides for a kind of immortality. Ironically, celibacy insures that mages will never enjoy the "immortality" inherent in passing on their genes. The recent books, knocking out this immortality clause, could then be read as more consistently conservative, truer to the author's intention, than they were before. Certainly, they now fall more clearly in line with Le Gun's Taoist sensibility. That would be denying their radical agenda, however.

As Suvin argues, this "second" trilogy has the property of cognition, what he calls "a transitive understanding, which the readers can transfer from the pages of fiction to their own personal and collective lives" (498). The new books reach past their fantasy packaging to suggest ways that we might enact change in our own lives. The recent additions to the Earthsea series do not just argue for living in the present. Like Pullman's *His Dark Materials,* they force a reexamination of the Christian tradition, a questioning of the origins of its core beliefs. The many parallels to the history of the Christian church, from its early inclusion of women, to the internal takeover by a male-oriented faction, its avowal of celibacy, and its campaign of disinformation about women, are too analogous to dismiss. To draw the analogy out, if Earthsea's mages are responsible for many of its social ills, to whom do we affix blame in our cognitive reality? If Suvin is right, and I believe he is, Le Guin forces a reexamination of beliefs long buttressed by patriarchal authority.

Works Cited

1. Cixous, Hélène. "The Laugh of the Medusa." *The Signs Reader.* Eds. Abel, Elizabeth and Emily Abel. Chicago: U of Chicago P, 1983. 279-297.

2. Comoletti, Laura B and Michael D. Drout. "How they do things with Words: Language, Power, Gender, and the Priestly Wizards of Ursula K. Le Guin's Earthsea Books." *Children's Litera-ture: Annual of the Modern Language Association Division on Children's Literature and the Children's Literature Association.* New Haven, CT: 2001, p. 113-141.

3. Hollindale, Peter. "The Last Dragon of Earthsea." *Children's Literature in Education* 34.3 (2003): 183-193.

4. Le Guin, Ursula K. *Always Coming Home.* New York: Harper and Row, 1985.

5. —. Interview with Nicholas O'Connell. *At the Field's End: Interviews with Twenty Pacific Northwest Writers*. Seattle: Madrona, 1987. 19-38.

6. —. *Earthsea Revisited*. Cambridge: Labute, 1993.

7. —. "Dreams Must Explain Themselves." *The Language of the Night*. Ed. Susan Wood. New York: Berkley Books, 1979. 47-56.

8. —. *The Left Hand of Darkness*. New York: Ace, 1969.

9. —. *The Other Wind*. New York: Harcourt, 2001.

10. —. *Tales from Earthsea*. New York: Harcourt, 2001.

11. —. *Tehanu*. New York: Atheneum, 1990.

12. —. *The Tombs of Atuan*. Toronto: Bantam, 1970.

13. —. *A Wizard of Earthsea*. Toronto: Bantam, 1968.

14. Manlove, C.N. "Conservatism in the Fantasy of Ursula K. Le Guin." *Extrapolation*, Vol 21, No 3, 1980. 287-289.

15. Suvin, Darko. "On U. K. Le Guin's '"Second Earthsea Trilogy" and Its Cognitions: A Commentary." *Extrapolation*. 47.3 (2006): 488-506.

Amy Clarke teaches in the University Writing Program at UC Davis. A science writing specialist, she also teaches Literature of Science Fiction and seminars on Ursula Le Guin and on the Harry Potter phenomenon. She is currently finishing a book on how feminism has shaped Le Guin's canon.

Circles and Lines: The Voyage in *The Left Hand of Darkness*

Vera Benczik

Eötvös Loránd University, Budapest

The voyage has been one of the basic themes in literature since the dawn of narratives, because it provides such a convenient means to externalize and generalize difficult personal, internal psychological processes of humanity. Joseph Campbell says:

> The passage of the mythological hero may be over-ground, incidentally; fundamentally it is inward—into depths where obscure resistances are overcome, and long lost, forgotten powers are revivified, to be made available for the transfiguration of the world. (27)

The physical journey invites metaphorical and symbolical interpretations as the hero's rite of passage from innocence to experience, from isolation to integration or re-integration into a community, or conversely, a departure from security and confidence into a world of danger, doubt and corruption.

SF as a genre provides an excellent framework for the voyage motif, which is used as a vehicle to encounter difference, a defining element of SF according to Adam Roberts (28). As Scott McCracken phrases it: "the meeting of self with other ... offers new possibilities of being and the exploration of new alternative realities..." (102). Yet it is not only an opportunity to explore the unknown, but a convenient means to access and reflect upon the collective Self, as Damien Broderick very aptly points out (52).

In particular, the journey or voyage presents a convenient means to establish the physical distance from the familiar world necessary to set up an environment of difference. Brian Stableford observes that in 17th-18th century narratives, what he calls utopian fantasies were usually presented as imaginary voyages set in contemporary reality (15), although some, especially when narrating interstellar journeys, took the form of dream stories, in the absence of a credible scientific explanation for crossing interplanetary space (Stableford 16). Following real-life explorations, "the gradual removal of terra incognita from maps of the Earth's surface" called for new territories of difference (Stableford 17), and the progress of science supplied the authors with a completely new array of possible devices and vehicles to displace themselves into the realms of Otherness.

Ursula Le Guin's work often uses the physical journey to reach its "territories" of difference. The voyage motif occupies a central position in her narratives, and is often a structuring element of her prose, used to parallel or counterbalance the rites of passage of her protagonists. Ged's coming of age in *A Wizard of Earthsea* or Shevek's personal transformation in *The Dispossessed* are all externalized by physical voyages to realms of difference. In *The Left Hand of Darkness* (henceforth LHD) the parallel journeys of Genly Ai and Therem Estraven may be read as the metaphoric realization of their relationship, and the transformation it undergoes in the course of the novel.

Warren G. Rochelle observes that the journeys in Le Guin's narratives also follow the pattern of "open spirals" (40), and Elizabeth Cummins states that these "unclosed circles... suggest that one's life is a series of changes or transformations." (39) The unfinished quality of such voyages does not only mean that the protagonist, transformed in the course of traveling will not enter the same dialogue at his/her starting point, but also that the transformative process is not a singular life event, and never complete.

Unclosed circles and constant change are also defining elements of Taoism, on which Le Guin frequently draws in both her SF and her fantasy (Bain 211). As a religious philosophy which places itself in a universe "constantly re-creating itself in a continuing evolution" (Robinet 7), Taoism is itself subject to continual change. No ultimate form of Taoism may be determined, as its present variants are a result of a millennia-long dialogue with Confucianism and Buddhism (Robinet 5), still constantly defining and re-defining themselves. Concerned with balance, the Taoist universe is built on pairs of opposites, which are indispensable to each others' existence:

> Difficult and easy complete one another.
> Long and short test one another;
> High and low determine one another.
> Pitch and mode give harmony to one another.
> Front and back give sequence to one another.
> (*Tao Te Ching* Ch. 11 in: Waley 143)

Cyclicity is another "constant Taoist leitmotiv... the end and the beginning join. Although the reference points are constants, ensuring rhythm and order, transformations are unceasing, and the possibilities of change through repetition, renewal and rediscovery are innumerable" (Robinet 14).

In her essay on *The Left Hand of Darkness* Dena C. Bain predominantly focuses on universal balance—especially the opposites of light and dark—and unlearning, or "ignorance" (Le Guin, LHD 60), that is, refraining from action and thus the "Not-being aspect of Tao" (219) as Taoist influences. I will concentrate on the Taoist framework as adapted to the voyage motif and all its paraphernalia within the novel, with special emphasis on the presence of cyclicity and recurring circles as indicators of Taoist elements.

Yet when analyzing the text's journey motifs we do not only find convenient circles, but some disturbing lines, and an array of linearities that do not fit the Taoist idiom, but rather evoke the linear mythological and historiographical tradition of Judeo-Christian philosophy, which favors a linear progress of the myth of mankind "from initial Fall to final Redemption" (Eliade 143, Glasenapp 2), from a distinct point of chaos in the past towards the ordered endpoint of a stagnant Heaven after the Apocalypse.

This dialogue between East and West suffuses LHD with a creative tension that externalizes the relationship between the two central characters, Genly Ai—the human First Mobile of the Ekumen positioned on the planet Gethen—and Therem Estraven, prime minister and later exile of Karhide. The narrative is defined by the direction of their journeys in respect to each other, which may be read as a pattern of CONVERGENCE—INTERSECTION—DIVERGENCE; that is, they move towards each other, meet and separate again at the end of the work.

This same pattern may be taken as one of the repetitive, cyclical elements of the work. Here it suggests the Taoist drive towards harmony: the protagonists meet and separate again and again until the dissonance in their levels of communication is eliminated. The repetition of the pattern is accompanied by the linear shift of focus: starting out on the utmost public level, the narrative slowly progresses towards intimacy, with the journey over the Gobrin Ice (Le Guin, LHD 200-262) as its climactic episode.

Genly Ai and Therem Estraven may also be read as two distinct traveler subtypes, whom I will call the Envoy and the Exile. Both variants may be interpreted as performing what I term linear voyagers: both are sent from point A to point B by official order: the Envoy journeys voluntarily, the Exile is forcibly evicted from his home territory. Both performances end when a return to point A is effected, as both roles require the dislocation from home and the placement in an environment of difference to be enacted.

Genly Ai is the Envoy whose profession is to go on journeys, sent by an official body on a political errand. His voyage is a voluntary act, a journey with a clear aim: the initiation of Gethen into the Ekumenical society (34). Even his official designation as the 'First Mobile' suggests constant motion, as he is by Ekumenical definition the first alien to openly declare himself in Gethen, the first glimpse of the Other presented to the humanity, the collective Self of a "new" world. The fact that the First Mobile is sent alone reduces the encounter with the Alien to the encounter with one single being. The aim is to eliminate generalization, to shift the encounter to the utmost personal level:

> Alone, I must listen, as well as speak. Alone, the relationship
> I finally make, if I make one, is not impersonal and not only
> political: it is individual, it is personal, it is both more and less
> than political. Not We and They; not I and It; but I and Thou.
> Not political, not pragmatic, but mystical. (259)

Yet Otherness as encountered by the Envoy still remains on the general plane; since s/he is immersed in an intact society, a situation which could be paraphrased as individual meets society (abstraction); the possibility of stereotyping remains. Peter Brigg accurately notes that "in the alien societies of Gethen, the mere ability to speak to people isn't quite the same thing as a genuine contact. So Genly... finds his goal shifting; he must now search for a contact in the social and mental universes" (38).

The Exile, on the other hand, is evicted from a place or community, and lives separated in space without the possibility to return home. Therem Estraven is a double Exile, as his banishment from Karhide is preceded by his expulsion from his home domain, Estre. It is implied that the former is a voluntary act of separation, self-induced punishment for a moral crime not enacted but committed in thought.

Both Genly and Estraven would have to relinquish their respective roles as linear voyagers in order to complete a circle back to the point of departure, but both are barred from the possibility of returning to their actual starting points. From this point of view the novel contains two linear voyages where "home" is never reached again. The first step in Genly's voyage is only referred to: his journey through space to Gethen. Its significance is aptly pointed out by Mike Cadden: "the space journey warps time—it requires NAFAL flight, which will forever displace the characters from both their own worlds and their own generations" (52). The Earth that Genly Ai calls home is 120 years "older" when the actual narrative takes place. It is never finalized or verbalized, only indicated that his voyage from Earth is linear, with no option to return to a place which would present him with an irreconcilable clash between the familiar and the alien. Estraven's exile puts him into a similar isolation, finalized by his death; this loneliness enables the two protagonists to meet as equals in the central episode of the narrative.

The narrative proper starts on the utmost public level, with a fairly formal micro-voyage: the parade at Erhenrang (Le Guin, LHD 1-21). A parade carries within it not only the motion from point A to point B, but often the completion of a circle. Such a procession is set in a rigid ritual framework that can be seen as the compact representation of a culture; it is by definition antithetical to most things personal. Apart from presenting many readers with the shock of immersion into alien society, this ritual voyage also presents us with the first intersection point of Genly Ai and Estraven.

The end of the parade sees their separation, only to converge again and meet at another formal occasion: a dinner. Ritual elements—such as *shifgrethor*, which formalizes and shapes Gethenian communication, or the social practice that forbids Gethenians from talking business while eating—again establish a certain ceremonial distance, and communication proves fruitless and frustrating for both. (19) Separation sees the transformation of Estraven—who until then plays the role of Prime Minister of Karhide, second only to king Argaven—into the Exile. This is the moment of his final isolation, a metamorphosis into the Other, as the definition of "exile" incorporates the separation from the territory and society called home. Prevented from any form of communication with his homeland by the Order of Exile, without the hope of returning (as Genly is denied access to his society by the gap in time), he arrives in Orgoreyn as an outsider (79) just as Genly Ai arrived on Gethen.

Estraven's exile also means a radical decrease in his political status, and contributes to the diminishing of Genly Ai's official position, both instances underlining the shift from the public to the personal level. Parallel to Estraven's journey into exile, Genly Ai takes a short detour, and a strangely mutilated mini-quest within Karhide: he visits Rotheren Fastness, a spiritual center in Old Karhide, which is Le Guin's analogue for Taoism. Genly's aim is twofold: he intends to gather information about the past and the future (42 and 98, respectively). The information Genly returns with strictly concerns public matters (scientific, historical and cultural information about Karhide, the Fastnesses; and the Foretelling about the chances of Gethen joining the interplanetary alliance). Faxe's pronouncement that Foretelling is practiced by the indwellers "to exhibit the complete uselessness of knowing the answer to the wrong question" (70) will reach full sense only when Genly's interests, and thus the questions he wants to ask (or would have asked) have moved to the personal level.

This voyage parallels Genly Ai's later journey to Pulefen Farm in many aspects: the pattern of ascent and descent over the mountains, the use of one of the slow-going trucks, whose noise level is so low that the traveler may "hear avalanches grumble down in the distance" (52). The mode of traveling is another reference to Taoist philosophy, and Genly Ai's remark about it beautifully exhibits the clash between the Western linear and Eastern cyclical traditions: "Terrans tend to feel they've got to *get ahead, make progress.* The people of Winter, who always live in the Year One, feel that *progress is less important than presence*" (50; italics mine).

While the similarities are obvious, there are remarkable disharmonies between Genly's two mini-voyages: the first is voluntary, made in comfort with Genly Ai and his concerns still in the public domain—he still "impersonates" the Envoy embarked on the quest to bring Gethen into the Ekumen. The second mini-voyage is undertaken as a private person, a prisoner without identity, under compulsion, spent in discomfort. There is an added emphasis on physicality: the nudity of the passengers, "the smell of excreta, vomit and sweat" (167), as opposed to the strong spiritual presence of the Fastness—especially via the account of the Foretelling (62-67)—in the first journey. Genly's spiritual receptiveness exhibits the same bipolar quality: while during the first mini-voyage even the emotionally and psychologically demanding act of the Foretelling interests Genly as a scientist rather than as a person, more intrigued by the mechanics of the procedure than the spiritual message (67), the apparent lack of a spiritual setting in the second mini-voyage finds him far more prepared to undertake the rite of passage required to undertake the central Journey in the novel.

The return to Erhenrang is thus rather low key, and the departure to Orgoreyn finally increases the personal involvement of Genly Ai in Estraven's affair, after Estraven's former kemmering asks Genly to serve as messenger and deliver a significant sum of money to the Exile (104-107).

The third meeting point in their lives comes in Orgoreyn, and although this encounter is less influenced by the rules of social conduct, it still proves fruitless. It is interesting to note that Estraven, whose status on the Orgota political scene is lower than Genly Ai's, turns to the other on a more personal level than the Envoy—still bound to the public level by enacting his political role—can at present handle; the personal dissonance prevails, thus separation ensues again, leaving Genly feeling like having been struck by an "electric shock" (132) and Estraven frustrated that his attempt to provide counsel had been misinterpreted (161). The personal discord is symbolized by a disharmony in their physical motion: their paths, despite the intersections, do not run parallel. One may argue that these intersections prove fruitless until society/culture is physically present in the meetings. Once this "obstacle" — the paraphernalia that mark "civilization" — is eliminated, and the shift from public to personal is completed, communication flows freely and assonance is achieved.

The politically and personally unsatisfactory meeting in Orgoreyn is followed again by diverging motion. It is Genly who moves ahead this time; the road to Pulefen Farm constitutes an inverse mirror image of the journey to the Fastness. Ascent and descent again, but no holy Grail at the end of the road, yet the voyage itself exhibits all the hardships required by a quest proper. It may be read as an act of ritual purification, a process of symbolically ridding the Envoy of his cultural background and the public dimension, readying him for the journey over the Gobrin Ice: he is deprived of his status and his name (the anonymity of the convicts objectifies them), his belongings, his clothes ("we were all naked..." 168), and spends the journey in the back of a truck, huddled together with twenty-five Gethenians for warmth. Symbolic in number, as twenty-six is the completeness of the lunar cycle for Gethen. Twenty-five alive, one dead; in the presence of the duality of death and life — another Taoist motif: harmony is only achieved when both members of a complementary pair are present — with only water to drink, involuntary fasting cleanses his body from within. He spends the journey covered in the blood of the dead Orgota, an image which carries an immense degree of inherent symbolism: blood is one of the most powerful liquids, both physically and spiritually, and the act of being covered by it evokes the dual image of birth — the newborn baby, naked yet covered in the blood of its mother — and christening, with one of the most powerful liquids human culture knows. Thus Genly, purged of his alien quality, his physical belongings, his status, his identity, properly prepared for the spiritual act by the purging of his body (fasting), is symbolically reborn into Gethenian society, ready to cross the threshold from the populated world to the isolated desert of the Gobrin Ice.

At this point the personal isolation for both Estraven and Genly Ai is complete, yet a whole world still stands behind the former. Its elimination is inevitable if the roles of Self/Other are to be presented as interchangeable, and harmony is to be achieved. The elimination of Gethenian society, or rather its reduction to one single being, comes when Estraven extracts Genly Ai from the labor camp, and their consequent isolation from all "human" culture. Now comes the novel's central episode, the Journey over the Gobrin Ice, where everything, the landscape, the natural surroundings, even the artificial objects, can be interpreted as devices aiding the narrator/s to emphasize certain aspects of the voyage.

The Journey occurs in a minimalist and dualist scenario: there is only ice and snow, sunshine and shadows, white and black, yin and yang. It is a land in *somer*, "...the silent vastness of fire and ice"(220). Seemingly sterile, yet full of dormant potential under the cold surface. Its seeming immobility is contradicted by the volcanoes in eruption (225), or the violence of the snow storms (223). Both may be read as the phases of Gethen in *kemmer*, crucial to the symbolic representation, for the Taoist drive requires harmony, which would be disrupted if only one sexual state was suggested and the other left hidden. It is no coincidence that the heavy sexual symbolism, the brutal and uncontrolled force of the eruption (227), and the image of the lava which may be read as a reference to menstrual blood, blood of the earth, is present during the sexually most tense episode in the novel.

The two tiny figures of Genly and Estraven pull a sledge together over the endless barrenness of the glaciers. This seemingly linear motion is in fact part of a cyclic journey; it brings the two protagonists back to Karhide, where they originally started. But the texture of the voyage is fundamentally different from the journey episodes observed previously.

Firstly, there are no minor characters present in the Gobrin Ice episode, and the dichotomy of motion and the immobility in the external environment results in a monotony not present there previously. The daily struggle for survival and the emptiness of the landscape eliminate anything beyond instinctive experiences from the external perceptions. Genly Ai's intolerance of *peshtry* meat (217) may be seen as an emphasis on the fact that any form of "communication" (as one may define eating, or digesting, as interiorizing the genetic information of a living form other than us, thus a form of "communication" with the surroundings on the cellular level) is exclusively reduced to the Genly Ai-Therem Estraven pair.

The sledge and the tent—artificial objects, remnants of Gethenian culture—both have an important symbolic function, as tools that aid the establishment of the complementary pairs that rule this part of the journey. The frequent references to a sledge in proverbs and sayings in the book establish it as an important symbolic artifact of Gethenian culture (e.g. LHD 116,); its rich and multilayered metaphorical use is exhibited at its full range on the Gobrin Ice. It is crucial for survival, yet it is heavy to pull. A furthering (it holds the food for the journey) and an obstructing device at the same time: in rainy weather, transformed into a cart "it was a bitch" (215). It yearns for snow to be easy to transport. It is the space for biological needs, since it carries their provision. A dichotomy in itself, and an object that creates dualism, it is both a means of connection and a separation: both characters pull the same sledge, work towards the same goal, yet it is sometimes physically wedged between them, and divides them according to their position into "puller" and "pusher" (213), a truly Taoist pair, who are opposites, yet work in harmony on furthering their object of focus in the journey towards its goal.

The other important cultural object concerned with traveling is the tent. In the narrative it is used as a tool to exhibit or accentuate a different set of dichotomies. In itself it is juxtaposed to the sledge, which symbolizes "outside," while the tent's emphasis is on the "inside," on "inner space.' One could say that in a Taoist division the sledge is yang, it is light, as it is pulled during the day, it is dynamic, as it is in motion. The tent, on the other hand, is yin: darkness (240), since it is used during nights and storms, it stands for inside, it is static. It is also just as separative and connective as the sledge (245). Yet its separative function concerns the borderline between nature and culture: it provides the space for the "cultural" needs; keeping out the cold and the wetness establishes the warm, safe place needed not only for survival but for the free flow of communication. Its connective function lies in aiding the dialogue between the main characters.

These two tools of the voyage are complementary, as the "existence," or the use of one never coincides with the use of the other. They add to the cyclic dimension as alternating, yet ever-present artifacts of the daily routine. Recurring episodes, like the waking ritual in the morning (240-41), further accentuate the static, cyclic quality of this journey; the external monotony of sledge-pulling is contrasted with the internal dynamism of Genly's and Estraven's relationship; thus the emphasis shifts from the circumstances of the voyage to the communication between the main characters, from outside, "death and cold" (245) to inside.

This internal progress of communication, which ultimately results in the partial achievement of harmony, is linear. A change in naming from land names and titles at first, then last names (212), and finally first names when utmost mental intimacy is achieved (253), marks the cornerstones of the progress in their relationship, as frequent misunderstanding gives way to mutual respect and understanding. The climax of this development is marked by telepathic communication, *mindspeech*: an extremely dynamic process, even more so when set against the staticity of the physical environment. Genly Ai and Estraven meet on the utmost mental plane possible for two people, with extreme honesty, since mindspeech renders conscious lying impossible. Harmony is achieved, yet it is disharmonious: a dichotomy in itself, marked by Estraven's uneasiness, caused by his lack of experience with this form of communication. The added strain of Genly Ai materializing in his mind as his dead brother—and love—Arek (252) makes this "bond... an obscure and austere one, not so much admitting further light... as showing the extent of the darkness." (255) At the same time, this is also the point when the most basic dichotomy of the novel, the human-alien opposition, is finally eliminated, and by this annihilation, fulfillment is achieved.

Very significantly, the most dynamic episode, in spiritual terms, is accompanied by and contrasted with a pronounced restraint on the physical level: the growing erotic tension between the two characters is not resolved like the spiritual progress, in fulfillment, in the utmost physical intimacy — the sexual act — because, as Genly puts it: "for us to meet sexually would be for us to meet once more as aliens. We had touched, in the only way we could touch. We left it at that. I do not know if we were right" (248-249). Genly seems to fear that a sexual encounter would endanger the harmony achieved on the mental plane. Focus would not only shift abruptly from the inside back to the outside, and thus break the linear development of the main characters' relationship, but physical sexuality would also disrupt the Taoist harmony inherent in Estraven's being as he is, "Cold, warmth. Female, male. ... Both and one. A shadow on snow" (257), since his sexual response to Genly would forever render him female, and thus deny him his "maleness."

As if in reply to this interior dischord, the physical environment reaches a state of utmost staticity: the weather termed unshadow, where light and dark become one, and contours are eliminated, thus producing the illusion of void: "sledge, tent, himself, myself: nothing else at all" (260). This stasis not only mirrors the main characters' relationship, but also presents them with a choice: remain forever suspended in this illusion of nothingness—which evokes the idea of Nirvana—or by traveling on again enter into the world of dualities. The choice is illusory: for one, remaining would mean certain death in the hostile environment. Additionally, after the *mindspeech*-episode, the original aim of Estraven's and Genly Ai's journey is introduced again, when the former theorizes about the possible courses of action King Argaven may take once Genly reappears alive in Karhidish territory (257). Thus driven by their original, political aim, and the need to survive, they have to continue traveling over the Ice.

There follows a ritual purification not unlike the one on Genly Ai's involuntary voyage to Pulefen Farm: the sledge is the first to go as the objects carried easily fit into backpacks (269). Food runs out, and the motif of fasting as preparation for the crossing of yet another threshold surfaces again (271). The return to a hearth (272), to society, sees the abandoning of the tent (277), and thus the acknowledgment that the voyage is nearing its end. The other objects, their sleeping bags, pieces of clothing etc., are given away as presents in return for hospitality. This gradual loss of the voyage paraphernalia is juxtaposed with society/ culture's slowly creeping back into the narrative. Yet because of the development in their relationship this does not prove the disruption it once was, and there is no return to the alien-Gethenian opposition. The end of the central journey does not only evoke feelings of relief, but also sadness, as "the saga was over; it belonged to the Ice" (277).

Yet spiritual readiness is required for a new journey waiting beyond. Purified, stripped of their personal belongings, voluntarily, this time, and anonymous to the world, they are left "without shelter, without food, without rest: nothing left but our companionship" (283) as crisis nears again: the journey over the Gobrin Ice is finalized by the last separation of Genly and Estraven. The latter's death by quasi-suicide (286) does not only put an end to his journey in time, that is, his life, but deprives him of the possibility of returning home, just as Genly's temporal dislocation had disabled him from going back. Communication between the two abruptly comes to an end, and the Taoist harmony gives way to another communicational void.

One could argue that Judeo-Christian linearity replaces the Taoist cyclicity, as Estraven crosses the threshold between life and death. And just as Genly's editorship of the narrative—Bickman calls him the "structuring consciousness" (43) of the novel—on the abstract level may be read as an effort at the ritual communication of his quest with his home community, left beyond the threshold of time, so may his editing of Estraven's journal be seen as a desperate attempt to interact with the persona of his friend left in his written notes. But both the abstract community and the personal friend are gone. Both instances of communication are one-sided, and thus fruitless. Hence the Taoist quest for harmony ultimately fails as it is robbed of ongoing interaction and mutual change.

The last part of the narrative is interspersed with a "presence of absence": Estraven. Genly's apathy, and then anger (285-286), his constant, often sarcastic remarks concerning Argaven's behavior towards Estraven during the audience with the King (291-93), the guilt Genly feels at having betrayed his dead friend (294), and finally his visit to

Estraven's family (299-301), all may be read as attempts to resurrect his friend, to reconstruct him from interaction with people around him. This strong personal theme is contrasted with Genly's apparent indifference to all matters political. Even Faxe's remark upon the landing of the ship, the climax to the political level of the narrative, as official contact is at last established between Gethen and the Ekumen, evokes memories of Estraven during their pull over the Ice (295).

The political aim of their overall voyages—bringing Gethen into the interplanetary alliance—is fulfilled. But because the emphasis during the journey had fully shifted to the personal level, the original aim of narration is annihilated, diminishing retrospectively the importance of this political achievement. Establishing communication between Gethen and the rest of the universe contrasts with the termination of interaction between Genly Ai and Estraven. The finality of both acts brings stasis in the narrative itself: all the journeys become fixed in the past. We leave the Taoist framework of constant, cyclic change, and this also signals the completion of the linear macro-journey which started with Genly's departure from Earth. But instead of solace waiting at the end of the road (300), it is purgatory at best that awaits the protagonist, who remains, presumably, on Gethen, if not, an alien, at least not in his own "home."

Conclusion

The multi-level use of the journey motif in *The Left Hand of Darkness* presents a complex pattern of cyclic and linear motion. The influence of Taoist and Judeo-Christian philosophical and religious traditions, respectively, structure the narrative to a point where the natural surroundings and the artificial objects can be interpreted as devices subordinated to the journey theme, aiding or opposing various aspects of the protagonists' attempts at communication.

This physical motion aids the gradual shift from the public to the personal level of communication, and the various parallel journeys in the text interact with one another, their similarities and differences both part of the dynamic pattern. But while the linear voyages are completed, the circular quests present in the novel are left unfinished, the narrative itself presenting an attempt at consummation. Yet the obvious replacement of the public with the personal level, the focal point of the narrative, remains fixed on the Gobrin Ice, or to put it in Genly Ai's words: "it is good to have an end to journey towards, but it is the journey that matters, in the end" (220).

Ursula K. Le Guin's narratives very often follow this Taoist principle of featuring the voyage over the destination. For Shevek, Ged or Rokannon, it is not the goal of their journey that counts—although a destination is certainly reached—but the process of getting there. The focus in these narratives is on the internal transformation of the characters, and various aspects of the physical voyage are used to accent or facilitate this process.

Works Cited

1. Bain, Dena C. "The 'Tao Te Ching' as Background to the Novels of Ursula K. Le Guin." In *Ursula K. Le Guin: Modern Critical Views,* ed. Harold Bloom. 211-224.

2. Bickman, Martin. "Le Guin's *Left Hand of Darkness*: Form and Content." SFS #11, 4:1 [March 1977].42-47.

3. Bloom, Harold, ed. *Ursula K. Le Guin: Modern Critical Views.* New York: Chelsea House, 1986.

4. Brigg, Peter. "The Archetype of the Journey in Ursula K. Le Guin's Fiction." In *Ursula K. Le Guin,* ed. by J.D. Olander and M.H. Greenberg. New York: Taplinger Publishing Co., 1979.

5. Broderick, Damien. *Reading by Starlight: Postmodern Science Fiction.* London: Routledge, 1995.

6. Cadden, Mike. *Ursula K. Le Guin Beyond Genre: Fiction For Children And Adults.* New York—London: Routledge, 2004.

7. Campbell, Joseph. *The Hero with a Thousand Faces.* Princeton, NJ: Princeton University Press, 2004 [Bollingen 2004 commemorative hardcover].

8. Cummins, Elizabeth. *Understanding Ursula K. Le Guin.* Columbia, SC: South Carolina Press, 1990.

9. Eliade, Mircea. *The Myth of the Eternal Return.* Pantheon Books, 1954.

10. Glasenapp, Helmuth von. *Die fünf grossen Religionen.* E. Diedrich, 1951.

11. James, Edward, and Farah Mendelssohn, eds. *The Cambridge Companion to Science Fiction.* Cambridge: Cambridge UP, 2003.

12. Ketterer, David. *New Worlds for Old: The Apocalyptic Imagination, Science Fiction, and American Literature.* Bloomington: Indiana University Press, 1974.

13. Le Guin, Ursula K. *The City of Illusions.* London: Vista, 1996.

14. —. *The Dispossessed*. London-Toronto: Granada, 1983.
14. —. *The Left Hand of Darkness*. New York: Ace Books, 1976.
15. —. *A Wizard of Earthsea*. New York: Bantam Books, 1984.
16. McCracken, Scott. *Pulp. Reading Popular Fiction*. Manchester: Manchester UP, 1998.
17. Roberts, Adam. *Science Fiction*. London: Routledge, 2000.
18. Robinet, Isabelle. *Taoism: Growth of a Religion*. Stanford, CA: Stanford UP, 1997.
19. Rochelle, Warren G. *Communities of the Heart: The Rhetoric of Myth in the Fiction of Ursula K. Le Guin*. Liverpool: Liverpool University Press, 2001.
20. Stableford, Brian. "Science Fiction before the Genre. The Genre's Prehistory." In *The Cambridge Companion to Science Fiction*, ed. by Edward James and Farah Mendelsohn. 15-31.
21. Waley, Arthur. *The Way and Its Power: A Study of the Tao Te Ching and Its Place in Chinese Thought*. London: George Allen & Unwin, 1934.

Vera Benczik, born in Budapest, Hungary, received her MAs in English and Assyriology from Eötvös Loránd University, Budapest. She is currently completing her PhD at the same institution. Her dissertation focuses on the voyage theme in Ursula K. Le Guin's science fiction.

The Lathe of Heaven
as Le Guin's Book of Changes

Kathleen Keating
Greensboro College

I think we all have archipelagoes in our minds. (Le Guin, "Books
Q & A")

Modern Chinese of course has a number of devices apt to contain
… fluidity and make the language more precise. Not so the archaic
language of the *Yi Jing*, in which the imaginal fields of single
ideograms stand next to each other as islands in an archipelago
or as figures in a dream…. (Ritsema and Sabbadini 19)

Daoist-oriented interpretations of Ursula K. Le Guin's fiction
sometimes polarize critics into two camps: those who "talk snake" and
those who "talk starfish." I borrow the categories from Le Guin's short
story "The Nna Mmoy Language" (2003). In the story, the narrator
describes an island destination frequented by tourists who arrive via
interplanar travel. Visitors to this "garden utopia" find its language
too foreign even for the translating machines to handle. However,
the narrator's well-travelled friend Laure has studied the language
impasse between plane-surfing tourists and the incomprehensible island
inhabitants. Laure uses a simple heuristic to explain the communication
problem: "We talk snake. A snake can go any direction but only one
direction at one time, following its head," whereas the Nna Mmoy "talk
starfish. A starfish doesn't go anywhere much. It has no head. It keeps
more choices handy, even if it doesn't use them" ("Nna Mmoy" 165).
Gingerly pressing this analogy into service, we might distinguish critics
who are starfish-talkers — those who uncover and explicate the still-point
of Daoist ideals, often through imagery and thematic analyses — from
snake-talkers, who find little narrative interest in Daoist readings.
  Snakes are not unwanted guests for Le Guin. Her playful "It Was a
Dark and Stormy Night" features the risk-taking "hoop snake," which
moves by biting its venomous tail and rolling along. "[V]ery few things,"
she writes, "come nearer the real Hoop Trick than a good story" (194).
Snake-talkers like a good story line, and they create lines of inquiry
that take us somewhere new, left or right. Starfish, on the other hand,

---

* I am greatly indebted to Sylvia A. Kelso, whose gifted editing has made all the
difference in this essay.

understand the world through five kinds of lefts or rights ("Nna Mmoy" 167), a relativist mapping that in narrative could easily collapse into a solipsistic series of impressions. With a few exceptions, the snake is generally a creature of the land; the starfish, of the sea. Readers may wonder whether the Nna Mmoy narrative pits the snake's "either/or" logic against the "either/or/or/or/or" (167) logic of the contentedly-centered starfish, who is somewhat reminiscent of the indecisive George Orr in *The Lathe of Heaven*. Does Le Guin ask us to privilege the starfish for out-"orring" the snake? Although the starfish way may critique the simple binary logic of the snake-talker, the critique itself spawns another binary either/or and thus reinscribes the dichotomous thinking it seeks to overturn.

In the "The Nna Mmoy Language," we catch a glimpse of another structure which might put starfish and snake in a different kind of relation:

> As well as [Laure] could figure out, the syllable *nen*, variously modified by the syllables that surround it, may signify a range of objects from a flash flood to a tiny iridescent beetle. He thought the central area of connotation of *nen* might be "things that move fast" or "events occurring quickly." It seems an odd name to give the timeless, grass-grown ruins that loom above the villages or serve as their foundations—the cracked and sunken tracts of pavement that are now the silted bottoms of shallow lakes—the immense chemical deserts where nothing grows except a thin, purplish bloom of bacteria on poisonous water seeps. (165)

This passage hints at a structure that moves beyond the starfish/snake dualism. The silt of starfish and poison of the snake are brought together in a strange shifting landscape of purplish water seeps and silted bottoms. Without count, pockets of land and water form the landscape. But if seen merely as either land or water, the landscape as represented would disintegrate, flattened into a two-dimensional diagram. The connections and extensions in space are equally important in spatializing relations in time: we see a field of action through which events, past and present, are manifested. The ruins of the past simultaneously present the marks of effacement, a process leaving its traces. Yet the future in Nna Mmoy also appears to be coming into being as the processes of sinking, silting, growing, seeping transform the space. This world is not locked in a single change, revolving-door style; it is a space of becoming and changing in different ways. Importantly, the space is the scene of language. The syllable, *nen*, escapes a single definition. Instead, it participates in signification by "surrounding" other syllables. Connoting a range of both "things" and "events," *nen* metonymically invokes languages beyond English. Can the "Dao of the West" reflect a set of relations beyond the familiar dualism of yin and yang, which so easily falls into fixity even when Western individuals "know" it is not a dichotomous opposition? This essay contends that Le Guin has in fact provided us with a realization of that possibility in her 1971 novel *The Lathe of Heaven*. In *Lathe*, the narrative structure is the experiment of writing the archipelago. Just as the Nna Mmoy's interspersed pockets of land and lake highlight the ways of starfish and snake, the archipelago mediates relations of surroundings and multiplicity. Much earlier than "The Nna Mmoy Language," the archipelagic art in *Lathe* finds its model in the 3000-year-old Chinese classic the Y*ijing (I Ching)*, more commonly known in the West as the *Book of Changes*.

Critics have sometimes expressed ambivalence about Daoist-oriented elements in Le Guin's work. Many have accepted early judgments that *Lathe* is conventional in form. Perhaps we have missed the experimental by focusing too much on the character contrasts between Haber and George Orr. It may not be coincidental that while the texts *Daodejing* (sometimes called *Laozi*) and *Zhuangzi* have been used to understand Le Guin's Daoist philosophy, the *Yijing* has not. Since my argument assumes that Le Guin's awareness of the *Yijing* also mediates her understanding of "Daoism," I provide a brief summary of recent sinological scholarship on Daoism.

The form of the *Yijing* is difficult to describe, much less analyze. One of its structural principles is correlative thinking, which I link with the archipelago as metaphor. Critics have argued passionately that SF has perhaps been underappreciated in the academy partly because it operates outside the conventions of realism. Despite such awareness, evaluations of *Lathe* often re-inscribe realist expectations. Yet if Le Guin's archipelagic aesthetic in *Lathe* draws on the *Yijing* and its philosophical implications, the novel would be better viewed as posing a radical challenge to Western epistemological assumptions regarding the process of subjectivity.

Critical discussions of Daoist thought in Le Guin's fiction can be loosely categorized without recourse to metaphors from land or sea. Since the 1970s, several approaches have emerged: early readings that identify and explain Daoist elements or the background of Daoist thought (Bain; Brown); analyses of "Daoist" imagery or of pairings and opposites (Cogell; Cummins); critical examinations of duality to be resolved or held in tension (Bittner; Theall); readings of Jungian archetypes or conflicts between individual and community, private and public (Spencer; Gunew; Crow and Erlich); paralleling Daoist concepts with magic (Galbreath); containment of "Daoism" through models of artistic development; political critique of "Le Guin's Taoist agenda" (Jameson 78); and synthetic explorations of Le Guin's philosophical and religious arguments (Erlich; Lindow).

Barbour's early assertion that *Lathe* is "practically a primer in Taoist thought" ("Taoist" 22), while undoubtedly revelatory and energizing, has since been difficult to dislodge. Critics have largely accepted the assertion that the protagonist functions as an exemplification of the Daoist sage, but this understandable judgment might be revisited given advances in the fields of classical Chinese and Eastern philosophy. In later essays, Barbour turns to the Hainish novels to explore images of "opposites yoked together": light/dark and yin/yang, for example ("Hainish" 166). Where Barbour pairs balance and *imbalance*, many later critics refer in shorthand to Le Guin's interest in "wholeness and balance," which are yoked in the titles of his essays. The slippage has meant that wholeness and balance have often been treated as privileged terms representing "Daoism." Critics after Barbour address holism and wholeness; balance and equilibrium; yin and yang as opposites; touch and separation; the Daoist sage; and *wu wei* (Slusser; Remington). Dualism, however mapped on the spectrum from static to dynamic, has become such a commonplace in Daoist interpretations that arguments challenging this structure have gone relatively unnoticed.

As early as 1975, another trend emerges in which scholars have insisted—each time prematurely—that Le Guin's Daoism has been just a phase in her growth as writer. Sometimes these positions focus on alleged genre violations, as in Watson's argument about the paranormal in *Lathe*. Others assume a teleological history of the progression of novels ending in explicit political commitment (Porter; Huntington). Suvin critiques Daoist strains for promoting "a static balancing of two yin-and-yang-type alternatives, two principles or opposites" (145). While Suvin's reading of stasis in the yin/yang relation veers from most accounts of Daoist philosophy, underlying his reading is acute psychological insight about Western difficulty with duality. At base, Suvin and Fredric Jameson suggest that Le Guin's incorporation of Daoism may be symptomatic of an incomplete radical politics.

These developmental arguments have fallen by the wayside with the persistence of Daoist thought in the fiction and public interviews. In 1998, Le Guin published *Lao Tzu: Tao Te Ching* (*LT*), her own poetic rendition of the well-known Daoist text *Daodejing* (*Tao Te Ching*).[1]

---

[1] To facilitate Chinese name recognition, the Pinyin will be followed by the Wade-Giles equivalent in parentheses on first mention.

A culmination of work beginning in her twenties, this version was a long-term effort of puzzling out passages "[e]very decade or so" (*LT* 107). Definitively belying the developmental models, *The Telling* (2000) seems to suggest the reverse tendency: increasing engagement with the historical and social specificity of Daoism. Sandra Lindow's essay on the novel explores a practical ethics that takes up political and social questions, thus moving the criticism beyond an either/or involving the political and Daoism. Richard D. Erlich's synthetic examinations of philosophical and religious thought demonstrate Le Guin's abiding interest in grappling with Judeo-Christian, Daoist, and other Eastern traditions. By approaching the fiction with attention to ontological and epistemological issues, such as transcendence and immanence, Erlich indirectly makes a good case for viewing Le Guin as much more than an "unconsistent Taoist" ("Ketterer" 139).

Unquestionably, *Daodejing* and *Zhuangzi* influence *Lathe*, so one might wonder what justifies a reading of the *Yijing* as particularly important in the novel. No epigraphs, after all, come from the *Yijing*. *Lathe's* title derives from *Zhuangzi*. Yet historical, archeological, and linguistic evidence confirm that the *Yijing* preceded any specifically Daoist texts by several centuries. The *Daodejing* and *Zhuangzi* are indebted to the *Yijing* rather than the other way around. It is, therefore, curious that the *Yijing* has remained unexplored in the criticism.

Yet the *Yijing* aside, even "Daoism" remains something of a mystery. The introduction to the one-thousand page *Daoism Handbook* warns that "Among the world's religions, Daoism is undoubtedly the most incompletely known and most poorly understood. As the twenty-first century opens, not only are the basic facts of Daoism known to very few, but the very concept of 'Daoism' remains unclear to most educated people and educators" (Kirkland, Barrett and Kohn xi).

Nor does Daoism fit neatly into typical Western conceptualizations of philosophy and religion. The term for religion, *zongjiao*, and philosophy in the Western sense, *zhexue*, did not exist in China until the nineteenth century (Ching 2-4). Sinologists point out that the English use of "Daoism" may be somewhat misleading because it implies a unified identity or system of thought.

In early China, texts such as the *Daodejing* and *Zhuangzi* developed in a milieu of "the hundred schools" of thought. These often-competing schools examined issues of governance, morality, and ritual. Historically, many teachers during the Warring States period advocated different *daos*, ways or paths that provide ethical, social, and political guidance. The various schools—including the *Daojia* as a school of the Way—were distinguished early in China's history in the work of Han scholars and were compared by Sima Dan, whose work was included in his son's famous *Records of the Grand Historian*. Over centuries, Daojia developed into different offshoots, including a religious strand with scriptures and deities. Traditionally credited as the author of *Daodejing*, Laozi (Lao Tzu) eventually was deified as one of the Three Pure Ones, which are part of a larger pantheon including the Eight Immortals. This religious extension of Daoist ideas uses elaborate rituals performed in temples along with exorcisms and blessings.

In recent years many scholars have moved away from linking Daoism with a perennial philosophy and critiqued the labeling of philosophical and religious Daoism as reinscribing Western imperialism. Others, however, have argued that treating Daoism and other Chinese philosophical thought as unique promotes a kind of orientalism as theorized by Edward Said and later postcolonial critics. Thus, although the single name "Daoism" has been viewed by some commentators as problematic due to its erasure of important variations in Chinese cultural practices, the idea of "slicing up" a field of interrelated behaviors and texts for Western convenience has been equally contested.

Beyond the problem of naming, a second pitfall in explicating "Daoism" is one common to comparativist projects. In the West, religion is typically viewed from within a Judeo-Christian framework. This framework assumes a logic of mutually exclusive spheres. In contrast, Confucianism, Daoism, Buddhism, and the so-called Chinese popular religion are not necessarily experienced as mutually exclusive systems of belief but rather as related traditions; the various strands form a braid of complementary practices that overlap in many ways with "Chinese culture." This braid of teachings is called *sanjiao* (san-chiao). It is thus not self-evident what should be classified as Daoist and what is better thought of as "syncretist."

Separate from Daoist texts is the *Yijing,* which at times has been vilified both in the People's Republic of China and in Western countries as a work of superstition, New Age-inspired irrationalism, or cryptic difficulty. C. G. Jung ironically remarks that the book is not "for intellectualists and rationalists. It is appropriate only for thoughtful and reflective people who like to think about what they do and what happens to them" (xxxiii). One might add that it is appropriate also for those who can bear with the uncertainty of its pre-classical Chinese. James Legge, one of the first English translators, spent decades trying to get a grip on the book and remarks: "There is hardly another work in the ancient literature of China that presents the same difficulties to the translator" (xv). John Blofeld's popular 1960s edition stresses the same concern: "the Chinese text is so difficult as to be largely incomprehensible to anyone who has not made it the object of special study" (26). However, even in the best English translations, those who make a first pass at the *Yijing* typically express bewilderment when confronted with its cryptic passages and a structure that has no fitting analogue in Western literature. Given the daunting nature of the text, one might ask whether Le Guin was well versed in the *Yijing*.

Le Guin would have encountered references to the text in her other reading, such as in the last book of *Zhuangzi*. Explicit naming of the work—as the *I Ching* rather than the now-standard Pinyin *Yijing*—occurs in her nonfiction, fiction, and poetry.[2] The nonfiction reveals that she has extensive experience working with the *Yijing*. In March 1976, Le Guin's response to the first special issue on her work mentions the *Yijing* by name twice as she denies belief in the paranormal: "one can go a very long way with Jung and the *I Ching*, as I do, without the slightest leaning towards occultism and obscurantism" ("Response" 46). In her short story "Intracom," published in 1974, one character hits another over the head with the *Yijing*—literally and metaphorically.

A substantive allusion to *Yijing* thought also occurs in the portrayal of the Handdara sect in *The Left Hand of Darkness*. From the safe distance of the narrator Genly Ai's perspective, the reader learns of the Handdara Foretellers, whose prophecies are legendary but explicable, or so he assumes, through "[o]racular ambiguity or statistical probability" with "discrepancies ... expunged by Faith" (*LHD* 55). Genly Ai's skepticism is, however, coupled with an awareness of his limited knowledge. Genly assumes the Foretelling is "on the plane of pure chance divination, along with yarrow stalks and flipped coins," which refer to divination technqiues. However, Faxe the Weaver disagrees and claims that in fact the process is "the reverse of chance" (61).

In an analogous manner, when asked in a 2003 interview about her writing process and the issue of conscious control, Le Guin responded:

---

[2] The *Yijing* appears in a 1976 *New Republic* article as well as in other essays ("Prophesy"; "Non-Euclidean"). The poem "Tui" published in *Hard Words* uses the "associated qualities" of Dui (Tui) described in the *Shuogua* of the Ten Wings. Correspondence with James Tiptree, Jr. also mentions the *Yijing* (Phillips). In *Coyote's Song*, Erlich suggests in passing that the patterning frame in *City of Illusions* operates like the *Yijing*, an important possibility that merits further argument.

When you're making something, a casserole or a clay pot or a
book, there are aspects of it that you have to be in full control of,
and then, once you know your craft through practice, there are
aspects of it that it might be better not to control—to let happen....
It is related to trusting the *I Ching*: Things are related; there is a
fullness of time, and what I need will come within my reach—but
we cannot understand how they are related, and so waiting and
being ready are of the greatest value. ("Life")

Le Guin's remark implies that a work may develop without conscious
understanding, and this openness to the idea of a creative unconscious
is not foreign to the *Yijing*. In summary, the evidence demonstrates
Le Guin's deep familiarity with the *Yijing* as far back as 1967 and as
recently as 2003.

The *Yijing* probably first took form as a Chinese divinatory manual.
The core of the book can be described as a composite of images and
words: the images consist of sixty-four diagrams called hexagrams. One
of its Western translators describes the work as "an anthology of omens,
popular sayings, prognostications, historical anecdotes, nature wisdom,
and the like, which have all been blended together and structured around
a framework of hexagrams" (Kunst 2-3). One can "read" the book,
but not in a linear way. It is usually portrayed as more like an intense
interaction with multiple interpretative levels.

The original text called for exegesis, and so the *Yijing* developed over
centuries and through contributions of an unknown number of authors.
Because the work has grown through layers of accretions, scholars
have sought to identify its different "strata." Philological studies and
comparisons of style with other ancient works suggest that the oral
tradition from which the written version emerged most likely brought
together a mix of actual divinations made over time by professional
diviners, certain historical events, proverb-like phrases and, possibly,
certain phrases from folk songs (Shaughnessy; H. Wilhelm). However,
the difficulty of piecing together the history of oral traditions preceding
the written form means that most accounts are still highly speculative.

The earliest strata of the written work, however, can be identified
as some version of a skeletal structure known as the *Zhouyi*, which
means "The Changes of the Zhou." When the Shang dynasty ended,
the conquering Zhou people absorbed several aspects of Shang culture,
possibly including ritual techniques. Knowledge of this period was
shadowy until Shang oracle bones were discovered in 1899 (Ching 16).
These bones and shells, which were carved with simple questions and
oracular answers, suggest that an early form of Chinese script existed

by 1200 BCE; the bones, scholars assume, predate the *Zhouyi*. Thus, the *Zhouyi* most likely took its written form between the eleventh and eighth centuries BCE.[3]

In the transition after the Zhou conquest, divination through astrology, omens, and bone-crack reading continued. This explains why the text may originally have served as a diviner's manual—to aid professional *fangshi*, who were individuals skilled in a range of divination practices and alchemical lore and were sought out by emperors to create life-preserving potions. Even this early stratum of the text, however, shows an appreciation of novelty and language play. The oracular text uses homophones, rhyme patterns, punning, pairings, parallelisms, and incremental repetition (Kunst; R. Smith 120-24). These devices imply a valuing of certain kinds of thinking: associational, relational, and correlative.

Identification of the second earliest stratum has been debated but includes at least some of the *Shiyi* or "Ten Wings," which are the collection of commentaries that became attached to the *Zhouyi*. The *Zhouyi* along with the Ten Wings became the *Yijing,* the very first of the so-called Confucian "Classics." This designation of a "classic" (often referred to as canonization) suggests the importance of the text, which was preserved from the infamous burning of the books near the end of the Warring States period in 213 BCE. A third stratum of the book includes the later wings and perhaps adjustments of earlier commentaries. All texts comprising the Ten Wings were most likely attached to the core oracular text before the end of the first century BCE.

At base, consultation of the "oracle" pivots on a question-and-answer format. The inquirer formulates the question ideally after much serious internal deliberation. The most frequently advocated methods to derive hexagrams are the use of yarrow stalks, wands, or coins. The yarrow stalk ("milfoil") method takes eighteen formal steps to yield a single hexagram. The faster and easier coin methods, attributed to Chinese Daoists from the Han period or before, remain popular. In this method, each toss of three coins (Chinese coins or others with contrasting sides) will yield a certain number of heads (a value of three) or tails (a value of two).

---

[3] Lynn dates the earliest written parts to the ninth century BCE, with the hexagrams themselves possibly much older (1-2). Kunst estimates 770 BCE, which is earlier than Shchutskii's 671 BCE (Kunst 5-9; Shchutskii 191).

Each value from a toss—totaling 6, 7, 8, or 9—is recorded through specific *Yijing* notation. There are two types of lines: solid (——) or broken (– –). The solid line represents firmness (*gang*), later associated with yang. The broken line represents yielding (*rou*). These forces are represented quite differently in the *taijitu* or Diagram of the Supreme Ultimate, which is shown at the bottom of Figure 1.

Fig. 1. Representations of Reality by Lines and Images

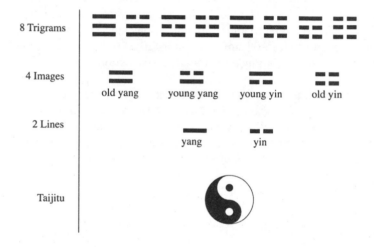

The cosmology behind the *taijitu* indicates that from the "nothing" of non-being emerges Dao, and from Dao emerges *qi* (ch'i). Dao produces the "ten thousand things" through *qi*, but *qi* itself is described by Western scholars in various ways. Common translations of *qi* are breath, force, or energy. A dynamic force that approximates self-perpetuating creativity, *qi* experiences constant change (*yi*).

It is from *qi* that yin and yang derive. The process by which *qi* bifurcates into yin and yang modes differs by commentator, with one such authority using an agricultural metaphor to explain that *taiji* produces yin and yang much like "a millwheel grinding out" coarse or refined "cosmic flour" (R. Smith 54). The metaphor may appeal to Western individuals in its material specificity but may also be misleading in that way, for yin and yang are neither substances nor states.

The "shapes of change" are explained in the *Dazhuan* commentary of the Ten Wings: "Therefore there is in the Changes the Great Primal Beginning. This generates the two primary forces. The two primary forces generate the four images. The four images generate the eight trigrams" (Wilhelm-Baynes 318-19; henceforth WB). Yet as Figure 1 also shows in the "four images," a dualistic model of yin and yang as the two basic building blocks of the universe is an oversimplification. If we imagine two main modes in which qi moves, and the different temporalities of those movements, we may perhaps get closer to the idea of the four images. Figure 2 shows the differences in notation, which is a necessary part of the reading process for most users. On the left of Figure 2, the "four images" show that what Westerners often assume are just "yin and yang" are better understood as four slices of development in time as yin and yang move in relation to each other. Ritsema and Sabbadini warn that yin and yang "cannot be adequately translated in Western terms.... Nothing is intrinsically Yin or Yang" (54-55). The problem is ontological rather than solely linguistic.

Fig. 2. *Yijing* Line Notations

Figures of Change	Phase	Notation symbol	Numerical Value	Moving line?	*Transforms into this line*:
▬	old yang	—0—	9	Yes	— —
▬▬	young yin	— —	8	No	
▬	old yin	—x—	6	Yes	——
▬▬	young yang	——	7	No	

Another implication of the four images is that yang and yin may be "young" or "mature," but they are involved in one of two processes: changing or transforming. That is, "change" itself is a moving process, according to one of the commentaries: "As the firm and the yielding lines displace one another, change and transformation arise" (WB 288). The term *yi* does indicate change, but it can also mean the kind of unexpected change that disrupts our lives or destroys the orderly world around us (Karcher, "Jung" 292). *Bian* is usually translated into English as "change" in a sense of alteration, while *hua* might be understood as "profound transformation" (Blair 942). The Chinese terms *fan* and *fu* designate different degrees of recurrence that are seen in change and transformation. *Fan* is explained by Ritsema and Sabbadini as to "turn and move in the opposite direction; turn around or upside down (180 degrees); change to the opposite position; contrary" (77). The English word *reversal* is a typical choice by which to render *fan*. Related but still differing in process is *fu*, typically translated as *return*, which means to "go back; turn or lead back; recur, reappear, come again; restore, renew, recover; return to an earlier time or place" (77). Thus, the four images involve grappling with change through movement, temporality, and pattern.

Four points in particular regarding the development of yin and yang should be kept in mind when considering the *Yijing*. First, the pair yin-yang is by no means restricted to Daoism and appears in other Chinese traditions. Second, the earliest core of the *Yijing* does not use the concepts of yin and yang. Third, yin and yang were formulated as part of a naturalist philosophy referred to as the Yin-Yang School or School of Naturalism that developed centuries *after* the oracular text was written down as the *Zhouyi* (Pas 4). Finally, although sometimes heaven and earth are called "pure yang" and "pure yin," the model of interdependence negates the possibility of having one kind of movement remain in a "superior" position.

Issues of interpreting change, then, come to the fore with the *Yijing*. Image and word co-exist but only in relation to a particular context, which has its own situation and timing. The specificity is supplied by the inquirer in the role of questioner/reader. Reading becomes a recursive and self-reflexive process that stretches its filiations both inward and outward, to past and future. So, too, can such readings stir up what Kunst calls "hermeneutic sedimentation" (93). The polysemous nature of the text thwarts any attempt to exhaust possible interpretations.

The *Yijing* emphasizes the particular insofar as the user's moment, situation, and question are critical factors in an "answer." The initiating act of questioning becomes a navigation of the multiple spaces of text and context. The process offers a kind of knowledge insofar as it suggests how one can best respond to change and transformation. For one consults the *Yijing* in times of crisis or when the mind feels stuck, as the commentary relates: "The Changes came into use in the period of middle antiquity. Those who composed the Changes had great care and sorrow" (WB 345). The commentary advises the wise person to meditate on the book in times of rest because it will be needed in a different way in times of crisis. The one who consults the text may feel, like George Orr, a sense of "no way out."

Sinologists argue that classical Chinese is better equipped than English to convey such nuances in the concept of change. One need only consider the catch-all nature of the English word "change" to understand this point. Whether it be family change, monetary change, mood changes, or "the change" in older women, the English word shaves away—lathe-like, perhaps—what otherwise might be subtleties, differing types, and duration. Western thought reflects a cultural difference in how we articulate and conceptualize change. Western individuals, Blair argues, "habitually set out to affirm that change is already contained by one or another of our essentialist categories or apocalyptic visions or totalizing theorics" (937). Le Guin's rejection of the apocalyptic reading of her novels may express much more than a displacement of the Judeo-Christian tradition, for by dispelling apocalypse, she also challenges the Western predilection for totalizing change ("Ketterer" 139).

Reading the *Yijing*, then, is not unlike encountering an archipelago. Simply defined, an archipelago is a cluster of islands. While we might wrest the idea from the literal geological context, there is no reason to do so since scientific models provide their own provocative evidence that an archipelago is multiple. No particular type of rock or formation is required, and these groupings of islands can be located anywhere. Scientists have identified several hundred different archipelagoes in mid-ocean as well as in shallow waters.

One might argue that the archipelago is an unsuitable metaphor to describe the *Yijing* since naturally islands do not move. Geomorphic scientists, though, measure what we cannot see. Not all time scales are anthropocentric, just as Daoist texts not infrequently decenter the human. Continental plates ride on the molten material inside the planet's core, mediated by different layers of heat and pressure. More startling, perhaps, is a recent theory that volcanic hotspots, which scientists long assumed were immobile while tectonic plates shifted over them, may themselves be on the move deep below the ocean. One long set of archipelagoes, the Hawaiian-Emperor island chain, may be the product of such a migrating hotspot located in the earth's mantle (Sager). According to Tarduno et al., it is the "land and seafloor that wander" while only "the spin and magnetic axes remain almost fixed in absolute space" (1069), a shocking idea that reminds us more of Earthsea's Immanent Grove than planet Earth. More familiarly, archipelagoes also change their surfaces and shores through the traversals of different plant and animal life on the surface as well as from the marine ecosystems submerged beneath the waves. They notoriously complicate international disputes involving property claims based on national borders. After all, the boundaries are fluid and untraceable.

The implications for a narrative structure modeled after the archipelago are numerous. Deliberately challenging the idea of a single island, the model is based on plurality and porosity. In terms of plurality, we might note that the archipelago is fundamentally oriented toward the multiple. Diversity in an archipelago takes the form of different local ecologies. The archipelago is inherently a relational structure that emphasizes shifting perspectives depending on one's position. Porosity can be seen in the model's use of correlative thinking. The small groupings of islands can form a system, but they also affect the larger system of the whole archipelago. Submerged connections are an obvious aspect of the archipelago. The sea typically hides the connections among land forms, and time and nature shape the land at different rates. The archipelagic is also a space of mediation on which different processes and inhabitants carve histories into meaningful places that pass away over time, much like the shifting landscape of the Nna Mmoy. It evokes both image and word; there is no "true" identity to an archipelago. Islands may exist in nature, but the archipelago is an understanding or way of viewing, mediated through human consciousness. It does not denominate a discrete separate object that exists in nature independently of the observer. Its model of plurality and porosity may challenge some of the dominant assumptions about subjectivity.

Archipelagoes, of course, form Le Guin's fantasy world Earthsea. The fictional universe is constituted by mapping the archipelago on the page or the screen; it appears from this bird's eye view at times to dissolve, not unlike a moving kaleidoscope of patterns. What "Earthsea" is, is impossible to know; what appears to be a unified map at first glance can shift into another pattern. The Earthsea of *The Farthest Shore* creates a secondary archipelago for the Children of the Open Sea. This tribe is part of the sea, not only moving across it from one raft to another, but also swimming within it. The floating rafts appear to be moving most of the time, and together they constitute a moving set of islands. In fact, when Arren asks tribe members where they are located, the chief answers, "The islands are there.... All the islands.... The sea" (116). In response to Arren's question about the land they come from, the chief replies simply enough, "No land." This model is the one that perhaps best approximates Le Guin's archipelagic art: a moving set of related islands that ungrounds.

Complex spaces may also map temporalities. In "Some Thoughts on Narrative" Le Guin opens with a consideration of Aristotle's view that narrative is "movement 'through' time for which spatial metaphor is adequate" (38). However, when she explains narrative, it is dreaming that she invokes. Using the terminology of dream researchers, she talks about the primary visual experience or "image-jumble" that takes place in the unconscious mind. Le Guin seems to concur with a basic psychoanalytic assumption that dream materials, as primary processes, are fundamentally irretrievable because they form in the unconscious. When awake, the dreamer may try to make sense of the materials by seizing upon events and ordering them causally through "secondary cognitive elaboration" (40), which becomes a story. The resulting "explanation" is really a fabrication, she notes, insofar as the links among the available images remain submerged, and thus the dreamer invents but under guise of rationalization. Offering an extended example, she narrates a possible dream full of bizarre and seemingly unrelated actions and images. Only afterwards does she introduce a *dreamer* in whose mind these dream images must have taken place. Her hypothetical dreamer is then named. Awakened, this Edith Driemer remembers only isolated bits from the dream. From these image bits, Le Guin hypothetically moves forward to imagine Edith's supposed actual day as "realistic narration of the day Edith woke up" (41). The dreamer almost seems to be constituted between the night dream and the next-day narrative, as if the process of subjectification can begin only from the indeterminate tissue connecting the dream-like images and the language of narrative.

Like a dream, the *Yijing* use breaks from the normal flow of life to create what Karcher describes as a "dragon hole in time" ("Jung" 292). For Le Guin, consciousness has its similar holes, through which images from the unconscious slip. Not insignificantly, James Miller uses a similar metaphor to describe Daoism: "Daoists seek primarily to realize a sort of transparency or porosity between their bodily identity and the economy of cosmic power in which it is embedded" (271). The archipelago seems to offer one of the most porous spaces that can be mapped, a mediation between dream and waking, the unconscious and consciousness, image and word. This mediation is, of course, what narrative also enacts. Asserting that, "I think we all have archipelagoes in our minds" ("Books Q & A"), Le Guin seems to embrace this ideal of multiple islands with channels of transparency in the waters between their rocks. It may not be coincidental that she seizes on a similar metaphor when asked about her role as a writer who crosses genres: "I do seem to be someone who has carried people across from realistic literature to fantasy and science fiction and back. I'm happy to do that. If I'm a stepping-stone, walk on me, for heaven's sake" (Le Guin and Heltzel 49).

The archipelagic appears in the *Lathe of Heaven* in two instantiations. First, it metonymically maps its own contours for readers through the association of islands set adrift in the narrative. I would agree, then, with Carl Malmgren's claim that *Lathe* has a metafictional dimension. Second, the archipelagic in *Lathe* complicates readings that otherwise focus on the self or singular identity. In Malmgren's reading of *Lathe* as hidden *Kunstlerroman*, for example, George is struggling to discover and realize his potential, to find out what he should be. While the narrative presentation of George, Haber, Heather may articulate attributes of their identities, the diegesis constitutively weaves these concerns together in a way that is more complex than a concern with singular consciousness. Suvin also sees self at the center of *Lathe*, and in fact faults the novel for projecting self onto universe. Where *Lathe* fails in its apparently solipsistic projection of self, "The New Atlantis" succeeds for Suvin through its guiding analogical movement. Ironically, Suvin applauds the "substitution of geology for history" in "New Atlantis" but sees no such movement in *Lathe* (267).

The archipelagic is mapped in *Lathe* as the narrative spatializes the experience of temporality through images of the changing landscape. We learn that some things are generally untouched by George's reality shifts: "Geography remained perfectly steady: the continents were where they were. So did national boundaries, and human nature, and so forth" (124). Yet later in the novel, when George seems to have greater insight and fortitude, he tries to explain to Haber:

> Everything dreams. The play of form, of being, is the dreaming of substance. Rocks have their dreams, and the earth changes.... But when the mind becomes conscious, when the rate of evolution speeds up, then you have to be careful.... A conscious mind must be part of the whole, intentionally and carefully — as the rock is part of the whole unconsciously. Do you see? (161)

George's explanation reveals that dream and form come together in different time scales represented as changing rocks of earth.

The narrative also calls attention to its archipelagic structure through scattered allusions to islands. The most notable, perhaps, is to More's *Utopia* through the trance code word, Antwerp. If that intertext is indeed operating, then one wonders why Antwerp rather than "Utopia?" More's narrative uses Antwerp as the site of human meeting, a crossing point that ultimately leads to the narration of the trip to the nowhere of Utopia. Utopia is, of course, an artificially created island structured to isolate, partly for defensive reasons. It is not entirely cut off from the world, but close. The word Antwerp, while serving as a threshold between dreaming and waking, also marks the crossing point where Orr and Haber meet. Other island intertexts appear in Haber's laudatory fantasies about the South Sea Islands, George's own dream about them, and the allusion to *Gulliver's Travels* as the Augmentor is refined. These otherwise disparate islands move into a new constellation with the snakebite scenario.

Although the Mato Grosso where Haber locates his hypothetical snakebite scenario may seem unrelated to islands, in fact this unusual region reflects an archipelagic structure. This Brazilian habitat is inland, roughly at the center of South America.[4] Yet the Mato Grosso experiences dramatic seasonal changes. Dry for about half the year, its floodplains are called the Pantanal, a heterogeneous mosaic of strange topographic features. Annually, the floodplains fill with several meters of water, which covers most of the land for months. The so-called hydromorphic savannas thus are submerged beneath rising waterways with interspersed island-like formations of high ground, often consisting of a circular grove of trees. The names used to describe these formations—raised islands, raised earth platforms, earthmounds, stands, or forest islands—suggest nothing less than an archipelago.

Haber's snakebite scenario in the Mato Grosso serves as a narrative lure about change and decision-making; courses of action that seem obvious are suddenly suspended. At his final psychiatric session, George questions the doctor's motives. The usually overbearing Haber paces a bit and then stands "pausing before the huge window" of his office, gazing at the "nonerupting" Mount St. Helen (136). The narrative seems to pause and appeal to readers' familiarity with the genre of the "moral dilemma" hypothetical scenario: "You're alone in the jungle, in the Mato Grosso," Haber says, "and you find a native woman lying on the path, dying of snakebite. You have serum in your kit, plenty of it, enough to cure thousands of snakebites. Do you withhold it because 'this is the way it is'—do you 'let her be'?" (136).

What may seem transparent to Haber—and perhaps to the reader as well—is not at all clear cut to Orr. Instead of affirming that he would of course administer life-saving and plentiful serum to the dying woman, George creates a space for himself by refusing the scenario frame:

> It would depend.... Well ... I don't know. If reincarnation is a fact, you might be keeping her from a better life and condemning her to live out a wretched one. Perhaps you cure her and she goes home and murders six people in the village. I know you'd give her the serum, because you have it, and feel sorry for her. But you don't know whether what you're doing is good or evil or both.... (136)

In this scene, Le Guin's irony resonates at a second level as Haber invents, only to render unconscious, a native woman curiously reminiscent of his query about South Seas island daydreams (36-38). The question is real: Given the constraints of subjectivity, how can we correctly read any situation that requires a choice and therefore change?

[4] On the Mato Grosso, I draw primarily on Zeilhofer and Schessl, as well as Ponce and da Cunha.

Haber has posed a snake-talking either/or choice, a "this or that," which George refuses to answer. Haber, eager to get on with the business at hand, dispenses with reasoning: "O.K.! Granted! I know what snakebite serum does, but I don't know what I'm doing.... I freely admit that I don't know, about 85 percent of the time, what the hell I'm doing with this screwball brain of yours, and you don't either, but we're *doing* it—so, can we get on with it?" (136). The "hypothetical scenario" regarding the Mato Grosso thus collapses, and so too does the semblance of reasoned discourse that can dialectically approach "truth." The narrative, too, "gets on with it," sweeping the reader into a web of complicity. Constraining the forward movement with a backwards reversal, however, we note that this dialogue has been preceded by Haber's unexpected prosopopoeia regarding the "entrails" of the Augmentor ("Just hooking a new ergismatch into Baby's hormocouple" [133]) along with an ill-fitting, almost dream-like allusion to Swift's *Gulliver's Travels* ("now to hook up the glumdalclitch with the brobdingnag" [134]). Swift's satire, of course, takes place on multiple islands, so the scene overlays two structures of islands here. The "hooking up" seems to be strangely framed on one end by Haber's words lifted from Swift, and on the other by Orr's dream of the Aldebaranian aliens. The snakebite scenario enacts suspension between these spaces by raising epistemological uncertainty ("It would depend.... I don't know"), possible future events ("You're alone in the jungle ... and you find a native woman"), and ethics ("Do you withhold it because 'this is the way it is'?").

In addition to island intertexts in the novel, the archipelagic is reflected in narrative structure. *Lathe* begins and ends in water, but the relationship with water is much more complex than merely an oceanic or maternal flux. One immediate question about narrative structure is the seemingly simple one of the opening: does the novel begin with a frame narrative? A vulnerable jellyfish that hangs, sways, and pulses in the powerful ocean is about to be thrust from dark sea currents onto the land. It is important to note how the contrastive land emerges: "But here rise the stubborn continents ... cliffs of rock break from the water.... And now, now the currents mislead and the waves betray, breaking their endless circle, to leap up in loud foam against rock and air, breaking..." (7). The "landing" of the jellyfish is about to occur. But the land is active: the continents "rise" and the rock cliffs "break" from the water, an active voice implying agency. Not only does the land "move," but the prose itself develops through polysyndeton: despite the moving action of the verbs, we are focalized on the process of widening perspective, an accumulation of details that expands and emerges, so that we get the feeling of "but here ... and there ... and there ... and now, now."

Lathe overlays two stories: a one-time cosmogenic event showing the creating of Earth through the accretion of matter; and on an entirely different time scale, the everyday phenomenon of tidal movement and engagement with the land through its shores. Two time scales, two stories, are layered together. They are both fused, insofar as we are able to read one narration, and yet also each positioned differently in the reader's mind while cohabiting the same space.

In this overlaying of time scales, the macrocosmic rise of "continents" and their "shelves of gravel" (7) is registered in a microcosm of daily tides around the smaller landmasses and their channels through which a jellyfish might be borne. This is one type of correlative relationship, and because we know how over time physical landmasses can indeed be radically affected by naturally-occurring oceanic events or human obstructions, we see that everyday events connect with larger systems. The appearance of continents here and there is co-present with this other everyday world of rocky landmasses surrounded by water that we extrapolate from our past experiences of beaches, shorelines, and other "breaks." The complex interrelation provides us with an archipelago. As the lyricism of the passage suggests, the archipelago is associated with currents, rhythmic movements, change, and some fear, for the ocean seems to "mislead" and "betray" to the "terrible outerspace" that our minds, like the jellyfish, must face.

At the very least, I would argue that the opening with the jellyfish landing cannot be reduced to an image or motif, but is seen to evoke indexically an encounter between the reader making interpretive acts, and a structuring on different layers. In narratological terms, the diegesis could be described as the fictional world in which the events of the characters George Orr, Haber, and Heather LeLache unfold. The extradiegetic has its own microstory and its own unknown narrator: the jellyfish as a synecdoche of "creature[s] made all of seadrift" (7) who has been drifting on the current is about to be landed—and presumably suffer greatly if not perish from sun and air. A question of suspense launches the main narrative: "What will the creature made all of seadrift do on the dry sand of daylight; what will the mind do each morning, waking?" This question in the future tense has neither answer nor prediction—only a hint that something is coming that will require action (what will "it" do) and therefore some kind of choice or decision-making.

Whether we call the narrative of the imminent jellyfish-landing a frame or extradiegetic narrative, we must tease out the implications of these different levels in the novel. One might argue, for example, that the novel structures itself to return to the water in order to enact the Le Guinian proverb-like bit of wisdom, "To go is to return" (175).

A piece of *Daodejing*, this maxim about the polar complementarity of yin/yang might first seem to suggest that we end up where we started. The problem with that interpretation is that continuous change implies more a spiraling than circling experience: we make a return kind of movement as signaled by the infinitive verb (to go, to return), but we cannot have the same experience twice. Continuous change does not involve a dualistic ping-pong effect. Instead, we would anticipate seeing a change or transformation in the return. The end of the novel in fact bears out this idea of continuous change, returning us to the extradiegetic frame. Heather has wandered into the store in which George now works, and she refers to her experience "before The Break," which occurred when Haber's void began unforming the current reality. But this "Break" also recalls the opening "breaking...". George notes that it is time for his "break," and invites Heather to go with him for coffee. As they leave the store to get to know each other (again), the alien "watched them from within the glass-fronted shop, as a sea creature might watch from an aquarium, seeing them pass and disappear into the mist" (175). These final words return us to the opening frame of sea creature in water, or so it seems. Instead of ocean waves breaking on rising land, the novel ends with explicit meditation, association, and analogy: the containing glass of the shop is *like* the glass of an enclosed aquarium, with the turtle-like alien inside. While the frame thus appears at first to close the loop of the circle in terms of imagery, there is not an exact return to the extradiegetic. We are not released back to the endless ocean, but rather continue to focus on the mediating seams between sea and land in the form of the aquarium. The archipelagic structure set up for us at the opening of the novel, with its interspersing of sea and land, remains.

An archipelagic structure thus would aim at invoking continuous change rather than a model of duality alternating back and forth. In its hexagrams, the *Yijing* provides an example of change that is relational; from a field of action, different slices of time, situations, and moments of development converge. The first two hexagrams have a kind of psychological importance because they are doubled trigrams. Hexagram 1, the Creative or Heaven, moves through its six lines much like a micronarrative. A "hidden dragon" in line one moves up to the second line: "Dragon appearing in the field. It furthers one to see the great man" (WB 7-8). The third line arcs through time: "All day long the superior man is creatively active. At nightfall his mind is still beset with cares. Danger." As the second trigram begins in line four, the dragon appears with "Wavering flight over the depths." The fifth and sixth lines of hexagrams generally are important indicators of "governing" positions. The fifth line notes a "Flying dragon in the heavens. It furthers one to see the great man," while the sixth gives pause: "Arrogant dragon will have cause to repent." In Hexagram 1, then, the *Yijing* reader follows a submerged dragon rising from its dark place to the open field, where it becomes visible. In line four, it takes flight over an abyss before flying higher in the sky. If the dragon flies too high, as signaled in the top line, it exceeds its own strength and therefore plummets. The order offers a story in progression, with each line symbolizing different changes. The beginning place is at the bottom. As we read from the bottom up, the lines reflect the dragon's flight.

While the dragon appears in five of the lines in this first hexagram, a moving line in the third position is anomalous: it shows the *junzi* (one who realizes Dao) engaging in a creative or productive activity in the day, but retreating in caution at night. This line has been interpreted as the junzi cautiously anticipating possible adversity that can arise in the dark unknown. Together, the lines open up an ambiguity: does the dragon of the first two lines transform into the junzi figure in that third line, becoming dragon in the top lines? Or is the dragon separate from the human junzi? While different commentarial traditions offer opinions about hexagrams, every *reading* is different, since the particular moment and situation of the question, along with the user's life as context, influence what interpretations would be most fitting. It is a fundamental experience when using the *Yijing* for readers to imagine themselves becoming other, whether it be dragon, goose, or other animal, or alternatively imagining the layering of realities: the becoming-dragon transformation, in this case, and a "becoming human." With the dragon appearing in five of the lines, transforming into the junzi requires a new act of imagination.

Yet hexagram relations do not end among the six lines. Roughly one quarter of the hexagrams are "interhexagrammatic," meaning that the incipient story in one hexagram may be resumed in another (Shaughnessy). We see this in the first two hexagrams (Creative/Heaven and Receptive/Earth). Hexagram 2 opens with a "mare," so that if the junzi "tries to lead, / He goes astray; / But if he follows, he finds guidance" (WB 11). Five of the lines provide a medley of images: frost; being straight and square; concealing ability; a tied-up sack; a yellow skirt (Kunst 243). The top line, however, carries forward Hexagram 1: "Dragons fight in the meadow. / Their blood is black and yellow" (WB 15). Thus the last line of the second hexagram takes us to a new place or action: the dragons are in a struggle and blood is drawn. The solo dragon of Hexagram 1 that began in a submerged or hidden position must now acknowledge others in an open field of action.

Hexagrams 1 and 2 show how change in the *Yijing* is more complex than a duality of yin and yang; continuous change and ongoing, dream-like associations occur in varying constellations of hexagrams. The hexagrammatic constellations and their lines shift much as the lines of the archipelago shift depending on one's position. If *Lathe* makes use of these *Yijing* lines and their different changes, we would expect to see continuous changes across space and time and throughout the narrative.

Indeed, George Orr enters the depths of dreams and the surface of experience; the narrative structure works by the principle of moving across time and space, from bottom to top or down to up rather than the reverse, which is the way English language texts proceed. Thus, the novel begins "down under," in the currents of the ocean's darkness. Just as a jellyfish can be thrown up by tidal forces onto the beach—something that humans might otherwise view deterministically as God's Providence or as the accident of chance, as in *Robinson Crusoe*—so we move from the dark ocean to the burning radiance of nuclear holocaust on land, all within the first chapter. The fourth paragraph of the novel shows George, prone, with his eyelids burned away. George then "sat up" on a set of steps. He "stood up" but feels imbalanced from radiation sickness. As he rushes toward the men's room, he falls ("the wall turned into the floor" [8]), but as realities converge he falls not in the nuclear wasteland but in his own apartment building. Once again, George is prone. The narrative is insistent in its details: "The elevator guard's face was hanging above him like a paper lantern" (8). This same pattern of moving from down to up in slices of time repeats throughout the first chapter: the medic is "coming up" from down on the fifteenth floor, associated with "the roar of breaking seas" (8). After treating George, the medic stands up from being seated on the bed. The chapter ends with Mannie the elevator guard sitting down on the bed, mixing the "faint smell, sweetish, like newly cut grass" with the upcoming "mist rising all around" (10). The movement is not simply thematic but structural as well.

The first chapter provides sudden transformation as well as gradual change several times, from nuclear holocaust and back again, a shifting perhaps native to dreams but also found in *Yijing* thought. The chapter has also shown a movement of continuous change, literally in terms of positional relations (lying down, sitting, standing) with the three characters interchanging places: George, the medic, and Mannie seem to be equally involved in this movement. Chapter one shows us George rising to consciousness, but specifically in relation with others. This is not, as Suvin might argue, a narrative projecting self *onto* universe; self and universe come as a package in correlative thinking.

We now expect to see some arc between chapters one and two, some link that will seem almost invisible based on continuous change. Mannie the elevator guard, once again hanging over George Orr on the bed, closes chapter one, while the next chapter moves us "higher" to "towering heights": it is Haber who contemplates his position on the 63rd floor of the Willamette East Tower. The tower, of course, is in part a symbol of Haber's career aspirations and his airy speeches about the human capacity to build up and out of squalor. Yet Haber finds himself bothered by the sound of the elevator coming up, with his new patient, George, inside. The whirring of the elevator going up seems to circle back to the end of the first chapter, with Mannie the *elevator* guard. Yet the narrative makes it clear that this is both return and novelty; there is no going back to the first place because events have occurred. This second chapter likewise appears to circle around, from the reproduction of a view of Mount Hood to the re-production of Mount Hood as the bay-maned horse. Yet the horse photograph ("the great racing stallion Tammany Hall at play in a grassy paddock" [27]) is explained by Haber as an exaggerated sex symbol; the horse is unbridled and "bearing down at a full gallop" (29). The energetic force of the horse is "bearing down" with notable speed and with a look as if "it was going to run me down" (27); George hopes to catch the bridle and leap up.

A structure of continuous change would mean the seam between chapters two and three will enact another correlative change. In fact, this happens. George descends into the Vancouver subway to get to Portland. Not coincidentally, he is unable to secure an overhead "strap or stanchion," so he finds himself subject to the force of crowding and gravity. The idea of wanting to seize hold of a strap above to deal with the pressure (from the moving subway train) bearing down on him is remarkably similar to the earlier bridle that he hopes to seize to avoid being trampled. While certainly both situations could be seen as expressing his feeling "emotionally off-balance" (35), and both could be viewed as a shared image (a loop, strip, strap), it serves an additional purpose of structurally bridging chapters.

Chapter three also transfers George from the soupy jungle-like atmosphere (mixing land and water) of the crowded city to Haber's fantasized South Sea Islands with their lack of crowding (36-37). After George's dream featuring coconuts and the South Seas (38), the chapter ends with a return to the subway, in which the imagery of straps returns but with a vengeance; the straps do not prevent him from swaying about. It is at this point that he realizes that Haber does indeed observe the moment of change from the effective dreams; he feels suddenly "goosed" (42). Later while speaking with Heather, George understands that he is like the goose that laid the golden eggs, with Haber collecting the spoils. Before George dreams the Aldebaranian aliens with their ovoid ships into existence, he dreams of a goose:

> Not quite night yet: late twilight on the fields. Clumps of trees looked black and moist. The road he was walking on picked up the faint, last light from the sky; it ran long and straight, an old country highway, cracked blacktop. A goose was walking ahead of him, about fifteen feet in advance and visible only as a white, bobbing blur. (83)

As Le Guin would know, a wild goose appears in the *Yijing's* Hexagram 53. The individual lines narrate the movement of the goose as, from bottom to top, it "gradually draws near the shore" and draws near a cliff, a plateau, a tree, a peak, and finally the clouds (WB 207-208). The goose ascends into the clouds toward the heavens, but "[i]ts feathers can be used for the sacred dance" (208). In the commentary on his own *Yijing* translation, Richard Wilhelm interprets this last line as a completion of one's work followed by inevitable death. As Kunst notes, another influential early work, *Shijing*, uses the wild goose as a symbol for an absent husband (77). Not unlike the flying dragon, the goose in the *Yijing* suggests multiple and continuous changes.

The flight may be replicated at the end of the chapter as George takes the elevator up to floor eighteen with its view of "the bright, life-encrusted hills," the West Hills of Portland "crammed with huge, glittering towers, heavy with lights and life" (42-3). The human dwellings have become part of the hills, connecting the natural mountains and the rising towers. Chapter four opens with an "automatic-elevator parking structure," the artificial creation of humans re-purposed as a place not for cars but humans to work. The structure is likened to the strata of the earth, which contain its history in fossils squeezed by pressure over time: "Its cement floors were stained with the excreta of innumerable engines, the wheelprints of the dinosaurs ... fossilized in the dust of its echoing halls" (44). This parking-structure-become-office at a "slant" convinces people they are not "standing quite upright" (44), perhaps recalling the opening of the novel when George topples before the elevator guard. The chapter ends with George telling Heather that he does not want to be used (like the parking structure) and Heather insists that all will be fine so long as he remains "on the level" (51). The narrative changes from Orr to Heather, metal (ore) to flower. Where the chapter opened with the "lineage" of buildings converted for human use but reminiscent of dinosaurs, it closes with her own lineage as the child of a mixed-race couple, emblematized for her as "that damn button her mother always kept in the bottom of her bead box, SCNN or SNCC or something she'd belonged to way back in the middle of the last century, the Black hand and the White hand joined together" (52). It is not merely a political button but rather a button at the *bottom* of a box. Once more from down, we go up in chapter five, with Haber going "up the steps" of the new building in which he works in a new reality.

Later chapters in fact continue this pattern of movement in the seams between scenes much as the lines in a hexagram develop continuous change. So, for example, from the "level sunlight of the heights" (73) of Haber's tower ending chapter five, the narrative resumes movement in chapter six not with Haber but George, from dragon or stallion to goose. George steps down from a trolley, walks up a hill to his apartment, and ascends the stairs, only to lie down again on his apartment floor. This chapter ends with George descending the steps of Haber's Institute in a mist whose blurring drops coalesce into the dark aquarium. Chapter seven begins from Heather's point of view, feeling down that George has stood her up for their lunch date at Dave's. George never arrives, but the chapter ends with the arrival of the aliens, showing up on Earth unexpectedly in their descent from the moon. The no-show of somebody becomes the showing up of nobody in the vacuity inside the turtle armor, a theme reinforced by the "unborn children singing in the water."

The role of the *Yijing* is not unlike another kind of song, that of the Beatles about getting help from friends. As the *Yijing* commentary notes, "with its help we can meet everything in the right way, and with its help can even assist the gods themselves" (WB 313). Present-day users of the *Yijing* continue to use this language of a lifeline being offered: "It reaches out to you with an offer of help" (Karcher, *How* 33). The Aldebaranian aliens seem to channel the voice of an oracle in their very first words of the novel: "'Do not do to others what you wish others not to do to you'" (118). Critics have assumed that this refers to the "Golden Rule" pronounced by Jesus Christ, and undoubtedly the similarity is there. However, the *Analects* of Confucius may match the words more precisely in what is sometimes called the "negative doctrine of the mean": "The Master said ... the saying about consideration: 'Never do to others what you would not like them to do to you'" (Waley 198;15.23). Two other passages in the *Analects* repeat this line (12.2; 5.11).

In other words, the aliens bring ancient Chinese philosophy to the foot of George Orr. The narrative underscores the importance of the aliens when George notes, "There was, he thought, something to the curious manner in which the Aliens communicated; but he was much too tired to decide what" (169). Certainly their advice is uttered in an oddly

disjointed language: "You are human capable of *iahklu'* as previously
noted. This troubles self.... Concepts cross in mist. Perception is difficult.
Volcanoes emit fire. Help is offered: refusably. Snakebite serum is
not prescribed for all. Before following directions leading in wrong
directions, auxiliary forces may be summoned, in immediate-following
fashion: *Er'perrehnne!*" (137-38). The strangeness of the language might
be likened to transliteration. For example, the *Yijing*'s Hexagram 11, Tai,
sounds equally strange when transliterated: "Enwrapped in wasteland.
/ Availing of crossing the watercourse. / Not putting-off abandoning. /
Partnering extinguished.... Without going, not returning.... Altogether
letting-go the substance indeed" (Ritsema and Sabbadini 174-77). The
narrative specifies that George listens to the Beatles' record eleven times,
and this event occurs in chapter eleven. The narrative may be playing
a number game by invoking the eleventh hexagram, Tai, whose image
is typically translated as "Peace." Thus, we see the "reverse of chance"
when the narrative specifies that American jet bombers pulverized the
"eleven-square-mile area" rumored to be hiding the Alien ship (111).

The bite of a snake, like the sting of a jellyfish, is an event implying
a relational encounter. The Aldebaranians insist that snakebites should
not be viewed fatalistically though they are indeed changes. As the
Yijing suggests, the nature of change is neither singular nor separable
from other contexts. One recalls that the Nna Mmoy, too, speak "ever-
varying phrases which seem to signify both permanent and temporary
relationships of consanguinity, of responsibility and dependence, of
contingent status, of a thousand social and emotional connections. I
could point to myself and say 'Laure,' but what relationship would that
signify?" (171). Subjectivity in *The Lathe of Heaven* is also mediated
through a kind of archipelagic aesthetic, a structuring that is perspectival
and constantly shifting.

My reading challenges the assumption that *Lathe* is a narrative focused
on individual consciousness, the Daoist sage, or the development of the
self. In fact, the novel's archipelagic structure reflects the fluid word-
image relations of the *Yijing*, in which "the imaginal fields of single
ideograms stand next to each other as islands in an archipelago or as
figures in a dream" (Ritsema and Sabbadini 19). As hidden dragon,
perhaps, in its experimental nature, *Lathe* finds a place beyond the binary
of starfish or snake talk. This place is the archipelago, with its interplay
of sea and land, fluidity and shore, lines and spaces. Not unlike the oracle
bones inherited from the Shang dynasty whose inscriptions eventually
became the first stratum of the *Yijing*, the Nna Mmoy's currency involves
shells, made of "the pearly-violet, translucent mantle ... left by ...
jellyfish. Found washed up on the sea beaches, these shells are traded

inland" for texts that may be "mandalas or scriptures" or nothing at all religious (164). Perhaps Le Guin's critics have viewed the novel's structure primarily through the lens of dualism because discussions of Daoist philosophy have not yet adequately acknowledged her interest in the *Yijing*. The larger implication of the archipelagic in *Lathe* is that the *Yijing* may mediate Le Guin's Daoist philosophy and thus require a new conception of change and subjectivity.

Works Cited

1. Bain, Dena C. "The *Tao Te Ching* as Background to the Novels of Ursula K. Le Guin." *Extrapolation* 21 (1980): 209-22.
2. Barbour, Douglas. "*The Lathe of Heaven*: Taoist Dream." *Algol: A Magazine about Science Fiction* 11 (1973): 22-24.
3. —. "Wholeness and Balance in the Hainish Novels of Ursula K. Le Guin." *Science-Fiction Studies* 1 (1974): 164-73.
4. Bittner, James. *Approaches to the Fiction of Ursula K. Le Guin.* Ann Arbor: UMI Research Press, 1984.
5. Blair, John C. "Change and Cultures: Reality Presumptions in China and the West." *New Literary History* 24 (1993): 927-45.
6. Blofeld, John. *I Ching (The Book of Change). A New Translation of the Ancient Chinese Text with Detailed Instructions for Its Practical Use in Divination.* 1965. NY: Penguin, 1991.
7. Brown, Barbara. "*The Left Hand of Darkness*: Androgyny, Future, Present, and Past." *Extrapolation* 21 (1980): 227-35.
8. Ching, Julia. *Chinese Religions.* Houndmills, UK: Macmillan, 1993.
9. Cogell, Elizabeth Cummins. "Taoist Configurations: *The Dispossessed.*" De Bolt 153-79.
10. Crow, John H., and Richard D. Erlich. "Words of Binding: Patterns of Integration in the Earthsea Trilogy." Olander and Greenberg 200-24.
11. Cummins, Elizabeth. *Understanding Ursula K. Le Guin.* Understanding Contemporary American Literature. Ed. Matthew J. Bruccoli. Columbia, SC: U South Carolina P, 1990.
12. De Bolt, Joseph, ed. *Ursula K. Le Guin: Voyage to Inner Lands and Outer Space.* Port Washington, NY: Kennikat Press, 1979.
13. Erlich, Richard D. *Coyote's Song: The Teaching Stories of Ursula K. Le Guin.* 2000. Science Fiction Research Association. 18 June 2007 <http://www.sfra.org/Coyote/CoyoteHome.htm>.

14. —. "Le Guin and God: Quarreling with the One, Critiquing Pure Reason." *Extrapolation* 47 (2006): 351-79.
15. Galbreath, Robert. "Holism, Openness and the Other: Le Guin's Use of the Occult." *Science-Fiction Studies* 7 (1980): 36-48.
16. —. "Taoist Magic in the Earthsea Trilogy." *Extrapolation* 21 (1980): 262-68.
17. Gunew, Sneja. "Mythic Reversals: The Evolution of the Shadow Motif." Olander and Greenberg 178-99.
18. Huntington, John. "Public and Private Imperatives in Le Guin's Novels." *Science-Fiction Studies* 2 (1975): 237-43.
19. Jameson, Fredric. *Archaeologies of the Future: The Desire Called Utopia and Other Science Fictions.* London: Verso, 2005.
20. Jung, C. G. "Foreword to the *I Ching*." 1950. Trans. Cary F. Baynes. *The I Ching or Book of Changes.* 3rd ed. New Jersey: Princeton, 1997. xxi-xxxix.
21. Karcher, Stephen. *How to Use the I Ching: A Guide to Working with the Oracle of Change.* NY: Barnes & Noble, 1999.
22. —. "Jung, the Tao, and the Classic of Change." *Journal of Religion and Health* 38 (1999): 287-304.
23. Kirkland, Russell, T.H. Barrett, and Livia Kohn. "Introduction." In *Daoism Handbook*, ed. by Livia Kohn. Handbook of Oriental Studies Section Four: China. Leiden: Brill, 2000. xi-xxxviii.
24. Kunst, Richard Alan. *The Original "Yijing": A Text, Phonetic Transcription, Translation, and Indexes, with Sample Glosses.* U California dissertation, Berkeley, 1985. Ann Arbor: UMI, 1985.
25. Le Guin, Ursula K. "Books Q & A: *Chronicles of Earthsea.*" *Guardian Unlimited.* 9 Feb. 2004. 25 Sept. 2007 <http://books/guardian.co.uk/print/0,,4855008-99935,00.html>.
26. —. *Dancing at the Edge of the World: Thoughts on Words, Women, Places.* New York: Grove Press, 1989.
27. —. *The Farthest Shore.* 1972. New York: Atheneum Bantam, 1983.
28. —. "Intracom." 1974. *The Compass Rose.* New York: Perennial-Harper, 2005. 183-206.
29. —. "It Was a Dark and Stormy Night: Or, Why are We Huddling about the Campfire?" *Critical Inquiry* 7 (1980): 191-99.
30. —. "Ketterer on *The Left Hand of Darkness.*" *Science-Fiction Studies* 2 (1975): 137-39.
31. —. *Lao Tzu: Tao Te Ching: A Book about the Way and the Power of the Way.* Boston: Shambala, 1998.

32. —. *The Lathe of Heaven*. 1971. New York: Perennial Classics, 2003.

33. —. *The Left Hand of Darkness*. New York: Ace, 1969.

34. —. "Life in the Wider Household of Being: An Interview with Ursula K. Le Guin." *West by Northwest.org*. 21 Nov. 2003. 25 Sept. 2007 <http://westbynorthwest.org/artman/publish/printer_634. shtml>.

35. —. "The Nna Mmoy Language." *Changing Planes*. New York: Ace Books, 2005. 161-74.

36. —. "A Non-Euclidean View of California as a Cold Place to Be." Le Guin, *Dancing* 80-100.

37. —. "A Response to the Le Guin Issue." *Science-Fiction Studies* 3 (1976): 44-46.

38. —. "Science Fiction as Prophesy." *New Republic* 30 Oct. 1976: 33-34.

39. —. "Some Thoughts on Narrative." Le Guin, *Dancing* 37-45.

40. —. *The Telling*. 2000. New York: Ace Books, 2001.

41. —. "Things Not Actually Present: On *The Book of Fantasy* and J. L. Borges." In *The Wave in the Mind: Talks and Essays on the Writer, the Reader, and the Imagination*. Boston: Shambhala, 2004. 38-45.

42. —. "Tui." *Hard Words and Other Poems*. New York: Harper & Row, 1981. 77.

43. Le Guin, Ursula K., and Ellen Emry Heltzel. "Portland Trailblazer: Ursula K. Le Guin." *Book: The Magazine* September-October 2000: 49.

44. Legge, James. *The Sacred Books of China: The Texts of Confucianism; Part II: The Yî King*. The Sacred Books of the East. Ed. F. Max Müller. Vol. 16. Oxford: Clarendon, 1882.

45. Lindow, Sandra J. "Sometimes It Takes a Leap: Decision Making and the Tao within the Work of Ursula K. Le Guin." *Foundation* 90 (2004): 71-80.

46. Lynn, Richard John. *The Classic of Changes: A New Translation of the I Ching as Interpreted by Wang Bi*. New York: Columbia UP, 1994.

47. Malmgren, Carl. "Meta-SF: The Examples of Dick, Le Guin, and Russ." *Extrapolation* 43 (2002): 22-35.

48. Miller, James. "Envisioning the Daoist Body in the Economy of Cosmic Power." *Daedalus* 130.4 (2001): 265-82.

49. Olander, Joseph D., and Martin Harry Greenberg, eds. *Ursula K. Le Guin*. New York: Taplinger, 1979.

50. Pas, Julian F. *Historical Dictionary of Taoism*. Historical Dictionaries of Religions, Philosophies, and Movements. Ed. Jon Woronoff. Lanham, MD: The Scarecrow Press, 1998.

51. Phillips, Julie. "Dear Starbear: Letters between Ursula K. Le Guin and James Tiptree Jr." *The Magazine of Fantasy and Science Fiction* 111.3 (2006): 76-106.

52. Ponce, Victor M., and Catia N. da Cunha. "Vegetated Earthmounds in Tropical Savannas of Central Brazil: A Synthesis: With Special Reference to the Pantanal do Mato Grosso." *Journal of Biogeography* 20 (1993): 219-25.

53. Porter, David L. "The Politics of Le Guin's Opus." *Science-Fiction Studies* 2.2 (1975): 243-48.

54. Remington, Thomas J. "The Other Side of Suffering: Touch as Theme and Metaphor in Le Guin's Science Fiction Novels." Olander and Greenberg 153-77.

55. —. "A Touch of Difference, A Touch of Love: Theme in Three Stories by Ursula K. Le Guin." *Extrapolation* 18 (1976): 28-41.

56. Ritsema, Rudolf, and Shantena Augusto Sabbadini, trans. *The Original I Ching Oracle: The Pure and Complete Texts with Concordance*. London: Eranos-Watkins, 2005.

57. Sager, William W. "Divergence between Paleomagnetic and Hotspot-Model-Predicted Polar Wander for the Pacific Plate with Implications for Hotspot Fixity." In *Plates, Plumes, and Planetary Processes*, ed. by Gillian R. Foulger and Donna M. Jurdy. Special Paper 430. Geological Society of America, 2007. 335-57.

58. Shaughnessy, Edward L. "Marriage, Divorce, and Revolution: Reading Between the Lines of the *Book of Changes*." *Journal of Asian Studies* 51 (1992): 587-99.

59. Shchutskii, Iulian K. *Researches on the I Ching*. 1960. Trans. William L. MacDonald, Tsuyoshi Hasegawa and Hellmut Wilhelm. Bollingen Series LXII. Vol. 2. Princeton: Princeton UP, 1979.

60. Slusser, George Edgar. *The Farthest Shores of Ursula K. Le Guin*. The Milford Series Popular Writers of Today. San Bernardino, CA: R. Reginald-Borgo Press, 1976.

61. Smith, Kidder. "Sima Tan and the Invention of Daoism, 'Legalism,' et cetera." *The Journal of Asian Studies* 62 (2003): 129-56.

62. Smith, Richard J. *Fortune-tellers and Philosophers: Divination in Traditional Chinese Society*. Boulder, CO: Westview Press, 1991.

63. Spencer, Kathleen L. "Exiles and Envoys: The SF of Ursula K. Le Guin." *Foundation* 20 (1980): 32-43.
64. Suvin, Darko. *Positions and Presuppositions in Science Fiction.* Kent, OH: Kent State UP, 1988.
65. Tarduno, John, A., et al. "The Emperor Seamounts: Southward Motion of the Hawaiian Hotspot Plume in Earth's Mantle." *Science* 22 Aug. 2003: 1064-69.
66. Theall, Donald F. "The Art of Social-Science Fiction: The Ambiguous Utopian Dialectics of Ursula K. Le Guin." *Science-Fiction Studies* 2 (1975): 256-65.
67. Waley, Arthur, trans. *The Analects of Confucius.* New York: Vintage-Random House, 1938.
68. Watson, Ian. "Le Guin's *Lathe of Heaven* and the Role of Dick: The False Reality as Mediator." *Science-Fiction Studies* 2 (1975): 67-75.
69. Wilhelm, Hellmut. *Heaven, Earth, and Man in the Book of Changes.* Publications on Asia of the Institute for Comparative and Foreign Area Studies. Seattle: U Washington P, 1977.
70. Wilhelm, Richard, and Cary F. Baynes, trans. *The I Ching or Book of Changes.* 1967. Bollingen Series. 3rd ed. New Jersey: Princeton UP, 1997.
71. Zeilhofer, Peter, and Michael Schessl. "Relationship between Vegetation and Environmental Conditions in the Northern Pantanal of Mato Grosso, Brazil." *Journal of Biogeography* 27 (2000): 159-68.

Kathleen Keating is a Professor of English at Greensboro College in North Carolina. She teaches courses in British literature, new media and technology studies, and science fiction and fantasy. Her current project focuses on narrative and cultural constructions of science as prophesy in the nineteenth century.

On *Almost* Meeting Ursula Le Guin

April Kendra
University of North Texas

I first encountered Ursula Le Guin about twenty years ago when a favorite college professor read "The Ones Who Walk Away from Omelas" out loud to our fantasy lit class. We also read the *Earthsea* trilogy, *The Lord of the Rings*, *The Wizard of Oz,* and *The Chronicles of Narnia*, but nothing had the impact of Le Guin's short story about the terrible price of utopia. I was transfixed, personally implicated by the image of a frightened child huddled miserably in a filthy basement closet while above him the townspeople of glorious Omelas celebrated the Festival of Summer, their perfect joy made possible by one child's unmitigated suffering.

Haunted by this story, I was driven to share it with everyone I knew. I talked about it constantly and read long passages to my friends, trying to repeat my own magical experience of hearing "Omelas" for the first time. I have a vague but embarrassing memory of knocking on dorm-room doors late one night, trying to find someone awake who would discuss "Omelas" with me. This was no passing fancy, you must understand. Years later, I took shameless advantage of young love by requiring a college boyfriend to sit on the floor of my sparsely-furnished apartment while I read the story to him in full.

I was absolutely thrilled when I learned that Le Guin would be visiting the University of Georgia Press, where I worked as an editorial assistant, to discuss a manuscript her husband was editing (*A Home-Concealed Woman: The Diaries of Magnolia Wynn Le Guin, 1901-1913*). Seeing my excitement, the executive editor, Malcolm Call, promised to introduce me to the object of my obsession, and I racked my brain for the appropriate thing to say. This would be my first experience of actually meeting an author I admired, and I agonized over how to express what her story had meant to me without sounding like every other starstruck fan in the world.

I was secretly terrified that I would lose all control and gush, "Oh, Ms. Le Guin, I just *love* all your books!" Oh dear God, there would be no recovering from that. I would have to go home and kill myself. Not only is "I just love all your books" the most unforgivably trite comment in fandom (followed closely by "Where do you get your ideas?" and "Would you mind looking at a story I wrote?"), but *it wasn't even true*. To the rest of the world, Ursula Le Guin was a pioneer in feminist science

fiction, but to me, she was simply the woman who had written "Omelas."
I cringed as I imagined admitting to my hero that I hadn't read *any* of her
books (I was too nervous at the time to remember *Earthsea*). Was that
the worst possible insult to an author of Le Guin's stature? Would she
think I was incredibly gauche and far too stupid to work at an academic
press? What if she persuaded her husband to take his book away from
UGA and publish it somewhere else? Hell, just hell.

The big day arrived. I was still trying to frame a statement that would
be dignified, truthful, and profound as I gathered all my books and papers
from the corner of the conference room that served as my "office." I had
just reached the door when I ran smack into Malcolm.

"April, I'd like you to meet Ursula Le Guin," he said.

Standing beside Malcolm was a petite woman with short-cropped hair.
She was smaller than I'd expected, but the room fairly crackled with
potential energy. I immediately thought of a coiled spring, a slender
electrical wire, images of tremendous power simply waiting to be
called forth. The newcomer gazed at me expectantly, her eyes sparkling
with eager intellect. Sadly, they met no answering spark in my own,
which I'm sure were glazed over in horror. I stared at her helplessly,
my arms so burdened with manuscripts that I couldn't have shaken her
hand even if I'd had the presence of mind to try. After several days of
feverish anticipation, I had nothing, not a single thing to say to Ursula
Le Guin.

No, there was one thing. I'd grown up in the South, after all, and some
habits are too deeply ingrained to be forgotten, no matter how dire the
situation. I drew in a deep breath and muttered, "Excuse me." Then I
scuttled past, my eyes on the carpet, and collapsed in the managing
editor's office, where I kicked myself for the next two hours. Two
decades later, I'm *still* kicking myself.

Perhaps the memory of my own cowardice has given me an even
greater appreciation for the moral courage of those who walk away from
Omelas. Certainly Le Guin's story continues to haunt me, and I am still
so eager to share it with others that I've included the story in every first-
year literature course I have ever taught. I usually restrain myself from
reading it to my students. Instead, I use "Omelas" as an icebreaker, the
basis of our first reading assignment and class discussion, and it has never
failed to spark passionate response. Is the story a moral litmus test, an
indictment of capitalism, a thought problem about social justice? Over
the years, my classes have offered these readings and more.

If I had another opportunity to meet Ursula Le Guin, I would like
to tell her about my students. I think she would be gratified by their
strong reactions to her story, and I'm sure she would be amused and

intrigued by the various, even contradictory, ways they interpret it. Many religious students regard the story as a Christian allegory in which an individual's undeserved punishment secures a blissful, guilt-free existence for everyone else; others, equally devout, view the story as an attack on Christianity, noting that the title characters reject the child's sacrifice by walking away from Omelas. Still others have hailed the story as a parable about self-determination, a declaration that no one is free, a savage attack on the democratic principle of majority-rule, and a proof that the needs of the many outweigh the needs of the few. They have written papers comparing "Omelas" to Shirley Jackson's "The Lottery," to the movie *Gattaca*, to the homeless problem. I have seen students almost come to blows during a debate and leave the classroom still arguing vehemently, which is perhaps the highest tribute college freshmen can pay any text.

While working on this essay, I am moved to pick up my battered anthology of short stories, which opens easily to "The Ones Who Walk Away from Omelas." Although no one is home but the cat and dog, I find myself reading the entire story aloud, enthralled once more by the passion, poignant longing, and stubborn hope that seethe just beneath Le Guin's cool and measured prose. I am again convicted as the story gently but irresistibly reminds me of the thousand compromises I make daily to secure, not the perfect beauty and unending joy of Omelas, but a little temporary comfort. Yet my fingers tingle with the electric possibility that it might not be too late, for me, for all of us. Even now, we might find the courage to leave home, make our way through the gates of our own personal Omelas, and walk confidently into the darkness.

I'd like to think I'm more self-possessed and articulate than the college student who became tongue-tied upon meeting Ursula Le Guin all those years ago. If I'm wrong, though, if I were to choke once again, I hope that instead of "Excuse me," I would at least manage to say, "Thank you."

April Kendra holds a Ph.D. from the University of Georgia in 19th-century British literature and teaches English at the University of North Texas. Her essays on the reception of women writers and the construction of popular genres have appeared in journals such as *Women's Writing*, *Nineteenth-Century Gender Studies*, and *Studies in the Humanities*. A passionate advocate of speculative fiction, she routinely includes Ursula Le Guin, Octavia Butler, and J. K. Rowling on her college syllabi, and she leads the Gryffindor Book Group at her local library for young readers of the magical, the fantastic, and the otherworldly.

Living in a Work of Art

Ursula K. Le Guin
Portland, Oregon

The extraordinary Palace of Fine Arts near the San Francisco marina—
you can see it from the freeway to the Golden Gate: a giant orange
upheld and surrounded
by very large, very
pensive ladies—was
contributed to the San
Francisco World's Fair
of 1915 by the architect
Bernard Maybeck.
Exposition buildings
weren't expected to
be permanent, and
Maybeck, a great
experimenter with

Palace of Fine Arts, San Francisco

materials, built the Palace out of chickenwire and plaster or some such
set of ephemeral ingredients. But it was so lovely in its utter originality,
and so beloved by the people of the city, that it wasn't knocked down
with the rest of the fair. When after six or seven decades it finally began
to crumble away, the city rebuilt it, repainting its dome the improbable
gold they assure us was the original color.

Born in New York, trained at the Ecole de Beaux-Arts in Paris,

Bernard Maybeck

Maybeck lived and worked in the Bay Area
from 1890 till his death in 1957. His best-known
buildings date from before the second World War.
He built churches, the most famous of which is
the Christian Science church in Berkeley, and at
least one of his buildings for the University of
California still stands, the old Women's Gym; but
he was principally a domestic architect. The house
I grew up in is known in the Maybeck canon as the
Schneider house. The Schneider family lived in
it eighteen years. My family, the Kroebers, lived
in it from 1925 to my mother's death in 1979,
fifty-four years. There are a couple of pictures of

the house in the excellent book *Bernard Maybeck: Artisan, Architect,
Artist,* by Kenneth H. Cardwell.

It seems to me that, while Frank Lloyd Wright remains more or less sacrosanct, and various old styles such as carpenter gothic, "Queen Anne," and Arts and Crafts, go in and out of fashion, we haven't given much real thought for decades now to domestic architecture. Are any beautiful houses built now in any but an imitation of some older style? The highrise apartment building, the splitlevel "ranch," the little-box development house, the McMansion in its grandiose banality, reveal the poverty of our thought about buildings for people to live in.

Maybeck was certainly in some ways a visionary, and his personality so marked his buildings that one can often identify "a Maybeck" at glance; but he had a pre-Modern understanding of the connection between dwelling-place and dweller. A "machine for living" would not be a useful description of a Maybeck house. In 1908, the year after he built the one I grew up in, he wrote:

> The house after all is only the shell and the real interest must come from those who are to live in it. If this is done carefully and with earnestness it will give the inmates a sense of satisfaction and rest and will have the same power over the mind as music or poetry or any healthy activity in any kind of human experience.

This consideration of the interaction of the house and its inhabitants is no less sophisticated and complex for being unfashionably modest. It is also a little mysterious: what does "this" refer to? I read it to mean "this consideration of the relationship of the shell to its living contents." Maybeck is, I think, saying that in planning a house, the architect establishes a relationship with the people who will dwell in it, whether he knows them or not, and that that relationship implies a responsibility towards them on his part– or so I interpret "earnestness." We are familiar with the idea that an architect should consider the natural environs and the social setting and make his building reflect or adorn them. We are not as used to this concept of a moral relationship with the individuals who will inhabit the house. Maybeck evidently would not have thought himself justified in subordinating that relationship to a theory he wished to illustrate or a "statement" he wished to make. I have been in Frank Lloyd Wright houses which clearly exhibit Wright's idea of architecture as self-expression; their inhabitants have no part in them but to accept and obey the whims of the Master. Maybeck's approach was quite different from that egocentrism. Though he was as interested as Wright in the aesthetic value of the work, to him aesthetic meaning was not a final declaration made by the architect, but the result of an ongoing dialogue between builder and dwellers. In its *inhabitation* a house's beauty would be active and fulfilled.

The house I grew up in was remarkably beautiful, comfortable, and almost entirely practical. If a dialogue between house and inhabitants was indeed what Maybeck had in mind, our house kept up its end wonderfully. Like most good conversationalists, though, it was not always predictable. If not self-expressive in the theoretical sense, Maybeck's style was intensely personal, sometimes going past the characteristic into quirkiness or real oddity. Our house, for example, had (or had had) no stairs to the basement.

"Maybeck was moody about stairs," my mother said. She claimed that he had also left them off one of his University of California buildings, or added them outside because they didn't look well inside, or something of the sort. I wonder if it was basements that Maybeck was moody about,

rather than stairs. Our basement was large but low, dim, and dreary. Its cement floor, practical for laundry, gave way to mere dirt at the back, behind the furnace, where the ground sloped up close to the ceiling. But Maybeck was a designer of joyously inventive staircases, as many houses in Berkeley still prove.

The main staircase of our house was a fine rise of wide, dark steps to a landing, where it met a very narrow back flight angling up in two turns from the pantry to the landing. Straight on

Ursula Le Guin's house in about 1950

up from the back stairs, or a 180-degree turn on the landing, brought you to the final flight: six quite narrow steps up to the second floor. (Furniture movers who had ascended the first flight with high hopes here met their doom.) A fine, short, broad banister rail beside this last flight made a single, but imperative, statement of slant; everything else was at right angles. Looked at from the top, the short straight waterfall of the top flight broke into two, a narrow sidestream angling down from the broad turn and fall of the main stair-river. The loftiness of the ceiling over the landing and the complexity of the joining angles of walls and ceiling-beams was a pleasure to the eye. It was literally uplifting to look at those high surfaces and high spaces, lit by the north light that came through a French door giving onto a little decorative balcony at the level

of the upper turn of the back stairs, which were so narrow they got triangular at the turns. If this sounds complicated, I mean it to. The whole staircase arrangement was organically

On the upstairs balcony of "the house" (age 7)

complicated, like the arrangements inside a living creature. It was fascinatingly complex, yet (unlike the balcony) expressed the purest structural necessity. And it consisted entirely of redwood. Air and redwood. Light and air and redwood. And shadows.

The house, with its notable beauty of material and proportion, was eminently habitable. Its proportions were human proportions. Proportion failed only at the top of the basement stairs.— For a flight of steps had been installed, I think by the Schneiders, so that you wouldn't have to go outside and all the way around two sides of the house from either the front door or the kitchen door to get into the basement by its single outside door. As the house was built into a hilltop slope, the ceiling over these steps was quite low; so if, standing in the tall, narrow hall at the foot of the back stairs, you flung open the door to the basement and started boldly down, you hit your head on a beam. King Somebody of Scotland was killed by hitting his head on a beam. My father told us this as a solemn warning, and put marks in white paint on the lintel, which he repainted every decade or so. We all crouched on the way to and from the basement. My brother Ted tells me that once coming up in a hurry he knocked himself to his knees and stayed there till the stars faded. I myself grew tall enough only to scrape the top of my head occasionally on the murderous beam, but whenever I opened that door I thought about the King of Scotland.

Aside from that, I can't think of anything out of proportion, or uncomfortable, or unfriendly about that house. It could be terrifying at night, but I will get to that later. Even in daylight it was shadowy in places, like a forest. Maybeck speaks somewhere in his few surviving writings of "dark heights," and our house had such dark heights. It was built entirely of redwood inside and out, and redwood darkens with age—but it was full of tall windows and glass-paned doors.

Because the walls and ceilings and spaces were so interesting in themselves, it seemed to require little furnishing. When I was a child we used only my grandmother's Navajo-Ute rugs, leaving much of the floor (fir, treated with boiled linseed oil) dark and bare. Most of our furniture was shabby: odd chairs, bamboo stools, a horsehair and mahogany sofa that it was easier to slide off than to sit on, my mother's mother's bed with the bullet embedded in the footboard, and so on. The dining table was one of our few elegant pieces, a broad redwood board, rather low as tables go, that sat eight comfortably and ten with a squeeze. Its elegance was purely that of material and proportion: Maybeck made it as a drafting table for his own use while building the house. The wise Schneiders persuaded him to leave it there. It had plain square legs and a simple skirting board, and the top was somewhat battered, since redwood is soft and scars easily; I found later on that if you beeswaxed it diligently it got a fine, deep glow, like a chestnut horse. There were triangular, glass-fronted cabinets built in two corners of the dining room in good Arts and Crafts style; and a seat like a windowseat ran along the inner living-room wall, at right angles to the huge firebrick hearth and chimney. That was comfortable. So were the little stone seats built out beside the hearth, where you could sit almost inside the fireplace and get really warm.

Except in the few, always threatened groves protected for tourists, there are no sequoias left like those from which that dining-room table was cut, or with which the whole house with its great rafters and wide, long, clear boards was built. *Sequoia sempervirens* were common in many northern parts of California, and their wood was as commonly used for building houses. It was cheap then, and it has remarkable virtues as lumber, resistance to dryrot and weather among them. Our house in the Napa Valley, a humble ordinary farmhouse of the 1870's, was built of redwood—painted and papered as if it were mere pine or fir. Maybeck's generation realised the extraordinary beauty of the wood, and used it bare and grand. What they didn't realise was the exhaustibility of the sequoias. I don't think anyone thought about that much in 1907. None of us thought much about it till the fifties. Then, as the price of redwood went up and up, and the Save the Redwoods people fought their endless struggle against the lumbermen and the politicians, we began to look up at those wide, sweet boards and beams with a guilty, grateful awe.

They were untreated, but sanded to a silken finish. Cardwell describes the color of a natural redwood interior very well:

The pink tone of new lumber mellows rapidly to a rich red-brown which is highlighted by an iridescent gold caused by the refraction of natural or incandescent light falling on the spring wood of the boards. (p. 58)

The house was not only built throughout of redwood but had several *Sequoia sempervirens* planted in front of it; they were very large and grand by the time I first remember them. The west front stood high above the street over a steep slope and a double flight of stone-walled steps; the whole exterior was in the general style of a mountain chalet, with peaked roofs, deep eaves, and wooden balconies jutting out on all four sides and from both stories. The beams and struts supporting the eaves and balconies made bold diagonals against the sky and against the batten walls – the lower story with horizontal, the upper with vertical battens. This sounds ornate in words, but the simplicity of the dark wood and the massive, splendid proportions of the house itself subordinated all its roof-angles and balconies to the tall, rather stern, and noble whole. Decorative elements, like that tiny north balcony, kept the nobility from being either boring or overwhelming. The house both soared up from its commanding position at the top of a hill-street, and echoed the slope of the hills as a whole in the long western downsweep of the main roof. In every aspect it was superbly suited and fitted to its landscape and community.

One of the bedroom balconies, intended as a sleeping-porch, was roofed and enclosed with windows to make a sunny, narrow playroom for the four children of my family; I don't know whether the Schneiders or we did that. We did a lot of things to that house. It was built for a family with only one child—Cardwell calls it "a modest house constructed on a modest budget."[p. 104] There were seven of us in it by 1929, and we must have been pretty crowded until my father added a wing to the east side: four rooms, two baths, two fireplaces, and a spacious attic. (The attic of the original house was a dreadful dark crawlspace, unusable except by black widows and bats.)

Nobody, I suppose, would dream of building on to a Maybeck house these days; the Great Man syndrome tells us that the Master's work is sacrosanct. I can only say that the wing designed by my father and his carpenter-builder, a Welshman named John Williams, fits seamlessly onto the house; no visitor I ever took round realised it wasn't part of Maybeck's original design. In proportions, the size and shape of windows, and so on, it matches the original, though without deep eaves or balconies, and without the fine details of iron latches, etc. in the William Morris style, which would have been out of fashion at the time and hard to find. This large addition perfected the comfortableness of the house for us, perhaps for children most of all—lots of rooms, built-in closets, corridors to race through, space to crowd into, space to be alone in, sunny corners of balconies, an enormous attic to set up the electric train and the armies of toy soldiers.

My mother always said that women didn't like that house and men did. I think this was one of my mother's theories. It did have a hunting-lodge quality, a certain rough, roomy starkness, which might be seen as virile, and so supposed to appeal to men and not to chintz-loving women; but then, we didn't know many chintz-loving women. The women and girls I knew that knew the house loved it.

The kitchen, maybe, wasn't the modern housewife's ideal – not many kitchens built in 1907 were. It was rather narrow (but there is convenience in being able to turn from the stove to the chopping board to the sink to the fridge in a few steps). It did have the one element that to me is essential in a kitchen, that is, a window over the sink. The window looked out north into the boughs of a crab-apple that blossomed wonderfully in spring. There were plenty of good kitchen cabinets and drawers, and a wall of shelves to keep and display china, with sliding wood-framed glassed doors from waist-level up to the ceiling. Those tall doors were well made, like everything belonging to the house; they continued to slide admirably all the decades we lived there. The pantry, off the narrow hall at the foot of the back stairs, across from the King of Scotland's door, was the kind with a screened opening to the outside to keep it cool; it was a tiny dark room full of shelves, smelling of apples and old pfeffernusse and other pantry things. I would go into the pantry sometimes just to smell it.

Its smell was partly redwood. The wood is aromatic; you can't easily catch the scent in a single piece as you can in a piece of cedar or fresh-cut pine, but an enclosed space built of it has a characteristic fragrance, dearly welcome to the nose to which it smells like home. To come into our house after a long absence was to know again how immediately and profoundly the nose is connected to the emotions.

Because it has nothing to do with sight or touch or hearing, the space in which smell takes place seems to me to be dark or at least shadowy; still; and without boundaries, therefore very large: mysterious and benign. In this it resembles the very earliest and most primitive impressions that I find in my memory of the house itself.

My brother Ted has pointed out to me how consciously and ingeniously Maybeck, like most of the California Arts and Crafts builders, integrated the house and its garden, its indoors and out. Sitting on the patio, one could see right through the house—through the French doors of the dining room and the French doors of the west balcony, clear to the Golden Gate. The many windows and glass-paned doors admitted the extraordinary light of the Bay Area, which combines inland sunshine with sea-reflected radiance. All the balconies but the little north one were fully usable for sitting or sleeping, and accessible by single or double glassed doors. The huge old Cecile Bruner rose that climbed the south balcony presented its flowers to the livingroom windows. Every window in every room had a view, either of our garden or other pleasant Berkeley gardens or, to south and west, the magnificent sweep of San Francisco Bay and its cities and bridges. Each window in itself was a pleasure, low-silled, but always tall enough to include the sky.

The original garden was laid out on the steep hillside lot by McLaren, the designer of Golden Gate Park. It had a rose plot and a fountain. It must have been formal, as the house was not. I do not remember this garden. I can just remember some flowerbeds and the fountain, which didn't fount, but dripped a little. The redwoods and ground-juniper and a pair of English yews in front of the house, a fine camphor tree south of it, a big abelia, a couple of very William-Morris weep-ing willows, were elements of it that remained through my childhood. I don't know whether the Schneiders kept the garden up or let it go; we certainly let it go. It all straggled along the way gardens of large families tend to do. In the mid-thirties, we acquired the lot adjoining ours to the north; part of that became a badminton court. I laid out acreage for my Britain's toy farm set between the old roses, and played in the secret passages under the

huge cumquat bushes, until my parents decided to build two houses on the north lot as rental properties. The crabapple tree remained in its glory, and both new houses had crowded, flowery little

Reading (age 7)

gardens, so our view while washing the dishes remained charming. As we children grew up, my parents had time to potter in their garden. My father planted and tended roses and dahlias, which he loved; my mother

had a gift for bonsai and grew little trees in pots on the sheltered, sunny
patio east of the house.

I realise I may be causing real pain in describing the desecration of a
unique Maybeck chalet and McLaren garden by an uncouth anthropologist,
a Welsh carpenter, and a swarm of brats. I am sorry if this is so. It seems
to me that we used both the house and the garden the best way we could.
We used every inch of it. We adapted ourselves to it and it to ourselves.
We lived in it intensely and completely. We adored it and abused it as
children do their mother. It was our house and we were its family. I think
this is exactly what Maybeck had in mind when he built it. I hope so. He
lived farther up the hill, in one of his chickenwire houses. I have a faint
recollection of a visit from him; I must have been very small, because I
remember looking up at the gentle curve of his belly, and he was a very
short man. It seems to me his trousers were fastened differently than other
men's trousers, with a single, central button placed somewhere high, but
I can't get the image clear. His presence was mysterious and benign.

I keep talking about practicality and impracticality, stairs, smells,
windows, and so on, when what I want to talk about is beauty; but I
don't know how to. It seems you can only describe beauty by describing
something else, the way you can only see the earliest star after sunset by
not looking directly at it.

Surely, if you live in a house from birth to age seventeen, and think of
it as home for years after that, you're going to find the house has become
entangled with your psyche. The degree of this entanglement may depend
somewhat on gender; women are said to identify themselves more with
their house, or their house with themselves, than most men do. The old
ranch in the Napa Valley was and is extremely dear to me, as is the house
in Portland I have lived in for nearly fifty years now. But the Berkeley
house was fundamental. If I recall my childhood, I recall that house. It
is where everything happened. It is where I happened.

And the space it allowed for me to happen in was truly extraordinary. It
was unusually beautiful. Not just pretty and pleasant: much more than that.
Maybeck's artistic standard was very high. Everything around us indoors,
under the scurf and scruff of children's stuff and the mess of daily living,
every surface and area, was nobly proportioned, handsome and generous
in material and workmanship, grave, genial, and spacious.

Cardwell says of the house, "Its ample feeling was developed by
Maybeck's skill in relating one volume to another, as well as by his astute
placement of voids in the walls that define them." (p104) The finest of
those voids, I think, was created by the single massive redwood-cased

pillar that supported the massive main beam of the livingroom ceiling, just as one came from the rather dark entry hall into the large, light living room, sunlit all afternoon. One was aware of the empty spaces around that pillar. One was aware of the movement of the air around it (indeed, the house was rather drafty, but in California that doesn't much matter.) One was aware of the clear, firm intention of the pillar itself. The house depends on me, it said, and I am dependable.

A house so carefully and deliberately planned and intended to give pleasure has got to have an influence on a person living in it, and perhaps most of all on a child: because for a little child the house is pretty much the world. If that world has been deliberately made beautiful, a familiarity with and expectation of beauty, on the human scale and in human terms, may develop in the child. As Maybeck said, such daily experience "will have the same power over the mind as music or poetry...". But the experience of music or poetry is brief, occasional. To a child living in it, the experience of the presence of a house is permanent and inclusive.

I fear I may seem to be describing a little princess growing up in a palace. That's not it. A palace may be beautiful or may not. Beauty's not its business. The business of a palace is to express power, wealth, importance, and so on. The modern McMansion is far more palatial in that sense than any Maybeck. When Maybeck built a palace, it wasn't for kings and princesses to live in or as a statement of grandeur and wealth, but to house and celebrate the public art display of a popular exposition. His buildings declare power only in the integrity and honesty of their design. The only purpose the Maybeck house might be said to share with a palace is the expression of order.

When the relationship of everything in the structure around you is harmonious, when the relationships are vigorous, peaceful, and orderly, one may be led to believe that there is order in the world, and that human beings can attain it.

What I am circling around here is the very difficult question of the expression of moral feeling, and the advancement of moral feeling, through aesthetic means.

Just growing up in a beautiful environment is not going to shape a child's mind favorably. The human, social element outweighs nature decisively. The extraordinary natural splendor of the Bay Area is probably not a very large factor in the development of kids growing up in poverty in the Oakland slums, though it may offer them some relief from decay and disorder. Even apart from social degradation and industrial ugliness, way out in the country, people who live among lovely, varied scenery don't seem to have more breadth of soul or nobility of purpose than those who never saw anything in their life but dreary scrubland. For the beauty of nature as such to brighten and enlarge the mind, I think a child needs either an unusual gift of observation, or a gradual training in observation and aesthetic perception, that will deepen with maturity. There is evidence that young children kept in a single room or a narrow apartment arrive at school with stunted intellectual, spatial, and social skills, mentally handicapped by the physical and visual limitations of the space they grew in. It is hard to doubt that the cramped, ugly, filthy, noisy, disorganised surroundings of slums and poor barrios foster depression and anger in children who live in them, and limit and darken their perception of the world as a whole. All the same, their awareness of human interdependence and mutual responsibility may be far more intense than that of the middle-class child brought up with a room of her own. Neither natural beauty nor deliberately created beauty is enough to foster moral perception and discrimination.

Junior High graduation (age 14)

But I think it possible that early and continuous experience of aesthetic beauty may foster an expectation of order and harmony that might in turn lead to an active desire for moral clarity.

I have trouble distinguishing the ethical from the aesthetic. Both my ethical and my aesthetic responses tend to be immediate to the point of suddenness; hesitant only in cases of real novelty or complexity; and stubborn, though capable of being educated and improved. They are so much alike that I am often uncertain whether I'm responding ethically or aesthetically. "That's right: that's wrong." Such spontaneous certainty seems shallow, but it is not: it is deep and deeply irrational, rising from old, tangled, multitudinous roots, reaching down to the depths of me. As soon as I try to justify it, to find its reason, I'm in deep. When I ask myself why I think the Gehry museum in Seattle is wrong and why I think the Palace of Fine Arts in San Francisco is right, I am involved in the same immensely laborious, ultimately unsatisfactory processes as in explaining why I think abortion on demand is right or why I think torture is wrong. And I do not feel a real difference in kind—or even of importance—between the ethical and the aesthetic inquiry. But to pursue that statement further would require some understanding of philosophy, and I have none.

I will not pursue abortion, torture, or Gehry, either, but will come back to the house I lived in. I think the house was built to an aesthetic ideal or concept which was indistinguishable from—or which I cannot distinguish from—a moral ideal or concept. Is it not fair to say that every building has a morality, in this sense, and not merely a metaphorical one, in the honesty and integrity of its design and materials, or the dishonesty expressed in incompetence, incoherence, shoddiness, fakery, snobbery, etc.?

I think I absorbed this morality of the building as I did the smell of redwood or the sense of complex space.

I think the moral conception of the building was as admirable as its aesthetic conception, from which it is, to me, inseparable.

"There is no Beauty which hath not some Strangeness in the Proportion," Francis Bacon said, which may or may not be true, but which is a useful idea. Our house had a great deal of strangeness in it.

Does anybody play Sardines any more? For Sardines, you have to have a large house, quite a lot of people, and darkness. One person is It. Everybody but It waits noisily in one room, long enough for It to find a hiding place somewhere else – under a bed, in the broom closet, in the bathtub – anywhere It pleases. Then the lights go off, and separately, in silence and darkness, everyone hunts for It. When you find It, you say nothing: you simply join It in the hiding place. If that's a broom closet there may be room for quite a few; if it's under a bed, there are problems. One by one other hunters find the site, and squash themselves into the sardine-can, and suffocate giggles, and try not to move, until at last the final hunter finds them and they all burst free at once. It's a good game. Our house, with its endless nooks and corners and unexpected spaces, was a perfect Sardines house.

That would be a benevolent side of its largeness, darkness, and unexpected spaces. Another aspect was revealed to anybody staying alone in it at night.

The first of our family to do so was a cousin of mine, who spent the night there before my father and mother moved in. He tried to sleep in the big bedroom at the top of the stairs. He leapt up because he quite clearly heard somebody coming up the stairs, step after step. He went to the top landing to challenge the intruder, but could not see anybody at all. He went back to bed. More people climbed the stairs. People walked across the floor of the room towards him, creak, creak, and still he could not see them. He ended up sleeping out on one of the balconies with the door shut, hoping the invisible people would stay inside the house.

Redwood floors have a kind of delayed resilience; compressed by a footfall, they snap back ... after a while ... hours perhaps. Once you understand the phenomenon, it is more or less endurable. As an adolescent I rather liked to hang over the deep well of the staircase and listen to the invisible people ascending it, or later, to lie in my small room and listen to myself walking around overhead in the attic, the floor repeating every step I had taken there that afternoon.

But as a young child, the explanations were not very helpful to me. I slept then in the big bedroom at the top of the stairs; and the house, deep in the night, was scary. It was limitlessly large and deeply dark. There was room in it for many and mysterious beings. I had night terrors for years after seeing *King Kong* at age six, but could handle them pretty well, so long as I knew people were in the house. The first time I was ever left alone in it, I went into a slow panic. I tried to be brave, but little by little the shadows and the creakings were too much for me. My older brothers were just across the street, and when I leaned from a balcony and wailed aloud, they came at once and were most comforting and remorseful. I wept apologetically, feeling very foolish. Why was I afraid of my own dear house? How could it have become so strange to me?

It had a strangeness in it; that is, I think, the truth.

Beauty is a very difficult word: I have already complained about not being able to approach it straight on. People don't use the word as freely as they used to, and many artists — painters, sculptors, photographers, architects, poets — reject it entirely; they deny that there is any common standard by which to judge it; they diminish it to prettiness and so righteously despise it; or they deliberately abandon it for truth, or self-expression, or edginess, or other values they prize more highly.

I don't pretend to be able to argue with such refusals of beauty, when I can't even offer a generally acceptable definition of the word. But I think it behoves artists to consider what the word means to them, no matter what it means to others. How do they interpret the aesthetic component of what they do, its importance, its weight? What, besides that component, makes it appropriate to call their work art? What, besides the search to make something beautiful, makes an artist? There are perhaps as many answers to those questions now as there are artists, and nothing gives me the right to ask them of other artists; but I do feel the obligation to ask them of myself, and answer as honestly as I can.

Novelists probably talk less than any other kind of artist about beauty, because the word is seldom used to describe what they make. It has always been an important word to me in thinking about my work, however, and in describing that of other novelists. For instance: *Pride and Prejudice* is, to me, an absolutely beautiful work of art. Exquisite accuracy of language, perfection of proportion, of gait, of rhythm, in the service of powerful intelligence and insight and strong moral feeling, forming a complete and vital whole—if that isn't beautiful, what is? If that makes sense to you, you may be willing to let me use the word beauty in describing novels of very different kinds, such as *Little Dorrit, War and Peace, To the Lighthouse,* or *The Lord of the Rings,* or to think of novels which you'd be willing to call beautiful.

Now, if *Pride and Prejudice* were a house, I think it would be a nobly proportioned, delightfully livable, English country house of the eighteenth century.

I don't know what novel our Maybeck house could be compared to, but it would contain darkness and radiant light; its beauty would arise from honest, bold, inventive construction, from geniality and generosity of spirit and mind, and would also have elements of fantasy and strangeness.

Writing this, I wonder if much of my understanding of what a novel ought to be was taught to me, ultimately, by living in that house; and so, if all my life I have been rebuilding it around me out of words.

photo by Joe Collins, Elliott Bay Book Company, Seattle, 2002

Always Coming Home
Ethnography, unBible, and Utopian Satire[1]

Richard D. Erlich
Miami University, Ohio

I may have just pissed off Ursula K. Le Guin. With my title. Satire has a dual and fairly bad reputation. On the one hand, it's frequently juvenile, obscene, and politically incorrect, insensitive, and/or indecent; on the other, it's necessarily at least a little judgmental and is often preachy, monologic, unfair, and, well, a lot judgmental.[2] In the case of her purest early satire, *The Word for World Is Forest* (*WWF*), Le Guin says in the Afterword to *WWF* in *Again, Dangerous Visions*, "Writing is usually hard work for me, and enjoyable; this story was easy to write, and disagreeable. [...] Writing it was a little like taking dictation from a boss with ulcers," a boss who "wanted to moralize" (I.126; also *Language of the Night* (*LoN*) 1979: 151-52, 1989/92: 144-47).[3]

So Le Guin might object to the "satire label," and Le Guin has definitely objected to calling her work utopian: "In the sense that it offers a glimpse of some imagined alternative to 'the way we live now,' much of my fiction can be called utopian," she says—but she continues "to resist the word." A number of her imagined societies seem to her "an improvement in one way or another on our own," but she finds "Utopia far too grand and too rigid a name for them. Utopia, and Dystopia, are intellectual places. I write from passion and playfulness." Le Guin insists that her fictions "are neither dire warnings nor blueprints for what we ought to do," finding most of them "comedies of human manners, reminders of the infinite variety of ways in which we always come back to pretty much the same place, and celebrations of that infinite variety by the invention of still more alternatives and possibilities." There is an obvious objection here, two of them, actually, and Le Guin anticipates them: "Even the

---

[1] This essay continues the argument in "Le Guin and God" (Erlich) and is based on my conference presentation "UKL: Eutopia, Antiutopia, Dystopia" and *Coyote's Song* (© 1997, 2001, 2006), published as an SFRA digital book, with pdf versions available of the hard-copy version prepared for library deposit.

[2] For authorial judgments in even the most "scenic," or dramatic of authors, see Wellek's critique of M. M. Bakhtin, esp. 32-33; keyword for on-line search: "Iago."

[3] See Sawyer 407 for *WWF* as "Le Guin's most pastoral (in the most general sense) work"; Sawyer offers an excellent sketch of the pastoral in SF generally and *Always Coming Home* particularly, including Pastoral as "a location for political and moral thought experiments" (412; see also 409, & passim).

novels *The Dispossessed (TD)* and *Always Coming Home (ACH)*, in which I worked out more methodically than usual certain variations on the uses of power, which I preferred to those that obtain in our world—even these are as much efforts to subvert as to display the ideal of an attainable social plan which would end injustice and inequality once and for all." Le Guin says her aim has not been to offer plans for "betterment but, by offering an imagined but persuasive alternative reality, to dislodge my mind, and so the reader's mind, from the lazy, timorous habit of thinking that the way we live now is the only way people can live. It is that inertia that allows the institutions of injustice to continue unquestioned" ("Utopia," "Only in Utopia" *Wave* 218).

Many eutopias (sic) do indicate "what we ought to do," with some giving detailed blueprints of how The Good Place should look; and dystopias usually imply "dire warnings"—including the disasters, dystopias, and dystopian traces in Le Guin's fiction, including *ACH* (cf. Sawyer 409). Still, that's not all there is to utopian writing. Sir Thomas More's *Utopia* (1516) describes Utopia in great detail, but "utopia" is The Good Place (*eutopos*) that is No Place (*outopos*); and the description of Utopia comes from Raphael Hythloday, a speaker of Healing (*Raphael* in Hebrew) Nonsense (the Greek implications of "Hythlodaeus" [see, e.g., Turner 8]). The detailed description of Utopia comes in Book II, following, unsurprisingly, Book I, which is set in Christian Europe and reviews the evils of Christian Europe. The rational pagans of Utopia and the unChristian republic of Utopia act as a satiric Norm by which Europe is to be judged and condemned. *Utopia* in this standard reading is a kind of satire in which the satiric Norm is a social-political system that gets developed in detail. Eutopias that are not blueprints, dystopias that are more than warnings, can be read as a variety of satire.

And utopian fiction can be pretty high art: not subtle, usually, but often erudite, sometimes complex and nuanced.

Like Le Guin's *The Dispossessed*, *ACH* can be read as critical utopia and critical dystopia (self-conscious works critical of themselves and of their parent genres), and as fictional ethnography and an "unBible."[4] But *ACH* is definitely in form a *satura*—an, overflowing plate, literary chop suey, a stuffed carrier-bag—and I think implied in Le Guin's disclaimer I quoted at length is the suggestion that *ACH* can be read also as an artful utopian satire. But that's *utopia* as I've sketched it for the ovular work, and satire with all the complexities of high-art satires: heard as many-voiced and rich and provocative. Good satires are teaching works where the teaching voices raise questions more than

---

[4] For critical dystopia and utopia, see Baccolini and Moylan, and Moylan.

preach the One Truth. Artistic satires, in Fredric Bogel's reading, ask us to question separations and rejections (46). Satires worth reading engage in what Dustin Griffin has analyzed as the rhetoric of "Display and Play"—they entertain while they may or may not passionately attack social evil (ch. 3). "The Satiric Plot," as Alvin Kernan suggested, seems to bring us "very nearly" back to "the same point where we began" (270). And "infinite variety" has long been the claim of satire (Juvenal I.85). Indeed, Northrop Frye insisted that satire's main job is endorsing complex movement over stultification "breaking up the lumber of stereotypes [...], pedantic dogmatisms, oppressive fashions, and all other things that impede the free movement"—not necessarily progress!—"of society" ("Nature" 328). In *Anatomy of Criticism*, Frye specifically applies Juvenal to contrast satire with the overselectivity and flattening of dogmatic philosophy (229), a "philosophical pedantry" seen satirically as "imposing of over-simplified ideals on experience," on the human comedy (231).

Le Guin has passionately and playfully written antiUtopia in *The Lathe of Heaven* (*LoH*, 1971) and both ambiguous eutopia and pretty direct dystopia in *The Dispossessed* (1974) and earlier in *The Left Hand of Darkness* (*LHD*, 1969). And so on up to the conflicting and contrasted societies in *Voices* (2006). One core satiric target is clear: the transcendent One. Not God exactly—Le Guin's a spiritual-minded atheist—but the One as the object of belief of the significantly named Unist Fathers of "Dancing to Ganam" and *The Telling*: more generally, any totalizing belief, from the mystic-vision of the Yomeshta in *LHD* to the alliance of church and state in the book-destroying, gods-fearing, mother-raping, bellicose priest-king, priests, and soldiers of Asudar in *Voices*.[5] Pre-eminently, Le Guin's target is the set of problems shown in the Condor People (the Dayao) in *ACH*.

The critique Le Guin consciously uses, with citation, is that of Holmes Welch: Lao Tzu and classical Daoism set against "the giant of Americanism" and the American "instinct [...] to play the male," and a macho male at that (169-74; "Part 4, Tao Today"—see also "A First Note" in *ACH*). Macho America, then, and more generally the "Judaeo-Christian-Rationalist West" (*LoH* 82; ch. 6) is the main butt of Le Guin's critique, but that Judeo-Christian target needs to be explained a bit more exactly.

---

[5] Le Guin's target "exactly" includes God, here for once an immanent one, in "Field of Vision": "the one true God, immanent in all things. Everywhere, forever" (*The Wind's Twelve Quarters* [*WTQ*] 234); see Abrash.

Émile Durkheim typified the sacred as "things set apart and forbidden"; Durkheim missed a major alternative tradition, the gentle mysticism Aldous Huxley called "The Perennial Philosophy," which sees the sacred in connection.[6] It is this separation that Le Guin most dislikes. Le Guin critiques explicitly "[…] the dreadful self-isolation of the Church, that soul-fortress towering over the dark abysms of the bestial/mortal/ World/Hell […]." As she continues in *Buffalo Gals* (*BG*), generalizing from the Church: "By climbing up into his head and shutting out every voice but his own, 'Civilized Man' has gone deaf. He can't hear the wolf calling him brother—not Master, but brother. He can't hear the earth calling him child—not Father, but son. He hears only his own words making up the world. He can't hear the animals […]. This is the myth of civilization, embodied in the monotheisms which assign soul to Man alone" (*BG* 11).

With rare exceptions, Le Guin is strongly and consistently unMonotheistic and anti-monotheistic. She opposes to monotheism, to monologism, law, logocentrism, idealism, and to separation, the Daoist Way: for Le Guin, "The central image/idea of Taoism is an important thing to be clear about, certainly not because it's a central theme in my work. It's a central theme, period" ("Response" 45). Daoism is a central theme, plus, as a complement and alternative, societies that embody that really old-time religion of The Perennial Philosophy and/or a polytheism and spirituality associated with societies that have not made The Big Mistake of entering history and civilization.[7]

In the 1972 dangerous vision, *WWF*, the local native Selver is a complex and deeply ambiguous hero, but a hero, leading, for a time—while he's a god—a well-balanced people who know how to live well. Don Davidson and the Terrans, representing high-tech, civilized Americans, are the antagonists, and Davidson is a villain. Le Guin may not have liked writing it, and the story itself may be "disagreeable," but "Word for World" was bracing and effective in novella form in 1972 and effective long afterwards as a book. In *ACH*, there is a similar clash between a richly complex, *sensibly*-technological culture and a people who are on the verge of committing the historical error of moving into civilization, patriarchy, and military hierarchy. Le Guin performs the

---

[6] Durkheim: *Formes élémentaires de la vie religieuse*, qtd. Jones, on line; see also Durkheim *Elementary Forms* 47 (ch. 1.4); *Durkheim on Religion* 123; Durkheim on sacred and profane, and hierarchy: *Elementary Forms* 37-38, *Durkheim on Religion* 112.

[7] For what I've called "The Big Mistake" in historical terms, the movement from Neolithic village culture into city life (civilization), see Mumford, and *Coyote's Song* ch. 10, search word, "Neolithic."

artist's Vonnegutian job of giving warning, and the poet's job of giving to an abstract conflict "a local habitation and a name," or names: Kesh and Condor, and Stone Telling, whose story moves from Kesh to Condor and back again, and provides a focus for *ACH*.[8] In doing so Le Guin does a novelist's work *and* commits, so to speak, acts of first-degree, first-rate satire.

STONE TELLING: Kesh v. Condors

Stone Telling tells her story in three parts: in the 523-page Harper & Row 1985 paperback, pp. 7-42, 173-201, 340-386, although the last ten pages are "Messages Concerning the Condor," finishing the story in other voices. One may read that story through, and then read or consult the rest of *ACH* as background. Or one may foreground the cultural materials and see Stone Telling's story as just a key example of Kesh narrative, illustrating the culture, and introducing the contrasting Condor people. Both ways are correct, and are wrong: *ACH* is a literary "figure and ground" illusion, and the "right" approach would be a double vision that allowed readers to see both at once, to see the world of the story and the story as both background and foreground.[9]

I privilege Stone Telling's story as a first-person novella within *ACH*, in the context of a *satura* that moves toward eutopian/dystopian satire. Stone Telling's story is the spine of an anatomy that is an experiment in the form of the novel, perhaps Le Guin's most extensive contribution to reshaping the novel in a less masculinist, more "Carrier-Bag" form. Stone Telling's story is high art, making the sort of nuanced judgments we associate with high art: life among the Kesh is far from perfect, but their way is much better than that of the Dayao/Condor people, and a major improvement on "'the way we live now.'" Indeed, the Kesh live short lives in a maimed world—a world despoiled by our culture—but still manage to undo much of the historical mistake of moving out of the Neolithic village and nature, our ancestors' mistake of moving out of immanence and into civilization, history, and transcendent projects.[10]

[8] Vonnegut suggested "that artists are useful to society because they are so sensitive. [...] like canaries in poison coal mines [...]. "Poets' giving "to airy nothing / A local habitation and a name": Shakespeare's Theseus, *A Midsummer's Night's Dream* 5.1.7-17.

[9] More exactly, we'd hear the voices in complex polyphony. But I don't know how to talk about aural "figure and ground" and have experienced music that way only when thoroughly stoned and only on a couple of occasions in the 1970s.

[10] I discuss immanence in a metaphysical/theological sense in "UKL and Arthur C. Clarke ...," in Simone de Beauvoir's sense of entrapment in domesticity in *Coyote's Song*, Introduction.

Stone Telling is a "liminal" person, one of Le Guin's "Exiles and Envoys" (Spencer). Her mother is Kesh, her father Dayao, and her quest for her self, for Home, takes her from the Valley to The City of the Condor—a City of Man—and then (fulfilling the quest pattern) back again, re-integrated into her world and, in *ACH, the* world: "*To be whole is to be part; true journey is return*" (Odo's tombstone, *TD* 68; ch. 3). Her spiral movement allows her to see and show us not only her eutopian world of the Kesh but also the imperialist dystopia of the Condor. In the movement between eutopian and dystopian worlds, she helps to answer the question, "*How shall a human being live well, then?*"[11] In the context of *ACH*, the question includes how we might set up cultures and societies that actively encourage—and avoiding creating cultures that discourage—good living.

A relevant analogy for the politics here is an earlier work that *ACH* reflects in a reversing and distorting mirror image: Yevgeny Zamyatin's, *We* (ca. 1920).[12] *We*'s male protagonist-narrator tells us, "Man ceased to be a savage only when we had built the Green Wall, when we had isolated our perfect mechanical world from the irrational, hideous world of trees, birds, animals [...]" (93; Seventeenth Entry), enclosing "infinity behind a wall" (40-41; Eighth Entry). In the backstory of *We* is "the Great Two Hundred Years' War—the war between the city and the village. [...] True, only 0.2 of the earth's population survived the war. But, cleansed of its millennial filth, how radiant the face of the earth has become! And those two tenths survived to taste the heights of bliss in the shining palace of the One State" (21; Fifth Entry). It turns out that a "small remnant" also survived outside the Wall, to become the wild, savage Mephi. These savages are the "half" that must unite with the civilized for full humanity (163); they represent nature and energy, opposing entropy (165; Twenty-eighth Entry). What's relevant here is the City/Village split and *ACH*'s literally re-evaluating some basic terms of Zamyatin's formula. Like Zamyatin, Le Guin puts her protoJudeo-Christians within the walls of the City and people integrated into nature into wall-less villages (in the shape of the double-spiral heyiya-if [*ACH* 3]); but it is the Condor who hold the promise of action, destruction, and "tormentingly endless movement," or, more exactly perhaps, busy-ness.

[11] The key question in UKL's variation on the theme of Job, the play of *Chandi*, *ACH* 226 f.

[12] For a discussion of mirror images and reversals, relating to *ACH*, see Selinger 135 f.

ACH starts sputteringly, as I have done and as is traditional with saturas/satires (see Jonathan Swift's longer works), but when we get past a rather analytical Contents and "A First Note," "The Quail Song" (a ten-line lyric), and a note moving us "Towards an Archeology of the Future"—then *ACH* moves into a plot with "Stone Telling," Part One.[13]

Part One (7-42)

We meet Stone Telling under her first name, North Owl, and she tells us her mother's names were Towhee (a bird), Willow, and Ashes and that as a girl she lived with her mother and her grandmother, Valiant. Her "father's name, Abhao, in the Valley means Kills." Stone Telling tells her story as a report on the Exchange, her world's high-tech communication/information system, so she talks to us as if we were human people of the Valley, and we have to tolerate some initial misunderstandings, e.g., "First Name" here doesn't mean first name in our binomial nomenclature, but the chronologically first name someone uses (7-8). We soon learn that young Stone Telling is teased by some children with epithets of "half-House" and called "half a person" (9). The mockery provides foreshadowing; it also shows that kids can be cruel even in eutopia (a good place, not some perfect place).

North Owl goes with her mother and maternal grandmother to visit her grandmother's mostly ex-husband, who they learn has changed from his middle name of Potter to (probably) a last name of Corruption (13). Corruption tells Valiant and us, "Your body is not real" and performs a trick upon himself and then North Owl demonstrating the maxim: he passes a potter's paddle through his hand and then through North Owl's arm. Corruption says, "This North Owl might come to the Warriors," teaching her a new word, with Valiant responding, "No chance of that. Your Warriors are all men," with Corruption answering back, "She can marry one." Willow may have been frightened by the power implied in Corruption's trick; North Owl seems impressed (14).

Very soon, North Owl sees men of the Condor for the first time and learns that her father may return (16), but nothing comes of the Condor visit for a while, and North Owl goes on being, mostly, a normal eight-year-old of her people: including one who recognizes dirt as "the mother of my mothers," and her kinship with Coyote (21-22), as with many real-world Indian groups a great Trickster and creator.

[13] The Harper 1st edn. pb has it Part I, Part Two, Part Three; I have regularized the section titles.

North Owl sees a condor — the bird — flying in a gyre, and her mother calls North Owl "Condor's Daughter," as if it were a name (23-24); and then news of the human Condor(s) arrive, and with the news a Kesh debate. Some say the Condor should be kept out, that they're sick, "that they have their heads on crooked" — a strong accusation in the folklore of the Kesh — and that for ten years there have been Valley people emulating the Condor, the "men of the Warrior's Lodge in the Upper Valley, and what are Warriors but people who make war?" The speaker of North Owl's heyimas sees no problem: "They can do us no harm. We walk the gyre."[14] He is answered with "And they walk the wheel, and the power builds!", a line we are not going to understand until we return to it after reading what the "Story of Flicker [...]" has to teach about wheels of power and understand that "gyre" means to the Kesh an important image of power moving properly. In this loaded context, North Owl finds a condor feather, which she tries to give to Cave Woman, who refuses the gift, saying it was for North Owl, and adding "Heya, Condor's Daughter, in the dry land, think of the creeks running! Heya, Condor's Daughter, in the dark house, think of the blue clay bowl!" The dry land in the universe of Earthsea is the land of death; here it is that symbolically, and the City of the Condor. The dark house is usually the grave; here it is symbolically that, plus the house of North Owl's father's family (25; see 359, [46], 420). Water in a dry land is a symbol for life; in other contexts, water is a symbol for passive strength. North Owl denies being the Condor's Daughter, but Cave Woman responds "It seems the condor says you are," and North Owl takes the phallic feather (Selinger 137): "If I had to be different from other people," North Owl thinks, "then let my difference be notable" (25).

When North Owl is nine, her father returned to the Valley. Looking back, the adult Stone Telling knows that he was "Terter Abhao, True Condor, Commander of the Army of the South, who was off duty with his troops for the autumn and winter, awaiting orders for the spring campaign" — who returns to be rejected by the town but accepted without recriminations by his wife and daughter (29-30).

The rest of Part One is the story of Abhao's stay in the Valley, especially North Owl's response to him and his men, until, inevitably, he leaves.

When she first sees her father's soldiers, North Owl isn't sure what to make of them and tries out theories. North Owl's observations defamiliarize uniforms, inviting us to see the weirdness of dressing a whole band of men identically and wonder what function the uniforms

---

[14] *Heyimas* is defined in the Glossary at The Back of the Book (*ACH* 515). To young North Owl, it would mean mostly "school," but school as an old-world village *Shul* or very small-town US high school.

fulfill. And here that sense of wonder isn't just a virtue in readers of SF but an ethical imperative: the organizers of the Condor military and the military in our world are neither crazy nor stupid (Wytenbroek 334-35). In Kesh terms, the Condor have their heads on, but their heads are on backwards. Uniforms for armies—real armies, not just armed bands—are rational.

"Kills" in the Valley is a stranger in a strange land, but an aristocratic one, too arrogant to learn to behave appropriately, since he is certain that his way is the only way for a True Condor (32). Kills is an officer and a gentleman, and gentility places severe limitations on what one may do without losing face; a gentleman is not a peasant who performs menial tasks. Valiant remains quiet, "but she could not hide her contempt for a man who would not herd or farm or even chop wood. He, holding herders and farmers and woodcutters in contempt, found this hard to bear."[15] And Willow loves Kills too much to insist that he work (31).

North Owl enjoys her father. For one thing, he has the largest horse she's ever seen and takes her for rides, giving her an aristocrat's view of the world. He also introduces her to a variety of thrill unavailable among the Kesh: shouting a command obeyed by the men working a low-tech piledriver. "Being the driver not the pile," she thought such power "was fine" (32).

North Owl is not the only one in the Valley to be attracted to unbalanced power. We have heard of Warrior Lodges growing up among the Kesh, and soon learn that they are organized by men who imitate the Condor in following a militaristic life. There is a mild confrontation with the Condor over building a bridge (33). The Condor wish to get their supply wagons across the river and don't want to go out of their way. Why not ford? Because "Soldiers don't carry loads on their backs." Besides, "Men of the Condor are not only brave fighters but great engineers. The roads and bridges in the lands around the City of the Condor are the wonder of the age" (34). Like the ancient Romans of the Republic and early Empire and, until recently, the Americans, the Condor are great builders, and builders build. To the people of the Valley, Abhao and his troops are building in their home, and they don't need foreign-built roads or bridges to get around in their own house ([34]-35).

What we have in this confrontation is less a misunderstanding than a minor clash between two groups of people who see the world in different ways and therefore have irreconcilable goals. The Condor wish to impose their corporate will upon the world and upon the Kesh, and the Condor are much more heavily armed than the Kesh and much more ready to

[15] Cf. the attitude toward "peasants" of Councillor (sic) Luis Falco et al., in *Eye of the Heron* (*EoH* [e.g., 65-67; ch. 5]).

kill people to get their way. We do get a misunderstanding when Terter Abhao says to his wife, "We must go before your World Dance, Willow," meaning by "we" he and his troops (39). Willow understands "we" as "you and I" (42). Willow quickly figures out what Kills mean, and tells him if he goes not to come back.

Willow puts Abhao's things outside the door and Willow's Blue Clay relations explain to Abhao "that a man may come and go as he likes, and a woman may take him back or not as she likes, but the house is hers, and if she shuts the door he may not open it." Abhao insists "But she belongs to me—the child belongs to me" and is mocked in what would be a comic scene if it were not narrated from the point of view of the pained North Owl (40). Part One ends with Abhao's departure, asking North Owl to wait for him, and with Willow going back to her name as a child (41). Abhao follows his orders, putting military business before his family.

If one reads through *ACH* beginning to end, Part Two of Stone Telling is introduced with the last subsection of the Time and the City section, called "Time in the Valley." This subsection includes a Valley Origin Myth; except we must note that it is "a" myth, one of them, not *the* myth; and the "myth" we hear may be more of a tale or an amusing story recently made up (165). The story includes the origin of humans. Our origin has to do with Coyote, a son and future mate Coyote delivers for herself, and a volcano: Maybe we came from he-coyote's afterbirth, maybe from Coyote's turds, maybe from Coyote's words made flesh—or maybe not. The volcano erupts, spewing out human people: "[...] so here we are, the children of Coyote and the Mountain, we are their turds and their words" (168). Le Guin is not earnest but is serious in this story. When we hear later of civilized views of "dirt people," keep in mind that one possible Kesh variation on *Adam* (Man) as dust + God's breath (Gen. 2.4-7), involves the origin of all humans in "turds and [...] words."[16]

The rest of this subsection is on time-keeping and calendars and the general resemblance of the Kesh to the Indians of Northern California in not being much concerned with exactness keeping time.[17] Pandora, fictional archeologist and intermittent Narrator of this fictional future, discusses time with Gather, a man of 60, an expert in using the Exchange, a student of domestic architecture, "whose lifelong passion has been

[16] Cf. humans as mud in the 1983 *EoH* (116-17, ch. 8; 176-77, ch. 11; & passim).

[17] A. L. Kroeber's *Handbook* Index has no entries for "time" or "calendar." See also *Handbook* 177 (ch. 11) for the usual lack of a word among the original Californians for "year," and for people not keeping track of their ages.

the retrieval of data concerning certain doings of human beings in the Valley of the Na. At last we have met a historically minded person […]" (169). Except she hasn't, not in our sense. Gather "spatializes time; it is not an arrow, not a river, but a house, the house he lives in" (171-72). Pandora is frustrated and leaves Gather, walking off with the Archivist of Wakwaha. "If you don't have a history," Pandora says to the Archivist, "how am I to tell your story?" The Archivist asks for a definition of history, and Pandora quotes, "the study of Man in Time." The Archivist is silent.

> "You aren't Man and you don't live in Time," I say bitterly. You live in the Dream Time."[18]
> "Always," says the Archivist of Wakwaha. "Right through Civilisation, we have lived in the Dream Time."[…]
> After a while […] [the Archivist] says, "Tell about the Condor. Let Stone Telling tell her story. That's as near history as we have come in my day, and nearer than we'll come again, I hope." (172)

And, if one is reading linearly, this brings one to Stone Telling Part Two.

Part Two (173-201)

Moving on in her story, Stone Telling tells us that her love has gone with her father, and she thought she didn't love her mother at all. North Owl's choice of beloved parent serves a psychological function for her, allowing her to feel, as foreshadowed earlier, not so much different as special (173; cf. 25). Soon the political becomes the personal for North Owl as her grandfather moves back in to help organize the town for the Warriors (175). North Owl's beloved cousin, Hops, becomes a Warrior and takes the middle name "Spear," whose phallic suggestions amuse North Owl (175-76). The household becomes strongly involved with not only the Warriors but also the Lamb Lodge: "a kind of woman Warriors" (176).

North Owl is caught up in the tension in her town. Spear tells her the new teaching "that there had never been sacredness in rocks or springs, but in the mindsoul, the spirit only. The rock and the springs and the body, he said, were screens that kept the spirit from true sacredness,

---

[18] For Le Guin on dream-time (sic) and world-time, see *WWF*, e.g., 136-137 (ch. 6).

true power." North Owl disagrees and says sacredness "was the rock, it was the water running, it was the person living." If the person breaks the relationship and says, "The sacredness has gone out of it," then the person had changed, not the rock. Coincident with North Owl's turning thirteen, there is a change in custom significantly juxtaposed with the introduction of this new philosophy. The Kesh had the tradition of "living on the Coast": a period of abstinence from sex in early adolescence (488-89). The change the Warriors introduced was "to forbid the young men even to speak to adolescent girls" (179), plus more explicit introductions of sexism. This part of the story sketches out the relationships among sexism, psychological hang-ups, and militarism. North Owl's adopted grandfather, Ninepoint, had a biological grandson who had gone over to the Warriors and taken the name "Vile," and Ninepoint accuses him of arrogance and implies that the lot of them may be "so afraid of girls you have to make war on them." Or so afraid of themselves that they have to fight themselves. Corruption comes to speak contemptuously of all women, and Valiant finally accuses him of "trying to be like those Condor men, who are so afraid of women they run [...] away from their own [...] to rape women they don't know!" (179). We will soon see the Condor close up, but insofar as we get within the story a psychological explanation of why they do what they do (or sexists generally do) the answer seems to be fear—a very popular and plausible theory. Keep in mind, though, North Owl's pleasure in "the power that originates in imbalance" (32).

North Owl comes to see her absent father as a symbol of her freedom and strength and asserts to her household, "I am a Condor woman!" (180).

And womanhood of some sort she is about to embark on, a vulnerable time in which she becomes infatuated with Spear, an impossible love because sex between them would be taboo. Spear goes the Warrior way and avoids North Owl and will not speak to her (183). Her personal problem with Spear becomes political. She was "swallowed up" in her love and had become "the servant" of that love. And so she joins the Lamb Lodge, where they "spoke of love, of service, of obedience, of sacrifice," and the love for a Warrior man as unambiguously good things—as they are in the Religion of Love in the Romance tradition and, in part, in Christianity. North Owl accepts such teachings for her love of Spear. As implied earlier in *ACH*, in a "Commentary on the War with the Pig People" (133-34), "The Lambs and Warriors were houses for adolescents, people who were not able to choose their own way yet, or unwilling ever to do so" (184).

At a low point in her relationship with her family—when North Owl has finally dropped the emotional big one and said to her grandmother, "I hate you!"—Terter Abhao returns (185). He gives North Owl a new name, Terter Ayatyu (Woman Born Above Others, of the clan of the Terter), and takes her away to live among the Condor (186-87). This is the first turning point, or major hinge, of the story and it leads to Stone Telling as a stranger in the land of the Condor, the Dayao. In terms of plot, Part Two takes us to Stone Telling's installation in the Terter household and her acceptance as granddaughter by her father's father, the clan chief. In terms of getting done the thematic/satiric work of the story, the crucial point is a brief ethnography of the Condor, and "a history" (192).

In terms of their ethnography and history, the Dayao are well on their way to epitomizing The Big Mistake in the evolution of (nowadays) most human societies.

The ruling Condor, *the* Condor, is Lewis Mumford's early Bronze Age King (in "Utopia, The City and The Machine") given not only a local habitation and a name but some high technology: a better-armed Genghis Khan or some Aryan chieftain converted to a city-based, militant, postMosaic monotheism; Joshua leading Israel into a Canaan with a much smaller and more pacific population.[19] In their combination of technology and hierarchy, the Condor people are in a line going back to the Gdemiar in Le Guin's "Semley's Necklace" (1964), and a temporary culmination of a line of thought that Le Guin had been nursing as a minor theme since *Planet of Exile* (*PE*) (1966). In that novel, "a new time" had come. Among the native peoples of the planet, the Gaal had stopped thinking of time and space in their traditional ways. Time to them had been "a lantern lighting a step before, a step behind—the rest was indistinguishable dark. [...] They looked ahead only to the next season at most. They did not look down over time but were in it [...]." For the Gaal until recently, "space was not a surface on which to draw boundaries but a range, a heartland, centered on the self and clan and tribe [...]." The Gaal had started to think of time and space in a civilized way, "in the linear, imperialistic fashion" (*PE* 74; ch. 9). A " great man" arose among the Gaal who "united all their tribes and made an army of them" (*PE* 23; ch. 2).[20]

[19] A. L. Kroeber describes the Aryans—Indo-Europeans, to use a less loaded term—who entered the Punjab as a "cityless, hut-dwelling, cattle-raiding, uncommercial Vedic people," with a culture that was tribal, without walls, "unbound, ready to pack up and move without being essentially nomadic; half peasantlike and half aristocratic; an uncitified semicivilization, pioneer rather than backwoods" (*Anthropology* 749; § 305).

[20] Note also the Nation of the Basnasska of *City of Illusions* that the protagonist Falk meets on his trip west across the North American Great Plains (68, 70; ch. 4).

In a "Carrier-Bag" ethnography of the Condor, I'd say the following are the most important points noted or shown in "Stone Telling" Parts Two and Three:

• The Condor people "lived outside the world" and are in theory, at war with everyone until they bring everyone "under the wing of the Condor"—or kill them (192-94).

• In the Condor City of Man—a civilized place for humans, plus aspects of The/A City of God—the men will "blind the eye or cut off the hand of a woman or farmer who writes a single word"; writing is sacred and limited to the True Condor elite, with only the One-Warriors, a kind of warrior priesthood, literate to a high degree. The Word of One is absolute truth, and "That word—'One'—is the end of talking as well as of writing, under the Condor's wing [...]" (192).

• The Condor status system starts with the One at the top, God. ("Hear, O Israel, the LORD our God, the LORD is one" [Deut. 6.4; qtd Mark 12.28-30]). Next under One is One's messenger, The Condor. Then come the nobles, "called True Condors"; others, also of high status are the "One-Warriors. No other people are called Condors. Men who are not of those families are all called *tyon*, farmers [cf. "peasant" as an insult], and must serve the True Condors." Women of elite families are called "Condor Women" and are inferior in rank to Condor Men but superior to and "may give orders to tyon and hontik. The hontik are all other women, foreigners, and animals" (i.e., nonhuman animals, "lower" animals in the view satirized in the Condor).

• Stone Telling correctly sees that the City of Man is "civilisation" and that to use *civilized* as a compliment and *barbaric* as an insult is problematic (193).

• Upon conquering a city, The Condor "killed and burned men and children and kept women to be fucked by Dayao men," penning the women with the cattle (193-94).

• The City of Man is built rectilinearly, "with walls of black basalt," a "magnificent bridge," "machines and engines of work and war," and many other "marvelous products of handmind." Stone Telling summarizes: "All I saw was great, and straight, and hard, and strong [...]" (194); the physical City is a kind of objective correlative for the way of a culture going very wrong: "without reversal or turning, straight, single, terrible" (201).

• Condor houses reflect "the winter dugouts and summer tents" the tribe used when they were "nomads of the Plains of

Grass," except in The City they're all-electric, usually brightly lit, and "very warm and comfortable, encompassing" (*ACH* 194 [see *LHD* 117; ch. 8]). Stone Telling speculates that "maybe their health as a people was in being nomads." When they built a city and lived in it, they "locked their energy into the wheel, and so began to lose their souls" (196).

• In a land low on metals, the Condor have plenty, and the City, generally, seems wealthy. "But their wealth did not flow; they did not give with pleasure" (195), so by Kesh standards they were poor.

• Condor women "lived under siege all their lives" and are rarely allowed to go outside or be alone; Stone Telling has no opportunity for solitude, nor for work beyond spinning and sewing (195, 199 [also 196]).

• Condor society is absolutely hierarchized and militarized: "Everything among the Dayao had to have a chief. [...] Even when people worked together one of them was chief of the work, as if working were making war [...]" (199).

• Women are not included in the life of the mind of the Condor. Stone Telling finds it notable that "It was not men there, but women, who told me that women have no souls" and so don't need to learn about "the soul's way" (200).

• Condor's wives are "expected to have babies continuously," in a big-litter theory appropriate to a warring people (345), but the peasant women "aborted more often than they bore" (349).

• Adulteresses are "killed by the husband's family [...] in public," in a formal execution because the wife belongs to the husband (346; as contrasted with murderous "jealousy and sexual rage," which Stone Telling accepts). Indeed, punishments generally are violent, frequent, and severe, and directed toward underlings (348); the Condor also practice group punishment, killing ten "hontik of the City [...] as punishment or payment for the deaths of [...] ten Condor killed" at a distant mine (353). Stone Telling sees group punishment as a sign of binary thinking: The killing of random slaves for punishment or payment "was fair, if all Condors were one and all non-Condors the other: either this, or that" (353).[21]

---

[21] Note *Either/Or* as the title of an 1843 work by Søren Kierkegaard, alluded to by Heather Lelache in *LoH* (90; ch. 7). Le Guin attacks thinking in binary oppositions but uses such oppositions—mindfully.

• Dayao women, even among the elite, come to think like slaves and lie to men, usually, "smiling and agreeing with everything and pretending" ignorance (358-59).

• Dayao women feel insecure outside the walls of a father's or husband's house "because to Dayao men all women unprotected by a man are victims" (360).

Stone Telling ends Part Two summarizing what she can infer about the ideology of the Condor—starting with their theology; this passage is crucial for ordering the data about the evils of Condor culture (everything, mostly, except their cooking) and determining what Le Guin is up to in *ACH* and what she had been leading up to in her teaching works for nearly two decades before. "One made everything out of nothing. One is a person, immortal. He is all-powerful [and a "he"—RDE]. Human men are imitations of him. One is not the universe; he made it, and gives it orders. Things are not part of him nor is he part of them, so you must not praise things, but only One. The One, however, reflects himself in the Condor; so the Condor is to be praised and obeyed" (200). Alternatively put, "I believe in one God, the Father Almighty, maker of heaven and earth" *ex nihilo* and as transcendent Creator, followed by standard theory on the divine right of kings.

The theology goes on to present a Great Chain of Humanity, with Platonic "reflection" metaphors, moving down from The Condor to the True Condors and One-Warriors, on to peasants. Peasants are still reflections of One, if dim ones, so are counted as human beings, but barely. "No other people are human," and only human people—noting that the Kesh use "people" more generally than we do—count in the Condor system. "The hontik [...] have nothing to do with One at all; they are [...] unclean, dirt people. They were made by One to obey and serve the Sons." That last part gets "a little complicated," and contradictory, "since Condor's Daughters gave orders to tyon [farmers] and talked about them as if they were dirt people" (200). Stone Telling speculates that things "must have been very different when the Dayao were nomads, but it may have started then, too, as a matter of sexual jealousy, the chief men trying to keep their wives and daughters 'clean,' and the women holding themselves apart from the strangers they met along their way, and finally all of them coming to think that to be a person at all is to be separate from and apart from everyone and everything" (200). This gets at the "Judeo" part in "Judeo-Christian religion": the nationalist part of Jewish doctrine (opposed to the Universalist part) that praises God for not making "us like unto the heathens of the earth, nor fashioned us like the godless of the land" (*High Holiday* ... e.g., 251). This part of Condor belief also undercuts doctrines that define purity through separation: "Blessed is the Eternal God, Ruler of the Universe, who separates" not just Israel from the heathen but "the sacred from the profane" (*Gates of Repentance* 526-27). If "To Be Whole Is To Be Part" (*TD* 68; ch. 3), and if the world is already sacred, then radical separation as a way to holiness is a big part of The Big Mistake. As suggested by Durkheim, it is a very common mistake.

The final bit of paralleled, binary thinking is primarily a satire against Apocalyptic Christianity. The Condor believe that even as there "was a time when One made everything, there will be a time when everything will stop being, when One will unmake everything. Then will begin the Time Outside of Time. One will throw away everything except the True Condors and One-Warriors who obeyed him in every way and were his slaves. They will become part of One then, and be forever" (201). In One, there is victory, and "no death!" (352).[22] Death is the final reintegration with the world, and the denial of death is a kind of untheistic original sin, as Le Guin can present directly in the fantasy, *The Other Wind* (2001). Koheleth (Greek: *Ecclesiastes*) dissociates "men [... from] the divine beings" and faces the fact that we "are beasts. For in respect of the fate of man and the fate of beast [...,] as one dies so dies the other, and both have the same lifebreath; man has no superiority over beast, since both amount to nothing. Both go to the same place; both came from dust and both return to dust" (Eccl. 3.18 21, *Tanakh*), and what humans can do, Koheleth tentatively concludes (all we can do and be sensible) is go about our work, try to find love, and put some effort into whatever we do, until we die and become dirt and no longer do anything (9.9-10, 11.4-6, & passim). Thus saith Koheleth; Le Guin agrees, but without the regret and the nicely melodramatic sense of "Utter futility! — said Koheleth — / Utter futility! All is futile!" (1.2). The alternative is to associate Man, or some men, with "the divine beings" and not our fellow beasts, and this mistake leads to trouble.

Part Three (340-86)

Stone Telling Part Three completes the Catalog of Abuses against the Condor, shows them clearly as a Judeo-Christian analog/sexist-militaristic culture, and completes the story. In terms of the political overplot of the rise and fall of the Condor, Part Three shows the fall

[22] See "Legends" 8 and Le Guin's "Ketterer" letter 139: her statement that "... all apocalypses are fake to me." See The Revelation to John 7.1-22.5 and 1 Corinthians 15.15.

foreshadowed in Stone Telling's earlier observation that even while stealing and slaying in the Volcano country and spreading the disease of their ideology among the Kesh, the Condor "were dying" (194). In terms of the personal history of Stone Telling, Part Three tells the story of her marriage among the Condor, her aborting the fetus produced by a marital rape, her later giving birth to a daughter, and her return to the Valley to become "Woman Coming Home," and then Stone Telling: a wife again, then mother and grandmother. Stone Telling, Part Three, is or includes a *māshāl*. According to Issac Rabinowitz, the word refers to a "likeness" in words and is "either the aptly stated analogue of a previously experienced reality, or it is the quasi-magical, verbal prefiguring of reality in the shape, for good and for ill, in which the utterer would like to encounter it [...]" (320). Part Three is a *māshāl* in bringing to a happy ending the story of the greatest threat to the Kesh and their uncivilized neighbors within their memory. And Part Three brings to a very happy ending the story of Stone Telling.

The Condor move toward a total war effort, trying to build "Great Weapons" that will allow them to conquer, well, ultimately, everything. About the time Stone Telling's daughter, Ekwerkwe, is born, the Condor bring out Destroyer and the Nestlings: a tank and aircraft (*ACH* 350). Stone Telling describes the tank as "huge and magnificent," "huge and blind, with a thick penis-snout" and three Condors inside. It breaks through the roof of a cave "and destroyed itself with its own great weight, thrusting and wedging itself into the lava tube," which makes for some interesting Freudian imagery; but a Jungian-ish reading may be more useful: the symbolic violation of the Earth Mother destroys the tank. The aircraft come to naught less symbolically: not enough petroleum for fuel, and the attempt to make alcohol fuel takes up a lot of grain (351). And, as we know from *The World for World Is Forest*, air power isn't useful against guerrillas, and high-tech cities are very vulnerable to attack from former slaves, of whom (probably) one "came at night and set fire to the fuel storage tanks," leaving the aircraft without fuel (352-53).

Primitive warfare went well for the early kings in part because there were plenty of resources around for what they needed, and only limited communication among the people they were out to subjugate. Post-civilization warfare goes ill for the Condor partly because we civilized folk have depleted the Earth of easily-gotten resources, and partly because the Condor's neighbors have the Exchange and can use it effectively: the cybernetic machines that evolved from primitive ancestors in our time are now AI(s) en masse (149)—"the City of Mind"—but they'll still perform "I.T." services that can give humans much knowledge, hence great strength.

In *ACH* Le Guin deals with what she sees as one of the most serious problems facing eutopia: the neighbors, specifically armed and dangerous neighbors like the Condor, and all the "dynamic, aggressive, ecology-breaking cultures" (*LHD* 233) for which they stand. Her last answer to why the imperialist Condor fail is the same satiric, probably inevitable answer she gave in *WWF,* combined with a common bit of wisdom from the antiwar movement of the late 1960s and early 1970s: "If you want to stop the War Machine, / Don't feed it." In *ACH,* Stone Telling tells us that "The sacrifices the Dayao were making were to win them wealth and comfort when the Nestlings went out to war. The trouble with the plan was that all the human peoples living anywhere near Dayao country had already moved away"—an option Le Guin often endorses (reservedly)—"or, if they remained, stayed to make war, not to give tribute [...]" (352).

As life got harder, among even the Condor elites, a number of women want to move away from their City "into more prosperous lands"; and their husbands listen, however much their ideology says women speak nothing of importance (352). Stone Telling suspects they fear the outside "because the Dayao said that everything belonged to One," so they "forced themselves to think in twos: either this, or that. They could not be [outside] among the many" (352-53).[23] Alternatively, they didn't want to go outside amidst nature: as the infinite (Zamyatin), or chaos (Mumford).

To move or not to move becomes a major issue, hence a major problem since the Dayao lacked democratic or even representative institutions to resolve disputes (352). Failure and dissension tend to bring on repression, and the City becomes "more and more like an ant-hill against which another ant-hill is making war." The executions of the ten City slaves destroys Stone Telling's desire "to be a woman of the Condor or to follow their way" (353), and the executions of other "enemies of the Condor" sickened her and scared her. She wants her politically endangered father to go with her and finish their journey, returning to the Valley. She had become bored again after Ekwerkwe has grown a bit, and now that boredom is punctuated—decorously in time of war—with terror, plus a growing disgust and what we might call guilt. "There is no way," Stone Telling thinks, "that men could make women into slaves and dependents if the women did not choose to be so. I had hated the Dayao men for always giving orders, but the women were more hateful for taking them," and Stone Telling grows very angry for her years in the City, possibly years of complicity (355). Stone Telling escapes, with

[23] See Psalm 24.1-2; see also Le Guin's story "Paradises Lost" (2000), esp. *Birthday of the World* (*BotW*) 325.

Ekwerkwe and her servant Esiryu, Esiryu escaping with her as Stone Telling's friend—and aided by two of Terter Abhao's soldiers (356), one of whom is shot and killed the first moment an ambush heard the men speak Dayao (357).

Stone Telling, as Woman Coming Home, arrives home in a flurry of significant words, stressing her return to the Valley of her being. And Woman Coming Home, Ekwerkwe, and Esiryu (renamed Shadow Woman) go to the Blue Clay heyimas at Kastoha and arrange for shelter. As most of the political action takes place offstage at the political climax of *LHD*, even so we learn here "that there had been a meeting of the Valley people about the Warriors, and that that lodge had stopped being." The scholars of the heyimas advise Woman Coming Home to post on the Exchange what she knows about "the doings and intentions of the Dayao people," which she will do when she gets back to her home town (361).

Woman Coming Home gets to her mothers' house and is admitted but not enthusiastically welcomed. Her grandmother is dead and her mother in bad shape. Politically, though, their small town seems better. Some walking wounded remain after the Condor crisis, but a sickness "had gone out of the Valley that had been there when the Condor was there" (365). Shadow likes it. She thought the City hard, "being was hard. Here's it's soft. [...] Animals live softly. They don't make it hard to live. Here people are animals. [...s] Here even the men are animals. Here everybody belongs to everybody. A Dayao man belongs to himself. He thinks everything else belongs to him [...]." Woman Coming Home says that the Kesh "call that living outside the world" (366-67). In terms of the satire, we can call it the hard Dayao way of living Life As We Know It, living in civilization, living in a culture that is monotheistic, rationalist, aristocratic, death-denying, death-dealing, high-tech, and macho; a culture that uses "ideal" as a compliment and "animal" as an insult, that can set up transcendent Goods that "justify" mundane horrors.

The love plot of Stone Telling's story gets resolved as the denouement of the story as such, but it is not Stone Telling—melodramatically violating an incest taboo—but Shadow who marries Spear (368). Woman Coming Home eventually does marry, gets rich—i.e., gives much—and ends her tale as Stone Telling and "the grandmother weaving at the loom" (376). She gets the last word on romantic love, before enacting a more stable love, concluding that her parents had seen in each other "a dream-woman, a god-man," and "their great passion and fidelity [...] was wasted [...]" (369). I wouldn't want to push the point with Le Guin—I will for Kurt Vonnegut—but it's possible that one of the causes of the "inertia that allows the institutions of injustice to continue unquestioned" is love like that of Willow: "To Willow, the Condor Abhao had been all the world—nothing mattered but him," while for him, Willow "had been a dream—waking life was all elsewhere," in the world of political/military action, the world of waging wars of conquest, giving Heroic aid to someone else's transcendent project (369).

The last words of the political overplot are comments by Pandora (as editor and annotator) and documents by people more politically engaged than Stone Telling and in some ways more knowledgeable; this set of documents and commentary give both an overview of the Condor people and the views of conscious opponents of the Condor.

Document 1 sketches a history of the Condor, sent by people in the town of Rekwit. Pandora has problems finding informants who think chronologically, but one person in the Rekwit area can state directly that "About a hundred and twelve years ago" the Dayao "began to become civilised," coming under the leadership of a man who led them west, died, and was succeeded by a son who started to re-democratize the people but was killed by a cousin, "a man [...] calling himself The Great Condor," who saw the finger of light in the Lava Beds and founded the City (377). The Dayao One People, under charismatic leadership, combine elements of the Mormons—a number of elements from the Mormon migration from the Midwest—the Israelites coming off the desert into Canaan, and others; they are a *māshāl* as "aptly stated analog" of a historical pattern.

The second and third documents are from people who agree with the concerned people of Rekwit. Reads of the Serpentine notes that "much infection has taken place" since the Condor came to the Valley; "Cults have arisen," presumably the Warriors and Lamb Lodge. "If fighting a war is necessary people will come from here to the fighting. If quarantine is possible it would be better"; and Reads asks that news of aggressive acts by the Condor people be entered on the Exchange. The third document notes simply that the Tahets "have been fighting a war with these sick people for two lifetimes." And from here Pandora notes "a flurry and then a steady crossflow of messages through the Exchanges of twenty-two different peoples of the regions." One notes the depredations of the Condor and says, "If you try to fight them you had better have guns and bullets. They do." Another, from a people far away, took up the "sick" motif. "Do not fight these sick people, cure them with human behavior." Pandora tells us that the Rekwit people responded "tersely, 'You come up north here and do that'" (378).

Pandora notes that had the Condor people attempted to increase their territory or move southward, they "would have met the concerted resistance by an alliance of all the people in the region. But the Condor dreams of empire were self-defeated." So, no war. But a major need for an explanation since, in the experience of most of us, people looking for fights usually find them, and evil, well-armed imperialists usually conquer nicer peoples who possess fewer weapons. Pandora suggests some possibilities:

• The Condor "seem to have been unusually self-isolated; their form of communication with other people was through aggression, domination, exploitation, and enforced acculturation. In this respect they were at a distinct disadvantage among the introverted but cooperative people native to the region." Also, they just couldn't use the Exchange very well. Between their fear of contamination and their dominance hierarchy, the Condor were under strong pressure to restrict use of the Exchange, which they did, limiting it to the priestly caste and The Condor himself.

• There were no documents in the Exchanges figuratively stamped TOP SECRET, and the AI City of Mind would release upon request information about weapons construction. What stopped the Condors' Great Weapons program was "the absence of the worldwide technological web [...] of the Industrial Age." Also, the Condor were relatively rich in metals, but they lacked "many of the fossil fuels and other materials from which the Industrial Age made itself" (379-80). Pandora notes that even at the height of the Industrial Age (our era) the expense "of making maintaining, fueling, and operating such machines [...] was incalculable, impoverishing the planet's substance forever and requiring the great majority of humankind to live in servitude and poverty. Perhaps the question concerning the Condor's failure to build an empire with its advanced weapons is not why did they fail, but why did they try."

• Some semi-dire warnings for our time are clear enough here, but there are still some questions just in terms of the world of the story. One obvious one is why didn't the Condor "use their superiority in metals not in a misguided effort to build anachronistic tanks and bombers, but in building up a good arsenal of guns, grenades, and other 'conventional' weapons until they were invincible among the almost defenseless and poorly armed peoples about them?" And Pandora/Le Guin adds significantly: "Then they might truly have made history!" Or restarted history: either way, a bad thing (380).

Pandora says here that the Valley people might have responded to such questions by observing that "Very sick people tend to die of their sickness" or that "Destruction destroys itself" (*ACH* 380). I stress that militaristic, competitive Condor society is operating in contradiction to its world—the world Le Guin has created for her future people—a world in which the Condor ideas of strength are weakness. The Condor attempt at conquest fails partly because Le Guin *wills* them to fail, *māshāl* fashion, but also because, *māshāl* fashion again, Le Guin presents a vision of a universe and a social world in which such attempts will fail. And we readers can accept that failure or reject it in terms of what we find plausible.[24] Stranger things have happened. The *māshāl* worked, so to speak, in *WWF*; the United States military did withdraw from Vietnam. And a motif of history as well as poetry is *Ubi sunt?*: Where are the empires of long ago—or the fairly recent Thousand-Year Reich? Nazi rule lasted a dozen years (although bringing down the Nazis took a major war).

Pandora does *not* deal with what made the war unnecessary, but goes on to suggest something biologically unlikely but quite possible in terms of cultural development. She suggests an optimistic, Kropotkinesque version of "the law of human evolution" (*TD* 177; ch. 7): that "natural selection had had time to work in social as well as physical and intellectual terms" and that her future Californians (newcomers like the Condor excepted) might be "healthier"—saner—than she, or we, can understand. "In leaving progress to the machines, in letting technology go forward on its own terms and selecting from it, with what seems to us excessive caution, modesty, or restraint," it is possible that "these people did in fact succeed in living human history with energy, liberty, and grace" (380-81).

The concluding section is "About a Meeting Concerning the Warriors" Lodge, by Bear Man, a member of the Doctors Lodge (381-86). It also concerns the Lamb Lodge, and the topic of the meeting is the dissolution of those lodges. The argument for the dissolution of the lodges is, as we would expect, that the Condor are sick, "Their heads are turned backwards," and that the people of the Valley "have let people with the plague come into our house," and "The people of the Warrior Lodge and some people in the Lamb Lodge have been infected" (381).

The Warriors and Lambs will be disestablished as lodges. Note, though, the reality of the debate going on with the final comment by Bear Man and the comments by the Warriors: words in male voices, and finally, after all this talk about sickness, by a physician. Bear Man tells us that "the sickness of Man is like the mutating viruses and the toxins: there will always be some form of it about [...]. It is a sickness of our being

[24] For a more negative suggestion, see Benford 17.

human, a fearful one. It would be unwise in us to forget the Warriors
[...], lest it need all be done and said again" (386). We now get a good
chance to be pretty sure of what Le Guin means by "the sickness of
Man": what the Warriors say. And what they say is that they are proud
to be Warriors; that they are not sick, but everyone else is. "[Y]ou're
dying and don't know it. You eat and drink and dance and talk and sleep
and die and there is nothing to you, like ants or fleas or gnats, your life is
nothing, it goes nowhere [...]. We are not insects, we are human people.
We serve a higher purpose" (382). Skull of Telina-na, a Warrior, says,
"Our sickness is our humanity. To be human is to be sick. The lion is well,
the hawk is well, the oak is well, they live and die in the mindfulness
of the sacred and need take no care," and thus far Skull could be Ged
lecturing Arren in *The Farthest Shore* (66; ch. 4). But here Skull comes
to a "But," and it's not Ged's "But" about human consciousness and our
need to "learn to keep the balance." Skull goes on,

> But from us sacredness has withdrawn care; in us is the mind
> of the sacred. So all we do is careful, and all our effort is to be
> mindful, and yet we are not whole. [...] You say that human
> people are not different from the other animals and the plants.
> You call yourself earth and stone. You deny that you are outcast
> from that fellowship, you deny that the soul of man has no
> house on earth. You pretend, you build up houses of desire and
> imagination, but you cannot live in them. (384)

This could be Orestes to Zeus in J-P Sartre's *The Flies* (121-23; Act
III): Skull has reinvented and inverted a couple of aspects of Sartrean
Existentialism and accuses his opponents of Bad Faith in denying the
human condition in a Godless world.[25] What Skull has to say so far is
definitely arguable: we humans are in culture and are conscious, and
by that amount we are "outside" of nature. Le Guin accepts the fact of
humans lacking a reliable instinctive connection with nature; and/so
since her first published story, "An die Musik," she has been advising
us to unbuild walls, unbuild houses, and go outside into Nature and
dance over the nearest figurative abyss. But then Skull takes a logical
leap—one of comfortable, True Believer belief, not Absurdist faith—and
shows not a figurative cloven hoof but a jackboot.[26] We cannot live in
our houses of desire:

[25] For Sartrean Man outside of nature, unconnected to God, forlorn and in despair,
see Erlich, *Coyote's Song* ch. 10, keyword: Orestes. For Le Guin's less-than-awestruck
view of Sartre, see "A Trip to the Head."

[26] For the leap of faith into the Absurd, see Kierkegaard's *Fear and Trembling*, a
meditation on The Binding of Isaac. SK's Abraham is ethically appalling (71), but he
accepts responsibility and isn't what Hoffer would long after call a "True Believer"
(Problems I and II, esp. 67, 86-90),

In them is no habitation. And for your denying, your lying, your comfort-seeking, you will be punished. The day of punishment is the day of war. Only in war is redemption; only the victorious warrior will know the truth, and knowing the truth will live forever. For in sickness is our health, in war our peace, and for us there is only one, one house. One Above All Persons, outside whom there is no health, no peace, no life, no thing [sic]! (384)

A slip here from Orestes into the Prophetic mode, but then quickly into something more ominous for readers with any knowledge of the Heroic doctrine most recently celebrated by the Nazis, and totalitarian word-twisting stamped across the twentieth century as "WAR IS PEACE / FREEDOM IS SLAVERY / IGNORANCE IS STRENGTH" (Orwell, *1984* 17; I.1). And to those who listen perhaps too intently for totalitarian allusions, "One Above All Persons" sounds ominously like *Deutschland über alles* ("Germany, Germany above all / Over everything in the world"). It is one formula for the complement to the denial of death in The Big Mistake: the setting up of a transcendent Good that is "Above All Persons," and upon whose orders men can—and some women, too—with clear consciences, commit atrocities.[27]

Much of *ACH* is pleasant and playful, in many voices and with an anthropologist-artist's delight in showing cultures and a world: poems and philosophy, dramatic works, recipes—even with the 1985 Harper & Row paperback, an audio cassette of *Music and Poetry of the Kesh*. Near its center though, at the void in the Hinge, are the massacred Indians of California (see Le Guin's "Legends"). At its center, from my point of view, is "the myth of civilization, embodied in the monotheisms which assign soul to Man alone" (*BG* 11), with "Man" gendered emphatically male. At its center is Le Guin continuing quarrel with the One, including her attacks on sacredness as separation, her attack on our denial of death and how death demonstrates very starkly our embededness, our immanence in nature and the world. In *ACH* Le Guin offers some passionate utopian satire—nuanced, rich and provocative, and with strong judgments—on what kind of cultures might provide fertile ground for evils, which might provide a chance that people can live well.

[27] In *LHD*, Genly Ai says that the mission he is on—a truly important, worthy mission—"overrides all personal debts and loyalties." The person he is talking to responds, "If so ... it is an immoral mission" (*LHD* 104-06; ch. 8). For real-world background (though not a source for Le Guin) on the dangers of following absolutist doctrines, see Hoffer, Part 3, "United Action and Self-Sacrifice," esp. sections 61, 63, 72, 92.

Works Cited

Ursula K. Le Guin's Works

1. *Always Coming Home*. New York: Harper & Row, 1985. *ACH*.
2. *The Birthday of the World and Other Stories*. New York: HarperCollins, 2002. *BotW*.
3. *Buffalo Gals And Other Animal Presences*. Santa Barbara: Capra P, 1987. Collection. *BG*.
4. "The Carrier-Bag Theory of Fiction." 1986. Coll. *DEW*.
5. *City of Illusions*. New York: Ace, 1967.
6. "Dancing to Ganam." *Amazing* Sept. 1993. Coll. *FIS*.
7. *Dancing at the Edge of The World: Thoughts on Words, Women, Places*. New York: Grove, 1989. *DEW*.
8. *The Dispossessed*. New York: Harper & Row, 1974. New York: Avon, 1975. *TD*.
9. "The Eye of the Heron." 1983. As novel, New York: Bantam, 1984. *EoH*.
10. *The Farthest Shore*. New York: Atheneum, 1972. New York: Bantam, 1975.
11. "The Field of Vision." *Galaxy* 1973. Coll. *WTQ*.
12. *A Fisherman of the Inland Sea*. New York: HarperPrism, 1994. Collection. *FIS*.
13. "Legends for a New Land." *Mythlore* 56.2 (Winter 1988): 4-10. *Legends*.
14. *Language of the Night*. New York: Putnam's, 1979. Rev. edn. 1989. New York: HarperCollins, 1992. *LoN*.
15. *The Lathe of Heaven*. New York: Scribner's, 1971. New York: Avon, 1973. *LoH*.
16. *The Left Hand of Darkness*. New York: Ace, 1969. Rpt. with Introd. New York: Ace, 1976. *Ursula K. Le Guin: Five Complete Novels*. New York: Avenel Books, 1985. *LHD*.
17. "On David Ketterer's *New Worlds for Old. SFS* #6 = 2.2 (July 1975): 130-48.
18. Only in Utopia section. In "A War without End." *Wave* 211-220.
19. *The Other Wind*. New York: Harcourt, 2001.
20. "Paradises Lost." Initial publication Le Guin's *BotW*.
21. *Planet of Exile*. New York: Ace, 1966. *PE*.
22. "A Response to the Le Guin Issue [of *SFS*]." *SFS* #8 = 3.1 (March 1976): 43-46.

23. *Rocannon's World*. New York: Ace, 1966. *RW*.
24. "Semley's Necklace" (vt. "The Dowry of the Angyar"). *Amazing* 1964. Rpt. opening of *RW*. Coll. *WTQ*.
25. *The Telling*. New York: Harcourt, 2000.
26. "A Trip to the Head." *Quark* 1 (1970). Coll. *WTQ*.
27. *Voices*. Orlando: Harcourt, 2006.
28. *The Wave in the Mind: Talks and Essays on the Writer, the Reader, and the Imagination*. Boston: Shambhala, 2004.
29. *The Wind's Twelve Quarters*. 1975. Toronto: Bantam, 1976. Collection. *WTQ*.
30. "The Word for World Is Forest." In *Again, Dangerous Visions*, ed. by Harlan Ellison. 1972/73. *The Word for World Is Forest*. New York: Berkley-Putnam, 1976. *WWF*.

Other Works Cited

1. Abrash, Merritt. "Le Guin's 'The Field of Vision': A Minority View on Ultimate Truth." *Extrapolation* 26.1 (Spring 1985): 5-15.
2. *Again, Dangerous Visions*, ed. by Harlan Ellison. New York : New American Library, 1972.
3. Baccolini, Raffaella, and Tom Moylan, eds. *Dark Horizons: Science Fiction and the Dystopian Imagination*. New York and London: Routledge, 2003.
4. Beauvoir, Simone de. *The Second Sex*. 1949. Trans. and ed. by H. M. Parshley. 1953. New York: Vintage-Random House, 1989.
5. Benford, Gregory. "Reactionary Utopias." 1987. *Australian Science Fiction Review*, 2nd series 3.3, whole number 14 (May 1988).
6. Bibles consulted: Vulgate, RSV, *Tanakh*, "Geneva," NEB.
7. Bogel, Fredric V. *The Difference Satire Makes: Rhetoric and Reading from Jonson to Byron*. Ithaca: Cornell UP, 2001.
8. Durkheim, Émile. "The Elementary Forms of the Religious Life: The Totemic System in Australia." 1912. Excerpted in *Durkheim on Religion*, ed. by W. S. F. Pickering. Atlanta: Scholars P, 1994.
9. —. *The Elementary Forms of the Religious Life: A Study in Religious Sociology*. 1912. Trans. Joseph Ward Swain. 1915. Glencoe: Free P, 1947.

10. Erlich, Richard D. *Coyote's Song: The Teaching Stories of Ursula K. Le Guin.* "A Science Fiction Research Association Digital Book." <http://wiz.cath.vt.edu/sfra/Coyote/Coyote-Home.htm>. Also available as a 5MB .pdf attachment, from <ErlichRD@MUOhio.edu>.

11. —. "Le Guin and God: Quarreling with the One, Critiquing Pure Reason." *Extrapolation* 47.3 (Winter 2006): 351-79.

12. —. "Ursula K. Le Guin and Arthur C. Clarke on Immanence, Transcendence, and Massacres." *Extrapolation* 28.2 (Summer 1987): 105-29.

13. —. "Ursula K. Le Guin: Eutopia, Antiutopia, Dystopia." Society for Utopian Studies Twenty-ninth Annual Conference, Toronto, 8 October 2004.

14. Frye, Northrop. "The Nature of Satire." *UTQ* 14 (October 1944). In *Satire: An Anthology*, ed. by Ashley Brown and John L. Kimmey. NY: Crowell / Harper & Row, 1977.

15. —. *Anatomy of Criticism: Four Essays.* 1954. New York: Atheneum, 1966. Third Essay: Archetypal Criticism: Theory of Myths.

16. *The Gates of Repentance.* The New Union Prayer book for the Days of Awe. New York: Central Conference of American Rabbis, 5738/1978, rev. 1996.

17. Griffin, Dustin. *Satire: A Critical Reintroduction.* Lexington: UP of Kentucky, 1994.

18. *High Holiday Prayer Book.* Morris Silverman, compiler and arranger. Bridgeport, CT: Prayer Book Press, 1951.

19. Hoffer, Eric. *The True Believer.* 1951. New York: Perennial-Harper, 1966. Reset 1989.

20. Huxley, Aldous, comp. *The Perennial Philosophy.* New York: Harper, 1945.

21. Jones, Robert A. *Emile Durkheim: An Introduction to Four Major Works.* Beverly Hills, CA: Sage Publications, Inc., 1986: 115-155. <http://www.relst.uiuc.edu/faculty/rajones/durkheim/Summaries/forms.html#pgfId=6641>. 11 Feb. 2006.

22. Juvenal. "All men's activities [... are] the hodge-podge [*farrago*] of my book." <http://www.fordham.edu/halsall/ancient/juvsat11lateng.html>, 10 Jan. 2008.

23. Kernan, Alvin. "A Theory of Satire." 1959. Rpt. *Satire: Modern Essays in Criticism*, ed. by Ronald Paulson. Englewood Cliffs, NJ: Prentice-Hall, 1971.

24. Kierkegaard, Søren. *Fear and Trembling* [1843] and *The Sickness Unto Death*. Walter Lowrie, trans., introd., notes. 1941, 1954. Garden City, NY: Doubleday, n.d.
25. Kroeber, A. L. *Anthropology: Race, Language, Culture, Psychology, Prehistory.* 1923. Rev. edn. New York: Harcourt, 1948. Mostly rpt. New York: Harbinger-Harcourt, 1963. As *Anthropology: Biology and Race* (chs. 1, 2, 4, 5, and 15), and *Anthropology: Culture Pattern and Processes* (chs. 1, 6-10).
26. —. *Handbook of the Indians of California.* Bulletin 78 of the Bureau of American Ethnology of the Smithsonian Institution. 1925. New York: Dover, 1976.
27. More, Thomas. *Utopia.* Trans. and introd. Paul Turner. London: Penguin Books, 1965.
28. Moylan, Tom. *Demand The Impossible: Science Fiction and the Utopian Imagination.* New York: Methuen, 1986.
29. Mumford, Lewis. "Utopia, The City and The Machine." 1965. In *Utopias and Utopian Thought*, ed. by Frank E. Manuel. Boston: Riverside & Houghton, 1966. 3-24.
30. Orwell, George (pseud. of Eric Blair). *Nineteen Eighty-Four.* 1949. Rpt. *1984.* New York: New AMerican Library, 1961.
31. Rabinowitz, Isaac. "Toward a Valid theory of Biblical Hebrew Literature." In *The Classical Tradition: Literary and Historical Studies in Honor of Harry Caplan,* ed. by Luitpold Wallach. Ithaca, NY: Cornell UP, 1966.
32. Sartre, Jean-Paul. *The Flies. Les Mouches* 1943. First English trans., 1946. Trans. Stuart Gilbert. In *No Exit and Three Other Plays.* New York: Vintage-Random House, n.d.
33. Sawyer, Andy. "Ursula Le Guin and the Pastoral Mode." *Extrapolation* 47.3 (Winter 2006): 396-416.
34. Selinger, Bernard. *Le Guin and Identity in Contemporary Fiction.* Ann Arbor: UMI Research P, 1988.
35. Spencer, Kathleen L. "Exiles and Envoys: the [sic] SF of Ursula K. Le Guin." *Foundation # 20* (Oct. 1980): 32-43.
36. Turner, Paul. Inrod. to More's *Utopia,* q.v. above.
37. Vonnegut, Kurt, Jr. "Physicist, Purge Thyself." *Chicago Tribune Magazine* 22 June 1969. <http://en.wikiquote.org/wiki/Kurt_Vonnegut>.
38. Welch, Holmes. *The Parting of the Way: Lao Tzu and the Taoist Movement.* Boston: Beacon, 1957.
39. Wellek, René. *"Bakhtin's View of Dostoevsky: 'Polyphony' and 'Carnivalesque.'" Dostoevsky Studies,* 1 (1980): 31-39. <http://www.utoronto.ca/tsq/DS/01/031.shtml> 3 Jan. 2008.

41. Wytenbroek, J. R. "*Always Coming Home*: Pacifism and Anarchy in Le Guin's Latest Utopia." *Extrapolation* 28.4 (Winter 1987): 330-39.
42. Zamyatin, Yevgeny (variously transliterated). *We*. Ca. 1920. Trans. Mirra Ginsburg. New York: Bantam, 1972.

Richard D. Erlich is professor emeritus in English at Miami University (Oxford, Ohio, USA), currently living in Ventura County, California. He is web-master for Frederik Pohl and is slowly working on *Clockworks 2*, a wiki sequel to Thom Dunn and his *Clockworks* list of *Works Useful for the Study of the Human/Machine Interface in SF,* <http://www.clockworks2.org/wiki/index.php?title=Main_Page >. He is the author of the Science Fiction Research Association Digital Book *Coyote's Song: The Teaching Stories of Ursula K. Le Guin* <http://www.sfra.org/Coyote/CoyoteHome.htm>.

Reconciliation in
"The Matter of Seggri"

Linda Wight
James Cook University, Townsville, Queensland, Australia

The fictional separatist society is one of the best recognised tropes of feminist SF, or, one might say, SF that concerns itself with foregrounding and exploring gender issues, as in the work of Joanna Russ, Suzy McKee Charnas, and Pamela Sargent. Unlike texts which depict men and women living together in either a patriarchal or matriarchal gender dystopia, separatist texts usually depict fictional worlds where men and women either live in spatially separate societies, or worlds from which men have been excluded altogether. Of course separatist texts can also include a gender hierarchy, with one gender enjoying more privileges and holding some sort of power over the other. In Ursula K. Le Guin's "The Matter of Seggri" (1994), for instance, women are perceived to be the superior gender.

In this story Le Guin continues the feminist tradition of using the separatist trope to critique certain traits such as violence and competitiveness which are also commonly identified as markers of masculinity in contemporary society. In particular, she expresses concern about what Ellen Jordan and Angela Cowan label the "warrior narratives" (128) of masculinity, which are still highly valued:

> By "warrior narratives," we mean narratives that assume that violence is legitimate and justified when it occurs within a struggle between good and evil. There is a tradition of such narratives, stretching from Hercules and Beowulf to Superman and Dirty Harry, where the male is depicted as the warrior, the knight-errant, the superhero, the good guy. (128)

Historically, feminist writers have explored the potential of the separatist society to protect women from the men who embrace such narratives, but Le Guin focuses on a society that favours women, suggesting that it is just as problematic as a male-dominated society. Le Guin implies that a separatist society may actually force men to embrace the warrior narrative, and by showing the suffering that this ethic can inflict on men, she argues for some sort of reconciliation between the sexes, where most separatist texts offer division as the best solution to the gender conflict.

Separatist SF

The primary concern of separatist SF writers has been a question that is central to feminism as a whole: what to do with or about men. As Thomas J. Morrissey puts it, separatist writers ask whether men and women can coexist peacefully, or whether women's happiness requires that men be held apart or exterminated (30). "The Matter of Seggri" can be read as one text in this long dialogue on the Man/Woman question. Suzy McKee Charnas' *Holdfast* series (1974-1999) traces some of the most important stages. In the first stage, represented by *Walk to the End of the World* (1974), writers present and destroy a dystopic male-dominated society in order to free women. In the second stage writers present a separatist all-female society. Drawing on the example of Charlotte Perkins Gilman's *Herland* (1915), a number of 1970s feminist SF texts including Charnas' *Motherlines* (1978), Joanna Russ' *The Female Man* (1975), and Sally Miller Gearhart's *Wanderground: Stories of the Hill Women* (1979), explore the potential of separatism to protect women from men, and to critique men's oppression of women. Brian Attebery observes that these separatist writers often employ the "filtration effect" (10) to prioritise everything that has traditionally been labelled feminine and thus dismissed as inferior in male-dominated societies (9-10). Joanna Russ recognises that such texts often approach the polemic: "[T]he authors are not subtle in their reasons for creating separatist utopias: if men are kept out of these societies, it is because men are dangerous. They also hog the good things of this world" (cited in Barr "Permissive" 188).

Robin Roberts and Sarah Lefanu argue that 1970s feminist writers also employ the separatist trope in an attempt to imagine how women might live, once free from patriarchal constraints and definitions. Roberts argues that separatism allows women access to the full range of human activities (67), while Lefanu contends that separatist worlds allow women physical freedom, access to the public world, and the freedom to express love for other women (55).

Some feminist writers were unsatisfied with separatism as a final solution, however, and Charnas' *The Furies* (1994) explores the first steps towards a way for men and women to live together. Several separatist texts published in the 1980s, including Pamela Sargent's *The Shore of Women* (1986), Joan Slonczewski's *A Door Into Ocean* (1986), and Sheri S. Tepper's *The Gate to Women's Country* (1988), convey a similar interest in reconciliation but, like *The Furies*, they indicate that it will be an extremely difficult task if women are to avoid again succumbing to a male-dominated gender dystopia. These texts trace the efforts of individual men and women to achieve reconciliation. But Jenny Wolmark suggests that for these writers the problem of how to incorporate the majority of men into a potentially utopian female community ultimately proves impossible to resolve (99).

This difficulty can be partially attributed to the consistent focus of 1970s and 1980s separatist writers on a white, straight, middle-class hegemonic ideal of masculinity. 1970s writers tend to group men under this default as the largely homogenous oppressors of women. 1980s writers differentiate between violent and non-violent men, but these alternatives are again largely confined within a white, straight, middle-class identity, omitting a consideration of race and class differences and alternate sexualities.

Published the same year as *The Furies*, Le Guin's "The Matter of Seggri" (hereafter "Seggri") attempts a more nuanced exploration of masculinities. Le Guin recognises that homosexuality may affect how some men engage with their society's hetero-normative masculine ideal. She maintains hope that such differences will enable some men to resist this dominant construction and encourage them to embrace alternative identities that will allow them to reconcile with women. However "Seggri" holds to the separatist tradition by omitting a consideration of race and class differences. Even a heterosexual ideal is finally reinstated by presenting marriage to a woman as the goal and symbol of the men's emancipation.

Nevertheless, Le Guin's focus on men's experiences of separatism reveals a shift in the way the trope is being employed. Writing "Seggri" approximately three decades after the beginning of second-wave feminism, Le Guin moves beyond an immediate concern with the protection of women. As a result, while earlier separatist writers focused on condemning the white, heterosexual, middle-class men who they identified as their oppressors, Le Guin explores the anxieties and contradictions that underlie this particular construction of masculinity. In particular, Le Guin differs from most of her predecessors by including male narrators who expose the costs that the warrior narrative inflicts on men. "Seggri" thus expresses a hope that was absent from most 1970s separatist texts: that these costs may encourage men to reject the violence of the warrior ethic, and work with women toward reconciliation.

"The Matter of Seggri"

Le Guin furthers her hope for reconciliation by presenting Seggri from five different viewpoints spanning fourteen-hundred years. Whereas other writers were unable to imagine a significant change to men's attitudes and behaviours, or to the separatist social structure within their texts' limited time-frames,[1] Le Guin's narrative scope allows her to identify and work through some of the myriad social and psychological elements that must be addressed for men to explore alternative ways of living and to achieve reconciliation with women.

Le Guin's first narrator, Captain Aolao-Olao, is a male visitor who interprets Seggri as a male-dominated utopia where men live an existence of privilege and power, served by the female "drudges" who perform the "common work of farm and mill" (Le Guin "Seggri" 347). He is impressed by the men's aggressive contests and assumes they are training to protect the helpless women "huddled" outside the Castle walls. Aolao-Olao's description of the fuckeries, actually male brothels, is further framed by his patriarchal mind-set: "At night they go to certain houses which they own in the town, where they may have their pick among the women and satisfy their lust upon them as they will" (347). His assumptions are quickly undermined by Merriment, a female visitor to Seggri, whose concern about the safety of her male colleague leads her to recognise the costs of the separatist society and its warrior ideal for men. Through Merriment, readers learn that Seggri boys are taken from their female relatives at age eleven and confined in all-male walled "Castles" where they spend their lives engaged in violent physical competitions, mock battles with other Castles, and meeting women's sexual and reproductive needs at the local "fuckeries." Only a handful of men are chosen to work in the fuckeries, however, leaving the majority completely separated from the women.

The remaining narratives show the suffering that this lifestyle can inflict on men, and traces their first tentative attempts to construct an alternative life. In the third narrative, Po recalls her brother's resistance to being sent to a Castle, and in the fourth, the Seggrian short story "Love Out of Place," Toddra reacts against his society's attempts to define him as a mere sexual object and pursues a forbidden relationship with his female lover, Azak. The final narrative by a Seggri man, Ardar Dez, draws these critiques together and signals Le Guin's primary concern with depicting the subjectivity of men suffering under the double oppression of a matriarchal hierarchy and values promoted by the warrior narrative of masculinity.

---

[1] Charnas' *Holdfast* series is one exception, however it is still limited to the social changes that can be achieved within the lifetime of its protagonists.

Thus, like *The Furies*, "Seggri" indicates that separatism is insufficient, but like Charnas' *The Conqueror's Child* (1999), it argues that gender inequities that favour women are unacceptable as well. Unlike Charnas, however, who addresses women's fears that an end to separatism will restore a male-dominated gender dystopia, Le Guin assumes that the men's rebellion will result in gender equity. Her critique of the separatist matriarchal society thus risks condemning women for a power that they have never actually held in contemporary male-dominated societies, and advocating the reinstatement of privileges that the majority of men have never lost in the real world.

Critique of the Warrior Narrative

Despite her sympathy for her male characters, Le Guin follows the separatist tradition of critiquing traditional masculine behaviours and ethics. Wolmark argues that Tepper undertakes a similar critique; both she and Le Guin depict the separatist male society as a kind of military garrison, creating a metaphor for what has also become a ritualised version of masculinity in contemporary society (92). Traits like physical strength, sexual prowess, bravery, aggression, competitiveness, and violence are all identified as aspects of the warrior narrative.

"Seggri" demonstrates that according to this narrative, a man's worth is determined by his place in the male hierarchy, which is precisely defined by military titles and rank. Merriment observes, "As they win trials they gain all kinds of titles and ranks you could translate as "generals" and the other names militarists have for all their power-grades" (Le Guin "Seggri" 354). Physical contests allow men to rise up the hierarchy. Like contemporary sporting teams, the Seggri Castles compete against each other in contests of strength, skill, and violence, hoping to win glory and status. Andrew Parker argues that sport is seen as a way for men to assert their masculinity in many contemporary societies. He observes that sport often combines notions of muscularity, strength, power, and fearless domination to produce images of the ideal man (131). "Seggri" reveals that such contests can socialise men into aggressive and violent behaviours as the games provide models for the everyday violence of the Castles.

In "Seggri," however, the supposed benefits of the warrior ideal are cancelled by a lack of freedom, choice, and practical skills. Merriment reflects:

> All they're allowed to do after age eleven is compete at games and sports inside the Castle, and compete in the fuckeries, after they're fifteen or so, for money and number of fucks and so on. Nothing else. No options. No trades. No skills of making. No travel unless they play in the big games. They aren't allowed into the colleges to gain any kind of freedom of mind. (Le Guin "Seggri" 354)

Even so, Le Guin insists on the attraction of a clearly defined warrior identity. Here she echoes the concerns of 1980s separatist writers who worried that the majority of men either cannot or will not change. Though Le Guin offers more hope that some men will do so, she also indicates that others will cling more fiercely to the warrior ideal when it is the only thing that offers them security and some kind of prestige in a matriarchal gender hierarchy. In particular, the men at the top of the Castle hierarchy vehemently oppose changes to the gender system. Lord Fassaw, for instance, argues against the establishment of the Boys' College because it threatens to undermine his power and control over other men.

To critique this, Le Guin employs what Attebery terms the "intaglio effect" (5), to reverse the traditional value attached to these familiar masculine traits. Captain Aolao-Olao initially interprets Seggri through his own patriarchal background, but each subsequent narrator further undermines his assumptions. The description of the fuckeries by Merriment reveals the Seggri reality:

> [M]en who don't win at things aren't allowed to go to the fuckeries. Only the champions. And boys between fifteen and nineteen, the ones the older women call *dippida*, baby animals, like puppies or kitties or lambies. They like to use the *dippida* for pleasure, and the champions when they go to the fuckery to get pregnant. (Le Guin "Seggri" 355-6)

Merriment believes that the gender imbalance of Seggri motivates the women to favour the men who win in the violent tournaments. Only one boy is born for every sixteen girls because of the genetic experiments her Hainish ancestors conducted when they settled Seggri millennia earlier. Merriment believes that, "Given their situation, they need strong, healthy men at their fuckery; it's social selection reinforcing natural selection" (353). However it is unclear why women, the majority of whom would expect to give birth to girls, would seek to pass on traits of violence and aggression. The unquestioned desirability of these men weakens Le Guin's attempt to devalue the warrior narrative.

Nevertheless, Le Guin further attempts to subvert its appeal by exposing the men's lack of freedom and choice. In a familiar refrain, Seggri men contemptuously dismiss many tasks as "women's work," but Aolao-Olao observes with unease:

> They have ... no notion of flight either in the air or in space, nor any curiosity about such things ... indeed I found that if I asked these great men about matters of common knowledge such as the working of machinery, the weaving of cloth, the transmission of holovision, they would soon chide me for taking an interest in womanish things as they called them, desiring me to talk as befit a man. (348-9)

Ardar Dez recognises these limitations when he admits that his warrior existence is unhappy and largely meaningless. Dez acknowledges that the masculine qualities celebrated in Seggri society encourage brutality and cruelty, thereby creating a miserable existence for the majority of men. His ability to question the warrior narrative shows that variations in masculinity can exist even within Seggri's strictly regimented gender order. Here, Le Guin follows writers such as Tepper and Slonczewski. Wolmark observes that in *The Gate to Women's Country* Tepper distinguishes between warriors and servitors (93), while Morrissey argues that Slonczewski's *A Door Into Ocean* shows that some men are eager to give up the male rat race (30).

However while Tepper and Slonczewski confine their alternatives to a white, straight, middle-class identity, Le Guin explores the potential for resistance among homosexual men. Thus it is the "Collegials," comprised largely of homosexual men and led by Kohadrat and his lover Ragaz, who most strongly oppose the brutality and violence of the Castles. Masculinities theorists have long recognised gay men's subversive potential. Lynne Segal argues that the 1970s radical gay movement was the first exhaustive critique and assertively self-conscious rejection of dominant forms of masculinity produced by men themselves (146). She suggests that this gave gay men the choice to embrace certain values that straight men have traditionally been encouraged to reject:

> [T]o assert the reality of tenderness, vulnerability and passivity in men, and to demand the liberation of sex and love from darkness and shame, encapsulate for me what has been significant in the homosexual challenge to the masculine ideal. (167)

These values are indeed emphasised by the Collegials who offer love, tenderness, comfort, and protection to the younger boys. The Collegials also reject the women's claims about inferior male intelligence by establishing secret colleges within the Castles. Le Guin thus implies that men who reject one aspect of the hegemonic ideal may be more willing to question its other assumptions.

The violent reaction of the "Traditionals," led by Lord Fassaw, exposes the perceived threat of this alternative to the straight male hierarchy:

> Lord Fassaw detested adult homosexuality and would have reinstituted the death penalty if the Town Council had allowed it .... [H]e punished consenting love between older boys with bizarre and appalling physical mutilations — ears cut into fringes, fingers branded with redhot iron rings. (Le Guin "Seggri" 374)

Nevertheless, Fassaw encourages his followers to rape the younger boys. The prevalence of sexual assaults within the Castles closely reflects a prison environment where, Stuart Turner argues, rape is motivated more by a desire for power than by the need for sexual gratification (80). Carol Polych and Donald Sabo agree that the act of prison rape is closely tied to the construction of inter-male dominance hierarchies (145), and this is illustrated in "Seggri" by the "Lordsmen" who regularly gang-rape the younger boys to assert their own power.

Le Guin avoids demonising heterosexual men by including "straight" men like Dez among the Collegials. Nevertheless, the social inferiority of the Seggri men allows Le Guin to evade the strength of resistance to change that we might expect from many men in contemporary societies, where hegemonic masculinity is commonly equated with superiority. Segal insists that no-one can assume that even gay men will automatically oppose dominant constructions of masculinity (144). In "Seggri," however, Dez claims that every homosexual man belongs to the Collegials, ignoring Fassaw's followers who perform technically "homosexual" acts. He avoids acknowledging that some homosexual men may perceive the benefits of remaining committed to the warrior narrative. Thus, overall, "Seggri's" exploration of alternative masculinities is limited both by its generalising about homosexual men, and by its failure to engage with race and class differences.

Critique of Separatism

Nevertheless, "Seggri" does indicate a shift in the separatist trope as it moves beyond a primary concern with the protection of women to imply that a gender hierarchy that favours women is as unacceptable as a male-dominated society. This is first apparent in the women's ideology of superiority, which, as with women in patriarchal societies, identifies men with their bodies' sexual and reproductive functions. Reduced to animal status, they are labelled "Sires" who exist to "service" women. Seggri women oppose men attending college, arguing that it would conflict with their natural function: "What goes to the brain takes from the testicles" (Le Guin "Seggri" 354). Recalling patriarchal arguments about debilitating female "humours," Seggri women further exclude men from public employment by claiming that male hormones make them unreliable.

Other writers have critiqued separatist matriarchies. Morrissey observes that Sargent's *The Shore of Women* inverts descriptors and logic borrowed from misogynist discourse to problematise the women's biological claims about men (29). Unlike Le Guin, however, Sargent includes an oppressive male-dominated society in her novel as a warning about one possible outcome of relinquishing female control. In contrast, "Seggri" reflects Le Guin's assumption that an end to separatism will result in gender equity rather than a reversal to a male-dominated society.

A further problem with critiquing the Seggri matriarchy is that it risks implying that the responsibility for changing the gender system rests predominantly with women. This is particularly evident in "Love Out of Place" which focuses on Azak's gradual realisation of the anguish that she has caused Toddra by using him as a sexual object. Azak's acceptance of responsibility reflects an ongoing insistence by Le Guin that women reject the role of the oppressor. In a 1983 address to women Le Guin states this explicitly: "I hope you live without the need to dominate, and without the need to be dominated. I hope you are never victims, but I hope you have no power over other people" ("Left-Handed" 117).

Le Guin does encourage women to take responsibility for rejecting separatism by emphasising what it costs them. Echoing Tepper and Sargent who ask what happens to sons in a separatist utopia (Donawerth 62-3), Le Guin exposes the pain that women experience when they reject their male loved ones. Po's memoir emphasises the depth of this grief. She rages when she is told about her brother Ittu working at the fuckery, unable to reconcile her memories of her brother as an equal and friend with her society's insistence that men are inferior animals, only useful for sex. Dez also remembers his mother's desolate eyes upon him in his boyhood as she contemplates their separation.

Beyond Separatism: Reconciliation

Like the separatist writers of the 1980s, Le Guin builds upon this critique to explore the possibility of reconciliation between the genders. Her work reveals a persistent concern with reconciliation, evident in recurring ideas of balance, mutuality, and wholeness (Clute & Nicholls 703). In *The Left Hand of Darkness* (1969), the myths of Gethen idealise a balance of light and shadow, life and death, male and female. In her "Introduction to *Planet of Exile*," Le Guin implies that these ideas often influence the way she engages with gender in her fiction:

> Both in one: or two making a whole. Yin does not occur without yang, nor yang without yin. Once I was asked what I thought the central, constant theme of my work was, and I said spontaneously, "Marriage." (143)

This emphasis on yin and yang is problematic because it implies that the sexes are fundamentally different and thus threatens to reinforce a naturalised gender binary. Furthermore, Le Guin's ideal of a marriage of complementary halves reveals a heterosexual bias which has been repeatedly critiqued by SF theorists. Lefanu argues that in Le Guin's fiction homosexuality is tolerated only as adolescent experimentation (141), and Tom Moylan complains about Le Guin's privileging of "heterosexual superiority and of the nuclear, monogamous family" (cited in Lefanu 141). These complaints can again be levelled at "Seggri." Although the homosexual men initially lead the Collegials' resistance, they disappear from the narrative once the Open Gate Law has been passed, allowing the men to live outside the Castles. Instead, Le Guin chooses Dez as her final narrator, and a hetero-normative ideal is reinstated through his dream of achieving emancipation by marrying a woman.

Le Guin's reliance on such "subversive" heterosexual relationships to overcome separatism must attract the criticism that Peter Fitting previously levelled at *The Shore of Women*. Fitting expressed concern that Birana's "conversion" to heterosexual love follows the scenario of many "flasher" anti-feminist novels where women abandon their power for love of a man (36). The repeated focus on such heterosexual relationships (i.e. Joshua and Margot in *The Gate to Women's Country*; Spinel and Lystra in *A Door Into Ocean*) suggests that this bias is common to separatist SF that favours reconciliation. Seeking to identify a force powerful enough to motivate their characters to reach across the separatist divide, the writers risk valorising heterosexual love at the expense of alternate sexualities.

In "Seggri," Le Guin repeats this defense of heterosexual love when Toddra comes to desire a relationship with Azak that would contravene his society's gender roles. Although Azak rejects Toddra for a socially acceptable same-sex marriage to a woman, Toddra's love also forces her to question her society's gender assumptions and recognise that she has caused Toddra's violence by treating him as a sexual object. Le Guin does not present love as an easy solution, however, because Toddra remains trapped within a system that can imagine love between a man and a woman only in terms of master and slave:

> 'I could live there,' he said urgently, bending over her. 'With you. I would always be there. You could have me every night. It would cost you nothing, except my food. I would serve you, service you, sweep your house, do anything, anything, Azak, please, my beloved, my mistress, let me be yours!' (Le Guin "Seggri" 365-6)

Dez's memoirs more hopefully recall his love for Emadr, a female college student. Although their relationship does not last, Dez presents it as an important step toward a reconciled world:

> It did not work very well or last very long, yet it was a great liberation for both of us, our liberation from the belief that the only communication or commonality possible between us was sexual, that an adult man and woman had nothing to join them but their genitals.... Its true significance was not as a consummation of desire, but as proof that we could trust each other. (383)

Linked to this personal experience of heterosexual love is the insistence that each individual take responsibility for social change. Marleen Barr remarks that Le Guin often creates characters who try to alter the structures that constitute them ("Humanist" 155), and Bülent Somay agrees that, for Le Guin, the utopian horizon exists only as a project of human agents (36). This is borne out in *The Left Hand of Darkness* where the Ekumen favour connecting to others on a personal level, and being prepared for personal change (259). Likewise, in *The Dispossessed* (1974), Shevek explains that revolution is something that each individual must carry out (242). In "Seggri," Le Guin insists that the resistance of individual men to their society's hegemonic masculine ideal can lead to change on a structural level. Thus, the actions that Dez and his friends take against the Castle Lords force the women to confront the misery inflicted by separatism and lead to the Open Gate Law. This provides an important balance to Le Guin's critique of the female-dominated society by insisting that men take responsibility for change as well.

Le Guin warns, however, that individuals may not always succeed, especially when they lack the support of an oppositional community. When Ittu attempts to run away, Po fears condemnation and refuses to help, and Ittu's attempt to flee alone is futile. Reflecting the gradual infiltration of feminist ideas into contemporary society, the slow process of questioning and tentative discussion that seems to have occurred in the hundred intervening years does allow Dez's society to consider the need for change. Again reflecting the experiences of the feminist movement, Dez succeeds where Ittu fails because he does not act alone, but as part of the Collegial community.

Change cannot occur, however, without education about alternatives. Thus Dez cannot construct an alternative to the warrior identity until he is educated about the life options that previously had been available only to women:

> [W]here I went and what kind of training I chose would depend on my interests, which I would go to a college to discover, since neither my schooling as a child nor my training at the Castle had really given me any idea of what there was to be interested in. (Le Guin "Seggri" 382)

The example of the Ekumen visitor, Mobile Noem, suggests that men can receive this education from other men who model alternative masculinities: "There were things for men to do, ways for men to live, he proved it by his mere existence" (381). However Le Guin assumes that this model will automatically help to produce gender equity. "Seggri" elides feminist fears about the reinstatement of male supremacy by ignoring the possibility that the men will seek to assert their superiority once Noem has made them aware of the existence of male-dominated societies.

Difficulty of Change

While this absence suggests an idealistic view of the possibilities of reconciliation, Le Guin does acknowledge the difficulty of changing dominant social structures, behaviours, and beliefs. These difficulties are signalled when the Open Gate Law simply shifts the system of segregation outside the Castle walls. Many men who leave the Castles end up working in competitive, male-only farming and construction teams managed by the women's companies. Others seek work in the fuckeries because the social structure provides no other place for them. Dez returns to his mother's home but feels that invisible walls remain: "They called us drones, and in fact we had no work, no function at all in the community" (377-8).

Le Guin recognises the difficulty of achieving the psychological transformations that are necessary to overcome these limitations (Jacobs 37). Many Seggri women resist male emancipation because they have been socialised to believe that men are inherently violent and irresponsible, and because they fear losing their social superiority. In an ironic role reversal, Noem warns Dez that even women who express goodwill towards men will struggle to alter their assumptions about inferior male intelligence. Significantly, many men also oppose the Open Gate Law as a contravention of the "natural" male role:

> Opposition to the new law had the fervent support of all the conservatives in the Castles, who pleaded eloquently for the gates to be closed and men to return to their proper station, pursuing the true, masculine glory of the games and the fuckeries. (Le Guin "Seggri" 378)

Noem warns that even Dez might find it hard to have his previously celebrated masculine behaviours devalued:

> [B]ecause you were trained at the Castle to compete, to want to excel, you may find it hard to be among people who either believe you incapable of excellence, or to whom the concept of competition, of winning and defeating, is valueless. (383)

The way that the men fight for change further reveals the persistent influence of gender socialisation. Dez realises that by murdering the Castle bullies, he and his friends risk becoming what they sought to oppose and that their violent resistance merely reinforces essentialist assumptions about the destructive nature of men: "How we played was what we won.... They treated us not as men, but as irrational, irresponsible creatures, untamable cattle" (377).

As Gregory Herek argues, even when men recognise the dysfunctional nature of the male role, they cannot change without a clear view of alternative ways of living (80). Women also struggle to imagine alternatives. Although Azak realises that her society is wrong to reduce men to sexual beasts, she is unable to conceptualise how change might occur: "She thought, 'My life is wrong.' But she did not know how to make it right" (Le Guin "Seggri" 372). Ragaz tells Dez that it is easier for the women to turn a blind eye to the suffering of the men: "Of course they don't want to know how we live. Why do they never come into the Castles? Oh, we keep them out, yes, but do you think we could keep them out if they wanted to enter?" (375). Segal implies that this resistance is to be expected when she asks if any group of people have ever given up power without struggle, pain, and conflict (303). However Ragaz's complaint critiques women at the expense of acknowledging the men's responsibility for their own suffering. Ragaz implies that the women could force their way into the Castles if they wished, yet it is the Seggri men who are trained in the use of force and violence. This begs the question of why the Seggri men have not left the Castles en masse and forced the women to accord them a place in their society.

Fear of the unknown is presented as a cause of the men's failure to pursue change. This issue again recurs throughout Le Guin's work. In "Old Music and the Slave Women" (1999), for instance, the slaves' resistance to revolution shows that even those who suffer most under the current system may cling to it rather than face an unknown future. In "Seggri" many men experience similar fears and choose to remain in the Castles. As Diane Crowder observes, it is often easier for the oppressed to remain in the hell they know, rather than strive for an unknown paradise that they can barely imagine (245).

In Le Guin's work, Warren Rochelle claims, experiences of change are recognisable by their complexity and pain (69). Nevertheless, Le Guin retains hope that reconciliation can be achieved, and the fourteen-hundred year time-frame of "Seggri" allows her to identify some of the steps in the slow process of change. Po's and Azak's awareness of the problems of their gender system can thus be seen as an important first step, despite their inability to translate their knowledge into action. Dez's feeling that his masculine existence is intolerable is also crucial as it motivates him to seek the education that will allow him to imagine an alternative life.

Rochelle also claims that for Le Guin revolution is an ongoing process (74), while Mike Cadden refers to her narratives as "creation unfinished" (349). These observations are supported by Le Guin's own explanation of her work:

> [W]hen I came to write science-fiction novels, I came lugging this great heavy sack of stuff ... full of beginnings without ends, of initiations, of losses, of transformations and translations, and far more tricks than conflicts, far fewer triumphs than snares and delusions; full of space ships that get stuck, missions that fail, and people who don't understand. ("Carrier Bag" 169)

Thus at the end of "Seggri" Dez emphasises that he still knows only with "uncertain certainty" (384) who he is. This uncertainty could signal Le Guin's refusal to replace one stable, closed concept of masculinity with another. On the other hand, it implies that despite its extended timeframe, "Seggri" moves little closer than earlier separatist texts to conceptualising what a fully reconciled society would actually look like. Dez's decision to leave Seggri and study on Hain hints at this failure of imagination. Although Dez signals his intention to return to Seggri to contribute to the ongoing process of change, his narrative provides no details about how the struggle towards reconciliation has progressed in his absence.

Conclusion

Although "Seggri" attempts to take the next step in the feminist discourse on separatism, it does not move much closer to actually envisaging reconciliation. Nevertheless, Le Guin's sympathetic presentation of male subjectivities in an oppressive gender hierarchy, and her implicit critique of a matriarchy, is a new step in the use of the separatist trope in feminist SF. However Le Guin's continued focus on white, straight, middle-class men suggests that, as yet, feminist writers have made limited use of the separatist trope to interrogate and explore multiple masculine identities. "Seggri's" exploration of the subversive potential of male homosexuality does signal a growing awareness of such multiplicity, but these nuances are finally pushed aside to reinstate a hetero-normative ideal. Because such heterosexual relationships have traditionally been seen as contributing to men's dominance of women, most feminist writers have been unable to imagine how these "subversive" relationships will lead to society-wide reconciliation without reinstating male privilege. Le Guin attempts to bypass this concern by combining the separatist trope with a role reversal, but this risks "Seggri" being read as a condemnation of women's power. "Seggri" argues that if men will only reject the violence of the warrior narrative, they may achieve a harmonious marriage of equals with women. This assumption, and "Seggri's" continued prioritisation of a white, straight, middle-class masculine identity, suggests that although Le Guin provides an important contribution to the feminist SF discourse about separatism and reconciliation, the conversation must continue.

Works Cited

1. Attebery, Brian. "Women Alone, Men Alone: Single-Sex Utopias." *Femspec* 1.2 (2000): 4-15.
2. Barr, Marleen. "Permissive, Unspectacular, a Little Baffling: Sex and the Single Feminist Utopian Quasi-Tribesperson." *Erotic Universe: Sexuality and Fantastic Literature.* Ed. Donald Palumbo. New York: Greenwood Press, 1986. 185-96.
3. —. "Ursula Le Guin's 'Sur' as Exemplary Humanist and Antihumanist Text." *Lost in Space: Probing Feminist Science Fiction and Beyond.* Chapel Hill, NC: University of North Carolina Press, 1993. 154-70.
4. Cadden, Mike. "Purposeful Movement among People and Places: The Sense of Home in Ursula K. Le Guin's Fiction for Children and Adults." *Extrapolation* 41.4 (2000): 338-50.
5. Charnas, Suzy McKee. *Walk to the End of the World.* 1974. *The Slave and the Free.* New York: Tom Doherty Associates, Inc., 1999. 1-215.
6. —. *Motherlines.* 1978. *The Slave and the Free.* New York: Tom Doherty Associates, Inc., 1999. 217-436.
7. —. *The Furies.* 1994. New York: Tom Doherty Associates, Inc., 2001.
8. —. *The Conqueror's Child.* 1999. New York: Tom Doherty Associates, Inc., 2000.
9. Clute, John and Peter Nicholls Eds. *The Encyclopedia of Science Fiction.* London: Orbit, 1993.
10. Crowder, Diane Griffin. "Separatism and Feminist Utopian Fiction." In *Sexual Practice/Textual Theory: Lesbian Cultural Criticism,* ed. by Susan J. Wolfe and Julia Penelope. Cambridge, MA: Blackwell, 1993. 237-50.
11. Donawerth, Jane. "The Feminist Dystopia of the 1990s: Record of Failure, Midwife of Hope." In *Future Females, the Next Generation: New Voices and Velocities in Feminist Science Fiction Criticism,* ed. by Marleen S. Barr. Lanham, MD: Rowman & Littlefield, 2000. 49-66.
12. Fitting, Peter. "Reconsiderations of the Separatist Paradigm in Recent Feminist Science Fiction." *Science Fiction Studies* 19 (1992): 32-48.
13. Gearhart, Sally Miller. *Wanderground: Stories of the Hill Women.* 1979. Denver: Spinsters Ink Books, 2002.
14. Gilman, Charlotte Perkins. *Herland.* 1915. London: The Women's Press, 2001.

15. Herek, Gregory M. "On Heterosexual Masculinity: Some Psychical Consequences of the Social Construction of Gender and Sexuality." In *Changing Men: New Directions in Research on Men and Masculinity*, ed. by Michael S. Kimmel. Newbury Park, CA: Sage Publications, 1987. 68-82.

16. Jacobs, Naomi. "Beyond Stasis and Symmetry: Lessing, Le Guin, and the Remodeling of Utopia." *Extrapolation* 29.1 (1988): 34-45.

17. Jordan, Ellen and Angela Cowan. "Warrior Narratives in the Kindergarten Classroom: Renegotiating the Social Contract?" In *Men's Lives*, ed. by Michael S. Kimmel and Michael A. Messner. 4th Ed. Boston: Allyn & Bacon, 1998. 127-40.

18. Lefanu, Sarah. *In the Chinks of the World Machine: Feminism and Science Fiction*. London: The Women's Press, 1988.

19. Le Guin, Ursula K. "The Carrier Bag Theory of Fiction." 1986. In *Dancing at the Edge of the World: Thoughts on Words, Women, Places*. London: Victor Gollancz Ltd, 1989. 165-70.

20. —. *The Dispossessed*. New York: Avon, 1974.

21. —. "Introduction to *Planet of Exile*." 1978. In *The Language of the Night: Essays on Fantasy and Science Fiction*, ed. by Susan Wood. New York: Perigee Books, 1979. 139-43.

22. —. *The Left Hand of Darkness*. New York: Ace Books, 1969.

23. —. "A Left-Handed Commencement Address." 1983. In *Dancing at the Edge of the World: Thoughts on Words, Women, Places*. London: Victor Gollancz Ltd, 1989. 115-7.

24. —. "The Matter of Seggri." 1994. In *Flying Cups & Saucers: Gender Explorations in Science Fiction and Fantasy*, ed. by Debbie Notkin & the Secret Feminist Cabal. Cambridge, MA: Edgewood Press, 1998. 347-384.

25. —. "Old Music and the Slave Women." 1999. In *The Birthday of the World and Other Stories*. New York: Harper Collins, 2002. 153-211.

26. Morrissey, Thomas J. "Review Essay: *The Shore of Women*." *SFRA Review* 271 (2005): 29-31.

27. Parker, Andrew. "Sporting Masculinities: Gender Relations and the Body." In *Understanding Masculinities: Social Relations and Cultural Arenas*, ed. by Máirtin Mac an Ghaill. Buckingham: Open University Press, 1996. 126-38.

28. Polych, Carol and Donald Sabo. "Gender Politics, Pain, and Illness." In *Men's Health and Illness: Gender, Power, and the Body*, ed. by Donald Sabo and David Frederick Gordon. Thousand Oaks: Sage Publications, 1995. 139-57.

29. Roberts, Robin. *A New Species: Gender and Science in Science Fiction*. Urbana: University of Illinois Press, 1993.
30. Rochelle, Warren G. *Communities of the Heart: The Rhetoric of Myth in the Fiction of Ursula K. Le Guin*. Liverpool: Liverpool University Press, 2001.
31. Russ, Joanna. *The Female Man*. 1975. London: The Women's Press Ltd, 1985.
32. Sargent, Pamela. *The Shore of Women*. 1986. London: Chatto & Windus, 1987.
33. Segal, Lynne. *Slow Motion: Changing Masculinities, Changing Men*. London: Virago, 1990.
34. Slonczewski, Joan. *A Door Into Ocean*. New York: Avon, 1986.
35. Somay, Bülent. "Towards an Open-Ended Utopia." *Science Fiction Studies* 11 (1984): 25-38.
36. Tepper, Sheri S. *The Gate to Women's Country*. New York: Foundation Books, 1988.
37. Turner, Stuart. "Surviving Sexual Assault and Sexual Torture." In *Male Victims of Sexual Assault*, ed. by Gillian C. Mezey and Michael B. King. Oxford: Oxford University Press, 1992. 75-86.
38. Wolmark, Jenny. *Aliens and Others: Science Fiction, Feminism and Postmodernism*. New York: Harvester Wheatsheaf, 1993.

Linda Wight is currently completing her PhD at James Cook University on images of men and masculinities in recent science fiction. This interest is reflected both in the essay published here, and in essays previously published on Marge Piercy's *He, She and It*. In addition to her studies, she serves as the Fiction Reviews editor of *LINQ*, and works as a research assistant for *AustLit: the Online Australian Literature Resource*.

Sympathy as Self-Discovery: The Significance of Caring for Others in "Betrayals"

Howard Sklar
University of Helsinki

The ethical self is an active relation between my actual self and a vision of my ideal self as one caring and cared-for. It is born of the fundamental recognition of relatedness; that which connects me naturally to the other, reconnects me through the other to myself. As I care for others and am cared for by them, I become able to care for myself. Nel Noddings (49)

In "Betrayals," the first of four novellas in *Four Ways to Forgiveness*, Ursula K. Le Guin provides a compelling portrayal of the implications of indifference, and the healing powers of sympathetic caring. In this essay, I will contend that Le Guin, like Noddings in the epigraph above, portrays caring as a continuously developing process by which we learn to give attention to, and to receive attention from, others. We find this particularly in Le Guin's depiction of Yoss, a character who finds herself, as well as a compelling reason to live, by caring for another. We come to recognize these changes through a form of "empathetic projection" (Keen, *Empathy* 129, 140) that enables us to share her thoughts and feelings through most of the novella. This narrative strategy moves us through continually revised assessments of, and feelings toward, the disgraced leader Abberkam. For his part, Abberkam, initially "indifferent to his own plight or hers" (Le Guin, "Betrayals" 18), discovers his own concern for Yoss, and ultimately is able to give of himself to the extent that he becomes both emotionally and physically vulnerable. We come to recognize that he is able to redeem himself only through the care that he extends to Yoss, and our initial contempt for him is gradually replaced by feelings of concern and tenderness. This conversion of our feelings toward him and the deepening of our feelings toward Yoss grow out of the narrative's structure of character disclosure, and the changing judgments this prompts us to make of the characters. I contend that by progressively allowing us to discover, assess, and ultimately appreciate Abberkam, the narrative provides an emotional opening for the reader through its elicitation of unexpected sympathy. This sympathy depends largely upon the response generated by the unfolding "complementarity" between the two characters, and especially by their recognition of the need to care for, and be cared for.

1. Sympathy and Empathy: Their Implications for Reader Response

Sympathy and empathy are frequently conflated or interchanged, both as real-life emotions and as forms of reader response. I will first clarify my use of the two terms and then make some important distinctions between them.[1]

Empathy commonly is thought to involve the absorption of the empathizer in the feelings or experiences of another. Social psychologist Liisa Myyry, for instance, suggests that "Empathy ... could be defined as an affective response more appropriate to another's situation than to one's own" (10).[2] Suzanne Keen, developing her theory of empathy's role in fiction, suggests: "In empathy ... we feel what we believe to be the emotions of others" (Empathy 5). Philosopher Martha Nussbaum broadens this definition, describing empathy as "an imaginative reconstruction of another person's experience, without any particular evaluation of that experience" (301-02).[3] Noddings proposes perhaps the most radical absorption in the experience of another, rejecting the "peculiarly rational, western, masculine way of looking at 'feeling with'" implied by the notion of "projecting one's personality into, and so fully understanding, the object of contemplation." She writes:

[1] While, clearly, the notions are interrelated, the precise ways in which they are connected tends to vary from scholar to scholar. Among social psychologists, for instance, Davis considers "empathic concern," which he defines as "feelings of warmth and sympathy" ("Individual Differences" 116; cf. Davis, Empathy), a constituent part of empathy. Hoffman likewise views "sympathetic distress" as a significant component of empathy (Empathy 95). Batson appears to exchange the terms, so that what he calls empathy actually is what Martha Nussbaum, a philosopher, terms "compassion" and what I call "sympathy" (see Eisenberg, "Development" 75; Nussbaum, Upheavals 331n).

[2] Myyry builds this definition on the work of Hoffman (Empathy).

[3] Nussbaum's formulation, by emphasizing an "imaginative reconstruction of another's experience," may seem to tend toward "cognitive role taking," which some scholars view "as distinct from empathy-related reactions because it lacks emotionality" (Myyry and Helkama, "Socio-cognitive" 251). Yet Nussbaum's focus, both in her discussion of empathy and of sympathy/compassion, is primarily directed to the emotional content of those experiences. To some extent, Nussbaum's definition integrates the two definitions of empathy delineated by Hoffman (2000: 29ff), e.g., empathy as "cognitive awareness" and as "the vicarious affective response to another person." Keen likewise addresses the emotional and cognitive components of empathy. She points especially to the implicitly cognitive aspect of narrative empathy, "for reading itself relies upon complex cognitive operations (Empathy 28).

The notion of "feeling with" that I have outlined does not involve projection but reception. I have called it "engrossment." I do not "put myself in the other's shoes," so to speak, by analyzing his reality as objective data and then asking, "How would I feel in such a situation?" ... I do not project; I receive the other into myself, and I see and feel with the other. I become a duality....
(Noddings 30; cited also in Juujärvi 44)

In each of these definitions, empathy operates as what I call a "chameleon emotion," in the sense that we take on the emotional experience of another as our own.[4] In empathy's relation to fiction, Keen suggests that, due to the distinction between an "author's empathy" (the author's empathy for the character as projected through the narrative) and "reader's empathy" (the experience that a reader receives), "narrative empathy" itself can be understood as "rhetorical"—as the "attempt [by authors] to persuade readers to feel with them" (*Empathy* 140). In some cases, our empathy with the feelings of an author may involve "feeling with" a particular character—of empathizing with her or him—as I have suggested that Le Guin prompts us to do with Yoss. In other cases, this process of empathizing with the *author's* feelings may lead us to feel other emotions that the author has projected, yet which are not shared by the character. "Betrayals" provides an interesting example of the shift in authorial empathy, in that it first leads us to experience that which Yoss experiences, before restoring the distance between her and us as we "witness" her interaction with Abberkam from the outside, as it were, in "feeling for" (sympathizing with) his own situation. From a social psychological perspective, this shift complies with the notion that empathy may act as a "precursor" to sympathy.[5]

[4] This engagement is dependent, as Nussbaum argues, on our ability to "think of [a character's] sufferings as 'things such as might happen,' and thus to consider, in a more general way, the vulnerability of human beings to reversals and sufferings" (Nussbaum 240). The dependence of the reader on the creation of this perception that the events "might happen" is no less relevant to works that depart from realistic conventions, as Sternberg suggests: "The reader's judgment as to the improbability of the fantastic elements is confirmed and even reinforced by the internal premises of the work itself....[P]robability ('truth') ... is to be judged not by external but mainly by immanent norms" (1976: 310). This suggests that the work itself, or the genre or mode to which it belongs, creates for itself its own "reality" against which plausibility is measured. See also Sklar ("Believable") for an extended discussion of these issues.

[5] Keen writes that "empathy is thought to be a precursor to its semantic close relative, *sympathy*," (Empathy 4). The key word here is "thought," since scholars remain divided on this issue. Indeed, as Eisenberg and Strayer noted in 1987, in their introduction to the seminal *Empathy and its Development*: "Whether or not

Empathy, then, essentially places readers inside the experience of a character. Our immersion in that experience, moreover, may bring us "too close" to view the character's reality "objectively."[6] Thus, Nussbaum emphasizes that, in empathy, our "imaginative reconstruction of another person's experience" occurs "without any particular evaluation of that experience"—that is, without forming a judgment. This last characteristic of empathy is critical to understanding the distinction between empathy and sympathy, as well as to conceptualizing the process by which we come to feel sympathy for Abberkam in the course of the novella. In my view, based on insights developed in social psychology, sociology and philosophy,[7] the most important elements in defining sympathy are:

(1) Awareness of suffering as something to be alleviated. (Wispé 318; cited also in Eisenberg and Strayer 6).
(2) Judgment of unfairness of suffering. Sympathy is based in part on the recognition, or judgment, of the *unfairness* of the suffering of another (see Nussbaum 302).

---

empathy always mediates sympathizing is an open question" (6). Myyry and Helkama, citing more recent work by Eisenberg, suggest that "pure empathy is not other-oriented...but by cognitive processing it can turn into sympathy, personal distress, or some combination" ("Socio-cognitive" 251). Nussbaum is more skeptical, but still believes that empathy may be "psychologically important as a guide" (330), in that empathy stimulates response, which in turn may lead to more judgment-related emotions such as sympathy. Candace Clark, whose study *Misery and Company: Sympathy in Everyday Life* examines sympathy from a sociological perspective, argues more emphatically for empathy's role in sympathy. She considers sympathy as comprised of "three components," of which empathy is the first and "a necessary precondition for both [of the other two components of sympathy,] sympathy sentiment and display" (Misery 34). However, Clark's terminology differs in important respects from that of social psychologists, as well as from Keen and Nussbaum: She views empathy as primarily a role-taking activity, unlike other, more emotion-related definitions (see note 3).

[6] When placed inside of a character's perspective, readers may find it difficult to judge that character from the outside; instead, I would argue, readers judge the situations that occur in the narrative from the character's point of view. Phelan himself advances this point with respect to what he calls "lyricality" (as opposed to "narrativity") in literary texts (Phelan, "Judgement" 117). I will discuss this further in section 3.

[7] This discussion condenses an extended examination (in Sklar, "Narrative") of the considerations that resulted in this definition. That essay, as well as the present one, directly relate to my doctoral dissertation, *Art of Sympathy*, which I will defend in October, 2008.

(3) "Negative" feelings on behalf of the sufferer. The recognition
    of another's suffering generally follows, produces or involves
    feelings (typically "negative" or unpleasant or uncomfortable)
    on behalf of the sufferer, or in relation to his/her situation
    ("sympathetic distress": see Hoffman 95; "sympathy
    sentiment": see Clark 44).
(4) Desire to help. Sympathy frequently (although not always)
    includes the *desire* to alleviate another's suffering (Oakley
    28; Eisenberg 76).

This definition of sympathy recognizes both "cognitive" *and* "affective"
aspects of sympathetic response, or what Justin Oakley calls *"complexes*
of cognitions, desires, and affects together"* (Oakley 93),[8] and is seen
as a social, and not merely psychological, phenomenon (see Clark).
Sympathy also is understood to involve "common-sense" notions of
fairness and suffering, in the sense that most people who describe what
they experience when they feel sympathy say that they "feel sorry for
someone" who is experiencing something difficult.[9] Sympathy for
those who are suffering is said to be a "negative emotion" involving
"sympathetic distress." Sympathy as an *emotion* generally is a *felt*
response, involving both physical and mental sensation.[10] Sympathy
either results from or produces the motivation ("desire") to eliminate its
cause. Finally, sympathy is viewed as an essentially *moral* response, to
the extent that it involves a judgment—sometimes explicit or conscious,
at other times implicit or intuitive—of another's situation. In fact,

---

[8] Social Psychologist Eisenberg notes Batson's contention that "sympathy is
associated with the *desire* to reduce another person's distress or need" (Eisenberg,
Development 76, emphasis added).

[9] Even though people generally have difficulty in articulating what sympathy means
to them (Clark 29-30), many very specifically associate the term with "feeling sorry"
for someone whose situation is somehow difficult, unfortunate or unpleasant. Clark,
in discussing respondents' attempts at defining sympathy, writes: "Among those who
ventured a definition, by far the most common was 'feeling sorry for somebody with
problems'" (30). I also found this to be true in tests that I conducted with adolescent
readers in response to texts that, like "Betrayals," produce sympathy in readers. I
will discuss these results briefly later. For a more detailed description of the tests
and the results, see Sklar (Narrative).

[10] I am not distinguishing here between what occurs as a bodily sensation (what
Damasio [2003] would call "emotion") and the mental sensation (for Damasio,
"feeling"). Unless otherwise specified, when I describe "emotions" or "feelings" I
am essentially referring to the same thing: to the complex of emotions and feelings
(in the sense meant by Damasio) as they occur together and/or in sequence.

sympathy gains its moral significance to the extent that, to cite Martha Nussbaum, it "includes a judgment that the other person's distress is bad" (302).[11]

In applying this definition to fictional characters, it may be helpful to look at the four elements of the definition (as well as each of the constituent properties that result from these elements) as operating on continua. Each may be said to contribute to a particular instance or expression of sympathy, but, depending upon the intensity of any one of these components, as well as the interaction between them, the expression of sympathy may take different forms: as concern, as sorrow, as outrage, as caring.

In all of these responses, though, a judgment of the unfairness of the character's situation lies at the heart of the sympathetic response. In understanding this phenomenon, it is helpful to consider Ed Tan's notion of "witness emotions," based on his research into the ways that films produce emotions in audiences. Tan contends that "viewers are led to imagine themselves an *invisible* witness in the fictional world" (Tan 16-17). This notion can be applied to written fiction, as well. In many narrative situations, we view the scenes as though we are in close proximity to the action, watching the events unfold, perhaps even responding emotionally to the characters or their predicaments. The events in such cases do not happen to *us* but to the characters within the narrative. By placing readers in the role of observers, narratives thus create the preconditions for judgment, as James Phelan points out:

> Narrativity encourages two main activities: observing and judging. The authorial audience perceives the characters as external to themselves and as distinct from their implied authors, and the authorial audience passes interpretive and ethical judgments on them, their situations, and their choices. The audience's observer role is what makes the judgment role possible, and the particular judgments are integral to our emotional responses as well as to our desires about future events. (*Experiencing* 7).

---

[11]Unlike Nussbaum, Kristján Kristjánsson argues that sympathy is considerably different from compassion in that, unlike compassion, it does not involve the determination that another's suffering is deserved or undeserved (300-01). For reasons beyond the scope of the present discussion, I tend to follow Nussbaum's characterization of the "contemporary usage" of sympathy as a rough "equivalent to what I call 'compassion,'" as well as her distinction between the two emotions as involving different levels of intensity (Nussbaum 302).

In the case of sympathy, this "observer" role dovetails with the "judgmental" nature of sympathy itself, in such a way that the process of judgment is made especially prominent. Already "integral to our emotional responses," judgment, when turned to sympathy, becomes virtually indistinguishable from that emotional response.

The activation of sympathetic judgment thus contrasts distinctly with the relative suspension of judgment that occurs in readers when they feel empathy for a character. I will now analyze how readers are moved, first, to understand Yoss without judgment, from within her consciousness, before moving outside of that consciousness to witness the dynamics of caring that unfold between Yoss and Abberkam.

2. Lost in the Marshlands:
Cognitive Estrangement and the Cultivation of Empathy

First, we need to examine Yoss's position when the story opens, since it is through her that much of the narrative's observations are filtered. We discover that she has chosen to live in a form of spiritual isolation on the marshlands, but we gradually realize that she considers herself inadequate to the pursuit of the inner peace that she craves. She tells herself:

> [W]hat a fool I was to think I could ever drink water and be silent! I'll never, never be able to let anything go, anything at all. I'll never be free, never be worthy of freedom. Even old age can't make me let go. Even losing Safnan can't make me let go. (Le Guin, "Betrayals" 5)

This last realization, that "even losing [her daughter] Safnan" can't bring her "freedom," suggests a more poignant cause for her feeling of inadequacy. Four years earlier, Yoss's daughter and granddaughter left Yeowe for Hain, a journey of eighty years. At the heart of Yoss's sense of loss is the realization — at least, as Yoss sees it — that her daughter rejected *her*: "They left me and I am dead" (11). As a result, she has come to live in the marshlands, a setting that seems to reflect her intense loneliness. The land contains "useless people on useless land. The freedom of desolation. And all through the marshes there were lonely houses" (9). This "desolation" reflects an even greater sense of "uselessness," of self-contempt, to the extent that those who go there to live essentially intend to die. As Yoss thinks, "I came here to be dead" (11).

The immediacy of these feelings is conveyed by the consistent focalization of the narrative through Yoss, as well as the fairly seamless, and frequent, transitions between "extradiegetic" (external to the story; in this case also: impersonal, omniscient, third-person) and free indirect (free indirect discourse, or FID) narration. The latter, by voicing Yoss's thoughts regarding the feelings and situations that she encounters, provides direct and intimate access to her state of mind, to the extent that "the tinting of the narrator's speech with the character's language and mode of experience may promote an empathetic identification on the part of the reader," (Rimmon-Kenan, *Narrative* 114). As I suggested earlier, this process of creating "empathetic identification" likewise leads to the suspension of judgment toward Yoss. The free indirect style, by placing readers in such a close "participatory" position, possesses what Phelan would term a "degree of lyricality":

> With lyricality, each element is different in some important way.... On the readerly side, ethical judgment drops out and is replaced by participation, an entering into the speaker's situation and perspective without judging it. That participation in turn influences the affective side of the experience—we share the speaker's feelings or take on the speaker's thoughts, beliefs, or attitudes. (Phelan, "Judgment" 117)

By providing access to Yoss's thoughts and feelings through FID, Le Guin postpones our judgment of Yoss, and we "unwittingly" adopt the latter's attitudes toward Abberkam, as well as her experience of estrangement as a whole.

This last point is crucial to an appreciation of Yoss's experience on the marshlands. As is well known, works of science fiction traditionally are thought to involve the production of what Darko Suvin termed "cognitive estrangement." As Patrick Parrinder summarizes this view: "It [science fiction] is cognitive by virtue of its affiliation to science and rationality, and estranged by its presentation of a conceptual 'new world' differing from the author's empirical reality" (*Science* 72). While I believe that "Betrayals" involves a form of estrangement, I do not consider that experience to be the product of what Suvin would call "a strange newness" or even "a domestication of the amazing" ("Estrangement" 4). In fact, the world represented in "Betrayals" remains largely familiar ... or is it?

To examine this issue, it is useful to look at the beginning of the second novella in *Four Ways to Forgiveness*, "Forgiveness Day": "Solly had been a space brat, a Mobile's child, living on this ship and that, this world and that; she'd travelled five hundred light-years by the time she was ten" (Le Guin, "Forgiveness" 47). In this novella, the reader is immediately "estranged" from what Suvin calls "the author's empirical environment" (4) and immersed in a world of intergalactic travel. "Betrayals" *seems* to begin similarly: "On the planet O there has not been a war for five thousand years,' she read, 'and on Gethen there has never been a war'" ("Betrayals" 1). The narrative begins by referring to other planets, but we immediately are drawn out of that estrangement when we reach "she read," for we too have just read that text in the first subtle shading of "character focalization." This sensation is reinforced (through the restored extradiegetic narrative perspective) in the following line: "She stopped reading, to rest her eyes and because she was trying to train herself to read slowly, not gobble words down in chunks the way Tikuli gulped his food" (1).

The experience, indeed, is largely *familiarizing*, and it is not until readers focalize on her experiences further that we come to recognize the type of estrangement that the story represents, which might properly be described as *existential*: By living far from others, Yoss is alienated socially; by living in a harsh and inhospitable land, she is physically estranged; by doubting her own purpose and reason for existence, she is psychologically a stranger to herself. None of these dimensions of Yoss's alienation, however, are necessarily exclusive to science fiction as a genre, or typical, in a generic sense, of "cognitive estrangement" as a theoretical construct. This is not to say that "Betrayals" succumbs to the tendency that Parrinder identifies in some works of science fiction that he considers inadequately estranging: "The estrangement-effect of the majority of SF stories is contained and neutralized by their conventionality in other respects. The result is that the familiar reality is replaced by an all too familiar unreality" (74). While I have suggested that "Betrayals" does not depend on radically estranging environments or situations, I nevertheless contend that the *experience* of estrangement for Yoss, and for us through her perception, is considerable. This estrangement, or defamiliarization, will play a considerable role in creating what I will term the "emotional estrangement" [12] (through Yoss) of our first impressions of Abberkam.

[12] By adopting the expression "emotional estrangement," I do not mean to imply that this effect is devoid of cognitive content, as my discussion earlier of the cognitive and affective components of sympathy should make clear. I do, however, wish to distinguish the experience that I claim readers undergo in reading "Betrayals" from the cognitive-"scientific" notion implied by Suvin's term. For an intriguing perspective on the way in which Le Guin "braids" together myth and science (and magic) in some of her works of science fiction—and thereby moves beyond the purely cognitive-scientific—see Bittner (20-21).

3. Abberkam as Other:
"Emotional Estrangement" and Reader Judgment

The frequent use of free indirect style provides us with considerable access to Yoss's internal experience. These thoughts, perceptions and emotions, in fact, somewhat rigidly focalize our first impressions of Abberkam through the lens of Yoss's attitudes towards him. Early in the narrative, for instance, Yoss worries that she will "soon be wandering around the marshes shouting aloud, like Abberkam," (Le Guin, "Betrayals" 6). This worry is reinforced by the specifics of Abberkam's behavior: His shouting in the night, his lips moving, his demeanor that is "wary as a wild animal" (6) — all suggest complete madness. While these descriptions alone might not be completely decisive in framing our impressions of Abberkam — Yoss even seems to feel an element of pity for the fallen leader, as demonstrated by her concern for his physical health in their first conversation (8) — they do suggest that there is something disturbing and perhaps even frightening about him, and these images create an unsettling foundation for the more directly critical descriptions that follow.

Indeed, shortly after these opening impressions, Yoss relates — in FID — some of the events that led to his downfall and the deep bitterness that she feels toward him for having taken part in them:

> "Let him die. How could he want to live knowing what he'd lost, his power, his honor, and what he'd done? Lied, betrayed his supporters, embezzled.... Big Chief Abberkam, hero of the Liberation, leader of the World Party, who had destroyed the World Party by his greed and folly. (8)

Yoss's bitterness, we learn, springs from Abberkam's having destroyed the dream of liberation of which he was the primary symbol. Yoss mentally builds on this later, when she recalls the specifics of his crimes:

> "He was certain to win the first free election ever held on Yeowe, to be Chief of the World Council. And then, nothing much at first, the rumors. The defections. His son's suicide. His son's mother's accusations of debauchery and gross luxury. The proof that he had embezzled great sums of money given his party for relief of districts left in poverty by the withdrawal of Werelian capital. The revelation of the secret plan to assassinate the Envoy of the Ekumen and put the blame on Abberkam's old friend and supporter Demeye.... (14).

Thus, as we learn of the suffering that Abberkam is believed to have caused, we grow progressively more contemptuous of him. Moreover, the FID approach allows us to interpret the descriptions as coming from Yoss, rather than from the narrator. "Hearing" her thoughts in this way, readers find it difficult to distance Yoss's feelings toward Abberkam from their own. Through Yoss, Abberkam becomes "alien," and our estrangement from him, mentally and especially emotionally, is virtually inevitable.

This process of naturalizing our impressions and feelings is one of the devices that narratives use to persuade us to unwittingly adopt attitudes or to feel in particular ways. As Mieke Bal writes,

> This so-called objectivity is, in fact, a form of *subjectivity* in disguise. This is most conspicuous when the meaning of the narrative resides in the reader's identification with the psychology of a character; this happens when characters are given the function of authenticating the narrative contents. (Bal, *Narrativity* 37, emphasis added)

In "Betrayals," our primary perspective, from the outset, is through Yoss, who has been "given the function of authenticating the narrative contents." Through this position, the focalizer enables us to share in her particular, subjective version of reality, and especially her feelings towards Abberkam.

A useful comparison with this strategy can be found in Meir Sternberg's analysis of William Faulkner's *Light in August*, a narrative that in important respects shares certain structural similarities with "Betrayals." Sternberg contends that Faulkner creates a "primacy effect"—a first impression—of the protagonist, Joe Christmas, that is wholly unflattering, that ultimately attributes Christmas's murderous behavior to his hidden black identity. Having established this impression, Faulkner spends a significant portion of the rest of the book countering this impression by revealing Christmas's painful past. According to Sternberg, then, "The unexpected retrospective illumination of Christmas's character and history, as well as the considerable increase in sympathy consequent upon the drastic shift in narrative perspective, compel the reader to retract or modify his adverse hypotheses and judgments one by one" (Sternberg, Expositional 100).

I have found some confirmation of this type of effect on readers by testing early adolescent readers' responses to Toni Cade Bambara's "The Hammer Man." In that story, we are introduced to the protagonist, Manny, through the descriptions of a first-person narrator. Based on these descriptions, through which we learn that Manny is "crazy" and violent, we form a distinctly negative impression of him. I hypothesized that readers, having only the narrator to focalize these impressions, would adopt these negative attitudes, only to have them reversed later. In general, the responses of nearly 200 readers suggest that they indeed tend to adopt these attitudes toward Manny, moving from relatively little sympathy in the early phases of the narrative toward a more pronounced sympathy for Manny as he is taken away, presumably to a mental health facility.[13]

Although the depiction of Abberkam is neither as negative nor as racially provocative as that of Christmas in *Light in August*, nor as unfathomable as Manny remains at the end of "The Hammer Man," I contend that Le Guin has created a similar rhetorical structure in "Betrayals": having "familiarized" us with the disgraced leader through an accumulation of unfavorable details about his past betrayals and his present deportment, the author prepares us to be reoriented—to view or experience this character in entirely new ways—through the presentation of subsequent details and events. This is made possible by the shift in perspective that we experience through the changing perspectives of the story's focalizer, Yoss.[14] We begin to reassess Abberkam's character, in fact, through Yoss's decision to care for him in his state of illness, and her growing uncertainty regarding her own attitudes toward him as a result of that caring relationship.

4. The Rehabilitation of Abberkam:
Revised Judgment and the Beginnings of Sympathy

Yoss's intervention on Abberkam's behalf rouses her from her condition of self-contempt to address the needs of someone who, at that particular moment, seems worse off than she. It is the memory of Safnan's near death in childhood from the same illness that Abberkam

---

[13] For a detailed account of the methodology and results of this testing, see Sklar ("Narrative"). In addition to Bambara's "The Hammer Man", I also tested readers' responses to Sherwood Anderson's short story "Hands." Results from this testing, as well as from "The Hammer Man", will be included in my doctoral dissertation (see note 7). For an earlier analysis of the narrative structure in "Hands," see Sklar ("Believable").

[14] Through their reader response tests, literary scholar David S. Miall and psychologist Don Kuiken have examined the connection between emotions that readers experience in response to fiction and the defamiliarizing strategies and "shifting perspectives" that fictional works employ. See Miall and Kuiken, "Foregrounding" and "Shifting."

endures that drives Yoss to visit him at his home, where she finds him "naked on the bed, writhing and raving in fever" (Le Guin, "Betrayals" 17). As Nel Noddings writes of the caring attitude,

> When I look at and think about how I am when I care, I realize that there is invariably this displacement of interest from my own reality to the reality of the other.... To be touched, to have aroused in me something that will disturb my own ethical reality, I must see the other's reality as a possibility for my own," (14).

When Yoss first encounters the ailing Abberkam, therefore, she is overwhelmed by the sight of his condition, by the degree to which he has deteriorated. The sight penetrates her awareness—"disturbs her ethical reality"—to the extent that she is moved spontaneously to act on his behalf. Yet *how* is this reality disturbed? What processes enable "this displacement of interest from my own reality to the reality of the other"? To explain this, let me recall my earlier discussion of the components of sympathy.

Yoss clearly recognizes that, despite Abberkam's abuses as a leader, the condition in which he finds himself is implicitly "unfair." As I claimed earlier, this recognition is one of the basic preconditions for the experience of sympathy. Yet, it is also important to realize that Yoss does not approach Abberkam, as it were, as a blank slate: She brings her own experience of pain, of loss, of human need. This cognitive dimension of emotional response is particularly significant, to paraphrase Noddings, in "arousing in Yoss something that disturbs her own ethical reality," of emotionally connecting her own experience with her judgment of Abberkam's situation. This arousal, however, would not help Abberkam without a concomitant desire to take action. The fact that Yoss's response involves each of the components of sympathy, including the final "*desire* to alleviate the suffering of another," prepares her for the act of caring, of altruism, that she performs for Abberkam. More importantly, this begins a process by which Abberkam is "rehabilitated" in the minds of readers.

Indeed, Yoss's efforts to nurse Abberkam back to health have a corollary effect in him; her actions lead him to reevaluate his own ethical reality and to respond in kind. To be sure, the capacity to *sustain* his focus on concerns other than his own takes some time. Abberkam's first expression of concern for something or someone outside of himself occurs when he asks about the ailing "foxdog," Tikuli (20). Not only does this simple but targeted question begin to humanize him, both for Yoss and for the reader, it also initiates a process by which Abberkam extends himself beyond his own needs. Nevertheless, the distance between this

relatively passive concern for Tikuli and the eventual rescue of Gubu
remains considerable, as Abberkam gives Yoss repeated reason to doubt
his sincerity. As Abberkam describes his childhood, for instance, Yoss
is uncertain of his honesty. She believes that the tale "has become his
stock answer, his standard myth" (22). She also resents his equation of
himself with the Lord Kamye ("What an ego!") (24). Ultimately, though,
she realizes that who or what she believed Abberkam to be was based
on a great deal of conflicting information. Indeed, she comes to see him
as a complex amalgam of influences:

> So who was he, this man? this big fellow? this sick old man, this
> little boy down in the mines in the dark, this bully, thief, and liar
> who thought he could speak for the Lord? (24)

In time, she realizes that, even though he sometimes remains self-
absorbed, gradually he becomes more aware of her:

> The chief was slow to get his strength back. Often he was sullen,
> dour, the uncouth man *she had first thought him*, sunk in a stupor
> of self-centered shame and rage. Other days he was ready to talk;
> even to listen, sometimes. (26-27, emphasis added)

This observation indicates a progressive change in Yoss's perception
of Abberkam. What "she had first thought him" has given way to more
nuanced impressions, as he has shown other aspects of his personality—
including some that are less "self-centered," such as listening.

It is Abberkam's recognition of her suffering, or her deep sense of grief
as though for one who has died, that signals a change in the balance of
their relationship. Abberkam asks her about Safnan's leaving, "Were
you willing for them to go?"

> "It was their choice."
> "Not yours."
> "I don't live their lives."
> "But you grieve," he said.
> The silence between them was heavy. (28)

Here the narrator has withdrawn from the internal perspective, to follow
the more extended exchange between them. As we witness this dialogue,
Abberkam's "But you grieve" cuts through Yoss's rationalization, "I
don't live their lives." Abberkam senses that which we as readers already
have come to understand about Yoss's feelings regarding the departure

of her daughter and grandchildren. In a certain sense, while Abberkam's own reputation serves as an impediment to Yoss trusting and feeling safe with him, the incisiveness of his observations makes her both resent and, ultimately, recognize the extent to which he is *paying attention* to her. Abberkam thus draws on his own sense of loss, of the grief he feels for the loss of the ideal for which he once lived, to identify Yoss's pain as akin to his own.

Such moments of identification between the characters occasionally are frustrated by Yoss's sense that Abberkam is trying to manipulate her emotionally. At one point, we learn that "She would not let him use her, play on her, have power over her" (29). This fear seems warranted by his subsequent attempt at flirtation, after which Yoss scolds herself for being a "Stupid, stupid, old, old woman" (32).

Abberkam's flirtation forms a distinct contrast, however, with his selflessness during and after the fire at Yoss's house. In that instance, he immediately realizes what concerns her, as Yoss imagines Gubu "Locked in: the bright, desperate eyes: the little voice crying—" (37). Indeed, while it soon becomes apparent that Abberkam's first concern was for Yoss's safety, he nevertheless demonstrates that something far deeper than flirtation lies at the heart of his connection to Yoss:

> "Oh my Lord, my sweet Lord, I thought you were in there. I thought you were in there. I thought you were in the house.... There was so much smoke, I couldn't tell if you were there. I went in, the little animal was hiding in a corner—I thought how you cried when the other one died...." (38)

Abberkam's concern for Yoss, as well as his recognition that Yoss's pets are significant companions in her life, marks an important shift in our understanding of the depth of his sympathy for her—a sympathy that, in fact, has motivated him to risk his own life on her behalf. In that moment of calming and comforting her, he becomes the caregiver, the "one-caring," and she learns to be the "cared-for." This important reversal allows Yoss to revise her impressions of him, and for Abberkam to begin to rehabilitate himself.

5. The Restoration of Self: Sympathetic Caring Comes Full-Circle

In much the same way that Abberkam's act of caring helps him to rebuild his own self-worth, Yoss's act of caring contains the seeds of her own restoration, the means which let her regain a sense of herself and begin to overcome the feeling of loss that originally drove her to live on the marshlands. As the epigraph at the beginning of this essay indicates, Noddings views the interaction of "one-caring" and "cared-for" as "born of the fundamental recognition of relatedness; that which connects me naturally to the other, reconnects me through the other to myself. As I care for others and am cared for by them, I become able to care for myself" (49). I will now briefly examine the dynamics that lead to Yoss's "reconnection through the other to herself."

Abberkam repeatedly gives Yoss reason to feel uncertain about his intentions or his commitment to her. Yet, when she sees that he has been injured while trying to rescue Gubu from the fire, she overcomes this feeling of doubt, symbolically completing the cycle of caring and being cared for by taking "his hands in hers." (42) One might say that the two experience a simultaneous recognition: Even as Yoss attempts to comfort him, it is her recognition of his ability to comfort *her*, to sympathize, to care for her as she has cared for him, that enables him finally to come to terms with his own betrayal of his ideals: "I betrayed my cause, I lied and stole in its name, because I could not admit I had lost faith in it" (45). He realizes, moreover, the role that she has played in this recognition: "But you give me this chance even now, this beautiful chance, to me, to hold you, hold you fast" (45). Given this "chance," he promises to "do my best" (46), and she agrees to stay with him "a while." This statement not only represents a significant shift in Abberkam's awareness, but the final reversal of the negative first impressions that we received in the early phases of the narrative. Yoss's nodded agreement shows that she, too, recognizes this change, and, as she has served to a considerable extent as our eyes throughout the novella, we are prepared to follow her lead.

Through the character of Yoss, in fact, Le Guin indirectly remedies a self-described shortcoming in the identification process that she feels takes place for readers of *The Left Hand of Darkness*. In the 1976 essay, "Is Gender Necessary?", Le Guin describes the role that male readers have in "completing" her work:

> It seems to be men, more often than women, who thus complete my work for me: I think because men are often more willing to identify as they read with poor, confused, defensive Genly, the Earthman, and therefore to participate in his painful and gradual discovery of love. (146)

Le Guin later came to feel that this access to her novel that men experienced was the product, in part, of the limited "voice" given to women there: she regrets "the only voice of a woman in the book" ("Redux" 146) occurs in but one chapter. "Betrayals" in a sense redresses Le Guin's critique by providing, through Yoss's indirect voice, a compelling portrait of a woman's perspective on the development of a relationship—a perspective that perhaps enables her female readers to "complete her work for her," as well.

Having said this, I do not want to neglect the suggestiveness of the completion by readers that Le Guin describes in that earlier essay. I would like to suggest that Le Guin, without expressly stating it, there describes the experience of feeling sympathy—in this case, on the part of her male readers for the struggles of Genly. And, although Le Guin refers specifically to a phenomenon that she claims has resulted from the "gender experiment" that she conducted in writing that novel, I consider her description of "poor, confused, defensive Genly" and his "painful and gradual discovery of love" to apply equally to Abberkam, who struggles so greatly to overcome his own stubbornness and history in order to discover and express his love for Yoss. Indeed, our exposure to Abberkam's difficult transition from corrupt politician to loving partner induces our sympathy.

Having reached this point, we suddenly are faced with a fundamental question: What do these two characters, seemingly so different, ultimately give to each other? I consider James W. Bittner's notion of "complementarity" to be particularly suggestive. In *Approaches to the Fiction of Ursula K. Le Guin*, Bittner identifies in Le Guin's works what he describes as the "complementary, correlative, or interdependent relationship between what we may perceive as opposites or dualisms, but which in reality are aspects of a whole, or moments in a continuous process" (x-xi). Elsewhere, Bittner connects this complementarity with Le Guin's conception of the traditional Chinese opposition between yin and yang. He cites Le Guin's suggestion (in "Is Gender Necessary?") that, rather than forming "a much healthier, sounder, more promising modality of integration and integrity," yin and yang have been "separated" into "dualistic" notions that "struggle for dominance" (Bittner 22). This sense of yin and yang as dualistic and struggling for dominance is particularly evident when we consider the way in which Abberkam and Yoss often are divided along intellectual or emotional lines. Abberkam adheres to his passionate advocacy for the expulsion of all "aliens" and views the fact that they are all descended from the same genetic source as irrelevant: "What is a 'fact' a million years old?" (Le Guin, "Betrayals" 27). Thus, he tends to dwell on the emotional dimension of the issues that they discuss, while Yoss deals with them matter-of-factly, dispassionately, and even seems to relish the "sense of teasing a bull"

(27) that sometimes characterizes her conversations with Abberkam. As they begin to approach each other, though, a subtle balance between these two sides occurs, a "complementarity" that enables them to draw from both intellectual and emotional resources. Rather than two parts that form a "complete" whole, I would suggest that the "whole" that is formed by Yoss and Abberkam is ever-evolving—"moments in a continuous process," as Bittner suggests. In this formulation, yin and yang stand not as struggling opposites, but, as Elizabeth Cummins evocatively puts it: "Acceptance of dualities as complementarities means ... that there is some truth in each, but there is no complete truth in only one" (82). Clearly, the novella's final scene, in which the two agree to try to live together, implies the continuation of this process by which the two come to discover the "truth" that is formed by their complementarity.

6. Conclusion

In this essay, I have attempted to examine the evolution of the relationship between Yoss and Abberkam in the novella "Betrayals." I have looked at the decisive role that the free indirect access to Yoss's thoughts provides the reader, particularly in terms of the development of the reader's attitudes and feelings toward Abberkam. I also have suggested that one important effect that the narrative exerts on readers takes the form of sympathy; that, as we follow Yoss's progressively more sympathetic attitude toward Abberkam, we likewise come to feel for him and his difficulties. I have also argued that the reader's experience of both characters is guided by the expression of caring that each extends to the other. In this regard, I consider Le Guin's novella "Betrayals" a deep and enduring expression of the dynamics that enable individuals who are divided to feel and care for each other.

Works Cited

1.   Anderson, Sherwood. "Hands." In *Winesburg, Ohio*, ed. by Charles E Modlin and Ray Lewis White. New York: W. W. Norton, 1996.
2.   Bambara, Toni Cade. "The Hammer Man." In *Gorilla, My Love*. London: The Women's Press, 1984.
3.   Bittner, James W. *Approaches to the Fiction of Ursula K. Le Guin*. Ann Arbor: UMI Research Press, 1984.

4. Clark, Candace. *Misery and Company: Sympathy in Everyday Life*. Chicago: University of Chicago Press, 1997.
5. Cummins, Elizabeth. *Understanding Ursula K. Le Guin*. Columbia, SC: University of South Carolina Press, 1993.
6. Davis, Mark H. "Measuring Individual Differences in Empathy: Evidence for a Multidimensional Approach." In *Journal of Personality and Social Psychology*, 44 (1), 113-126, 1983.
7. —. *Empathy: A Social Psychological Approach*. Madison, WI: Westview Press, 1996.
8. Eisenberg, Nancy. "The Development of Empathy-Related Responding." In *Moral Motivation through the Life Span*, ed. by Gustavo Carlo and Carolyn Pope Edwards. 2005.
9. Eisenberg, Nancy and Janet Strayer. "Critical Issues in the Study of Empathy." In *Empathy and Its Development*, ed. by Nancy Eisenberg and Janet Strayer. Cambridge: Cambridge University Press, 1987.
10. Hoffman, Martin. *Empathy and Moral Development: Implications for Caring and Justice*. Cambridge: Cambridge University Press, 2000.
11. Hogan, Patrick Colm. *Cognitive Science, Literature, and the Arts: A Guide for Humanists*. London: Routledge, 2003.
12. Juujärvi, Soile. *The Ethic of Care and Its Development: A Longitudinal Study Among Practical Nursing, Bachelor Degree Social Work and Law Enforcement Students*. Social Psychological Studies 8, University of Helsinki, 2003.
13. Keen, Suzanne. *Empathy and the Novel* Oxford: Oxford University Press, 2007.
14. —. *Narrative Form*. Hampshire, UK: Palgrave Macmillan, 2003.
15. —. "A Theory of Narrative Empathy." *Narrative*, 14 (3), 2006.
16. Kristjánsson, Kristján. "Empathy, sympathy, justice and the child." In *Journal of Moral Education* 33 (3), 291-305, 2004.
17. Le Guin, Ursula K. "Betrayals." In *Four Ways to Forgiveness*. New York: HarperPrism, 1995.
18. —. "Forgiveness Day." In *Four Ways to Forgiveness*. New York: HarperPrism, 1995.
19. —. "Is Gender Necessary?" In *The Language of the Night: Essays on Fantasy and Science Fiction*, ed. by Susan Wood and Ursula K. Le Guin. London: The Women's Press, 1989.

20. —. "Is Gender Necessary? Redux." In *The Language of the Night: Essays on Fantasy and Science Fiction*, ed. by Susan Wood and Ursula K. Le Guin. London: The Women's Press, 1989.

21. Miall, David S. and Don Kuiken. "Foregrounding, Defamiliarization, and Affect Response to Literary Stories." *Poetics*, 22: 389-407, 1994.

22. —. "Shifting Perspectives: Readers' Feelings and Literary Response." In *New Perspectives on Narrative Perspective*, ed. by Willie van Peer and Seymour Chatman. Albany, New York: State University of New York, 2001.

23. Myyry, Liisa. *Components of Morality: A Professional Ethics Perspective on Moral Motivation, Moral Sensitivity, Moral Reasoning and Related Constructs Among University Students.* Helsinki: Helsinki University Press, 2003.

24. Myyry, Liisa and Klaus Helkama. "Socio-Cognitive Conflict, Emotions and Complexity of Thought in Real-Life Morality." *Scandinavian Journal of Psychology* 48: 247-259, 2007.

25. Nussbaum, Martha. *Upheavals of Thought: The Intelligence of Emotions.* Cambridge, UK: Cambridge University Press, 2001.

26. Noddings, Nel. *Caring: A Feminine Approach to Ethics and Moral Education.* Berkeley: University of California Press, 1993.

27. Oakley, Justin. *Morality and the Emotions.* London: Routledge, 1993.

28. Parrinder, Patrick. *Science Fiction: Its Criticism and Teaching.* London: Methuen, 1980.

29. Pettersson, Bo. "The Many Faces of Unreliable Narration: A Cognitive Narratological Reorientation." In *Cognition and Literary Interpretation in Practice*, ed. by Harri Veivo, Bo Pettersson and Merja Polvinen. Helsinki: Helsinki University Press, 2005.

30. Phelan, James. *Experiencing Fiction: Judgements, Progressions, and the Rhetorical Theory of Narrative.* Columbus, OH: Ohio State University Press, 2007.

31. —. "Judgment, Progression, and Ethics in Portrait Narratives: The Case of Alice Munro's 'Prue'." In *Partial Answers: Journal of Literature and the History of Ideas* 4 (2), 2006.

32. —. *Living to Tell about It: A Rhetoric and Ethics of Character Narration.* Ithaca, NY: Cornell University Press, 2005.

33. Rimmon-Kenan, Shlomith. *Narrative Fiction: Contemporary Poetics.* London and New York: Routledge, 1983.

34. Sklar, Howard. *The Art of Sympathy: Forms of Moral and Emotional Persuasion in Fiction.* University of Helsinki doctoral dissertation. Helsinki: Helsinki University Press, forthcoming.

35. —. "Believable Fictions: The Moral Implications of Story-Based Emotions." In *Cognition and Literary Interpretation in Practice.* Harri Veivo, Bo Pettersson and Merja Polvinen, eds. Helsinki: Helsinki University Press, 2005.

36. —. "Narrative Structuring of Sympathetic Response: Theoretical and Empirical Approaches to Toni Cade Bambara's 'The Hammer Man'," submitted.

37. Sternberg, Meir. *Expositional Modes and Temporal Ordering in Fiction.* Baltimore: The Johns Hopkins University Press, 1978.

38. —. "Temporal Ordering, Modes of Expositional Distribution, and Three Models of Rhetorical Control in the Narrative Text: Faulkner, Balzac and Austen." *PTL: A Journal for Descriptive Poetics and Theory of Literature* 1: 310, 1976.

39. Suvin, Darko. "Estrangement and Cognition." In *Metamorphoses of Science Fiction: On the Poetics and History of a Literary Genre.* New Haven, CT: Yale University Press, 1979.

40. Tan, Ed S-H. "Film-induced affect as a witness emotion." *Poetics* 23: 7-32, 1994.

41. Wispé, Lauren. "The Distinction Between Sympathy and Empathy: To Call Forth a Concept, A Word is Needed." *Journal of Personality and Social Psychology,* 50, 2, 314-321, 1986.

Howard Sklar is a doctoral student in the Department of English at the University of Helsinki, Finland. The title of his dissertation is *The Art of Sympathy: Forms of Moral and Emotional Persuasion in Fiction.* He has recently contributed essays on the dynamics of reader sympathy to academic journals and essay collections. He teaches "Fiction, Ethics and the Significance of Reading." In addition, Sklar teaches English in the public schools of Espoo, Finland. He has been a secondary school English teacher, in the United States or in Finland, since 1987.

Feminism, Animals, and Science in Le Guin's Animal Stories

Kasi Jackson

West Virginia University

The experiment is performed, the question is asked, in the mind. [...] One of the essential functions of science fiction, I think, is precisely this kind of question-asking: reversals of a habitual way of thinking, metaphors for what our language has no words for as yet, experiments in imagination. (Le Guin, "Is Gender Necessary? Redux," 9)

In her short story "Schrödinger's Cat," Le Guin plays with Erwin Schrödinger's famous thought experiment in which a cat is placed in a box with a photon emitter, a half-silvered mirror and a gun. There is a 50% chance that the emitted photon will be reflected by the mirror and a 50% that it will pass through the mirror—thus causing the gun to shoot the cat. Since the outcome can only be decided by the opening of the box, while the box is closed the cat is neither dead nor alive. To Le Guin, Schrödinger's own cat "[...] was a parable-cat, a figment-cat, the amusing embodiment of a daring hypothesis" (*Buffalo Gals*, 187). However, Le Guin's cat is "[...] an actual, biographico-historical cat (his name was Laurel, and his visit during the writing of the story is described exactly as [during the time that] it occurred), and so changes the thought-experiment, and its results, profoundly. So it is a story about animal presence—and absence" (187).

Le Guin's narrator also meets Rover—simultaneously a small, annoying dog and a small, annoying human. Rover recreates the thought experiment for the narrator. As the representative of Man, he has difficulty accepting that his perspective will influence the outcome of the experiment. According to James Bittner, Rover "[...] does not want the issue complicated by involving the observer in his system. He wants to keep things restricted to the box and confined within the categorical boxes of his binary thinking. Either the cat will be dead or not dead" (*Approaches*, 80). When Rover and the narrator open the box, "[t]he cat was, of course, not there" (*Buffalo Gals*, 198). Rover asks where the cat is and the narrator counters by asking where the box is. When Rover responds that the box is, "Here," the narrator asks "Where's here?" Rover answers, "Here is now." But the narrator continues to shift perspectives and replies, "We used to think so, but really we could use bigger boxes" (198-9). In the last scene, Rover and the narrator become part of the thought experiment: The roof is lifted off of the house and the narrator identifies the note that has been sounding as "[…] the note A, the one that drove the composer Schumann mad. It is a beautiful, clear tone, much clearer now that the stars are visible. I shall miss the cat. I wonder if he found what it was we lost" (199). Part of what we have lost is the ability to see ourselves in intra-action with the world and to acknowledge how assumptions about that world determine human descriptions of it—feminist, scientific and otherwise.

To reclaim what has been lost, Le Guin encourages us to think about the "habitual ways" human knowledge systems, including scientific and feminist accounts, construct the animal. She complicates animal models in ways consistent with feminist critiques of science and with the animal behavior scientist's goal of understanding and encouraging understanding of/appreciation for/communication with animals. Animal behaviorists, including those who adopt feminist empiricist goals like Marlene Zuk, Patricia Gowaty, and Sarah Blaffer Hrdy, often posit an evolutionary continuity between animals and humans. This animal/human link can then be used to argue for preservation of animals and nature because humans are animals and are, therefore, a part of nature. However, for some feminists this is problematic because animals are objectified and, therefore, the animal/human link leads to the objectification of humans. Some feminists fear that this opens the way for human behaviors, specifically those that contribute to the oppression of women, to be seen as biologically or genetically determined and natural. For example, Anne Fausto-Sterling offers a substantive critique of how use of the term "rape" to describe apparently forced copulations draws false parallels between humans and other animals, thus leading to inaccurate portrayal of both human and animal behavior (*Myths of Gender*, 156-62). One possible strategy is to respond that although these theories might apply correctly to animals, humans are too complex for biologically based explanations of behavior, but this can also become problematic. According to Lynda Birke, "[…] what we have implicitly accepted in feminist work is the notion that animals are little more than their biology; this is what constitutes their animalness" (*Feminism, Animals and Science*, 11). Because links will be made between humans and other animals "[…] if animals are 'mere' biology, puppets of their genes, then there will inevitably be inferences made about the mere biology at the heart of human nature" (11).

This can be, therefore, an area of contention between feminist empiricist animal behavioral ecologists and feminist scholars who study science from social constructivist perspectives. Specifically, Zuk,

Gowaty and Hrdy see science as a method that provides ever more accurate representations of a Nature "out there" separate from human influence. Therefore, they often employ the visual metaphor of science as a lens through which the scientist obtains a view of nature. Gender bias and androcentrism block this clear view. By applying feminist insights, scientific methodology can be improved, thus clarifying the view and getting closer to "reality." Other feminist scholars like Birke or Donna Haraway critique this presupposition of a Nature outside of human culture—they argue that the human activity of science is part of a larger discourse that constrains the production of knowledge. However, according to Karen Barad, both of these positions share a set of assumptions that privilege human activity because "[...] the representationalist belief in the power of words to mirror preexisting phenomena is the metaphysical substrate that supports social constructivist, as well as traditional realist, beliefs" ("Posthumanist Performativity," 802). Realists and social constructivists differ on "[...] whether scientific knowledge represents things in the world as they really are (i.e., 'Nature') or 'objects' that are the product of social activities (i.e., 'Culture'), but both groups subscribe to representationalism" (806).

In this paper, I argue that the fiction of Ursula K. Le Guin offers a potential resolution to the dilemma identified by Barad in which: "Language matters. Discourse matters. Culture matters. There is an important sense in which the only thing that does not seem to matter anymore is matter" (801). Le Guin acknowledges the power of language, discourse, and culture, but in her fictional accounts of and critical essays about animals, matter matters. Le Guin grounds her fiction in an attempt to inhabit the worldview of the animal that is informed by science, and yet critiques the "habitual ways" that scientific accounts sometimes deny animal subjectivity and agency.

The scientific debates that parallel Le Guin's thinking can be tracked first from feminist interventions in science like the feminist empiricist critique of animal behavior science. Feminist empiricists problematize some gendered assumptions, specifically an androcentric bias that neglects female agency. For example, animal behaviorist and phylogenist Deborah McLennan began to study the role of female coloration in the stickleback, a fish species in which many studies had examined the function of male color patterns in courtship. She looked at communication as a process involving mutuality and exchange between male and female. When contextualizing her work, she discussed how previous models assumed communication was a one-way process, between males or from male to female because...

The classical story of stickleback courtship, brightly colored males vying for the attention of cryptic but choosy females, has strong parallels with heraldic competitions in medieval England. During these competitions, burnished knights arrayed in their lady's preferred colors would joust for the love of said lady, while the modestly clad object of the ritualized contest remained in the background. ("Integrating Phylogenetic," 262)

McLennan uses this example to argue that expectations based on human society distorted studies of animal behavior—scientists fitted stickleback fish into paradigms created in human myths and legends. She argues that stickleback courtship is best viewed as a "duet."

In the same way Hrdy critiques Bateman's important work on fruit flies (*Drosophila*). Bateman's paper has been used to ground many of the arguments about sex roles in humans and other animals. His experiment has been "[...] cited fifteen times before and nearly a thousand times after the birth of sociobiology" (Snyder and Gowaty, "Reappraisal," 2457). Bateman found that males had greater variation in number of mates and reproductive success (number of offspring). He argued that this meant males were under more selective pressure than females; males would therefore be more sexually aggressive and competitive for mates—hence the coy female and the ardent male (Bateman, "Intrasexual Selection"). Hrdy asks

When generalizations persist for decades after evidence invalidating them is also known, can there be much doubt that some bias was involved? We were predisposed to imagine males as ardent, females as coy; males as polygynists, females monandrous. How else could the *Drosophila* to primate extrapolation have entered modern evolutionary thinking unchallenged? ("Empathy, Polyandry," 134-5)

Hrdy goes on to wonder why researchers rejected the coy female/ardent male stereotypes. She argues that a gender analysis is crucial to understanding this shift because of "[...] the possibility that the empathy for other females subjectively felt by women researchers may have been instrumental in expanding the scope of sexual selection theory" (120). Or as Gowaty puts it: "Being self-conscious about my politics has helped to make my experiments better than they might otherwise be, because I institute a variety of controls that others might also use, and would no doubt use, if they were more aware of their own biases" ("Sexual Natures," 917).

Gowaty, in particular, rejects the argument that fields such as behavioral ecology and sociobiology are inherently biologically deterministic and therefore antithetical to feminist goals. According to Gowaty (writing with Jonathan Waage), theories derived from these fields complement feminist theories and other explanations and, therefore, provide "[…] just one level of analysis of causation" ("Myths," 609). They argue that "[o]ur views are consonant with the notion that the fault of many, perhaps most human ills, lies not 'in our genes' but in the variable ecological (including social) conditions that individuals land in" (609). They conclude, "[…] without an evolutionary theory inclusive of the interests of women and other females, natural selection models will remain incomplete and inappropriate sources of insight into human behavioral variation" (609). Important is the phrasing "women and other females" indicating that an important role for the feminist scientist is to extend feminist theorizing beyond the boundaries of the human because "[…] the human-animal dichotomy and the genes-environment one fail because they are biologically impossible alternatives" (586). Thus, rather than abandon the desire to understand the evolution of *human* behavior, scientists must instead complicate their view of *animal* behavior, and feminist theories offer a good way to accomplish this.

Though feminist empiricists like Gowaty emphasize the evolved nature of human and non-human behavior, they focus on variation in behavior rather than fixed sex roles. For example, Gowaty's theorizing explores sex role flexibility in response to environmental circumstances such as how much control of their reproductive choices individuals can exercise ("Sexual Dialectics," 369-78 and "Chance," 931). Gowaty, Zuk and Fausto-Sterling are strong critics of evolutionary psychologists because they argue that, "[w]hether for finned fish or legged people, evolutionary models of behavior are almost never as static […]" as suggested by theorizing in evolutionary psychology. In contrast, "[w]hen Darwinian feminists apply their concepts to modern human cultures, a central fact emerges: women and men have choices" ("Evolutionary Psychology," 411-12).

However, writers such as Donna Haraway critique the feminist empiricist approach for not being self-reflective enough to recognize how it is constrained by colonialist, heterosexist, racist, and sexist ideologies. It may, therefore, reproduce those same ideologies, even against the wishes of feminist empiricists themselves. Accordingly, these writers focus their criticism on the practice of science itself and problematize scientific and feminist conceptions of human-animal interactions.

For example, according to Haraway, those who study animals should be careful that they are not merely using animals as a proxy to tell human stories (especially the ones they want to hear). Haraway argues, "[...] people reaffirm many of their beliefs about each other and about what kind of planet the earth can be by telling each other what they think they are seeing as they watch the animals" ("Otherworldly Conversations," 68-9). In *The Companion Species Manifesto*, she writes that treating animals as if they were human is potentially harmful for both humans and for animals (33-9). But she cautions that we can't totally separate humans and animals. We have to look at both as biosocial creations—we have affected the biological evolution of our companion species, but they have also affected our evolution (26-32). Thus, Haraway questions the division between nature and culture and the assignment of animals to nature and humans to culture because "[...] it is a mistake to see the alterations of dogs' bodies and minds as biological and the changes in human bodies and lives, for example in the emergence of herding or agricultural societies, as cultural, and so not about coevolution" (31). Thus, while Haraway cautions scientists to attend to the ideological underpinnings of their studies of animal behavior, at the same time she urges feminist theorists to attend seriously to the non-human, rather than to segregate humans from animals. Like Haraway, Birke posits that "[...] feminism unwittingly relies on evolutionary discontinuity" because "[...] the flexibility implied by social constructionism extends only to human behavior [...] the behavior of nonhuman animals remains largely in the realm of biology, outside the remit of most feminist inquiry" ("Intimate Familiarities," 430).

The aforementioned "evolutionary discontinuity" is in part responsible for some feminist empiricists' reluctance to adopt the critiques of theorists like Haraway. From an empiricist perspective, it may not be readily apparent how to apply insights about the embeddedness of science in larger cultural practices, to the actual experiments, observational work and other data gathering required of the scientist. For example, like Barad, Haraway and Birke, Zuk resists the assignment of humans strictly to culture and animals strictly to nature. However, Haraway, Birke and Barad interrogate the perceived distinction between science and nature with critical attention to how ideology mediates scientific accounts of "nature" and "[d]iscursive practices define what counts as meaningful statements" ("Posthumanist Performativity," 819). In contrast, Zuk argues that feminist methods of gender analysis provide a tool to remove cultural biases that prevent science from getting a clear picture of nature (*Sexual Selections*, 4).

Therefore, Zuk reacts strongly against what she identifies as ecofeminist positions that link scientific methods with "masculine" domination and control of a "feminine" nature. Zuk's concern is that "[t]his aspect of ecofeminism also leads to the suggestion that science itself is bad for women [...]" (36). Zuk is also skeptical of essentialist claims that women are more attuned to nature, and are more likely to pursue peaceful coexistence with nature (a critique which is shared by Haraway and other feminist theorists). Rather than dominating and imposing masculine control over nature, for Zuk, science is the way to understand nature because "[s]cientists are people who pay attention to the natural world, and I do not see how one can truly interact with nature without paying this attention" (44). Zuk's concern is that critiques of science practice will overemphasize culture and humans to the neglect of the actual study of nature; Zuk wants to study animals to learn something about animals, rather than humans, because "[...] what kind of partnership can we have with creatures we know little about, because studying them represents a controlling patriarchy? If we simply rely on feeling a connection with them, but don't know how they breathe or reproduce or find food, we have learned more about ourselves than about them" (44).

This feminist empiricist critique emphasizes an image of scientists "looking at" an external nature obscured by preconceived notions that science, informed by feminist analyses of androcentrism and other gendered biases, helps remove. However, this model does not fully address the complexities of the relationships among feminism, gender and animal behavior research. Specifically, the project at hand is not to reinscribe the divisions among women, nature and science, but rather to elucidate how these kinds of discourses constrain scientific knowledge production. For example, critiquing the argument that a feminist science would be more holistic and, therefore, "better" than masculinist accounts, Haraway cautions that all perspectives are situated and political—feminist ones just as much as androcentric ones. She calls for feminists to examine their own ideologies: "What is the generative structure of oppositional discourse that insists on privileging 'unity' at the expense of painful self-critical analyses of power and violence in one's own politics?" (*Primate Visions*, 257). According to Barad, one way to accomplish this kind of "self critical analysis" is to shift "[...] the focus from questions of correspondence between descriptions and reality (e.g., do they mirror nature or culture?) to matters of practices/doings/actions" (802).

In scientific research on animal behavior a large part of "practices/doings/actions" concerns the avoidance of anthropomorphism, or the assumption that animals share the emotions, perceptions and reactions of humans. Both Haraway and Zuk recognize the difficulties that anthropomorphism poses to the scientist who studies animals. For this reason, Haraway believes that "[...] the apparatus of the animal laboratory can be read as an elaborate defense against boundary transgressions" (*Primate Visions*, 249). Although Zuk recognizes that "[s]cientists may even encourage such empathy, misplaced or not, because it makes the public more likely to support research into the habits of the animals themselves," ultimately, she problematizes such "boundary transgressions" because of "[...] the risk that if we claim our kinship too insistently we will not see what the animals actually do, because we will see only behaviors that reflect our own preconceived ideas" (23).

Ironically, however, the avoidance of anthropomorphism can lead to the objectification of the animal. Eileen Crist, in *Images of Animals* (1999), points out the consequences of that set of assumptions. She argues that the writing styles of Darwin and other early naturalists allowed for animal intentionality but the adoption of a "technical-causal language" by early ethologists inadvertently promoted a mechanomorphic view, in which "animals appear mindless" (203-4). Crist argues that if anthropomorphism, or assuming animals are like humans, is biased, then so is assuming that they are NOT like humans — either assumption, and particularly the kinds of language use it entails, carries a set of biases that will have consequences for models of animal behavior (209-10).

Because some scientists use animals to understand aspects of human behavior, these assumptions also have consequences for the study of humans. Therefore, feminist analyses must not neglect animals. Barbara Noske argues that the unwillingness of feminists and others concerned with social justice to engage with the study of animals has left the development of models of animal behavior solely up to those who employ reductionist models (*Beyond Boundaries*, 114). Yet, ultimately, "[e]quality does not necessarily lie in sharp distinctions between humans and animals" (117). Along these lines, Birke, Bryld, and Lykke posit that Barad's work offers a method by which to encourage boundary crossing between animal studies and feminist theory because "[u]sing concepts of performativity can [...] help us to challenge that separation of non-humans from humans; both human and animal can conjointly be engaged in reconfiguring the world [...]"; however, they caution, "that must be done in ways that allow for animal agency, participation, and performativity — whether they are stag beetles, laboratory rodents, or companions by the feminist fireside" ("Animal Performances," 178).

The collection *Buffalo Gals and other Animal Presences* demonstrates how Le Guin encourages us to think about the "habitual ways" human knowledge systems, including scientific and feminist accounts, construct the animal. One of her central concerns is for human relations with the non-human world, and the gendering thereof. Le Guin posits in the introduction that, "[i]n literature, as in 'real life,' women, children, and animals are the obscure matter upon which Civilization erects itself, phallologically. That they are Other is (*vide* Lacan et al.) the foundation of language, the Father Tongue" (*Buffalo Gals*, 9). Le Guin's interrogation of the gendering of boundaries between nature/culture may upon first glance appear to reinscribe, rather than dissolve, borders. However, I argue that Le Guin employs several border-crossing strategies that recognize "[…] that the environment and humans (both female and male) have evolved an intricate and highly complex web of interactions" (Wayne, *Redefining Moral Education*, 139). Like Barad, Le Guin seeks to avoid the privileging of language over matter shared by social constructivist and representationalist accounts; Le Guin's work requires "[…] that 'nature' be conceived of as more than inert matter that is probed and penetrated; that it have metaphorical status as a speaking, feeling, alive subject" (Legler, "Ecofeminist Literary Criticism," 232). I argue that Le Guin's work in *Buffalo Gals and other Animal Presences* envisions what Barad's agential reality would look like in actual practice.

Le Guin refuses to be content with an easy resolution to moral/ethical divisions—she does not fall into the error Haraway points out, in which reductive science is all bad and holism is all good. Le Guin's self critical reflection encourages the reader first to empathize with the Other, but also to consider the dangers for women of a close association with the animals. In addition, she problematizes the potential for empathy to lead to anthropocentrism and essentialism. Finally, Le Guin offers a way out of this dilemma—drawing on scientific accounts to inform her writing of animals (as Gowaty, Hrdy and Zuk urge) and simultaneously critiquing the objectification science requires (as suggested by Crist as well as Birke, Bryld, and Lykke).

First, to encourage empathy, Le Guin invites her reader to adopt the perspective of the non-human Other. Indeed, in some cases she goes further and tricks the reader into seeing the world through the Other's eyes. In "The Wife's Story," Le Guin uses this technique to play a trick upon her readers, creating the impression that a human wife is telling how her husband transforms into a werewolf, when actually the wife is a wolf, and the husband is a wolf who is becoming human. Le Guin provides clues as to the correct species identification of her characters. Her clues originate from the perspective of the animal, yet the narrator's "voice" sounds human thus inspiring empathy in the reader. For example, when the narrator describes what first attracted her to her husband she mentions his gentle nature. One day she encountered him and "[h]e hadn't got any game at all, not so much as a field mouse, but he wasn't cast down about it" (77). She continues that this is what attracted her to him: "[...] he didn't grouch and whine when things didn't go his way" (77). These descriptions could apply equally to a human or a wolf—especially the descriptors "grouch" and "whine"—thus blurring the human/animal boundary and building sympathy for the species typically on the "bad" side of the species divide in werewolf tales.

Le Guin's experiments with empathy go beyond even the animal/ human divide. Though the collection is entitled *Buffalo Gals and other Animal Presences*, Le Guin describes it as "[...] a sort of Twenty Questions anthology—animal, vegetable, or mineral?" (8). The inclusion of poems and stories about plants, and even rocks, forces a greater confrontation with what it means to be human—or even to be animal—by guiding the reader to think about what humans or animals would look like to the non-animal, the non-motile and even the non-"living" in the conventional sense. Thus, this tactic creates a unity among animal life possible only when animals (including humans) are Others to the non-human. In "Direction of the Road," a tree observes the changes wrought by the human invention of the automobile. The reader sees how humans would look from the tree's view. The tree describes a walking human thusly: "There he'd be, working his arms and legs the way they do [...]" (99). From the perspective of the tree, the tree approaches the man: "[...] I was abreast of him and hung above him, loomed, towered, overshadowed him" (99). In addition, the character provides a tree's perspective on human modifications of natural organisms. The tree describes apple trees (whose "genes have been tampered with" by humans) as "tame," "herd creatures"; finally the tree concludes, "[...] no orchard tree can really form an opinion of its own" (102). Overall, the story provides a comment upon how humanity's alterations upon the natural landscape (agriculture, roads, cars, etc) impact the non-human, but this perspective shift also encourages the human reader to reflect upon the negative impacts of modern, progress-driven life for humans as well—in their hurry to get from place to place humans no longer take the time to notice trees.

Though Le Guin encourages empathy with the non-human Other (both animal and plant) she does this with a critical insight into the dangers that this can pose to women's self-determination, due to the historical linkage between Woman and animal—and the use of this linkage to further the oppression of both women and animals. In "May's Lion," "The White Donkey" and "Horse Camp," Le Guin demonstrates that Woman's unity with animals makes the freedom of both Woman and animal vulnerable to threats from Man. Mike Cadden describes these stories, along with "The Wife's Tale" as dealing with "[...] betrayal across gender, age and species" in ways that "[...] rethink status using anthropomorphism as the metaphor of difference" (*Ursula K. Le Guin Beyond Genre*, 4).

Le Guin describes "The White Donkey" as a "last contact" story—a fantasy in particular because "[...] the creature in question is not an 'alien' or an extraterrestrial, but just the opposite. It is an animal whose habitat is restricted to the human imagination" (167). In the story, a young girl develops a friendship with a unicorn that will end when the girl is married. Crucial to the story is the mystery inherent in the appearance of the creature to the girl. She does not know the animal is a unicorn because the beast "[...] flourishes only within the Western European ecosystem, where a few years ago it experienced quite a population explosion, reproducing itself all over greeting cards, posters, book covers, and other curious ecological niches," but the heroine of the story—Sita—is not a native of a Western European culture (167).

Through the eyes of a child with no reference for a unicorn, Le Guin creates the beauty of the creature anew for those readers who have become jaded by its ubiquitous pop culture appearances. Having no reference for a unicorn, Sita fits it into her own culture—at her first glimpse; she thinks it is a goat. Next, she describes it as "whiter than a Brahminee bull" and then she identifies it as a donkey because of "[...] the neat round rump and the tail like a rope with a tassel [...]" (169). Eventually, she decides it must be a god "[...] because it had a third eye in the middle of its forehead like Shiva. But when it turned she saw that that was not an eye, but a horn—not curved like a cow's or a goat's horns, a straight spike like a deer's [...]" (169). The horn is a phallic symbol; this is significant for Sita's story because she will soon be married to a man who has been watching her take the goats to graze.

Sita does not try to capture or tame the white donkey—indeed she doesn't even ask anyone about it—instead she offers it kerala flowers and simply enjoys its company. Initially, "Sita was a little afraid of it, and thought it might be a little afraid of her [...]" but eventually trust forms between the two and soon "[...] her friend the donkey came out of the forest every day, and accepted her offering, and kept her company" (170). The immediate sentences after this image of peace and trust are a jarring contrast—"'One bullock and one hundred rupees cash,' said Uncle Hira, 'you're crazy if you think we can marry her for less!'" (170). Thus, Cadden says that the uncle "[...] betrays the relationship and mediation between the girl and the mythical beast" (5). It is clear that Sita's life after her marriage will not be idyllic because her prospective husband is "dirty and lazy" (170). In fact, while herding her goats, Sita had "[...] seen him watching her across the road, but had never looked at him. She did not want to look at him" (171). Unicorns are associated with virginity and after her marriage Sita will no longer be virginal, she will also lose the freedom she had as the goatherd, for her younger brother will take over that role. Sita tries to put a brave face on her fate for her friend—she tells the white donkey about her wedding clothes (Nana's red sari and a golden bangle), the henna that will decorate her hands, as well as the sweet rice she will eat. But in the end, she cries when she says goodbye to the donkey and her freedom (171). Thus, "The White Donkey" emphasizes the fragility of the Woman/animal bond, when women and animals live in patriarchal societies.

"May's Lion" also concerns women's ability to determine their own futures and make their own choices. "May's Lion" has two parts: In the first, Le Guin's elderly neighbor May relates a story in which a sick mountain lion comes to her house; after she calls the masculine authorities, they shoot the cat—an outcome which she did not intend. In the second telling, May becomes the woman, Rains End, who sings to the cat as it dies of natural causes. The first section is Le Guin's recounting of what May had related to her when Le Guin was a child. There is some dispute about the proper species identification of the cat—May's nephew remembers it as a bobcat, but May said it was a mountain lion. Though Le Guin concedes that the cat was probably a bobcat, she acknowledges the truth of May's version because "[...] you can't trust a good story-teller not to make the story suit herself, or get the facts to fit the story better" (214).

In "May's Lion" Le Guin further develops some of the juxtapositions that are present in "The White Donkey," particularly how the relationship between Woman and animal offers freedom, but is at the same time potentially dangerous and threatening. Le Guin opens the story with a description of the animals that May had—chickens, cows, a workhorse, a fox terrier, the black cats in the barn. Le Guin devotes some time to figuring out which animals were there, and part of the story, and which were gone by the time the lion came and, finally she decides, that it was just May, Rosie the cow and the cats in the barn. Le Guin doesn't romanticize the lion's visit. She knows the danger that it posed; she notes that May no longer had chickens, so they weren't in the story and "[i]t might have been quite different if they had been" (215), thus implying the potential violence toward other animals of the lion's approach. This juxtaposition of approach and retreat due to threat is treated humorously in the passage where May first sees the lion:

> So she went to the kitchen door, opened it, and looked out. Then
> she shut the kitchen door and went to the kitchen window to

look out, because there was a mountain lion under the fig tree.
(216)

May recounts, "I do believe it come here because it was looking for
help. Or just for company, maybe" (217). So, she gives it water. She
begins to worry about milking the cow and to fret because the lion
has her shut in her house. She literally tries to shoo it off, but it won't
leave. Her neighbor advises her to call the sheriff because the lion might
have rabies and so she does. When May gets to this part of her story,
her voice becomes "dry and quiet" as she recounts what happens after
the two carloads of police arrive: "I guess there was nothing else they
knew how to do. So they shot it" (218). The police say that she must
have been scared; however, May says, "But I wasn't. I didn't want him
shot. But I didn't know what to do for him. And I did need to get to
Rosie" (218).

In the retelling, Le Guin provides Rains End with some strategies to
respect the lion's desire for company in its dying and simultaneously
to defend against the potential danger it posed, non-violently. After
recounting the story that May told, Le Guin wants to "[…] tell it as
fiction, yet without taking it from her: rather to give it back to her if I can
do so" (218). So May becomes Rains End who is currently living in her
summer camp that is shaded by a fig tree planted by her grandmother.
After she hears the lion's yowl: "She looked at him from her house. He
looked at her from his" (220). This passage mirrors May's retreat into
her kitchen, but shifts things so that both lion and woman have a clear
space within which they can comfortably co-exist. Le Guin advises the
reader that the stories are almost the same until this point: "[…] the old
woman; the lion; and, down by the creek, the cow" (220). Rains End
sings to the lion and then begins to worry about her cow—she doesn't
want to leave her house because that could upset the lion and "[…] she
did not want to frighten him or to become frightened of him" (221). She
realizes that he is probably sick, but that he may also carry a message.
She considers asking a neighbor for help as May finally did, but doesn't
because she fears that one of the teenagers who live with the neighbor
will shoot the lion "[…] to boast that he's saved old Rains End from
getting clawed to bits and eaten" (222). Therefore, Rains End is able to
avoid the tragic end that befell May's lion. Rains End realizes that the
lion has come for company while he dies, and, thus, will not harm her;
so, she goes to milk the cow, which is nervous about the lion. Rains End
reassures Rose the cow that she won't let him hurt her but "[s]he did
not say how she planned to stop him" (223). This indicates that here,
as in the story about May, the lion does pose a potential threat to those

for whom Rains End is responsible. Ultimately, Rains End is able to resolve the threat in the way that May wished to—keeping herself safe and fulfilling her responsibilities to her animals, but respecting the lion's death. Rains End sings to the lion as he dies.

Le Guin keeps the basic elements of the story the same—the things that Rains End surmises about the lion are the same interpretations that May came to. In the two tellings the women's motivations and reactions to the lion remain largely the same, but May lacks an appropriate context for action. Cadden argues that Le Guin places an actual gap of a few lines of white space in the text between the two parts—"[…] a gap as significant as that among animal, woman and man in the story"—the subsequent retelling offers a way to close the gap (6). This technique is similar to the discordance that Le Guin evoked in "The White Donkey" by transitioning from a sentence about Sita's friendship with the donkey to her uncle's decision to sell her for "one bullock and one hundred rupees cash". Le Guin concludes:

> It's still your story, Aunt May; it was your lion. He came to you. He brought his death to you, a gift; but the men with the guns won't take gifts, they think they own death already. And so they took from you the honor he did you, and you felt that loss. (225)

Le Guin uses the lion to achieve the healing that Cadden finds in the re-telling because "[i]t is only the lion who crosses between history and dream unchanged" (*Buffalo Gals*, 213). Rains End's resolution to the dilemma posed by the lion is an option that neither May nor Sita could attain in their patriarchal cultures.

In "Horse Camp" (companion piece to "The White Donkey"), instead of gaps or discordant sentences to emphasize the barriers Man creates between women and animals, Le Guin problematizes the links between Woman and animal by blurring the animal/human boundary. In the story, girls attend a summer camp, where they appear to be transformed into horses. Le Guin's writing sometimes indicates that the girls are human, sometimes horse, and on occasion it is unclear which. In the opening of the story, Norah's older sister Sal –who has delighted her younger sister for 3 years with tales from the horse camp—is giving Norah and her friend Ev some last minute advice before they board separate buses to go to camp (172-3). The campers are separated by gender as well as age—the boys board another bus (173); however, Sal asks Norah to tell old Meredy, the horse handler who was a jockey in his teens, hello (173). Norah and Ev ask many worried questions about finding the right cabin. In contrast, "Sal was cool, a tower of ivory" (172) and, after giving advice, she walked "[...] lightfoot and buxom across the black gap to the others of her kind who enclosed her, greeting her [...]" (173). In contrast, "Ev was twitching and nickering [...]" (173). Though the girls are clearly human at this point, the descriptions of Ev and Sal could describe horse behaviors as well. Also, this passage sets up a clear division between the younger campers and the older ones, like Sal, who are becoming sexually mature and "buxom."

Once they arrive at the camp, the description indicates that the cabins are inhabited by girls—iron cots, styling mousse, paperbacks, insect repellent, combs, flashlights, T-shirts (174). Though the Counselors are described by hair color in a way that could also refer to horses' coats—"Red Ginger, blonde Kimmy and beautiful black Sue"—their skill with the actual horses is indicated for "[t]he Counselors know what it is to be known. [...] they know the vices of Pal and how to keep Trigger from putting her head down and drinking for ten minutes from every creek" (174). The counselors also convey disdain for boys: "'Who needs 'em'" says Sue, yawning" (174)—except for Meredy, who provides instruction in horsemanship (175-6). It is under the tutelage of Meredy, that the horse/girl boundary blurs. Meredy slaps Philly on the hip to get her up and moving and "[s]tep by step, watching, Norah went with her. Inside her body there was still a deep trembling. As she passed him, the handler just nodded. 'You're all right,' he meant. She was all right" (175). In this passage, the description of Norah could apply equally to a skittish, young filly looking to Meredy for reassurance—it could also imply that Norah has a crush on Meredy—one that was perhaps shared by her sister Sal. Later, Norah "[...] leans her head against Ev's firm and silken side" while "Sue comes striding by, winks wordlessly, beautiful as a burning coal, lazy and purposeful, bound for the shade of the willows" (176)—both of these passages would seem more apt for horses than girls.

As in "The White Donkey" the advent of sexuality and, specifically, sexual relations with men, marks a change in the Woman/animal relationship—but in "Horse Camp," the sexually mature campers retain their horse characteristics, though they seem to fall under the control of boys. In the closing passages, the campers Ev and Norah see Norah's sister Sal being ridden by a young man—"One hand was on his thigh, the other on the reins, guiding her" (177). Norah pursues calling "No, No," but they are unable to get Sal's attention and she and her companions enter the forest. Norah and Ev return to the horse camp and freedom, but where is Sal going? Sal has already been described as being too old to return as a camper next year—she is crossing the child/woman divide to puberty and sex. Le Guin's choice to leave Sal in horse form at the end indicates that the link between woman and animal remains. However, the implication that the boy is controlling Sal indicates that this link does not signify Sal's own freedom, but a more ambiguous position. In fact, Le Guin wrote in her introduction to the story that "Horse Camp" bothers some because "[...] one can hear in it a yell of freedom and a scream from the trap in the same voice at the same time" (168). Or as Cadden puts it, the story demonstrates what awaits both girls and horses in a world where "[...] she and the horse are both ridden" (5).

In contrast to the ambivalence of "Horse Camp," in "She Unnames Them," identification with animals becomes "[...] not an act of self-sacrifice but of empowerment" (Scholtmeijer, "The Power of Otherness," 233). In this story, Eve and the animals give their names back to Adam so that "[...] animal indifference to language shows a woman the way out of the stories culture tells about women and animal" (255). Le Guin resists the need to take sides; according to her, "She Unnames Them" "[...] states (equivocally, of course) whose side (so long as sides must be taken) I am on [...]," (229). As part of this equivocation, Le Guin draws a distinction between personal names and "generic appellations." Dogs and some birds hesitate at parting with their personal names, but they agree as soon as they realize that "the issue was precisely one of individual choice" and those who wanted to continue to use personal names could do so (234). And finally, Eve does not surrender her own name without anxiety, nor does she leave Adam without regret: when he does not react (because he's not really listening) she "put some things away and fiddled around a little" hoping that he would notice, but he does not (236). Finally, Eve leaves "[w]ith them, you know" but she recognizes that surrendering names will have as many implications as being assigned them by someone else for...

> I could not chatter away as I used to, taking it all for granted. My words now must be as slow, as new, as single, as tentative as the steps I took going down the path away from the house, between the dark-branched, tall dancers motionless against the winter shining. (236)

Whereas "She Unnames Them" provides a whimsical resolution to Othering, Le Guin's "Vaster than Empires and More Slow" foregrounds the issue of whether empathy always facilitates communication and understanding of the Other, or whether it can sometimes be an impediment. In this work, a group of dysfunctional scientists investigates what they initially perceive as an uninhabited world. Eventually, they realize that the planet is composed of one singular plant mind, which reacts with fear to the intrusion of humans—a fear that is detected by the empathic crewmember Osden. This novella is about the Other and how we react to the Other. It's also about perspective—who the Other is depends on whose perspective is being taken—Osden is disliked by the rest of the crew, the plant mind is Other to the landing party, whereas the landing party provides the plant mind's first experience with the Other. For most of the story, the reader sees Osden as the rest of the mission team sees him—unpleasant: if he's an empath, why doesn't he feel compassion, why doesn't he treat people better? It's not until the end (141) that the reader gets Osden's perspective—he is trapped by the feelings of the Others (to him) in an endless feedback loop— he mirrors their dislike, which triggers more dislike. The point is that we project onto the Other all of the things we don't want to admit about ourselves. The clearest example of this is when Osden is attacked by a crewmate, but the crew wants to blame the plants (129-33). Once discovered, the attacker rationalizes his action as self-defense against the threat posed by Osden (139). Osden resolves the situation by disappearing into the forest to merge with the plant mind: "He had learned the love of the Other, and thereby had been given his whole self. —But this is not in the vocabulary of reason" (154). Richard Ehrlich interprets the panic experienced by both the plant mind and the landing party and Osden's final sacrifice in terms of the Greek god Pan who represents the dissolution of boundaries. Therefore "[p]art of *pan*ic is the loss of the boundary between human passion and reason [...]" arising from "[...]the fear of loss of self, the ultimate dissolution of boundaries, when we stand in a forest or approach the ocean or any other vastness that reminds us that the price of our individuality is triviality" ("Coda").

As exemplified above, working through the difficulties that empathy presents is the second way that Le Guin's border crossings reflect feminist critiques in and of science. Empathy, according to feminist empiricist accounts such as the one given by Hrdy, provided the impetus for female researchers to attend to the lives of female animals and to revise androcentric theories about animal behavior. However, empathy is a problematic concept for science due to the potential for anthropomorphistic bias; it is also problematic for feminism due to the potential for essentialism. Le Guin's resolution shows how one can empathize without idolizing or idealizing; her approach meets the empiricists' desire to study animals to understand animals. Yet, while she acknowledges that science is one of the primary avenues to construct the human/animal relationship, Le Guin recognizes how scientific accounts can be rooted in ideology. Le Guin's descriptions of animal nature, which employ both empathetic renderings and scientific observation, attend to Barad's "practices/doings/actions" and answer Barad's call to attend to "[…] the nature of material-discursive practices, such as those very practices through which different distinctions get drawn, including those between the 'social' and the 'scientific'" (816). Le Guin employs various methods in this process, including some that echo scientific approaches.

First, Le Guin employs keen "scientific" observation. In the poem "What is Going on in the Oaks Around the Barn" in which "The Acorn Woodpeckers/are constructing an Implacable/Pecking Machine to attack oaks/and whack holes to stack acorns in" (158), Le Guin draws upon her own detailed observations of the woodpeckers, as well as some of their natural history. In her introduction to the poem, she describes them as "[…] still common in Northern California, splendidly marked, with a red cap, and a white circle round the eye giving them a clown's mad stare" (157). She describes their breeding system, in which kin groups work together to raise their offspring (157). Yet she moves easily between scientific detachment and fancy — including both the Latin name of the species (*Melanerpes formicivorus*) and the name used by the Kesh people in her novel *Always Coming Home* (boso). And she provides a whimsical description of their vocalizations that include "[…] the loud yacka-yacka call, and all kinds of mutters, whirs, purrs, comments, criticisms, and gossip […]" (157). Though Le Guin provides information from scientific accounts in her introduction to the poem, she also dryly comments upon the limits of science: "Why they make holes and drop acorns into them when they can't get the acorns back out of the holes is still a question (to ornithologists — not to acorn woodpeckers)" (157).

The novella "Buffalo Gals, Won't You Come Out Tonight" is an excellent example of the delicate balance that Le Guin manages between observations of animal behavior that foreground the non-human, and a careful anthropomorphism that draws the reader into identification with the non-human characters. In the novella, an injured child, Myra, develops a relationship with the legendary Coyote figure and other First People, who have both human and non-human aspects. Karla Armbruster commends Le Guin because while she eliminates "[…] the boundary that excludes the non-human from discourse" (109), her characterizations resist essentialized stereotypes about women and nature — Myra's female gender does not enable a special bond with the First People and though Coyote cares for Myra, she is irresponsible rather than nurturing ("Buffalo Gals, Won't You," 108).

The child protagonist's loss of vision in one eye and the new eye created for her by Jay show that in Le Guin's perspective, humans must change how we look at the world—specifically by learning to see animals clearly. Though Armbruster argues that Myra learns to "[…] step beyond her culturally constructed human perception and, at least temporarily, perceive as the non-human" (112), Cadden argues that this mediation is imperfect because "[…] it is difficult for Myra to see herself from the perspective of the other, and difficult for her to see the animals through her one eye" and her new eye only produces an "unsatisfactory synthesis" (9). Le Guin uses Myra's imperfect border crossing to emphasize the instability of the animal/human boundary—Coyote, Jay and the rest of the First People move back and forth between anthropomorphized (with animal attitudes) and purely animal forms. When Jay does the dance to fix the child's eye his human description matches the animal persona of a blue jay: "A man in new jeans, with a bright blue velveteen vest over a clean, faded blue workshirt, came forward to meet them, very handsome, tense and important. 'All right, Gal!' he said in a harsh, loud voice […]" (28). The other First People have similar descriptions including Young Owl who is "broad and tall, with powerful hands, a big head, a short neck […]. When he blinked, it was like the passing of a hand before a candleflame" (25) and Doe, who has "[…] a severely elegant walk, small steps, like a woman in high heels, quick, precise, very light" (33). Doe, Jay, and Young Owl are fanciful anthropomorphic renderings of animals, yet their characters are grounded in details that reflect the movement patterns of real deer, blue jays, and owls. Significantly, Le Guin does not shy away from the less appealing (to human sensibilities) aspects of animal behavior. In one scene, Le Guin's description of Coyote flips between a woman cooking at a fire and a coyote eating a dead crow (21). The act is disgusting from a human perspective but scavenging provides a legitimate food source for coyotes.

Thus, Le Guin's distinctive application of anthropomorphism presents the animal in a form with which the human reader can empathize and yet retains the essential difference inherent in the animal's nature, rather than recasting it as simply human. Cadden describes Le Guin's selection of animals as "purposeful," and he posits that Le Guin's work visualizes a continuum between animal and human with various points where the two can meet (2). Scholtmeijer commends Le Guin's talking animal stories, because instead of showing "[…] human aggression toward the animal's natural being" by replacing the Otherness of the animal with human traits, in Le Guin's work "[…] animal speech is used to communicate, rather than erase, animal otherness" (242). For example, in "She Unnames Them" the descriptions of how the animals rid themselves of their names evoke the nature of the animals themselves—by referring to their habitats, their behavioral traits, their physical features, or their vocalizations. Therefore, "[t]he insects parted with their names in vast clouds and swarms of ephemeral syllables buzzing and stinging and humming and flitting and crawling and tunneling away" and the fish's names "[...] dispersed from them in silence throughout the oceans like faint, dark blurs of cuttlefish ink, and drifted off on the currents without a trace" (235).

In the preceding passages from "She Unnames Them," as with the acorn woodpeckers, Le Guin's vision blends scientific observation and poetical renderings and she draws upon the best aspects of both to create a vision of animals that is truly unique. To accomplish this, she uses scientific and feminist theorizing to complement each other. First, she realizes that science can inform feminism's treatment of the animal Other by encouraging appreciation of the connections between animal and human and of the differences and variation among animals. For example, Le Guin appreciates all animals regardless of whether humans "naturally" empathize with or appreciate them:

> We find the bowerbird's designs exquisite, the perfume of the rose and the dance of the heron wonderful; but what about such sexual attractors as the chimp's swollen anus, the billy goat's stink, the slime trail a slug leaves for another slug to find so that the two slugs can couple, dangling from a slime thread, on a rainy night? ("Collectors," 174)

Le Guin's descriptions (even of unappealing behaviors) resist objectification. In this, she considers Darwin an ally because "[i]t is like him to say that the bowerbird makes its elegant passage 'for playing in'—thus leaving the bowerbird room to play, to enjoy his architecture and his treasures and his dance in his own mysterious fashion" (174). Her interpretation of behavior acknowledges significance and meaning, in addition to function. Birds sing to attract mates, but "[t]he functional message becomes complicated with a lot of 'useless noise' because the pleasure of it—the beauty of it, as we say—is the noise: the trouble taken, the elaboration and repetition, the play" (177).

Critically, Le Guin has the self-awareness to address her own limitations—particularly in the question of how to render animal subjectivity. Acknowledging the tension between objectifying and anthropomorphizing animals, she worries "[...] how is the experimenter to avoid anthropomorphizing, carrying the analogy too far?" ("Silent Partners," 292). Le Guin's poem "For Leonard, Darko and Burton Watson" locates this tension in the authorship of the piece. The author describes both her actions (reading) and the cat's ("waves his tail, suns his belly") and at the end asks: "Whose poem is this?" (*Buffalo Gals*, 184). The author is writing a poem about the cat, but the cat controls the action, so who is actually writing the poem? Therefore, though she appreciates science and is sensitive to the scientist's desire to avoid anthropomorphism, Le Guin concludes that refusing to accept animals as subjects is the greater danger because "[t]he attitude of the human supremacist is expressed in a vocabulary very close to that of the male supremacist, and both positions probably rise from a terror of losing control of 'nature' defined as an object of human exploitation" ("Silent Partners," 295). Overall, Le Guin wants to cross, rather than reinscribe boundaries, but to do so in a way that recognizes animal difference from humans while simultaneously acknowledging animal subjectivity. In her view, a strict adherence to avoiding anthropomorphism is a failed attempt to do so because it reduces the animal to an object. Therefore, Le Guin utilizes feminist theorizing to question scientific accounts of the animal/human boundary by exploring what it means to produce knowledge and who can do this.

For example, the stories "Mazes" and "The Author of the Acacia Seeds" describe scientific experiments in which the experimenter's acceptance of or resistance to animal subjectivity determines the experiment's outcome. "Mazes" shows how refusal to acknowledge animal subjectivity limits the ability of the experimenter to communicate with the animal, thus predetermining the outcome of the experiment—in this case tragically. The scientist (identified as the "alien" by the narrator, who is the subject of the experiment) keeps placing the narrator in a maze, a form with great significance in the narrator's culture. The narrator assumes that this is an effort to communicate, and interprets the scientist's lack of response as deliberate cruelty. The narrator dances the "Eighth Maluvian" within the maze (72). The beautiful description demonstrates the narrator's capacity for creativity and appreciation for beauty—higher functions that are supposed to define humanity by excluding animals. The alien responds by replacing the narrator in the shortest, simplest maze—"the maze for little children who have not yet learned how to talk" (72-73). The scientist assumes the animal's perceptions are impoverished—that very assumption limits what can be learned about the animal and, in fact, precludes the kind of working partnership and trust that communication requires.

The final example provides a positive view of the possibilities when the experimenter is open to redefining science. With "The Author of the Acacia Seeds" Le Guin makes the linkage even more explicit—the story demonstrates how assumptions affect what is actually defined as science—or as art, for that matter. According to Le Guin, the story

"[...] grew in part out of arguments over the experiments in language acquisition by great apes (in which, of course, if the ape is not approached as a grammatical subject, failure of the experiment is guaranteed)" (188). The story is a series of reports written in the field of therolinguistics — the study of the language of animals, plants, and perhaps "even rocks, someday." The reports ask what is language, what is communication, what is art, and what properties does a being have to possess to make language or art or to communicate. Each report identifies assumptions that have prevented advances in therolinguistics. For example, the scientists forgot penguins were birds and they tried to use Dolphin in order to understand them (204). Though they will never be able to fully understand the language of the Adelie because it is a performance by multiple beings (205-6), the author is more hopeful about study of the "individualist" emperors (207). Notably, the physical actions of these animals are what create the language, described as poetry (207). When thinking about animal communication, scientists and others who study and work with animals must think more broadly than human-type communications; they have to observe animals' actions and their very being as well.

The final section questions the assumption that the purpose of art must be to communicate and that the capacity for communication is limited to kinetic beings — which would mean that plants are incapable. The author rejects that and says that therolinguists simply haven't learned what to look for or how to interpret plants (208-10). The report concludes with the hope to eventually learn

> [...] the still less communicative, still more passive, wholly atemporal, cold, volcanic poetry of the rocks: each one a word spoken, how long ago, by the earth itself, in the immense solitude, the immenser community, of space. (210)

The authors in the pieces show a willingness to acknowledge the limits of their research and to conceive that there may be alternate ways of thinking that make new results possible. They acknowledge that to comprehend the world "[...] we must re-think the very elements of our science, and learn a whole new set of techniques" (209). Thus, Le Guin's therolinguists are on the way to regaining what the narrator of "Schrödinger's Cat" laments that "we have lost" — which can be expressed in Barad's words as follows:

> We do not obtain knowledge by standing outside of the world; we know because "we" are of the world. [...] *Onto-epistem-*

ology—the study of practices of knowing in being—is probably a better way to think about the kind of understandings that are needed to come to terms with how specific intra-actions matter. (829)

In order to gain what has been lost—that study of "knowing in being"—Le Guin envisions the intra-actions and relationships between the biological and the social, the human and the non-human, words and matter. She attends to the effect of the narrator's (or scientist's) subject position on his or her organization of data and experience of the Other. Her essays and stories about animals urge those studying animal behavior to think carefully about how their view of animal subjectivity affects the outcomes of their research. She reminds us that, "[…] the real presence of an animal in a laboratory—that is, an animal perceived by the experimenting scientist [...] as a subject in the philosophical/grammatical sense of a sentient existence of the same order as the scientist's [...] would profoundly change the nature, and probably the results, of the experiments" (157).

Works Cited

1. Armbruster, Karla. ""Buffalo Gals, Won't You Come Out To-night": A Call for Boundary-Crossing in Ecofeminist Literary Criticism." In *Ecofeminist Literary Criticism: Theory, Interpretation, Pedagogy*, ed. by Greta Gaard and Patrick D. Murphy. Urbana and Chicago: University of Illinois P, 1998. 97-122.
2. Barad, Karen. "Posthumanist Performativity: Toward an Understanding of How Matter Comes to Matter." *Signs: Journal of Women in Culture and Society* 28(3) (2003): 801-31.
3. Bateman, A. J. "Intra-sexual Selection in Drosophila." *Heredity* 2 (1948): 349- 68.
4. Birke, Lynda. *Feminism, Animals and Science: The Naming of the Shrew*. Bristol, PA: Open University Press, 1994.
5. —. "Intimate Familiarities? Feminism and Human-Animal Studies." *Society and Animals* 10(4) (2002): 429-36.
6. Birke, Lynda, Mette Bryld, and Nina Lykke. "Animal Performances: An Exploration of Intersections between Feminist Science Studies and Studies of Human/Animal Relationships." *Feminist Theory* 5(2) (2004): 167-83.
7. Bittner, James W. *Approaches to the Fiction of Ursula K. Le Guin*. Ann Arbor, MI: UMI Research Press, 1984.

8. Cadden, Mike. *Ursula K. Le Guin Beyond Genre: Fiction for Children and Adults*. New York: Routledge, 2005.

9. Crist, Eileen. *Images of Animals: Anthropomorphism and Animal Mind*. Philadelphia: Temple UP, 1999.

10. Ehrlich, Richard D. "Coda: Buffalo Gals and other Animal Presences." *Coyote's Song: The Teaching Stories of Ursula K. Le Guin*. Science Fiction Research Association. http://www.sfra. org/: accessed 9/1/07.

11. Fausto-Sterling, Anne. *Myths of Gender: Biological Theories about Women and Men*, Revised Edition. New York: Harper Collins Publishers, Inc., 1992.

12. Fausto-Sterling, Anne, Patricia Adair Gowaty, and Marlene Zuk. "Evolutionary Psychology and Darwinian Feminism." *Feminist Studies* 23(2) (1997): 403-17.

13. Gowaty, Patricia Adair. "Sexual Dialectics, Sexual Selection, and Variation in Reproductive Behavior." In *Feminism and Evolutionary Biology: Boundaries, Intersections and Frontiers*, ed. by Patricia Adair Gowaty. New York: Chapman and Hall, 1997. 351-84.

14. —. "Sexual Natures: How Feminism Changed Evolutionary Biology." *Signs: Journal of Women in Culture and Society* 28(3) (2003): 901-21.

15. Gowaty, Patricia Adair and Stephen P. Hubble. "Chance, Time Allocation, and The Evolution of Adaptively Flexible Sex Role Behavior." *Integrative and Comparative Biology* 45 (2005): 931-44.

16. Haraway, Donna. *Primate Visions: Gender, Race, and Nature in the World of Modern Science*. New York: Routledge, 1989.

17. —. "Otherworldly Conversations; Terran Topics; Local Terms." *Science As Culture* 3(1) (1991): 64-98.

18. —. *The Companion Species Manifesto: Dogs, People and Significant Otherness*. Chicago: Prickly Paradigm Press, LLC, 2003.

19. Hrdy, Sarah Blaffer. "Empathy, Polyandry and the Myth of the Coy Female." In *Feminist Approaches to Science*, ed. by Ruth Bleier. Elmsford: Pergamon Press, Inc., 1986. 119-46.

20. Legler, Gretchen T. "Ecofeminist Literary Criticism." In *Ecofeminism: Women, Culture, Nature*, ed. by Karen J. Warren. Bloomington: Indiana UP, 1997. 227-38.

21. Le Guin, Ursula K. "'The Author of the Acacia Seeds' and Other Extracts from *The Journal of the Association of Therolinguistics*." In *Buffalo Gals* 200-10.

22. —. *Buffalo Gals and other Animal Presences*. New York: Penguin, 1987.

23. —. "Buffalo Gals, Won't You Come Out Tonight." In *Buffalo Gals* 17-60.

24. —."Collectors, Rhymesters, and Drummers." In *The Wave in the Mind: Talks and Essays on the Writer, the Reader, and the Imagination*. Boston: Shambala Publications, Inc., 2004. 171-84.

25. —. "Direction of the Road." In *Buffalo Gals* 99-108.

26. —. "For Leonard, Darko, and Burton Watson." In *Buffalo Gals* 184.

27. —. "Horse Camp." In *Buffalo Gals* 172-7.

28. —."Is Gender Necessary? Redux." 1976/1987. In *Dancing at the Edge of the World: Thoughts on Words, Women, Places*. New York: Grove Press, 1989. 7-16.

29. —. "May's Lion." In *Buffalo Gals* 214-25.

30. —. "Mazes." In *Buffalo Gals* 69-76.

31. —. "Review of *Silent Partners* by Eugene Linden." 1986. *Dancing at the Edge of the World: Thoughts on Words, Women, Places*. New York: Grove Press, 1989. 291-6.

32. —. "Schrödinger's Cat." In *Buffalo Gals* 188-99.

33. —. "She Unnames Them." In *Buffalo Gals* 233-6.

34. —. "Vaster Than Empires and More Slow." In *Buffalo Gals* 109-154.

35. —. "What is Going on in the Oaks Around the Barn." In *Buffalo Gals* 158-9.

36. —. "The White Donkey." In *Buffalo Gals* 168-71.

37. —. "The Wife's Story." In *Buffalo Gals* 77-83.

38. McLennan, Deborah. "Integrating Phylogenetic and Experimental Analyses: The Evolution of Male and Female Nuptial Coloration in the Stickleback Fishes (Gasterosteidae)." *Systematic Biology* 45(3) (1996): 261-77.

39. Noske, Barbara. *Beyond Boundaries: Humans and Animals*. Montréal, Quebec: Black Rose Books, 1997.

40. Scholtmeijer, Marian. "The Power of Otherness: Animals in Women's Fiction." In *Animals and Women: Feminist Theoretical Explorations*. Durham: Duke UP, 1995.

41. Snyder, Brian F., and Patricia Adair Gowaty. "A Reappraisal of Bateman's Classic Study of Intrasexual Selection." *Evolution* 61(11) (2007): 2457-68.

42. Waage, Jonathan K., and Patricia Adair Gowaty. "Myths of
    Genetic Determinism." In *Feminism and Evolutionary Biology:
    Boundaries, Intersections and Frontiers*, ed. by Patricia Adair
    Gowaty. New York: Chapman and Hall, 1997. 585-613.
43. Wayne, Katherine Ross. *Redefining Moral Education: Life, Le
    Guin and Language*. Bethesda: Austin & Winfield, Publishers,
    1995.
44. Zuk, Marlene. *Sexual Selections: What We Can and Can't Learn
    about Sex from Animals*. Berkeley: University of California P,
    2002.

Kasi Jackson completed a PhD in biology (2003), specializing in animal
behavior and evolutionary biology, and a graduate certificate in women's
studies (2000) at the University of Kentucky in Lexington. She teaches
courses on women and nature, women in movies, feminist theory, and
women and gender in science. In addition to her work on gender and
animal behavior, her scholarly efforts include work on the representation
of female mad scientists in film and the application of feminist science
studies to nanotechnology. In addition, she is involved in various efforts
to enhance science and engineering education by linking science content
to popular culture, as well as societal and ethical issues.

Articulating Ghost Stories: Haunted Humanity in Ursula K. Le Guin's "Newton's Sleep"

Jenny Gal-Or
Bristol, Great Britain

I wish to set aside the Enlightenment figures of... masterful subjectivity, the...legitimate sons with access to...the power to represent... with... rational clarity, the...founders of states, and fathers of families, bombs, and scientific theories—in short, Man as we have come to know and love him.... Instead... [m]y focus is the figure of a broken and suffering humanity, signifying—in ambiguity [and] contradiction...—a possible hope... [in] an unending series of...counterfeit events implicated in the great genocides and holocausts of ancient and modern history.
(Haraway, *Ecce Homo* 48)

From the viewpoint reached through stories of future worlds, we can look back to earth and listen to the echoes reverberating from the past through to the future and back to us in the present, so as to reconfigure, and re-understand, their messages. In Ursula Le Guin's "Newton's Sleep", (1991) the haunting figures "of a broken and suffering humanity" have emerged as ghosts in the midst of the community on Spes—a suspended spacecraft re-homing humans who no longer consider Earth "a viable option" (Le Guin 311)—signalling an urgent need to redress exactly what, or who, is human.

The concept of "simultaneity"—the existence of contradictory alliances, and paradoxical partnerships—like the relationship between the siblings, "Hey Es" (Esther) and "Hey No" (Noah) (Le Guin 329 my emphasis) in "Newton's Sleep"—has always ensured that "SF[1] ...is an especially apt sign under which to conduct an inquiry" (Haraway, *Promises* 70) into embodied contradictions, awkward subjectivities, and (im)possible worlds.

The relationship that exists between SF and Earth, between the cultures of storytelling and science—formed because although "the domains of SF seem the negation of earthly regions... this negation is the real

[1] "[S]cience fiction, speculative futures, science fantasy, speculative fiction" (Haraway, *Promises* 70).

illusion" (106)—is why I'm positioning Spes as the focus world—the place for enquiry into humanity—and why I'm presenting Haraway's theories as a network around it. Her theories constitute the articulating environment within and by which this world is able to exist. In this way they may be reliant upon, and accountable for, each other.

Haraway's theories are particularly needed in this essay in order to connect and communicate with the ghosts haunting Le Guin's text, because it is Haraway who asks: "What kind of topic is the 'human' place in 'nature'... in worlds shaped by techno-science" (*Otherworldly Conversions* 134) and "[w]ho speaks for the earth?" (*Promises* 97); questions which resonate throughout the text of "Newton's Sleep."

The answers, I'm sure, will not shape themselves smoothly either into consciousness, or into narrative. This will not be the gleaming knifelike sweep through space to ensure that what we conventionally understand of "humanity" and of the individual human prevails. The "male utopian communities... reproduc[ing]... the idealization of independence" (Pfaelzer 95) will not be allowed to form themselves unquestioned, because the fantasies of Le Guin, among others, are rallying for "utopian communities forged through [conflicted] dependence" (96). Recalling humanity and an environment within which it can articulate more fairly is a painfully necessary process. So neither will this be a passive encounter with ghosts. It is much more likely to be "a struggle over life and death" (Haraway, *Manifesto* 8).

The world according to I/ke, and his "dead past" (Le Guin 316)

In "Newton's Sleep," Western Mankind stars as I/ke—well-meaning—benignly relying on his own interpretation of what constitutes reason and logic to decide the fate of less privileged worlds. Ike is the "engineering physicist, handpicked... as Spes's chief specialist... [and] leader of the Environmental Design group for the... Spes ship" (Le Guin 315), which was designed to relocate into space specially selected families, in order to save humanity from the dying planet-Earth. Ike is installed as Caretaker for the space-station-world suspended above the weather-wrecked, diseased and poverty-stricken planet-Earth. Spes is a pristine environment—composed of smooth, white surfaces and cutting-edge technology—ordered, rational and promising. Existence is heaven-bound, and the world is this way because Ike designed it. He knows where everything is, because he did all the positioning: "Reason's the compass that brought us through" (313). He knows what everything does, because he oversaw its production: "He knew... all the specifications, all the materials... He had reasoned them. He had planned them" (337). Ike is the controller around which the world Spes and its inhabitants revolve in perfect, complex patterns, never malfunctioning, never colliding....

In the production of Spes "immense resources have been expended to stabilize and materialize nature" (Haraway, *Promises* 64). To shape the construction of the community's own "natural" environment, the boundaries of what is nature on Spes have needed to be heavily drawn and then closed-off, in order to then be "producible." As " [t]hese people are innovators, intellectually courageous" (Le Guin 320) professionals, chosen for Spes because they are genetically and mentally superior, their assured positions of governance over Spes demonstrate how society installs the scientist as "the perfect representative of nature, that is, of the permanently and constitutively speechless objective world" (Haraway, *Promises* 88). Its interpreted speechlessness transports nature smoothly along the productivity conveyor belt: it is now available as potential commodity. On Spes nature is carved out of nothing, traced in the air —not even an artefact, but the simulacra of one—from the sweeping production on a massive scale of virtual "natural" landscapes, down to the minute manipulation of each human genome: "The light in Vermont Quadrant was just the right number of degrees off vertical" (Le Guin 315) and "fortunately" Esther's "defect was developmental, not genetically coded" (312). On Spes, "[n]ature is [indeed] the programme" (Haraway, *Otherworldly Conversions* 138). But what those images depict is not nature, as the residents think, but "the image of commodity production itself" (*Promises* 66).

As "biotechnology is... making commodities out of the least elements of living nature—amino acids and genes" (Young, *Darwin's Metaphor* 247, cited in Haraway, *Otherworldly Conversions* 136), everything around Ike is reducible to improvable components: his world, his community, his daughter: all are his building blocks. And this manufacture includes his own identity and humanness, since "man makes everything, including himself, out of the world that can only be resource and potency to his project and active agency" (Haraway, *Promises* 67).

Then ghosts begin to appear on Spes, revealing themselves to others but not to Ike. Suddenly his world is no longer cooperating: "Noah... telling ghost stories... about white-eyed phantoms... was discouraging" (Le Guin 321). With the complacency of his assured-subject-positioning, Ike has signed the warrant for his own unmaking. He realises, too late, that he's severed his connection to his own construction, and that it is in fact he, and not those who can see the ghosts, who is suffering from "environmental deprivation" (329) Having pulled out layers and disconnected limbs, Ike finds himself teetering on a precarious precipice of his own engineering.

Ike will deny the existence of ghosts because he knows that "[t]he world of 'autonomous' subjects is the world of objects, and this world works by the law of the annihilation of defended selves imploding with their deadly projections" (Haraway, *Otherworldly Conversions* 142). He knows what the ghosts are a projection of: that they are not his reflection. They cause the disintegration of his "defended self" because they provide no affirming mirror-image. This is why, when the first ghost appears, she seems "afraid of being seen" (Le Guin 321).

The ghosts are the ungovernable, and therefore unbelievable, messengers of (white, Western) Man's oppressive subjectivity. They do not confirm Man's subject-positioning, and to make matters worse, there is the possibility that despite Ike's inability to see *them*, "they might be seeing us" (332). By initiating a gaze he cannot return, the ghosts reveal the oppressive marking processes "Man" has been using, and so deconstruct the subjectivity that has been based upon these fraudulent and flawed processes. In other words, Ike's subjectivity cannot exist if ghosts do.

"Newton's Sleep" follows Ike through all his stages of denial and deconstruction, until the point of his eventual surrender, when he is rewarded with the new pair of eyes he was in so much greater need of than his far-sighted (but physically almost-blind) daughter, Esther. His centrality to the world has been irrevocably displaced. Ike is no longer the subject and it is dawning on him, in the "clear light" (338) of the mountains, that he never really was.

It would be dangerous, however, to compare Ike's awakening with any Enlightenment fallacies of rebirth. His subjectivity has been dispersed, but what remains of him is still active: a variant on agency shared by his daughter and the ghost of his dead mother, who "died of RMV-3" (314) back on Earth.

The ghosts have also shown Ike that just as "[n]ature cannot pre-exist its construction" (Haraway, *Promises* 65), so it also cannot *post*-exist its *de*struction: what remains is Man's memory of his construction, which he has attempted on Spes to re-construct, devoid of all the actors that/who were configuring this construction on Earth: a memory which he manifests into a product, projects this onto whatever he can for appropriation of that particular component, and calls it "nature."

Through the destruction of the planet-Earth in "Newton's Sleep," we learn that this is what (white Western) Man has always done: to project his desires, his prescribed requirements, onto a canvas that is dense, diverse, non-static and, most importantly, anything but blank. That the humans on finding themselves in an entirely new space feel immediately secure enough to reassert an assumed authority over their new environment is testament to the apparently limitless human ego, for whom the "act of taking over a territory seemed like a fairly straightforward... technoscientific project" (*Cyborgs* 322).

This presumptuousness is swiftly addressed by the emergence of ghosts, who set about undermining the illusionary control prematurely asserted by the human. This they do by re-imagining the environment and destabilising its context: walking on the world in apparent disregard for its humanly defined boundaries. Moreover, these new actors of an imminently new "natural" environment are, at least in some form, human themselves: effectively mutinying against everything Ike assumes to be "human," these "humans" embody absence: they *are* absences—they *are not*.

Given Ike's explanation of why no people of African origin were permitted entry to Spes, because "there had been no way around the fact that... every single person must be fit, not only genetically, but intellectually" (Le Guin 322), and this had meant that though they "had been wonderful people... [this] wasn't enough" (322), it's little wonder that the ghosts appear predominantly to be African women: "all those people that used to live where that was before the desert, right, Africa?" (324). For "racist/sexist logic... made the very flesh of the black person in the New World indecipherable, doubtful, out of place, confounding—ungrammatical" (Haraway, *Ecce Homo* 53). Traditionally, white Man's identification processes have obliterated "the invisible bodies of people of color who have never counted as able to represent humanity in Western iconography" (*Promises* 81).

Only such frigidly linear thought processes could assume that eradication from the past secures a race's elimination from the future, just because white Man's elite consider themselves to be "future oriented" (Le Guin 320), and assume that the position of authorship, of representation, is a lifelong guarantee. But when the ghosts begin to emerge to others but not to Ike, what he begins to see instead is a disturbingly distorted but more accurate image of his self-hood: ghostly, intangible, and unbelievable—that his authorship, his identity as subject and self, is the apparition, the impossible—his self-assured governance is the ghost. And there is a part of Ike that knows this already: the part that forces him to acknowledge his own embodiments of difference, when anti-Semitism succeeds in infiltrating Spes. As Ike exclaims: "We can keep out every virus, every bacteria... but this—this gets in? How?" (319).

The "how" has to do with the markings of difference, and again, why the ghosts on Spes are mostly manifesting as African women: because "a black woman [was not considered]... a coherent substance... but an oxymoronic singularity who stood for an entire excluded and dangerously promising humanity..." (Haraway, *Ecce Homo* 53). Traditionally these women have been ignored into invisibility and illegitimacy as human subjects: now, *through* this invisibility, they are able to redefine and destabilise not only subjectivity, but also the humanity denied them for so long.

In Vermont-sized[2] mural messages, the unreasoned, (unseasoned!), contrived, galactic-scale egocentricity, and the unsustainable illusion that white Man has manufactured out of thin-air (or thin-space) for himself, is illustrated. From his elevated position, Ike surveys the damage he has caused and the vertiginous distance he has created through murderous severance—through the desire to turn off the monitors that survey the devastation on Earth because it's "a tie, an umbilicus" (Le Guin 315) that he wishes to cut. And then he wonders why, when on the brink of sleep, he feels a sensation of panic and an abstract vacuum gaping open... threatening to consume him in waves of otherness he is responsible for creating, and yet completely unwilling to be held accountable for: a fatal error when at the core of "Newton's Sleep" is a belief in "the necessity of political accountability" (Haraway, *Cyborgs* 336)[3] for all of humankind's erroneous practices.

In deciding that he is a self by whom everything else must be measured and compared for sameness or difference, Ike unleashes on himself a flood of difference bursting all the aesthetically perfect damns he has painstakingly constructed. He has not yet understood that

> [n]ature is not a text to be read in... codes.... It is not the Other who offers origin... and service. Neither mother... nor slave, nature is not matrix, resource, mirror, nor tool for the reproduction of that... ethnocentric, phallogocentric, ...universal being called Man. (*Otherworldly Conversions* 126)

The gradual realisation that he is not central to existence trips him up with virtual rocks. He cannot see them, but he does *feel* "something rough, irregular, painful" (Le Guin 338), as if to directly address Robins's and Levidow's fears that in technological systems of power "[s]eeing was split off from feeling; the visible was separated from the sense of pain and death" (107). Until, eventually, Ike finds himself seeking solace in,

---

[2] "The Roses lived in Vermont... So their unit faced on Vermont Common" (Le Guin 314).

[3] As in the varying and not necessarily conventional ways knowledge can manifest and distribute itself very differently from knowledge-according-to-Man.

and asking for assistance from, the women and others he'd tried with such vigour to erase from the world, and from the future: "Esther, I can't see. Show me how to see!" (Le Guin 338).

With the help of his daughter, son, his wife Susan, and his dead mother, Ike slowly begins to see the world again—to come to terms with the knowledge that "[t]here will be no nature without justice" (Haraway, *Promises* 86). In other words, if justice, if self-definition, alternative agencies, and responsibility for others, are not sought and found, then nature as the human knows it will do as it has in Spes and refuse to *be*. It will refuse Man his categorisations and disrupt all ordering processes, until the world is unrecognisable to the human subject: the world will reorder, layering the landscape with ghostly manifestations of forgotten, faulty f/actors and misshapen activity.

As we descend from the mountain down "the steep, dusty trail" (Le Guin 338) with Esther, Ike and his ghost mother, there is an unspoken understanding that it is

> not a "happy ending" we need, but a non-ending. That's why none of the narratives of masculinist, patriarchal apocalypses will do. The System is not closed; the sacred image of the same is not coming. (Haraway, *Promises* 110)

Here's what *is* (or *isn't*) coming...

"There is nothing there" (Le Guin 331)
Ghosts on Spes, and Embodiments of Absence

> It seems to me that we need a whole kinship system of figurations as critical figures... The cyborg can quickly become banal, and mainstream... [providing] an alibi that makes the technoscientific bourgeois figure comfortable. (Haraway, *Cyborgs* 327)

Ike's plans to operate on Esther's eyes make Spes a world where cyborgs have been appropriated by Man and absorbed into his obsession with bodily perfection. That which Haraway feared might happen to cyborg figurations *has* happened. As a result there must again be a challenge to conventions, and inappropriate/d others must "erupt in powerful new tropes, new figures of speech, [and] new turns of historical possibility" (*Ecce Homo* 47).

So ghosts emerge, not as subjects but as figurations: they are not central, they are positioned on the edge; they are edgy. The ghosts use their "bodies" to rework the living environment; a conversational process of networking the world that pushes all supposedly central subjects, including Ike, to the edge of their subject-positioning; an edge the ghosts themselves inhabit. Perhaps for the first time a figuration is emerging from outside of human classification processes: the name "ghost" describes something which isn't. Man has no category for nothingness, no way to describe it beyond otherness, no way to explain it that doesn't discredit it. Vexingly for Ike, this frees the ghosts to be self-organising. By dodging the processes of "exclusion through naming" (*Manifesto* 13), the ghosts are free to define themselves and set the conditions of their own agencies.

In another figurative sense, the ghosts are a manifestation of our dead selves, now that we are "finished *as* subjects" (*Otherworldly Conversions* 142). "Once the world of subjects and objects is put into question" (144) by objectification-denying actors, what emerges through the deconstruction of man-made systems is a "promising form of life [in which] conversation defies the autonomization of the self, as well as the objectification of the other" (144), because conversation is a communal activity, formed through equality between actors. Thus the form-changing habits of the ghosts make a mockery of the conventional subject's chosen form—the complete and bounded human. They expose Ike's flaws and they do it in the shadows, echoes and rumours of the subject's memory of the bodies that he abandoned broken and, he hoped, left without trace. But these *are* the traces; these are the outlines self-forming and expressing everything that he doesn't want to hear and travelled a million miles into space to escape.

> Dawn Dietrich remarks on how the euphoric praise nearly always associated with virtual systems can act as a... smokescreen, in which an emphasis on the end obscures any clear understanding of the means used to get there. This disparity between rhetoric and reality has the most devastating consequences for women, who are usually structured at the bases of operations (174).

As Ike begins to see, so he also begins to remember those he had forgotten, or dismissed, embedded within the intricate complexities of production that have enabled his privileged position in his technological paradise. He had denied that "the germs... and funguses... the radiation and the rain" (Le Guin 324) in any way constituted his ascent, or could not be made separate from it. The matrix, from which he has attempted to extract himself, though noisy with conversation has, historically, existed unseen and unheard by a subject who is afraid to look down.

Ike doesn't want to look down because the descent, the fall, is a reminder of death—the destruction and decomposition of the body he has striven to polish and perfect. These ghostly, unclassifiable actors slipping between the literal and the figurative, are reminders of the human subject's mortality. They speak of worlds beyond death (still in connection and communication with the living world) and all that is beyond the subject's knowledge and ability to explain. They wrench the subject from his comfort zone, to a place created not by a singular god—not by any god at all—but by the multiple layering of actors conversing in the residue of expansive melted boundaries, drawing the subject down into them, to an infinitely connective world, which to Esther, and to most of Spes's residents—who are prepared to learn "how to coexist with ghosts" (Le Guin 334)—"seems like a good place to inhabit" (Haraway, *Cyborgs* 323).

"[T]he tension of holding incompatible things together... is... a rhetorical strategy and a political method" (*Manifesto* 7). Through this embodied ambiguity with political agency—because they are and are not—and because they are seen and unseen—the ghosts convey the difficulties of classification as a process. Their contradictory embodiment defies consistency and predictability, and so effectively refuses any actor the right to speak on behalf of any entity other than itself. The ghosts themselves cannot speak for abandoned humanity, or for cheated nature. They speak *between* these classifications. As it is for Haraway, "it is the undecidability, the wiliness of other actors, the 'negativity,' that give me confidence in the... *unrepresentability* of social nature" (*Promises* 89).

Ghosts have come to inform Ike and the other humans about the relationality, about these accountable partnerships, between humans and every other actor—not to speak *for* those "integral" partners (85). They take it upon their (un-doing)selves to deny all forms of representation—including that of the context from which they are assumed to have come and are therefore, regardless of relevance or tangibility, associated with. In this blown open world where the subject has no more complete walls behind which to hide, "the simultaneously semiotic and political ambiguity of representation is glaring" (88-89).

The ghosts *are* our memories: although they are most certainly not composed *only* of our consciousness, our consciousness is amongst the elements of their configuration. "Refiguring conversations with those who are not 'us'" (*Otherworldly Conversions* 139) is vital to the project, but so is remembering those who *do* partially, though silently and almost invisibly, make up the "us": forgotten subjects who are now ghosts. They are the ghostly versions of "us" — the abandoned members of "we." "Newton's Sleep" requests that we readdress, with reawakened responsibility, "the arrogant ravages of our technophilic civilization" (*Promises* 66) — all the while remembering our inimitable inability to completely and finally detach ourselves from the members of "us" we feel uncomfortable sharing our humanness with.

At the same time, Le Guin creates an apparently deliberate ambivalence concerning the origin of the memories which conjure the ghosts. That the ghosts seem unaware of the humanly-perceived incongruity of their positioning on a hi-tech space-craft — of the "vine growing by the front door" (Le Guin 335) and "the goldfish… [that] came out of the tap" (333) — may imply that they are manifested as much by the environment's memory of a humanity absent from its configurations, as they are by the humans' memory. In other words, the "nature" of Spes, far from being the carefully crafted and tightly controlled product of Ike and his team, is drawing up an active agency of its own, in the form of memory, to conjure the vital elements — the vitality, perhaps — dismissed by the humans as obsolete — to bolster a deeper living world — a world where death is integral and not escapable, as the humans had hoped when abandoning the dying planet-Earth.

It was women and all others (who are not white Man) who bore "the violent erasures of that history-making move" (Haraway, *Otherworldly Conversions* 140) when the star-ship left the planet and its inhabitants to almost (un)certain death, and removed the hierarchically select few from the earth's poverty and untidiness — from the "chemical marshlands… [and] the fungal plague[s]" (Le Guin 311). Uncountable (and unaccounted for) "erasures" took place in this move that, though seemingly apocalyptic and momentous, were in fact merely exaggerations of destructive measures practiced throughout our non-fictional history against the planet and its inhabitants.

Witnessing the explosion of definitions in "Newton's Sleep" confronts us with the necessity of re-imagining and unlearning our own world. Its "nature" is irrevocably changed and there can be no way back. It is constant nostalgia for the world as it never was that has imprisoned so many within the fraudulent and unrelated categories which were never their home. "Where we need to move is not 'back' to nature, but *elsewhere*" (Haraway, *Promises* 90).

In the same way, Ike has failed to make and fill the world of Spes, and through the gaping holes new voices are erupting with partial definitions of their own — interconnected, empathetic and "insubstantial." These voices are rewriting the future from the past — from outside of life even:

vocalising a perpetually rewritable universe. They have new shapes for an "earthly" existence that breaks down not only the confines of the usual categories—human, natural, technological—but of existence itself—of life and death.

Esther: out of sight and "out of control" (Le Guin 327)

Ike's daughter, Esther, is the first in line for his New World's project of improved existence and enhanced being. Esther is to undergo surgery on her almost-blind eyes. She chooses, under Ike's little-short-of coercive advice: "You'll make the reasonable choice. I have confidence in you, Daughter. Show me that it's justified" (327). Ike implements Esther's improvement—she is implement for Ike's project of all-encompassing governance. Esther is appropriated for Ike's "extraterrestrial man-in-space project… [becoming] a science fictional figure out of a largely male-defined science fiction" (Haraway, cited in Wolmark 231), plied as she is with "electronic implants… [and] sonar headbands for periods of visual nonfunction" (Le Guin 330).

Le Guin is not the first to predict that cyborg figures who/that promised such liberation for deviant actors could, in future tales, be compromised by the conventional subject. Her concerns are shared by John R. R. Christie, who expresses his doubt of the "questionable hope" (174) associated with a figuration

> [p]ossessed of a scrupulous infidelity to origins, dislocated from the organic, the reproductive, and hence the Oedipal… [and intended]… to serve… as resource for an emancipatory, postmodern narratology. (173)

So those wishing to articulate must arrange for whole new un(fore)seen embodiments, utterly re-configured, never encountered nor explained before, if they are to have an effect upon what it means to be human, or to have a body of any kind.

Esther is a seer of such possible agencies and these potentially new ways of being, because her own embodied differences and her imperfect sight grant her a share in "Le Guin's vision of utopian space as dialectical space. The self and others, the self and society, create political space in which the self evolves through relationships rather than quests" (Pfaelzer 98).

Her blurred conventional sight denies Esther the means to operate the processes of othering performed by the traditional subject, and this allows her a clarity of sight, uninfluenced, unaffected, by that subject's usual practices of self-identification. She has never been mirrored—never used an-*other* to reassert, or reassure her of, her subject positioning—and so she is not disturbed by the ghosts' embodied refusal of these processes. Her sight instigates diffraction, not reflection, because what she does see is unstable, inconclusive and with indefinite boundary lines and "[t]hese diffracting rays compose interference patterns, not reflecting images" (Haraway, *Promises* 69).

Esther thus embodies incompletion and imperfection and accepts the articulating activity of others who share her incompletion and imperfection, however differently or alternatively the forms of these identities materialise. As she says herself, ghosts "could be walking in front of me right now and... I'd think it was just somebody that belonged" (Le Guin 325). She understands that "the body is a collective;... an historical artifact constituted by human as well as organic and technological unhuman actors" (Haraway, *Promises* 86) and not an autonomous, single entity, closed off from the world it inhabits, and in complete command of itself and its environment. Indeed, the "perfection of the fully defended, 'victorious' self is a chilling fantasy, linking... space-voyaging man cannibalizing the earth" (100). It is through Ike's narrow ambitions for Esther that she, we as readers, and the other humans on Spes, can see clearly the potential ruthlessness of the human subject's dominance and desires.

Without comparison, but with empathetic connection, and without representation, through refusing Ike's version of subjectivity, through denying a "victorious" self—which Esther does when her operation fails and her eyesight refuses to improve—Esther and the ghosts together utilise the nothingness left to them in order to prevent Ike from realising this fantasy. She recognises that "[a]ctors are entities which... have effects, build worlds in concatenation with other *unlike* actors" (*Promises* 86) and that there is no thread of sameness connecting us, only disjointed connections of difference, and the subject (I/ke) is not in any way an exception to these un-rules.

Her uncooperative eyes have made Esther as slippery a character as a ghost. Her unruly body enables her to sense the speech of other deficiencies. Ike has concluded that neither Esther nor the ghosts are complete humans. But he does not fully realise the freeing extent of the title, "Unrestricted" (Le Guin 312), with which he himself has labelled Esther, and by which she is freed to join "in conversation with Trinh [T] Minh-ha's inappropriate/d other, the personal and collective being to whom history has forbidden the strategic illusion of self-identity" (Haraway, *Promises* 112)—that is, the ghosts—because Esther's sightlessness makes a connection with the ghosts of speechlessness.

So Esther is not a victim. Rather, she is a crucial and active component in a rapidly reconfiguring world. She is the linchpin-with-a-pulse between the conventional humans and the new social partners flooding the world: she is the storyteller—of the failures of the world they left and of the world they're building—and she is an empathetic interpreter in the conversation, fragmentally translating the communal texts, (the texts which she helps to make communal). For example: the "note from Susan... in Esther's sprawling hand" (Le Guin 337), which has been delivered by the ghost of "[t]he little black girl" (337) is intended for Ike to intercept. It informs him that Esther is "going up in the mountains for a while" (337), and so, crucially, requests his active inclusion in the conversation going on between all the other articulating partners.

It is Esther who sparks up these imperative conversations and it is Esther who asks the awkward questions. She also gives Ike hope by acting as a guide out of his personal apocalypse. She is simultaneously the reason he enters the matrix, his mentor in new ways to see there, and his companion out. He enters alone and emerges, as the ghosts have, in mutual and equal connection with any number—with a whole series—of actors and companions.

According to Haraway, "[b]y the late twentieth century, very few cracks, indeed, are allowed to show in the solid cultural complex of WCHP[4] constructionism" (*Otherworldly Conversions* 137). But in "Newton's Sleep" a great many cracks have finally broken through this seemingly impenetrable perfection of the human subject's ego, until an entire chorus of indefinable diversity has flooded the arena. Nature and otherness, so often forced into incongruous and unsought-for mutual association by the white male human subject, have subverted that anything-but-obvious alliance to confront the subject with the consequences of his dismissive and repressive assumptions.

From that point, it's only a matter of time before Ike "stumble[s] violently" (Le Guin 338)—falling, literally and metaphorically, into the environment that has as much hold on him as he has had on it. Only on the mountain where his living daughter sits talking with his dead mother does Ike begin to appreciate the complexity of contextual existence and the extent to which it is multiply configured: the human and the natural world are not severable or independent, and yet they are also not one-and-the-same.

---

[4] White Capitalist Heterosexist Patriarchy

The Beginnings of Conclusions:
"It was a long way, and he was never sure he was not lost" (Le Guin 338)

Self-representing, inappropriate/d others, like the ghosts, or their original embodied subjectivities, call for an upheaval of the roots of current classification and representation. They call for revolutions, where all actors—the altered subject included—inhabit the conversational hooks-like third-spaces[5] where all connectivity and communication will take place, thus rendering ineffective and redundant the previous categories from which each party attempted conversation across impenetrable borders and chasm-like distances, or else not at all: chasms that were never real, only ever virtual—enforced and policed at the subject's insistence. When visionary blindness alters sight and seeing on Spes, distances are bridged and crevices re-connected, the vibrations of which wake Ike at last from his constricting slumber.

Eventually accepting this untidy mass that is the worlds of other subjectivities, with all their tangled threads and circular arguments, is a hard (fragmented, open-ended) journey for a man like Ike, who has seen only the reassuring stretch of smooth, open road with a beaming, godly, light at the end of it. That is until the moment when, just as he is "relaxed, a thrill of terror jolted through him, stiffening every muscle for a moment—the old fear from far, far back, the fear of being helpless, mindless, the fear of 'sleep itself" (323); when he finds himself on that edge of sleep… and about to drop off … into space … which should be the perfect ground upon which to re-imagine and re-understand the mechanics of social cultures. Yet rather than embrace this opportunity, the humans in "Newton's Sleep" embark on a return to Earth—a return through a re-genesis—not of new beginnings, but another Beginning—and a perpetuation of patriarchal order—where Ike is the Creator installed in the godlike position in the sky, overseeing his Earth below, having gained his position through forced Oedipal severance, by the murder of his mother.

However, Ike's mother arrives (not returns) with the others on Spes to figure—and to speak—and to change I/ke into Isaac, by asking; "Isaac, dear, are you awake?" (338). She does this along with, and in place beside, every other actor in the network—and not to figure as the Freudian special case—since that would be to accept a body with meaning only the subject authorised: to confirm, and to conform with, Ike's centrality to the plot and to the world. This "is not a Freudian

[5] For a closer look at bell hooks' analyses of third-space, see: hooks, bell. 'Homeplace: a site of resistance', in *Yearning: Race, Gender, and Cultural Politics.* Boston: South End Press, 1990. 41-49

unconscious. There is a different kind of dreamwork going on here; it is not ethical, it is not edenic, it is not about origin stories in the garden" (Haraway, *Cyborgs* 323). In such dreamwork

> The tools are often stories, retold stories... In retelling origin stories, cyborg authors subvert the central myths of the origin of Western culture. We have all been colonized by those origin myths, with their longing for fulfilment in apocalypse. (*Manifesto* 33)

Colonization by origin myths for the purpose of fulfilment in apocalypse describes perfectly the processes at work by the human subject in "Newton's Sleep," who seeks to establish and ensure its almighty governance through replication of the Origin story, this time without the flaws and the hiccoughs, this time without the Fall of Man, and this time with Man in place of God.

From his elevated position Man in the form of Ike can continue processes terrifyingly similar to those practiced on Earth in hi-tech military combat. Robins and Levidow outline such experiences as being "tele-engaged in the theater of war" (106) where "psychologically invisible" (106) actors are killed while both the directors and audience are distanced by "the computer screen" (106) through which they observe and direct; all the while retaining a "moral dissociation... [because] the targeted 'things' on screen do not seem to implicate... [them] in a moral relationship" (106). Ike has positioned himself in the Overseer's glass-fronted, hi-tech, executive suite from where he has a perfect—because dislocated—view of the detonation of his previous creation. He is free, both physically and morally, to build again, to rewrite history, the present, and the future.

But there are some things he has failed to consider. For one, he is not the only actor to understand that stories are tools. Esther and the ghosts also know that the "boundary is permeable between tool and myth... Indeed, myth and tool mutually constitute each other" (Haraway, *Manifesto* 23). In other words, ghosts and humans alike *are* their own myths: they write themselves into being, tell their stories through their embodied forms of existence, and use these embodiments to shape their tools which write the myths. They also know that storytelling is a communal facility that the subject can neither monopolise nor regulate or silence, and they have only to tell a different story to cast doubt on his, to unravel its meaning, to reveal its agenda. They can turn the story of the Fall of Man into a gentle descent into his no-longer-deniable place amongst, and in the equitable company of, others.

The second crucial consideration Ike missed is that there was no apocalypse. He is mistaken in thinking that he defines apocalypse —that his earthly world will be destroyed according to *his* measures of destruction and that because he can no longer inhabit his earthly world, so no-body or no-thing else can either. In the worlds of "Others," however, moments of apocalypse are neither definite nor all-encompassing. Theirs has always been a position of adaptability, elusion and shape-shifting, for survival in the subject's inhospitable world. The disruptions to the planet have simply triggered the necessity for further transformation. Apocalypse for every-body but Ike is not earth-bound or earth-dependent. All others are not bound by the origin stories of "Man"—the ones he manufactured for his own assurance and installation into hierarchical status—and don't rely upon the central, core pull of one subject-planet for their existence. And now that he is removed from Earth, "Man" finds he was mistaken in thinking he was also the centre of the universe. The moment of Ike's realisation of this is the more authentic apocalypse: the deposing of the conventional subject—he is One no longer. The first, planetary, apocalypse was a false end.... The result, for the subject—for Ike—is the panic and dislocation of vertigo and Goya-like nightmares.[6]

Through fables like "Newton's Sleep" we are, like Ike, "unblinding ourselves from the sun-worshipping stories about the history of science and technology as paradigms of rationalism" (66). If we are to find equality and equal forms of something like agency in present and future worlds we must, by working out the possibilities through re-imagined myths and new fables, "refigure the actors" (66): it may not be "something we were trained in" (Le Guin 334) but it is just something we will "have to learn... to do... as we go along" (334).

From a position of dismantled subjectivity and re-imagined agency in an articulate and interconnected environment of conversational systems without hierarchy,

> [s]cience becomes the myth not of what escapes agency and responsibility in a realm above the fray, but rather of accountability and responsibility for translations...linking the cacophonous visions and visionary voices that characterize the knowledges of the marked bodies of history. (Haraway, *Promises* 69)

The re-emerging world of changed humanness in "Newton's Sleep," where illegitimacy and deviance ensure that there can never be "a true

[6] Esther describes the engraving of "The Sleep of Reason engenders monsters" by Goya (Le Guin 325) in relation to what is happening on Spes.

human community" (Le Guin 320), celebrates embodied-contradictory ways of being, and environments for equal articulation which "suggest a rich topography of combinatorial possibility" (Haraway, *Promises* 110). And death is just one of those possibilities. Death, like the actors who do not fit the categories of nature, human and technology "is just one of the [unclassifiable] 'cacophonous agencies' (66) that must be admitted to the narrative of collective life" (66, cited in Wolmark 245).

I share with Haraway an interest in "the way of conceiving of us all as communication systems, whether we are animate or inanimate, whether we are... human beings or the planet herself... or machines of various kinds" (*Cyborgs* 322): the "horses and the whales and the old women and the sick babies. They're just us, we're them" (Le Guin 336). Every kind of connection and conversation is possible in this newly articulate world, now that there is a shared understanding that *all* categories of every kind of f/actor must be equally encoded into *all* lived (and dying) spaces. We must learn "to recognize 'oneself' as fully implicated in the world" (Haraway, *Manifesto* 34) and that regardless of our individual configurations we are accountable for each other, and for who or what "we" is and can be—to persistently demand of ourselves "who [(in)exactly] do we think we are?" (Le Guin 336).

In "Newton's Sleep" the ghosts, and in time the humans also, instigate dialogue in all worldly (which is other-worldly) directions, composing the nature/s, technologies and humanity of those worlds as they go; leaving trails of the "[m]eaningless clutter" (316) Ike finds so distasteful. In all of these conversations there'll be so many "more things going on than you thought" (*Cyborgs* 321) that we'll hardly even notice the decline of imposing subjects, as they descend in a flurry of connectivity until "we can [all] go down" (Le Guin 338) together.

Works Cited

1. Christie, John R. R. A Tragedy for Cyborgs. *Configurations* 1.1 (1993): 171-196.
2. Dietrich, Dawn. (Re)-Fashioning the Techno-Erotic Woman: Gender and Textuality in the Cybercultural Matrix. In *Virtual Culture: Identity and Communication in Cybersociety,* ed. by Steven G. Jones. London: SAGE Publications Ltd, 1997. 169-184.
3. Haraway, Donna. *A Cyborg Manifesto: Science, Technology, and Socialist-Feminism in the Late Twentieth Century.* 1985. In *The Haraway Reader,* ed. by Donna Haraway. New York: Routledge, 2004. 7-45.

4. —. Ecce Homo, Ain't (Ar'n't) I a Woman, and Inappropriate/d Others: The Human in a Post-Humanist Landscape. 1989. In *The Haraway Reader*, ed. by Donna Haraway. New York: Routledge, 2004. 47-61.

5. —. The Promises of Monsters: A Regenerative Politics for Inappropriate/d Others. 1992a. In *The Haraway Reader*, ed. by Donna Haraway. New York: Routledge, 2004. 63-123.

6. —. *Otherworldly Conversions; Terran Topics; Local Terms.* 1992b. In *The Haraway Reader*, ed. by Donna Haraway. New York: Routledge, 2004. 125-150.

7. —. Cyborgs, Coyotes, and Dogs: A Kinship of Feminist Figurations and There Are Always More Things Going On Than You Thought! Methodologies As Thinking Technologies. In *The Haraway Reader*, ed. by Donna Haraway. New York: Routledge, 2004. 321-344.

8. Le Guin, Ursula K. "Newton's Sleep" 1991. In *Future Primitive: The New Ecotopias*, ed. by Kim Stanley Robinson. New York: TOR, 1994. 311-338.

9. Pfaelzer, Jean. Subjectivity as Feminist Utopia. In *Utopian and Science Fiction by Women: Worlds of Difference*, ed. by Jane L. Donawerth & Carol A. Kolmerten. Liverpool: Liverpool University Press, 1994. 93-106.

10. Robins, Kevin & Les Levidow. Soldier, Cyborg, Citizen. In *Resisting the Virtual Life: Culture and Politics of Information*, ed. by James Brooks & Iain Boal. San Francisco: City Lights, 1995. 105-113.

11. Wolmark, Jenny. The Postmodern Romances of Feminist Science Fiction. 1995. In *Cybersexualities: a Reader on Feminist Theory, Cyborgs and Cyberspace*, ed. by Wolmark. Edinburgh University Press, 1999. 230-239.

12. —. *Cybersexualities: a Reader on Feminist Theory, Cyborgs and Cyberspace.* Edinburgh: Edinburgh University Press, 1999. 239-247.

Jenny Gal-Or is co-authoring a photo/imagery and creative-text book about Angola where she set up and edited a local newspaper in Portuguese. Currently, she blogs here: <http://www.inthecompanyofwolves.blogspot.com>. She graduated with an MA in Gender Studies from University College London with Distinction, and is hoping to embark on doctoral research either into technological environments in visual culture, or the writing of speculative futures. This is her first published essay.

Ursula Le Guin's "Sur": Defamiliarizing the Frontier

Traci Thomas-Card
University of Wisconsin – Eau Claire

Ursula K. Le Guin's "Sur" (1982) is a rich exploration of what it means to be defined as masculine or feminine; she creates a vision of a world in which women are free to explore not only a frontier, but also the social construction of gender and sexuality that exists in contemporary society. Janice Hocker Rushing points out that in the myth of the American frontier,

> ... women were rarely the center of action in the *myth*; those heroines who did appear were usually caricatures, masculine personalities in female bodies. Ever-present in the background as helpmates, mothers, captives of the Indians, schoolmarms, and saloon girls, women were nevertheless primarily *supplements*. (1)

In "Sur," Le Guin estranges the myth by featuring women who have been released from the constraints of patriarchal tradition. In Antarctica, the women are no longer forced to abide by the notion that they are subservient to men. They are the dominant gender there, indeed, the only gender. This process matches Darko Suvin's understanding of "science fiction as the *literature of cognitive estrangement*" (6). He notes that the

> ... use of estrangement both as underlying attitude and dominant formal device is found also in the *myth*, a "timeless" and religious approach looking in its own way beneath (or above) the empiric surface. However, science fiction sees the norms of any age, including emphatically its own, as unique, changeable, and therefore subject to a *cognitive* view. (7)

Similarly, Patrick Brantlinger suggests "the conventions of both Gothic and science fiction involve a rejection or a symbolic putting to sleep of reason ... Darko Suvin's 'estrangement'" (31). The women's journey to Antarctica reflects both Suvin and Brantlinger's arguments by challenging us to see the mythic frontier norm transformed.

Though "Sur" is a definitive Le Guin text, published over two decades ago, little criticism has been written on the work. The four primary pieces include Barbara Brown's, "Feminist Myth in Le Guin's 'Sur,'" Marleen S. Barr's "Ursula K. Le Guin's 'Sur' as Exemplary Humanist and Antihumanist Text," Anne Kaler's "Carvings in Water: Journeys/Journals and the Image of Women's Writings in Ursula Le Guin's 'Sur,'" and Elena Glasberg's "Refusing History at the End of the Earth: Ursula Le Guin's 'Sur' and the 2000-01 Women's Antarctica Crossing." Though analyzing different aspects, each scholar concludes that "Sur" critiques the social construction of gender and sexuality in a male dominated age.

In "Sur," Le Guin combines elements of science fiction with historical fiction to form the utopic setting of her story. As the women set out on their challenging journey, it is evident that the plot of "Sur" takes its pattern from familiar frontier myths. Whereas the traditional frontier connotes a place of territorial and cultural and racial skirmishes at the point of actual settlement and (usually) whites claiming the land, the North and South Poles are more the explorer's frontier, a matter of finding and (re)naming. As Hocker Rushing states, "myths that endure over time and place have both archetypal and rhetorical aspects" (2). For the Antarctic explorer, the archetype is a strong, independent male figure who is brave, fearless, and heroic. He is unlike frontier settlers in that he does not set out to claim land; rather, the Antarctic explorer sets out on his quest with the purpose of discovering the unknown and to become famous.

In contrast, the worldview Le Guin creates is not focused on the figure of the explorer, or his independence, or his heroism in tackling the Antarctic. As Le Guin declares elsewhere "the men's wilderness is real; it is where men can go hunting and exploring and having all-male adventures, away from the village, the shared center, and it is accessible to and structured by language" ("Wilderness"163). Instead, in "Sur" she defamiliarizes this archetypal imagery of Antarctic exploration by featuring South American women who prove to be resoundingly successful in what has traditionally been considered male territory. For them the Antarctic becomes a "utopia" where they are released from the constraints of their lives at home, to explore the possibilities and opportunities of courage, adventure, and their own type of heroism.

This contrast will emerge clearly as I focus on comparing details in Robert Falcon Scott's narrative of the *Discovery* expedition to details in Le Guin's narrative of the fictitious *Yelcho* expedition. I chose Scott's narrative rather than other expeditions mentioned in Le Guin's text because the narrator explicitly states, "all these exploits were to

me but forerunners of the British National Antarctic expedition ...
and the wonderful account of that expedition by Captain Scott" (257).
In particular I will examine similarities and differences between the
formation of the crews, their acquisition of funding and supplies, the
expeditions' treatment of the environment, and the system of naming
used by each.

The early 1900s saw a flurry of activity in expeditions to the Antarctic
region. Though expeditions to Antarctica had been mounted since the
1700s, the territory remained largely uncharted because of the high
dangers in traversing the icy land, but the world was eager to discover
the unknown. In 1873 Sir Clements Markham of England decided to
send an expedition, led by Robert Falcon Scott, to Antarctica. Eight long
years later, the *Discovery* left port in London.

By contrast, the narrator and her companions in Le Guin's "Sur" are
able to leave for Antarctica within a year of their expedition's conception.
As evidenced by Le Guin's subtitle: "A Summary Report of the *Yelcho*
Expedition to the Antarctic, 1909-1910," their story begins two years
before Roald Amundsen became the first man to reach the South Pole on
December 14th, 1911. The choice of such a subtitle serves to familiarize
her readers with the type of story—exploration narrative—that Le Guin
rewrites in "Sur." However, readers learn almost immediately that rather
than traditional male European explorers bent on conquering uncharted
lands, the expedition comprises nine women from various countries in
South America who have no intention of conquering anything.

Both Scott and Le Guin's narratives reflect briefly on the history of
those who had gone to Antarctica before. While the tone of Scott's
account is somewhat condescending at times, Le Guin's narrator only
praises and envies those who had the freedom to venture on such
journeys. Nevertheless, the language used by both Scott and the narrator
of "Sur" conveys admiration for their predecessors. Scott writes "one
cannot read the simple, unaffected narratives of these voyages without
being assured of their veracity, and without being struck with the
wonderful pertinacity and courage which they display" (14). Le Guin's
narrator writes of the "wonderful account of that expedition by Captain
Scott ... which [she] ordered from London and reread a thousand times"
(257). From his use of the word "veracity," Scott does not even consider
that previous explorers may not have told the whole truth regarding
their adventures into the frontier. Le Guin's narrator, from her use of the
phrase "wonderful account," quite obviously considers this a possibility.
Their admiration of past expeditions is intriguing because their praise
points to a striking similarity in each expedition's definition of what it
means to be a hero. Both recognize the patriarchal notion of "hero" as

the strong white male so commonly portrayed in exploration narratives. Yet only Scott's expedition attempts to *imitate* this ideal. Instead, as Brown observes, for "Sur,"

> ... on the one hand, there is a "cover story"—the concealment of the expedition—on the other hand, Le Guin creates a counter story, which is both a contrast to the way men reached the Pole and a whole counter-culture established by the women in Antarctica. (56)

The men do not need a cover story, nor do they create a counter-culture. The *Discovery* expedition crewmembers undertake a typical explorer's mission to Antarctica. They brave the icy waters to chart the territory and collect specimens, and return to their native land. Everything about the nature of their expedition is considered heroic, and the men are perceived as "heroes" because of their work.

Though the women understand the "hero" concept, they see no need to imitate it. The narrator comments that she "deeply respect[s] the scientific accomplishments of Captain Scott's expedition ... but having had no training in any science, nor any opportunity for such training, my ignorance obliged me to forego any thought of adding to the body of scientific knowledge concerning Antarctica" (Le Guin 257). This statement underscores the women's success. Despite their lack of formal education, they trained themselves to haul sledges, to make observations regarding the land and wildlife they encountered, and to take measurements in order to map/chart their progress to the South Pole; in general, to survive comfortably in an environment that kills those not equipped to deal with it. The narrator's statement, one of the few direct comments on the limitations women experience in comparison to explorers and males in general, also explains to some degree the women's approach to living in Antarctica. It contextualizes their humility and lack of "heroism" in the traditional sense. Le Guin ponders elsewhere conventional notions of heroism. She writes,

> ... what is false is the military image; what is foolish is the egoism; what is pernicious is the identification of "Nature" as enemy. We are asked to believe that the Antarctic continent became aware that four Englishmen were penetrating her virgin whiteness and so unleashed upon them the punishing fury of her revenge, the mighty weaponry of wind and blizzard, and so forth and so on. Well, I don't believe it. I don't believe that Nature is either an enemy, or a woman, to humanity. Nobody has ever

thought so but Man; and the thought is, to one not Man, no longer acceptable even as a poetic metaphor. ("Heroes" 173)

Her modest narrator in "Sur" makes a virtue of her ignorance, and points up the women's actual efficiency in handling this environment, in contrast to the more "heroic" males.

Though Scott is anything but modest, he begins his narrative by excusing his ineptness at writing, and states that he will attempt to tell his tale "objectively" for the use of explorers who follow. He writes that the "first object in writing an account of a Polar voyage was the guidance of future voyagers; the first duty of the writer was to his successors" (Scott vii). It is clear that Scott intends his report to be read by a male audience. This is evident from Scott's use of the phrase "his successors" as well as the contemporary belief that only men were considered capable of success in frontier exploration. The narrator in "Sur" begins her account by explaining that she is adding a final note to a report she "has no intention of publishing" but one she hopes a grandchild or even a great grandchild might someday read (Le Guin "Sur" 255). This implies there is more to her story than practical information, that there is content for interpretation and the text itself may be discovered and explored. It is telling that the narrator Le Guin creates for "Sur" makes none of Scott's claims of "responsibility" to future explorers. The women's actions and the "non-heroic" nature of their account both undercut the tone of Scott's narrative, and at the same time insist that another sort of "successor" will nevertheless discover their accomplishments.

This is not to say that Le Guin's narrator does not have an audience in mind. Whereas Scott clearly addresses a male audience, and very likely a European upper-class audience, Le Guin's narrator draws an implicit parallel between the discovery of Antarctica and the discovery of her text, and in doing so emphasizes that her report is intended, less exclusively, for a male *and* female audience. Brantlinger writes that in science fiction, "there is a break from present reality, a radical disjunction from the world as we know it, a displacement in time or space or both" (35). The break from "reality," in "Sur" is not only the women's journey to the South Pole, but also the time displacement the narrator intentionally arranges for the discovery of their expedition. She indicates that a grandchild or great-grandchild might someday read the report. However, the word "somebody's" grandchild, opens the possibility for her report to have an even wider audience. Le Guin's narrator addresses a future generation, a nameless audience who may not even exist yet. Indeed, with this statement she provides even for the possibility of a non-scientific, non-adventuresome audience for her report.

Funding & Equipment

Both Scott and the narrator of "Sur" devote a good portion of their narratives to explaining how their expeditions originated. However, Scott pays far more attention to acquiring the necessary funding than does the narrator of "Sur." This is natural considering that Scott was obligated to give due credit to each of his patrons. The men of the *Discovery* waited many years before finally having enough patrons to finance their expedition, while the women of the *Yelcho* expedition had only one. After reading and re-reading Scott's account of his expedition, the narrator of "Sur" shares her wonder over his adventures with Juana, who proposes they write to Carlota. It is through Carlota that the women are able to find an unnamed benefactor. The women's use of an "old girl" network is as inconspicuous as the lack of fuss about their funding, again in high contrast to Scott's "heroic" treatment of the matter. It also provides a vital narrative link in the final reversal of supposed gender superiority. Because the women did not have to solicit funds for years as did Scott and his patrons, the *Yelcho* expedition arrived at the South Pole prior to Amundsen.

A further strong contrast appears in the way each narrative discusses the equipment and supplies for its expedition. Scott devotes a large section to describing the effort that went into securing proper equipment and supplies. He writes, "few people can realise what an extraordinary variety of articles is required on such an expedition as ours, where a ship and its crew are to be banished from all sources of supply for a lengthened period" (Scott 39). Scott and his men categorized supplies according to the needs of various men aboard ship; creating separate lists of equipment for the boatswain, the carpenter, the engineer, etc., not to mention the supplies ordered solely for the officers' personal comfort—Scott writes that they ordered "tobacco, soap, glass, crockery, furniture, mattresses, and all such requisites for personal comfort" (40). The items on this list show that Scott and his men had very high expectations regarding their personal comfort in Antarctica. The realization that society viewed them as "heroes" for undertaking such a conquest allowed them to demand a certain amount of respect (and goods) be given for their willingness to isolate themselves from the comfortable surroundings of "civilized" society.

In contrast, the women of "Sur" seem perfectly capable of surviving on "limited" supplies. Certainly they are very content with the provisions provided by their benefactor, described by the narrator as both "plentiful and fine" (Le Guin "Sur" 255). Kaler's essay argues that Le Guin's narrator speaks of her expedition using "a journal/tale form which revolves on three 'feminine' or intuitive and creative principles of order—disorder, dislocation, and reversal" (52). Indeed, Le Guin disdains the list-form that Scott and other Antarctic explorers used to structure their descriptions of supplies. Instead, she uses the journal-form that Kaler's essay refers to and artfully integrates mentions of supplies used into the text. For example, the story opens with the narrator adding her report to the trunk in the attic that holds "Rosita's christening dress and Juanito's silver rattle and [her] wedding shoes and finneskos[1]" (Le Guin "Sur" 255). Later in the narrative, she notes that their success at sledge hauling is in part due to "the quantity and quality" of their food supply, observing that the "fifteen percent of dried fruits in our pemmican helped prevent scurvy; and the potatoes, frozen and dried according to an ancient Andean Indian method, were very nourishing yet very light and compact" (266).

Glasberg remarks on the women's technique of utilizing nontraditional equipment and supplies, finding it an "awareness of subaltern cultures" (109) who, like them, had no need for the luxurious items desired by Scott and his party. This adds a multicultural awareness to this expedition not seen in Scott's. One item of luxury to note is the Veuve Clicquot the women partake of during their journey. According to the Veuve Clicquot website, at age 27, "Madame Clicquot (Barbe Nicole Ponsardin) railed against the traditions of the day and took the reins of the family business" following her husband's death. Although she struggled against those who felt she was incapable of doing so, she was extremely successful and created a name for herself that is still known around the world ("History: 1805"). This item first indicates that the women's high economic status is a match for Scott and his men's. Second, the story of Madame Clicquot aligns the women's expedition in the text's usual unpretentious manner with another woman who fought to gain her right to work outside the house.

Formation of Crew

Both narrators write about the selection of their expedition's crewmembers; however their methods differed widely. Representatives from The Royal Society and the Royal Geographic Society assisted Scott in conferring and deciding upon members of the *Discovery* expedition. Once Scott received his appointment as Commander, he then made certain demands regarding the remainder of the crew. Scott states, "from

[1] A boot made of birch-tanned reindeer skin with the hair left on the outside.

a very early date I had set my mind on obtaining a naval crew. I felt sure that their sense of discipline would be an immense acquisition, and I had grave doubts as to my own ability to deal with any other class of men" (36). It is not surprising to note that Scott's narrative frequently makes use of the word "I." The possessive way he refers to both ship and crew indicates his hierarchical sense of ownership as Commander of the expedition. His references to "other classes" of men also indicate Scott's sense of his leader's status, and the economic status expected of Antarctic explorers.

The *Yelcho* expedition was formed in a much more casual, though secretive, manner. The narrator explains that it was Juana's idea to go in the first place, and Juana who suggested they write Carlota. She adds that they asked many women to accompany them, and recalls, "so few of those we asked even knew what we were talking about—so many thought we were mad, or wicked, or both! And of those few who shared our folly, still fewer were able, when it came to the point, to leave their daily duties and commit themselves to a voyage of at least six months" (Le Guin "Sur" 258). This passage emphasizes that at the time of recruitment, women were confined to the home. The desire to *leave* home was what society considered transgressive; had they been men this desire would not have been questioned.

It is more interesting to note that the women of the *Yelcho* expedition, according to the narrator, "were, and are, by birth and upbringing, unequivocally and irrevocably, all crew" (260). There are indications to the contrary embedded within the tale. For instance, the justification they give for being away six months; "going on retreat in a Bolivian convent, which some of us were forced to employ (while the rest of us said we were going to Paris for the winter season)" are not activities that women of poor economic status could afford (258). The narrator also mentions "a child with only ignorant or incompetent servants to look after it," implying that they didn't ask women who couldn't afford servants (258). Glasberg points out that in contrast to Scott and his men, the women "are conscious of their reliance on the domestic labor of native servants to cover their temporary absences" (109). Though the narrator does acknowledge the existence of these servants, there is no evidence in the story that these "friends" are or should be identified as such. The narrator observes that she looks "back with regret to those friends who wished to come with us but could not, by any contrivance, get free," making it more likely that she regrets the absence of companions such as Maria, of whom they had "received word that [her] husband, in Quito, was ill, and she must stay to nurse him" (259). The economic status of these women provides an interesting parallel to the economic status of Scott and his officers; neither is richer nor poorer than the other.

Leadership and Crews

A comparison of leadership styles in each narrative reveals the constraints and power relationships of a patriarchal social structure, though Scott's reflection on the matter is unintentional. Scott held the position of Commander on the *Discovery*, although there were many people aboard who possessed fine leadership qualities. Each person had a role on board, and there was no room for improvisation. Though Scott takes time to acknowledge each of the officers in his narrative, the same cannot be said for his crew. He writes,

> I pass on to that long list of petty officers and men which completes the roll of honour of the "Discovery." I would that space permitted me to give each that notice which his services deserved ... reluctantly I leave the personalities of my sailor friends to emerge in a more casual manner from its pages. (74-75)

His language is tactful, yet it is clearly understood that his officers were more deserving of attention simply because of their status in the ship's hierarchy.

The leadership style of the *Yelcho* expedition differs dramatically. As Brown notes, "the heroic is the realm of the individual ... there is a tendency to let the leader stand for the whole expedition.... [T]he women choose a 'leader,' yet they do not need one" (57). The women make some pretense of electing leaders, and agree that

> ... if a situation arose of such urgent danger that one voice must be obeyed without present question, the unenviable honor of speaking with that voice should fall first upon myself; if I were incapacitated, upon Carlota; if she, then upon Berta. (Le Guin "Sur" 259)

It is obvious from the narrator's use of the word "unenviable" that she has no desire to have the power to control. Unlike Scott, she is not possessive about authority, and in fact is nervous about assuming it. But she recalls that

> ... as it came out, to my very great pleasure and relief, my qualities as a "leader" were never tested; the nine of us worked things out amongst us from beginning to end without any orders being given by anybody, and only two or three times with

recourse to a vote by voice or show of hands. To be sure, we argued a good deal. But then, we had time to argue. And one way or another the arguments always ended up in a decision, upon which action could be taken. (259)

Unlike Scott's expedition, which saw leadership as roles to be enforced for the duration, the women of Le Guin's tale discuss it in a situational context. In "Sur," a sole individual is not responsible for the successes or failures of the whole. Rather the women of the *Yelcho* expedition formed a true democracy, in which everyone was given a voice. The narrator's further comment about the women arguing implies their acceptance that a difference of opinion is healthy and even necessary to the "success" of the mission as they define it. This very different style of operation points up the possible alternatives to Scott's hierarchically based leadership. It is not necessary, the Yelcho expedition suggests, that heroism always be a matter for individuals. Through the narrator's descriptions of each woman's talent and specific characteristics, their individuality is expressed at the same time that a sense of community and sisterhood is created.

The Journey—Environment and Strategies of Exploration

An article by Fred H. Besthorn and Diane Pearson McMillen is useful in identifying several elements of Ecofeminism in "Sur." According to them, an Ecofeminist worldview considers that "oppression and value based hierarchical ranking are inseparable," that "human/nature relationships and all forms of social domination are feminist concerns" and finally, that "ecofeminist philosophy envisages the idea of *interconnectedness*. Interconnectedness for ecofeminists is a view that the parts of all energy, matter, and reality are related to the greater whole" (225). This notion is repeatedly expressed and embodied in "Sur."

The women's interaction with the environment differs greatly from that of the known Antarctic explorers, which reflects the relation of environmental domination to social domination referred to by Besthorn and Pearson McMillen. The women do not expect any profit to arise from their journey, a aesthetic in direct opposition to the goals of Scott and his men. In fact, the women have none of the obligations that might incite them to act aggressively towards the wildlife they encounter. This respect for the environment implies a somewhat anachronistic recourse to the discourse of Ecofeminism.

One of the most telling comparisons is found in Scott's description of the Emperor penguins that they encounter. Scott writes,

> ... our zoologist pointed out that here was the chance to complete our collection of skins, as the birds would now be in their finest plumage; and in spite of the weather a large party had soon surrounded the unfortunate birds. I was not present myself, but I hear there was much excitement. It is no easy matter to hold an Emperor; they are extraordinarily strong both in their legs and flippers, and are capable of moving even with a man on top of them. They could of course have been clubbed, but this would have damaged them as specimens. (286)

Scott's description conveys his sense of drama and satisfaction in the hunt, though he was not even present.

Traditional explorers' tales often involve scenarios like Scott's tale of the penguins—brave men, heroes—defying danger for the good of the people. Scott justifies their hunt by stating it was necessary for the advancement of science. He writes,

> It was late at night before sufficient specimens had been slain, and then the party returned with a plentiful supply of frost-bites of which they had been quite oblivious in the excitement of the chase ... we never slew animals except for the practical object of obtaining food or specimens or both; and, indeed, the more we came to see the extraordinary, unsuspicious tameness of the animal life about us, the more compunction we were forced to feel at the necessity of killing at all. (287)

His use of the word "force" is interesting in that with its use he victimizes himself and the men involved in the hunt rather than the penguins. And yet, the "compunction" Scott writes of is one of the rare instances when his narrative conveys a departure from the macho explorer mythos. As with the reference to the "unfortunate birds" in the previous description, the sense of emotion portrayed—or perhaps betrayed—in this passage undercuts archetypes of the strong men associated with Antarctic exploration narratives.

The women's experience with penguins is quite unlike Scott's account. There is no indication whatsoever that the women ever considered killing the animals. If anything, the women welcomed the encounter with other living creatures in such a barren land. The narrator personifies the penguins she and her companions encounter, creating a dialogue with them, recalling how they asked, "'where on earth have you been? What took you so long? The Hut is around this way. Please come this way. Mind the rocks!'" (Le Guin "Sur" 261). The interaction demonstrates an alternative theory of scientific observation, one that doesn't view the wildlife of Antarctica as something to be conquered. Further, while Scott's narrative suggests the men's encounter with the penguins was dangerous and involved personal risk to their lives, Le Guin's narrator suggests just the opposite. Admittedly, the penguins were of a different breed, the Adelie being somewhat smaller than the Emperor. The very word "emperor" has patriarchal connotations, and could very well be the reason Le Guin chose to use the Adelie. Genevieve Anderson notes the Adelie were named after the wife of Dumont D'Urville, an early Antarctic explorer ("Penguins" par. 6). However, the fact that the women bonded with the wildlife of Antarctica on an equal level reinforces Le Guin's critique of the power dynamics associated with masculinist notions of "success" in 19th century exploration.

The two narrators' accounts of the Hut used by the Southern Cross Expedition[2] and its environs also contrast. Scott writes, "the hut is in very good condition ... should some future explorers traverse this region, it is well to know that here they possess a retreat in case of emergency." He adds, "although they may not find all the provisions in good condition ... at this spot there would always be abundance of food in the shape of seals or penguins" (136). Scott never considers that future explorers may dislike the disorderly conditions of the camp, nor does he consider the possibility of using the land itself as a retreat like the women of "Sur" do.

The women of the *Yelcho* expedition find the hut deplorable. The narrator describes the exterior as "a kind of graveyard of seal skins, seal bones, penguin bones, and rubbish" and the interior as "less offensive, but very dreary ... it was dirty, and had about it a mean disorder" (Le Guin "Sur" 262). This description strongly critiques the traditionally accepted behavior of 19th century male explorers toward their kill and the land it came from. It re-emphasizes the fact that the women kill no animals on their expedition. The women's suggestions about what to do with the structure reinforce this critique. "Teresa proposed we use the hut as our camp. Zoe counterproposed that we set fire to it. We finally shut the door and left it as we found it. The penguins appeared to approve" (262). Barr notes that the women "are more concerned about penguins' approval then men's approval" (162).

[2] The Antartic Heritage Trust Organization notes that the huts built by the British Southern Cross expedition of 1898-1900 who "arrived at Cape Adare, the largest Adelie penguin rookery in Antarctica, in February 1899. A beach ridge was selected as a site for their two prefabricated huts."

I believe it extremely important that the women decide to leave the structure without a trace of their existence. Here, once again, the women's desire to remain unnoticed shapes another kind of heroism, the anonymous type that women have shown for generations, retrieved only by the work of feminist historians. It is possible that these women are more "penguin" than "man"—that is to say, Le Guin is implying that some women are more connected to the Earth—an old, old idea. The idea that this notion is true for the women of the Yelcho expedition is supported by Le Guin elsewhere. She writes,

> ... the experience of women as women, their experience unshared with men, that experience is the wilderness or the wildness that is utterly other—that is in fact, to Man, unnatural. That is what civilization has left out, what culture excludes, what the Dominants call animal, bestial, primitive, undeveloped, unauthentic—what has not been spoken and when spoken, has not been heard—what we are just beginning to find words for, our words, not their words: the experience of women. (Le Guin "Wilderness" 163)

The women's distaste for the hut clearly derives from their domestic experience. Le Guin suggests that the notion of pride in the beauty and efficiency of one's shelter brings the women of the *Yelcho* expedition a good deal closer to nature than Scott's crew were.

The vast difference in the expeditions' modes of domesticity is at the heart of Le Guin's creation of an alternative exploration narrative. Whereas previous explorers built shelters for themselves, and imported supplies for comfort and entertainment, as evidenced by Scott's narrative, the women of the *Yelcho* expedition "dug out a series of cubicles in the ice itself, lined them with hay insulation and pine boarding, and roofed them with canvas over bamboo poles, covered with snow for weight and insulation." Their beds were "very small, mere tubes into which one crawled feet first ... the sailors called them 'coffins' and 'wormholes' and looked with horror on our burrows in the ice" (Le Guin "Sur" 264). It is telling that neither Scott's expedition, nor any previous Antarctic explorers, ever consider the possibility of using the ice and snow as a means to shelter themselves from the wind, and this supports Glasberg's notion that the women were aware of and utilized survival strategies from "subaltern" cultures.

The Return Home

In part because they are in declining health and spirits, but also in part due to their desire for reward, Scott and his men look forward to returning to the comforts of home. They want the glory and honor of public acknowledgement for some amount of success in their voyage. Scott writes in the final pages of his narrative, "to attempt to describe the hearty welcome which we received from our country-men, and the generous tributes which have been paid to our efforts, would be beyond the scope of this book." He concludes, "although this inevitable parting has taken place, we hope that as the years roll on we may meet again, and we know that when such meetings come they will renew old friendships and recall some of the pleasantest memories of our lives" (403).

In contrast, the women of the Yelcho expedition grieve at the idea of returning home. Upon the ship's arrival, the narrator remembers that Juana "burst into tears—she who had never wept in all our weeks of pain and weariness on the long haul" (Le Guin "Sur" 273). The excitement the narrator conveys in her memories of the start of their journey is conspicuously absent now. The narrator says succinctly: "of the return voyage there is nothing to tell. We came back safe" (Le Guin 273). In an interview Paul Mandelbaum asks Le Guin why the women of "Sur" feel so at home in Antarctica. She responds, "there is nobody telling them it doesn't belong to them, that men own everything, do everything, are everything … by suggesting it indirectly, the story says it better than any interpretation can do" (206). This comment plays with the idea that there actually *is* no indigenous culture in Antarctica. The cultures created there are a direct reflection of the identities of those who land there. Where the men ventured into what they considered peril and isolation, the women are leaving what to them has been the utopic space of travel and adventure, and returning to the "estrangement" of "captivity."

Because the women have no intention of making their expedition known to the public, they also have no desire for the recognition and glory that are traditionally part of such a journey. In fact, the only remnants of their trip are the narrative, the sketches of various landmarks in the women's attics, and the narrator's finneskos. Even little Rosa del Sur, a physical memory of their trip, dies from scarlet fever at the age of five, and so the women are left only with their memories. Le Guin's narrator concludes by writing "over the years we have lost touch with one another. It is very difficult for women to meet, when they live so far apart as we do" (273). Scott is hopeful that he and his shipmates will meet again, whereas the narrator of the *Yelcho* expedition recognizes an end to the women's community. Adrienne Rich explains the sense of loss that the narrator of "Sur" and her companions feel over the end of their time together as she notes that

> ... woman-identification is a source of energy, a potential springhead of female power, violently curtailed and wasted under the institution of heterosexuality. The denial of reality and visibility to women's passion for women, women's choice of women as allies, life companions and community; the forcing of such relationships into dissimulation and their disintegration under intense pressure, have meant an incalculable loss to the power of all women *to change the social relations of the sexes to liberate ourselves and each other.* (657)

Naming

As Barr points out, "in terms of structural fabulation, man names the system of the universe," (159), as evidenced by the choice to name the ship *Discovery*. Scott makes only a brief mention of naming in his account, writing about choosing a name for the expedition; "it was generally considered that the most appropriate plan was to revive some old time-honoured title, and as it was seen that few names carried a greater record than 'Discovery,' that name was chosen" (49). It is doubtful that Scott and his patrons would have picked a name that was unknown, or that they would have revived a name without a good "record." Naming the ship *Discovery* connects this expedition to the history of previous explorers, and the bravery and courage that was associated with Scott's mission to "discover" the last unknown frontier.

There is a wealth of meaning behind Le Guin's choice of title, names of characters, and places in the story, so it proves useful to examine not only the intertextual references of names themselves, but also instances where Le Guin purposely chooses *not* to provide a name.

By far, most of the scholarly attention regarding Le Guin's use of naming in "Sur" is on the significance of her title. In the Mandelbaum interview, Le Guin claims that the title "is a homage to Jorge Luis Borges, for his story 'El Sur' and for being Borges" (205). Kaler touches on the idea that "Sur" referred to "Sur, the bi-monthly magazine about feminist literature published from 1931-70 by Victoria Ocampo in Buenos Aires," of which Borges was a regular contributor (52). But further scrutiny suggests that the symbolism behind the name "Sur," is far richer than Le Guin's original intention to simply pay homage to Borges. Four other potential meanings are reflected in the title: "Sur" as south, "Sur" as sir, "Sur" in biblical references, and "Sur" as a prefix for surname.

"Sur" means south in Spanish; the women travel to the South Pole, and they name their base in Antarctica "South South America." Kaler notes a "reversal in [Le Guin's] pun on the word 'sur'... [T]o a person from the northern hemisphere, south means warm; to a South American, however, south means the cold and ice of Antarctica" (52). This reversal would certainly be estranging for readers in the northern hemisphere. Though the focus on directional change is interesting, it is as likely that close readers would simply associate "sur" with the Spanish term "south," and attribute the word to the fact that the women hail from South America.

"Sur" is also a cognate of "sir." Barr notes

> "Sur" rewrites *sir*; the former word superimposes the ethnic (*sur* is Spanish for south) and the female (*sur* is the surname of Rosa del Sur, the daughter born at the South Pole in Le Guin's story) upon the latter word's usual implications regarding white male power. The word *sur* articulates the existence of non-WASP, nonmale people and emphasizes the individuals called "sir" are not the only viable people in the world. (158-159)

As Barr suggests, Le Guin could rewrite "sir" for "sur" to indicate the existence of a successful, heroic, and yet non-dominant culture.

Kaler also reveals that "in the Scriptures, Sur is the desert land toward which Sarai's Egyptian handmaid Hagar flees to escape from her mistress' wrath (Gen.16:7)" (52). Kaler claims that "by setting her short story in Antarctica, Le Guin builds on the connotation of Sur as a desert experience where spiritual cleansing takes place" (52). As Besthorn and McMillen note, the connection of women to nature and spirit is a quality of Ecofeminism, and Le Guin certainly conveys a sense of spirituality amongst the women. That Hagar is pregnant when she reaches Shur is a nod to Theresa's pregnancy when the women reach Antarctica.

Close readers will also perceive a connection between the title "Sur," and Le Guin's narrator's choice to give no surnames "lest this report fall into strangers' hands at last, and embarrassment or unpleasant notoriety thus be brought upon unsuspecting husbands, sons, etc" (258). She doesn't reference wives and daughters but "husbands, sons," and in doing so emphasizes the idea that the men of their families would actually be perceived as "unmanly" for staying at home. But her choice to give no surnames also allows the women to protect themselves; it is also possible that the title "Sur" serves as a kind of surname for all the women of the expedition.

Kaler writes extensively about the possible significance behind the
"'portmanteau' names" of less prominently featured characters from
the *Yelcho* expedition.

> Carlota suggests several pioneer women who explored male
> territory: Charlotte Perkins Gilman and Carlota Montez ...
> Zoe, the zealous one, means "life" in all its forms ... Berta, the
> sculptor, may suggest Berta Hummel ... Pepita, a short form of
> Joseph, is known only for her illness, although she may be the
> prototypical woman writer Jo in Alcott's *Little Women*. (55)

If "Zoe" represents one who is zealous, recall that she was the member
of the expedition "who arrived in a tiny pirogue manned by Indians, her
yacht having sprung a leak" (Le Guin "Sur" 259). Her eagerness and
passion to be a part of the journey to Antarctica made her take any risk
to arrive in time. She is also the character who proposes they "set fire"
to Hut Point. Similarly, if "Berta" represents Berta Hummel, recall that
she was both architect and artist of the expedition; "when she had done
all she could to make South South America livable, she dug out one
more cell just under the ice surface ... alone, she worked at sculptures.
They were beautiful forms" (265).

Le Guin also mentions several landmarks later given "official" names
by male explorers.

> Zoe and Juana had called the vast ice river that flowed through
> that gateway the Florence Nightingale Glacier, wishing to
> honor the British, who had been the inspiration and guide of
> our expedition; that very brave and very peculiar lady seemed to
> represent so much that is best, and strangest, in the island race.
> On maps, of course, this glacier bears the name Mr. Shackleton
> gave it, the Beardmore. (267)

Nightingale too railed against societal standards that called for an
educated woman to thrive only at home and in social circles. Like the
women of "Sur," she challenged normative ideas regarding success and
the heroic. It is also intriguing to note that the women choose Nightingale
to honor the whole of Britain, their "inspiration and guide," rather than
Scott, other previous Antarctic explorers, or a South American ancestor.
Sadly, like so much other women's history, "Nightingale" was replaced
with "Beardmore," never again to be heard of.

With the Polar peaks, the narrator explains,

> ... we gave names to these peaks, not very seriously, since
> we did not expect our discoveries to come to the attention of
> geographers. Zoe had a gift for naming, and it is thanks to her
> that certain sketch maps in various suburban South American
> attics bear such curious features as "Bolivar's Big Nose," "I Am
> General Rosas," "The Cloudmaker," "Whose Toe?" and "Throne
> of Our Lady of the Southern Cross." (269)

Barr remarks

> Conforming to humanist rhetoric, the female explorers struggle
> to map the South Pole, to create a narrative (a history) for the
> South Pole. Conforming to antihumanist rhetoric, by making no
> effort to communicate their narrative (their history) to others,
> they deconstruct subjectivity. (159)

I would add that Le Guin is mocking the masculinist tradition to associate
power with a specific name. The women's choice of landmark names
has none of the territorial identity that Scott's narrative conveys. The
lightheartedness with which they approach the question is refreshing.
It indicates that the women of the *Yelcho* expedition have no need to
lay claim to territory.

Readers never learn the name of "Sur's" narrator, though Le Guin
does provide the first names of her companions. Kaler believes that
"if Le Guin's narrator does not have a name, she may well represent
Everywoman as the ubiquitous older, wiser woman" (53). Brown, on the
other hand, believes that because the narrator is unnamed "she cannot
come to stand for the whole" (57). In part I agree with both Kaler and
Brown. As Kaler notes, the unnamed narrator connotes Everywoman
in that she is considered "lesser" than men. Brown's clever explanation
is just as likely; readers cannot hold the narrator "accountable" for the
actions of the expedition because they do not know her.

Conclusion

"Sur" is a powerful critique of the masculinist 19th century explorer
mythos, with its construction of white individual "heroes." By
persistently opposing the discourse and values revealed by Scott's
narrative, with its emphasis on hierarchy, glory, and individual effort,

"Sur" reveals a "yin-centered" story of heroism that is democratic, low-key, expressive of modern views on the environment, and yet presented efficient beyond that of any actual Antarctic explorer, including Amundsen. Le Guin defamiliarizes Antarctic exploration, indeed frontier exploration, and pushes the concept in a new direction by focusing the story around women of South American descent. Le Guin estranges her characters from patriarchal traditions, and creates an alternative definition to the vision of the heroic. "Sur" offers an alternative to how the frontier myth is conceptualized, particularly as it relates to Antarctic exploration narratives.

As previously mentioned, Le Guin intended her criticism to be, for the most part, embedded within the text itself. However, one of the few explicit critiques is when the narrator of "Sur" shares what she has learned from her experience: that the "backside of heroism is often rather sad; women and servants know that. They know also that the heroism may be no less real for that. But achievement is smaller than men think. What is large is the sky, the earth, the sea, the soul" (263). The women's modesty at their success here points to the notion of self-silencing, and indicates that at least to some extent the women have internalized the oppressions placed on them by contemporary society. And yet the narrator demonstrates that to be successful and to be considered a "hero" one need not compromise herself or her environment. The women of the *Yelcho* expedition, unlike the men of the *Discovery* expedition, learn that in relation to the harsh conditions of the Antarctic environment, success and heroism as they have been conceptualized in the traditional sense are insignificant. Indeed, this is perhaps the most significant variation between the two narratives, the "paradoxa" to the explorer mythos—the women in "Sur" don't *want* to become famous—they don't need the glory. For them, the heroism is enough.

Works Cited

1.   Andersen, Margaret. "Thinking About Women." *Gender and Society* 19.4 (2005): 437-455.
2.   Anderson, Genevieve. "Penguins in Antarctica." *Biological Sciences*. 2003. Santa Barbara City College. 15 July 2007 <http://www.biosbcc.net/ocean/AApenguins.htm>.
3.   Barr, Marlene S. "Ursula K. Le Guin's 'Sur' as Exemplary Humanist and Antihumanist Text." In *Lost in Space: Probing Feminist Science Fiction and Beyond*. 154-170.

4. Besthorn, Fred and Diane Pearson McMillen. "The Oppression of Women and Nature: Ecofeminism as a Framework for an Expanded Ecological Social Work." *Families in Society: The Journal of Contemporary Human Services.* 83.3 (2002): 221-232.

5. Brantlinger, Patrick. "The Gothic Origins of Science Fiction." *NOVEL: A Forum on Fiction.* 14.1 (1980): 30-43.

6. Brown, Barbara. "Feminist Myth in Le Guin's Sur." In *Mythlore: A Journal of J.R.R. Tolkien, C.S. Lewis, Charles Williams, and the Genres of Myth and Fantastic Studies.* 16.4 (1990): 56-59.

7. "Finnesko." *Oxford English Dictionary.* 2nd ed. 1989.

8. Glasberg, Elena. "Refusing History at the End of the Earth: Ursula Le Guin's 'Sur' and the 2000-01 Women's Antarctica Crossing." *Tulsa Studies in Women's Literature.* 21.1 (2002): 99-121.

9. "History: 1805." *Veuve-Clicquot Ponsardin Champagne.* 15 July 2007 < http://www.veuveclicquot.com/home.asp?path=us/en/the_house/history>.

10. Hocker Rushing, Janice. "Evolution of 'The New Frontier' in *Alien* and *Aliens*: Patriarchal Co-Optation of the Feminine Archetype." *The Quarterly Journal of Speech.* 75.1 (1989): 1-24.

11. Kaler, Anne. "Carvings in Water: Journeys/Journals and the Image of Women's Writings in Ursula Le Guin's Sur." *Literary Interpretation Theory.* 7.1 (1996): 51-62.

12. Le Guin, Ursula K. "Heroes." In *Dancing at the Edge of the World: Thoughts on Words, Women, Places.* New York: Grove Press, 1989. 171-175.

13. —. "Sur." *The Compass Rose.* New York: Harper & Row, 1982. 255-273.

14. —. "Women/Wilderness." In *Dancing at the Edge of the World: Thoughts on Words, Women, Places.* New York: Grove Press, 1989. 161-164.

15. Mandelbaum, Paul. "Ursula K. Le Guin: Sur." *12 Short Stories and Their Making.* New York: Persea Books, 2005. 205-213.

16. Rich, Adrienne. "Compulsory Heterosexuality and Lesbian Existence." *Signs* 5.4 (1980): 631-660.

17. "Roald Amundsen." *Encyclopedia Brittanica.* 2006. Encyclopedia Britannica Online. 30 July 2006 <http://search.eb.com/eb/article-9007288>.

18. Scott, Robert F. *The Voyage of the Discovery.* 2 vols. 1905. New York: Greenwood Press, 1969.

19. "Southern Cross Expedition." June 2006 Antarctic Heritage Trust. 2 June 2006 <http://www.heritage-antarctica.org/index.cfm/Human/Borchgrevink0/>.

20 Suvin, Darko. *Metamorphoses of Science Fiction*. New Haven and London: Yale University Press, 1979.

Traci Thomas-Card is an Associate Lecturer of English at the University of Wisconsin-Eau Claire where she teaches courses in composition, literature, and English as a second language. She also serves as co-advisor for the Theta Zeta chapter of Sigma Tau Delta, the International English Honor Society. Her current research interests focus on studies of gender and sexuality in contemporary literature and popular culture.

Changing Planes:
The First Post 9/11 Feminist SF Text
Embraces When It Changed

Marleen S. Barr

Fordham University

An unnamed narrator, perhaps a "changed plane" version of Ursula Le Guin herself, tells the stories about strangers in strange lands which constitute *Changing Planes*. Like emissary Genly Ai, the narrator makes her "report as if I told a story" (Le Guin *Left Hand of Darkness* 7). The American government's use of stories—fictions—as a means to report truth is a sign of the post-9/11 times. Stories delivered in the form of reports emanating from Bushworld (Maureen Dowd's term)—such as Condoleezza Rice's infamous "mushroom cloud" comment and the pervasive false assertions that Iraq caused the 9/11 terrorist attacks—influence American reality. These fictions are so many alternative history science fiction stories. Genly's words, then, apply both to his own world and the post 9/11 American political world: "I was taught ... on my homeworld that Truth is a matter of the imagination" (Le Guin *Left Hand of Darkness* 7), he says. September 11, 2001, and the Al-Qaeda attacks on American installations occurring prior to this date, mark when it—American reality—changed. The attacks and the planes caused a change which can be described as when Americans, like Genly, lost their home world. We can't go home again.

According to the narrator of *Changing Planes*, protagonist Sita Dulip of Cincinnati discovers that experiencing post 9/11 wretched travel conditions causes airports to act as portals to changed planes, other-worldly fantasy locales. Le Guin substitutes things imagined for 9/11 induced "things fall apart" in a series of linked tales (what Le Guin calls a "story suite"— (*Birthday of the World "Foreword,"* xii) about how the fantastic travel method Dulip discovers enables airports to serve as portals to different worlds.[1] Dulip visits places akin to the fantastic locations described in *Gulliver's Travels* and to Italo Calvino's *Invisible Cities*. In response to the wreckage which ensues after terrorists cause things to fall apart, Le Guin transforms the negative and mundane into the fantastic and the new. The Borgesian infinite, recast as the seemingly endless horror of "sitting for over an hour on a blue plastic chair with

---

[1] The "story suite" which comprises *Changing Planes* consists of sixteen stories. Six of these stories were previously published between 1998 and 2002.

metal tubes for legs bolted to the floor in a row of people sitting in blue
plastic chairs with metal tubes for legs bolted to the floor facing a row
of people sitting in blue plastic chairs with metal tubes for legs bolted
to the floor" ("Sita Dulip's Method" 4), changes airports into a science
fiction gateways to, say, voyages to Arcturus. This transformation is
a creative response to when it changed, when terrorists positioned an
airport as a portal enabling them to deploy mundane commercial planes
as horrific weapons. Against the Western capitalist world Le Guin
imagines changing the terrorists' planes by remodeling their altered
airport as a means to change planes (places of being situated); this
difference creatively illuminates the "everything" capitalism includes.
The terrorists read "changing planes" to denote mass destruction.
Changing Planes can be read in terms of juxtapositions which emerge
from constructive creativity. *Changing Planes* is replete with instances
in which the mundane becomes extraordinary. Le Guin's references to
her own writing and the writing of her fellow fantastic fiction authors
accompany Dulip's travels to other realms. These references emphasize
Le Guin's connection to Joanna Russ, assert that she and Russ are
on the same plane. More specifically, *Changing Planes* as a totality
embraces Russ's "When It Changed"; Le Guin's story suite—which
when presented together reads as a linked whole—implies that she
was never on a higher plane in relation to twentieth century feminist
science fiction.[2]

Other representative post 9/11 science fiction and mainstream novels
have focused upon the terrorist attacks.[3] I include two science fiction
novels—William Gibson's *Spook Country* (2007) and Brian Francis
Slattery's *Spaceman Blues: A Love Story* (2007)—and three mainstream
novels: Don DeLillo's *Falling Up* (2007), Jonathan Safran Foer's
Extremely Loud & Incredibly Close (2005), and John Updike's *Terrorist*
(2006). Novels which focus upon 9/11 best exemplify the relationship
between our science fictional real world and the "new normal"
ludicrousness of branding science fiction as being inferior to realistic
literature. *Changing Planes*, however, is the first post 9/11 feminist
science fiction work that directly addresses the terrorist attacks.

---

[2] I of course realize that some of the stories were written before September 11,
2001. Viewed as a whole, however, the stories in *Changing Plane* reflect a temporally
fluid *zeitgeist* rather than a specific calendar date. I refer to the fact that Al-Qaeda
attacked two United States embassies and the USS Cole prior to September 11, 2001.
What we call "the 60's" did not end when the clock struck midnight on December
31, 1969; what we call "9/11" was in evidence before September 11, 2001.

[3] Throughout this essay, when I refer to the "post 9/11 novel," I specifically mean
novels which focus upon the terrorist attacks.

I. It's a Mad, Mad, Mad, Mad Science Fiction World

The 1963 film *It's a Mad, Mad, Mad, Mad World* includes almost every major comedian of the time participating in a mad-cap hunt for nefariously garnered money buried under a giant "W" symbol. Follow the misbegotten money to "W?" Did time travelers from the future inspire this movie to communicate an early warning signal about the post-9/11 doings of the president known as "W?" I recognize that this notion is far fetched. William Gibson, though, tells us that contemporary reality is a mad, mad, mad, mad science fiction scenario world. This is his answer to Deborah Solomon's question about when American life became stranger than science fiction: "If I had gone into a publisher in New York in 1981 and told them I wanted to write a novel that is set in a world where the climate is out of whack and Mideast terrorists have hijacked airplanes and in response the U.S. has invaded the wrong country—it's too much. Contemporary reality is like an overlapping set of dire science fiction scenarios" (Solomon 13).

Gibson's new novel, *Spook Country*, which rather realistically portrays the present, could not have been published in the recent past; it would have been perceived as being too outlandishly over the top. Contemporary reality is science fictional to the extent that it goes beyond the parameters of 1981 genre science fiction. By necessity, the contemporary mainstream realistic novel resembles yesterday's 1981 science fiction. There is, then, a new affinity existing between what was once 1981 science fiction and today's realistic novels. The latter works must reflect the overlapping science fiction scenarios which comprise present reality. Science fiction is the new realism; elitist barriers erected to separate "high brow" realistic mainstream literature and "low brow" genre science fiction are as yesterday as telegrams—and post 9/11 novels enable us to read all about it. The convergence between the science fictional and the real that Gibson describes establishes a telegramesque STOP to the discrimination against science fiction I have called "textism."[4] Mainstream writers now embrace the alien, that is to say the immigrant. Science fiction writers eschew such fantastic locales as Annarres, Urras, and Gethen in favor of New York City—and even Cincinnati. Mainstream and science fiction post 9/11 writers, instead of differentiating themselves by choosing either to exclude or include such science fiction accoutrements as warp drives and zap guns, jettison flying saucers and locate their work in the same boat: the recognizable here and now. Science fiction about 9/11 has become less fantastic; mainstream literature about 9/11 revolves around aliens.

---

[4] See Marleen S. Barr, "Textism—An Emancipation Proclamation.".

John Updike's *Terrorist* exemplifies this trend. The exceedingly multicultural Central High School located in very blue collar New Prospect, New Jersey, is the milieu of protagonist Ahmad Mulloy Ashmawy. The upper class people Updike places in *Couples* would react to Ashmawy and his classmates in terms of cognitive estrangement. Le Guin's narrator seems to express the reaction I attribute to those who inhabit *Couples* with these words: "Wasn't there something I could do? Click my heels and say, 'I want to be in Kansas?'" (Le Guin "Confusions of Uni" 243). Resistance to change, to the brave new science fiction real world, accomplished via clicking heels is futile—for real people and protagonists of mainstream novels alike. One of Kansas's favorite sons is a brilliant and exciting black senator who is running for president. I don't think we are in what was recently WASP hegemonic Kansas anymore. And *Terrorist* is most certainly not set in Rabbit Angstrom's America anymore.

And neither is Jonathan Safran Foer's *Extremely Loud & Incredibly Close*, one of the first mainstream novels published in response to 9/11. *Extremely Loud* evokes Germany, that most alien Other locale in relation to American Jews. The tambourine playing protagonist, Oskar Schell, of course alludes to Gunter Grass's Oskar Matzerath. *Extremely Loud* focuses upon the bombing of Dresden as recalled by Oskar's grandfather. I don't think that the young New York Jewish hipster readers of *Heeb Magazine* are in the old country German world anymore. Further, Foer, to exemplify his affinity with the fantastic, turns the final pages of *Extremely Loud* into a flip book; these pages literally cause a man who jumps from the World Trade Center to appear to be falling up. Updike and Foer write post 9/11 novels which position old elitist designations between science fiction and mainstream literature as things which have fallen apart.

Spook Country, like Updike's *Terrorist*, features a protagonist who is alien in relation to Caucasian America: Gibson's Tito, a young Cuban-Chinese immigrant who speaks Russian, is almost as unusual in regard to the American mainstream as alien little green men. In the manner of *Spook Country,* debut science fiction novelist Brian Francis Slattery's *Spaceman Blues: A Love Story* shows how science fiction about 9/11 is set in the science fiction scenario which forms the present reality. The title of Will Hermes's review of *Spaceman,* "The Tentacles of Foreigners," aptly describes the real aliens who populate post 9/11 science fiction. *Spaceman* involves the doings of Manuel de Guzman Gonzalez, Swami Horowitz, and Masoud Azzi. These protagonists inhabit a New York City world which is, in reality, Other in relation to the real Manhattan. In Hermes's words: "the book is not so much about immigrants as the immigrant experience…. *Spaceman's Blues* suggests that in New York's multicultural arcade, we are all immigrants. His novel hits Coney Island and Red Hook, chills in Breezy Point and the Rockaways, hangs in the stank [sic] of the Gowanus Canal" (Hermes 58).

The post 9/11 mainstream and science fiction novels I mention are devoid of flying saucers; the protagonists are more comfortable on subways. They can all take the mundane subway the MTA calls "the train to the plane"—go to Kennedy Airport and change planes. They must do so in a way that coincides with reality, however. Changing planes in the manner of *Changing Planes* is not an option for them. This is not to say that the fantastic is off limits to all the protagonists. Yes, Foer's Oskar is tied to the real world. The man who falls up in *Extremely Loud*, however, might be appropriately situated in Don DeLillo's *Falling Man* (2007), the most critically acclaimed mainstream post 9/11 novel.

According to Frank Rich, in *Falling Man* DeLillo creates an alternative reality scenario which teeters between the real and the unreal. DeLillo, then, writes in the vein of Foer, Gibson, Slattery, and Updike—and, as I will explain in detail, of Le Guin. Rich says: "While there are just enough signposts to keep 'Falling Man' tethered to a recognizable reality, it's an askew, alternative-reality variation on the literal.... The entire city, not just downtown, is in the physical and emotional limbo of a frozen zone.... This time the falling men and women tumble before the reader with no safety harness, no net or simile or irony, nothing to break their fall. It is not performance art, but the real thing, and it brings at least a measure of memory, tenderness and meaning to all that howling space" (8, 9). Like DeLillo, Le Guin tackles "the real thing" that constituted 9/11 via the unreal. Her protagonists literally do escape to infinite locations positioned in all that howling other world space. Her vision is much more unreal and bold than that of her male science fiction colleagues. Slattery becomes exotic when he ignores Gibson's Manhattan to spotlight outer borough reality, not outer space. The places that Le Guin calls Islac and Mahigul for example, unlike Brooklyn and Queens, contain no "train to the plane" stations. She comments upon our world by creating new worlds.

II. The Rain In "Spane" No Longer Stays Mainly In Our Plane

Changing Planes can be understood in terms of Rich's reading of *Falling Man* because like De Lillo's novel, Le Guin's text is replete with both recognizable reality signposts and askew alternative realities. Sita Dulip, like the Parsons women portrayed in James Tiptree's "The Women Men Don't See" (1975), matter of factly, without pomp and circumstance, leaves our world and goes to another one. Dulip and the Parsons women respond to being powerless in a manner analogous to *Spook Country* protagonists in the same circumstance. Dave Itzkoff explains: "More than a post-9/11 novel, it [*Spook Country*] is arguably the first example of the post-post-9/11 novel, whose characters are tired of being pushed around by forces larger than they are—bureaucracy, history and, always, technology—and are at long last ready to start pushing back" (4). The number of "posts" Itzkoff calls for aside, he alludes to why *Changing Planes* is a specifically feminist post-9/11 work. Dulip changes the effect of larger than life forces which are definitely not with her. While closely encountering the combined forces of bureaucracy, history, and technology which form the extreme unpleasantness characterizing the contemporary airport, this person— doubly powerless as an immigrant woman—changes her powerlessness into a powerful means to push back. Her "push back," the term used to describe a plane initially moving away from an airport gate, functions as a "gate to women's country"—transportation to places located beyond patriarchal reality. Dulip discovers a feminist version of what Itzkoff calls Gibson's "playing on the word 'spook,' not just in the slang sense of a spy, but also in the more traditional sense of a ghost—of figures who pass through the world unnoticed and unrecognized, and who are about to find out how empowering anonymity can be" (Itzkoff 4). Like the unnoticed and unrecognized "ordinary" women appearing in Le Guin's "Sur," women who journey to Antarctica without recognition, Dulip is empowered by experiencing anonymous—and feminist—adventure beyond the boundaries of patriarchy. Itzkoff explains that Gibson and the *Spook Country* protagonists interpret the future as "a clean slate for all of them, and whether his characters realize it or not, the author surely understands that this is a symbol of ultimate freedom" (4). Le Guin's feminist version of this clean slate involves creating a feminist science fiction analogue to the feminist empowerment Susan Gubar attributes to Isak Dinesen's "The Blank Page."[5] Le Guin fills blank pages with stories about how an ordinary/extraordinary woman like Dulip can, with benign safety analogous to a *Star Trek* Holodeck altered reality, undertake leaving patriarchy. Traveling far far away from patriarchy constitutes the ultimate freedom for women. What a *New York Times* editorial calls a post 9/11 "dread of flying" (Editorial A16) enables Dulip to escape what Erica Jong famously described as the specifically female "fear of flying." Since Dulip is afraid of post 9/11 "normal" flying, she evades the airports' "reality planes."

[5] See Susan Gubar, "'The Blank Page' and the Issues of Female Creativity."

Itzkoff points out that in *Pattern Recognition* and *Spook Country,* Gibson steps away from the technological fantasy worlds he once created (Itzkoff 4). So too for Le Guin. *Changing Planes,* which is even devoid of the literally story-fueled spaceships which figure in *A Fisherman of the Inland Sea,* emphasizes a nonmechanical fantastic: Teddy Bears who are living pets, dreamers whose dreams form a biologically based internet, human hybrids of animals and vegetables, and people who fly with flesh-made wings. Those wishing to visit winged people "may spend a week in Gy without ever seeing a winged native or learning that what they took for a bird or a jet was a woman on her way across the sky" (Le Guin "The Fliers of Gy" 197). Influenced by the jeopardy characterizing the post 9/11 world, Le Guin alludes to the most stereotypical of all science fiction questions—and she provides a new feminist answer. Is it a bird? Is it a plane? No. It's an "ordinary" Gy "super" flying woman. Her answer involves changing reality planes to encounter difference: observing bird/people, for example. Le Guin's response also refers to the marginalization of science fiction and fantasy literature. "Why Are Americans Afraid of Dragons?" Le Guin once asked in an essay title. The fear of fantasy Le Guin discusses—a cognitive estrangement from the strange—is so twentieth century. Many Americans, now newly obsessed with being afraid of terrorists, no longer have the luxury of being afraid of dragons. Many Americans would currently give anything to go back to the twentieth century science fiction/fantasy future where imaginatively changing locational planes involved close encounters with the then despised dragons and flying saucers. The marginalizing displeasure once directed toward science fiction characters, such as the *Star Wars* Wookie and Eleanor Arnason's fur creatures, has been supplanted by hatred for alien terrorists, the real men who really live in caves. Fantasy lions and tigers and bears, oh my; Wookies, fur people, and Le Guin's plant people are now welcomed in an atavistic harkening back to the late twentieth century world. The new response to once outlandish fantasy and science fiction characters: bring 'em on. As Michael Moore's *Fahrenheit 9/11* makes so patently clear, Bush, for one, could not manage to tear himself away from a juvenile story—"My Pet Goat"—and face the inception of 9/11 reality.

Changing Planes has more in common with twentieth century genre feminist science fiction than with the recent mainstream and science fiction post 9/11 novels written by men I have described. This affinity to a literary past involving writers such as Tiptree and Russ is logical. The planes the terrorists hijacked did change everything—except patriarchal reality.[6] Like Tiptree's women men don't see, Sita Dulip, a spectator,

[6] For a feminist analysis of how 9/11 impacted patriarchal reality see Susan Faludi, *The Terror Dream: Fear and Fantasy in Post-9/11 America.*

might fare better in another, nonpatriarchal world. What has plainly not changed from Tiptree's time to the present is that, upon departure, Dulip and the Parsons women will not be missed. Despite the new affinity existing between the post 9/11 mainstream and science fiction novel, the women men don't see, invisible women, are still with us. Le Guin, instead of writing in the vein of Gibson or Slattery, stresses this point. She positions *Changing Planes* as a vehicle to declare her affinity to twentieth century feminist science fiction. The work's authorial voice affirms that Le Guin does not welcome being positioned as the serene science fiction grande dame who stands apart from the strident Russ, Tiptree, and Suzy McKee Charnas. Or, in terms of two women who are not known for writing science fiction, Le Guin prefers not to play Brooke Astor in relation to irreverent feminist science fiction writers characterized as Bella Abzug.[7]

Changing Planes emphasizes that the pre 9/11 late twentieth century world is now a once upon a time or, in terms of the conclusion to Russ's "When It Changed, "for a while." It took Americans "a while" to understand the nature of this change. "Children learn what is real and what isn't" (Le Guin "Social Dreaming of the Frin" 80); not so for the Americans who still believe that Iraqis were responsible for 9/11.[8]

Changing Planes is also post 9/11 feminist science fiction which emphasizes that science fiction is serious literature. The text itself metafictionally points toward this reading. The "Author's Note" placed at the beginning of *Changing Planes* directly mentions the 9/11 perpetrators, the "bigots with beards in caves." Le Guin describes exceedingly fantastic scenarios which reflect contemporary American politics. The "Elder of Isu," for example, lists utterances which describe the forever war Bush calls the War on Terror: "2. It is almost ready [or] Be ready for it soon. 3. Unexpected. 4. It will never cease…. 11. It will not cease." (Le Guin "The Silence of the Asonu" 23). The "Premier of Islac," who Islac citizens can "never, ever get rid of," is "a pious hypocrite and a greedy, petty, stupid, mean-minded crook" ("Porridge on Islac" 15, 16). Le Guin takes no chance that readers will miss her intended message that a story about never ever getting rid of Bush is a horror story beyond imagination. The title of her story "She Unnames Them" does not figure here. She names him directly: Accommodations on the fourth island include the "George W. Bush Grand Luxury Hotel and Suites. (It was

---

[7] Bella Abzug (1920-1998), was a Bronx-born daughter of Russian immigrants who became a politician known for her feminism and stridency. Brooke Astor (1902-2007) was a philanthropist, socialite, and author who epitomized propriety.

[8] For a discussion of the political implications of this misconception, see Al Gore, *The Assault on Reason*.

foolish of me to hope for a grim motel with hourly rates called The Last Resort of Scoundrels)" ("Great Joy" 143). The fourth island, replete with nightly Iwo Jima fireworks displays, patriotic steak houses, and godly prayer chapels, is a paradise for conservative Republicans. Luckily, I do not think that conservative Republicans read Le Guin. If they did, Republican hordes might be seen sitting in airport lounges trying to imitate Sita Dulip. This effort might take the form of a reverse Nexium commercial scenario in which people try "to induce the necessary stress and indigestion" ("Great Joy" 133) which, as we are aware, would enable them to change planes and attend the 2008 Republican National Convention located on the fourth island. The reality of "the funny name in Florida" (145), presumably hanging chads, is sufficiently nauseating to induce *Changing Planes* changed plane mode. How can we try to travel with Dulip? Based upon the absolutely justifiable and welcome Bush bashing, I quote above, I think Le Guin would agree that Bushworld can induce enough distress and nausea in liberals to forever serve as their Borgesian infinite frequent flyer miles to changed planes.

Contemporary American ideological political separation aside, *Changing Planes* discusses itself and asserts that it should not be categorized as marginalized genre fiction, that literature should not be divided into separate and unequal planes. As Le Guin is not subtle about her distaste for Bush in particular and Republicans in general, she directly indicates her displeasure for how science fiction writers, herself included, are disconnected from the valorized canonical literary heritage. She asserts that the exalted Swift also wrote linked fantasy stories and that she descends from him. To do so, again rejecting "unnaming," she directly mentions Swift: "*Gulliver's Travels*" and "Swift's works" ("The Island of the Immortals" 215, 216) name Le Guin's right on target insistence upon being a contemporary literary figure who is connected to literary tradition. Here Le Guin and Russ share the same emphasis: Russ positions her "little book" *The Female Man* (1975) (213-14) firmly in the Chaucerian and Swiftian tradition. Further, *Changing Planes* also directly expresses its connection to the renowned father of postmodern literature, Jorge Luis Borges. "Social Dreaming of the Frin" refers to the Borgesian trope of many dreamers sharing dreams: "'the doctor already knows what the patient dreamed last night, because the doctor dreamed it too; and the patient also dreamed what the doctor dreamed; and so did everyone else in the neighborhood' (Le Guin 76). In addition, "The Building" names one of the most recognizably Borgesian tropes of all: "a maze, a labyrinth" (192). Even more directly, Le Guin's narrator links herself to Borges and his love of libraries: "I, like Borges, think of heaven as something very like a library" ("Woeful Tales from Mahigul"

106). Le Guin's "I, like Borges" functions as emphasis added to Donna Haraway's manifesto about respecting science fiction cyborgs—sans excluding the ones women authors imagine. (Le Guin mentions "Mills College Press" in "Social Dreaming of the Frin" (77). Mills College is the oldest institution of higher education for women in the United States and the first women's college to offer a computer science major. Mills College Press, then, would be an appropriate publication venue for the manifesto I describe.)

Le Guin, of course, refers to venerated women writers. The "constant alertness, like that of a mother who ... is listening every moment for the cry of her baby in another room" ("The Silence of the Asonu" 22) is analogous to the mother incessantly listening for the "child cry" Tillie Olsen emphasizes in *Silences* (1980.) "All the Warriors of Akagraj were now women" ("The Ire of the Veksi" 44) is a statement which seemingly alludes to Maxine Hong Kingston's *The Woman Warrior* (1975) as well as to the woman warrior science fiction subgenre Jessica Amanda Salmonson's work epitomizes. The character who is "being squashed by a pair of giant breasts, huge ones, with pointy nipples," ("Social Dreaming of the Frin" 78) would recognize the giant mammary gland which is the central focus of Philip Roth's *The Breast* (1972.) *The Breast*—and Roth's alternative history novel *The Plot Against America* (2004)—are written by a mainstream "great American novelist" who incorporates science fiction in his work.

Le Guin also alludes to acknowledged great writers who remain true to genre science fiction. The "Daqo attempted to use the Aq as slaves for domestic or factory work but failed" ("The Building" 182). According to Le Guin's more humane version of H. G. Wells' science fiction scenario, the Daqo are analogous to failed Morlocks and the Aq luckily enjoy better circumstances than the Eloi.

Le Guin alludes to Tiptree and Joan Slonczewski as well as to Wells and Roth. "The rest of the world is ocean" ("The Seasons of the Ansarac" 54) instantly recalls the water world called Ocean in Joan Slonczewski's *A Door Into Ocean* (1987). The "airborne germ that would sterilise all Hy Brisalian males" ("Wake Island" 152) is one with the modus operandi of the aliens in Tiptree's "The Screwfly Solution."(1978). In "Screwfly," the aliens do the sterilizing; in the essay I call "The Females Do the Fathering,"[9] I explore how Tiptree's work questions using gender stereotypes as a basis for assigning parenting roles. Le Guin's protagonist in "The Seasons of the Ansarac" follows my line of thought in regard to Tiptree's work: "Why should a child be left to the mother only?" (72).

[9] See Marleen S. Barr, "'The Females Do the Fathering': James Tiptree's Male Matriarchs and Adult Human Gametes."

This question could have been asked by a number of Tiptree's characters and a large number of second wave feminists alike.

Today, many young parents would agree that a child who is left to the mother only is being reared in terms of rigid lack of vision. *Changing Planes* does not include these real people. Unlike her colleagues who set their post 9/11 texts in the recognizably real present, Le Guin emphasizes science fiction locales and her oeuvre's connection to them. Within her stories, such fantastic places as Hegn and Mahigul signal her connection to the history of genre science fiction. Le Guin, then, treats her own work as a source of allusion, as she treats Tiptree's and Wells' texts.

"The king was pregnant" (*Left Hand of Darkness* 90), Le Guin once wrote; murder of gender stereotypes, she wrote. I quote the most startling sentence in *The Left Hand of Darkness*. With one stroke of her pen, Le Guin rewrote roles women and men played throughout history. She is at it again in *Changing Planes*. "The Royals of Hegn" contains a very other-worldly sentence: "Everybody is a member of the royal family" (90). So much for class barriers. Those who have difficulty understanding the meaning of eradicating class and gender categories can avail themselves of a "translatomat" ("Feeling At Home With The Hennebet" 37), the latest version of the communicating device Le Guin previously called the "ansible."

The two separate species who inhabit the plane of Qoq in "The Building" do not need a translatomat. Despite their disparate locations — "The Aq inhabited the southern continent, the Daqo were in the northern hemisphere" (180) — they do not have a communication problem. Like the separated people who live on the planets Urras and Annares in *The Dispossessed,* the Aq and the Daqo experience political rather than linguistic differences. (Perhaps Le Guin is suggesting that the language of science fiction is worth listening to as a means to assuage real national differences.)

Two distinct sentient species also appear in "The Seasons of the Ansarac": "They were a great people, full of knowledge, with high sciences and great ease and luxury of life. To them we truly were little more than animals" (71), explains Kergemmeg, a native host and guide. This relationship between two peoples of differing technological abilities is akin to the primitive furry forest dwellers who encounter technologically more advanced people in Le Guin's *The Word for World Is Forest*. Kergemmeg points to another connection between "The Seasons of the Ansarac" and an earlier work written by Le Guin: "Kergemmeg said that while they [his people] are in the south, they do not miss their sexuality at all." (69). Kergemmeg's people, like the Gethenians in *The Left Hand of Darkness*, engage in sex only under certain conditions. They migrate between northern and southern continents and become sexual when they are in the north. Kergemmeg explains further: "Because our lives in the north and the south are so different that they seem, to you others, incoherent, incomplete. And we cannot connect them rationally" (70). He describes two separations: his people's locationally determined sexual behavior difference and their difference from the "others" who visit from different planes. Here, again, the schism existing between Urras and Annares is evoked. However, in terms of Le Guin's previous work, convergence also characterizes Kergemmeg's description. When Kergemmeg—whose name sharply recalls the polysyllabic "K" name Kurremkarmerruk in Le Guin's Earthsee—describes separation, his words invoke the plots of *The Left Hand of Darkness* and *The Dispossessed*. In *The Left Hand of Darkness,* people can only have sex during rigidly specific times; in *The Dispossessed*, people inhabit two separated communities. Le Guin then turns to her own work to emphasize juxtaposition. Her self-referential mergers function as a self-made construction which speaks against the destructive breaking apart which Al-Qaeda makes real.

While metafictionally connecting itself to Le Guin's previous work, *Changing Planes* openly comments upon her relationship to twentieth century feminist science fiction. For many years, science fiction scholars placed Le Guin on a pedestal, valorized her as the token great woman science fiction writer. Labeled as "humanist" rather than as a "feminist," she was separated from her sister women science fiction writers. I, for one, remember very purposefully often not writing about Le Guin in the early 1990s because, in order to counter the "all Le Guin all the time" science fiction criticism penchant of the time, I wanted to direct attention to other women science fiction writers. The emphasis upon juxtaposition characterizing *Changing Planes* now manifests itself in terms of Le Guin's relationship with her women colleagues. I think that Le Guin wishes belatedly to connect herself to unruly, irreverent twentieth century feminist science fiction. In *Changing Planes,* she echoes the circa 1970s (and still pertinent) feminist science fiction insistence that women can be even better at performing certain important jobs than men.[10] "The

[10] The feminist arguments from the 1970s are unfortunately not old fashioned. For example, Lisa Belkin explains that "Catalyst's [an organization that studies women in the workplace] research is often an exploration of why, 30 years after women entered the work force in large numbers, the default mental image of a leader is still male. Most recent is the report titled 'Damned if You Do, Doomed if You Don't,' which surveyed 1,231 senior executives from the United States and Europe. It found that women who act in ways that are consistent with gender stereotypes . . . are considered less competent. But if they act in ways that are seen as more 'male' . . . they are seen as 'too tough' and 'unfeminine.' Women can't win" (Belkin G1-G2). Further, the fact

Fliers of Gy," for example, points out that the women of Gy, due to their lighter bodies, are the best long distance flyers ("Gy" 202). As I have mentioned, Gy plane women fly with wings, not planes. What is true for them is also true for human female pilots, though. Even today people still deny this biologically determined truth about women and flying: women, who are usually smaller than men, have the logical right stuff to fit in small space travel vehicles and fighter plane cockpits. So, if Le Guin presently wishes to affirm and emphasize her connection to the last century's strident feminist science fiction chorus, *Changing Planes* has not missed the feminist social critique boat. As the woman Gy fliers question human gender based work role stereotypes, a woman shipmaster, in the manner of the Freegans who now garner the media spotlight, questions capitalist economic imperatives.[11] The shipmaster believes that it is normal sometimes to do some work without pay, to function outside capitalism ("The Building" 188).

Le Guin's most noticeable effort to connect herself to the history of feminist science fiction in *Changing Planes* comes via one sentence, a twenty first century version of "[t]he king was pregnant (*Left Hand of Darkness* 90): "Many pair bonds are between two men or two women" ("The Seasons of the Ansarac" 63). Here Le Guin, the "acceptable" heterosexual wife and mother, incorporates homosexuality, aligns her writing with feminist lesbian science fiction. She echoes her stories "Another Story, or A Fisherman of the Inland Sea" and "Mountain Ways" which describe the bisexuality and polyfidelity marriage system practiced on the planet O.[12] The echo serves as an emphasis to underscore that her writing is not so acceptable after all. A stronger emphasis on this point comes in another such echo: "The large, many-roomed omedra contain households, usually a group of related women and their children or sexually partnered women and their children. Men—relatives, sexual

---

that today's young adult women routinely position their mothers as their advisers also shows that 1970s feminist ideas are not antiquated. According to Stephanie Rosenbloom, "There have always been close-knit mother-daughter relationships. But social, demographic and technological changes have made it more common for adult daughters to keep their mothers' apron strings tied tighter—and for longer, say researchers who study the transition into young adulthood. Today, it is not unusual for unmarried middle-class women in their 20s or 30s to share with their mothers the diary-worthy details of their lives . . . and call the Mommy Batphone when they need help" (Rosenbloom G1). Rather than dredging up obsolete material, when Le Guin evokes 1970s feminist science fiction, she writes in terms of a new twenty first century feminist science fiction trope made real: "the Mommy Batphone."

[11] See Steven Kurutz, "Not Buying It."

[12] Other works by Le Guin which describe complex family relationships include "Coming of Age in Karhide" and *The Telling*. Separatism is depicted in "Solititude" and "The Matter of Seggri."

partners, and friends—can join a household only on invitation, may leave at will, and must leave if ordered out by the women. If they don't leave, all the women and most of the other men attack them savagely, drive them away bleeding, and throw stones at them if they try to return" ("The Ire of the Veksi" 43). Although "The Ire of the Veksi" is more reserved than Tiptree's "Houston, Houston Do You Read" (in which women kill men), the passage I quote is written in the vein of Pamela Sargent's *The Shore of Women* (1986), in which women expel men from their all-female society. Le Guin now embraces feminist separatist science fiction, a category which does not include the critically lauded *The Left Hand of Darkness* and *The Dispossessed*. She signals that the time has come to elevate such fiction, to applaud it, to remove it from its status as a subgenre positioned within a still often maligned genre. Russ's *The Female Man* is as great as *The Left Hand of Darkness* and *The Dispossessed*.

The passage in "The Ire of the Veksi" also relates to a 2007 separatist novel, Doris Lessing's *The Cleft*.[13] The feminist science fiction community has not, to say the least, welcomed this separatist utopia written by one of the world's greatest living novelists. Like the critical uproar which greeted "When It Changed," *The Cleft* has generated much controversy. "When It Changed" was too feminist for its time; *The Cleft* is not feminist enough for our time. Le Guin is not happy with Lessing: "men achieve; women nag. Much of the presentation of this is familiar from the literature of misogyny.... They're [Lessing's separatist female protagonists] a lot of slobbering walruses, till the Prince comes along" ("Saved by a Squirt"). Le Guin positions Lessing as an object of science fiction community derision, a new version of the ridicule that was once aimed at Russ. I wonder if, in the future, *The Cleft*, like "When It Changed," will be belatedly accepted and respected. Perhaps critics will eventually conclude that just as the denizens of twentieth century women's separatist communities had the right to do nonheroic things such as fight among themselves, their early twenty first century sisters have the right to be slobbering walruses. When men land on Russ's Whileaway, they encounter a feminist separatist community and ask, "Where are all your people?" ("When It Changed" 273). As we are now well aware, defining "people" according to one particular limited interpretation is not a good thing to do. It is also shortsighted to approach a women's separatist community in terms of the women feminists want to see. Perhaps Lessing is purposely changing the plane regarding the expected characteristics of women's separatist communities. Perhaps feminists are railing against how *The Cleft* signals

[13] My comments about Lessing were written before she won the Nobel Prize.

when women's separatist utopias changed. Lessing is clearly changing
the plane of feminist science fiction in a manner which is inconsistent
with *Changing Planes.*
"The time has come, the walrus said, to talk of many things." Once
upon a time during my early career, I could never have imagined that in
my future—in what was to become the post 9/11 world—I would talk of
Le Guin calling Lessing's protagonists a plethora of slobbering walruses!
Even in the heyday of reaction against separatist feminist science fiction,
no one ever equated this literature with slobbering walruses! Russ's essay
"Amor Vincit Foeminam: The Battle of the Sexes in Science Fiction"
(1980) differentiates between feminist utopias and the antifeminist
novels about all-female societies written by men. *Changing Planes* seems
to address the content of this essay: "All that will change. You will see"
(Le Guin "The Seasons of the Ansarac" 73). The battle of the sexes in
science fiction has changed. The new battle involves Le Guin, in no
uncertain terms, railing that Lessing attaches herself to the literature of
misogyny. Lessing, who is even more revered by feminists and literary
critics than Le Guin, now creates separatist science fiction which is as
maligned as Russ's separatist fiction (and her own science fiction series
which began with *Shikasta,*) once were. In response to *Shikasta* and
its nonrealistic fiction ilk, the mainstream critical establishment took a
negative view of Lessing's turn toward science fiction. In response to
Lessing's portrayal of female separatists, the feminist science fiction
critical community finds fault with her depiction of separatist women.
Elizabeth Bear, for example, calls *The Cleft* "an actively bad novel"—(
BWO2). Now is when it changed. Le Guin's criticism of Lessing is a
clash of the women science fiction writer titans, devoid of the Prince, a
changed plane. Protagonists of feminist utopias assert that women are
people; hence, these protagonists have the right to get down off their
pedestals and clash.

III. (Extra)Ordinary People: Ursula Le Guin/Joanna Russ—and Ita Aber

On a more positive note in relation to Le Guin and Russ, the critical
response cleft which once separated them has changed from a great divide
into a union. Le Guin stood outside the controversy which accompanied
the publication of "When It Changed." As *Changing Planes* exemplifies,
Le Guin now writes in a manner which, in the manner of Russ's oeuvre,
is specifically feminist. In 1986, Brian Aldiss used the word "angry" to
characterize Russ's work—not Le Guin's (Aldiss 364). Thousands of
years of sexism is certainly something to be angry about. Even though

Le Guin has been publicly angry since she wrote "Is Gender Necessary? Redux" in 1987, Russ, not Le Guin, bore the brunt of misogynistic responses to feminist science fiction. Le Guin, who by repeating her anger signals that she is open to brunt bearing, seems to wish that this penchant for disassociating her from rancor might change. Perhaps the basis of her exalted elevation can be attributed Robert Scholes' often cited 1974 essay about Le Guin "The Good Witch of the West." When Scholes described "our already considerable debt of gratitude for the benevolent magic of [Le Guin] the Good Witch of the West" (12), he typecast her as Glinda. Just as the range of, for example, Sally Field's artistic power is not limited to her role in "The Flying Nun," the range of Le Guin's artistic power is not limited to being a Glinda-esque goody goody. *Changing Planes* articulates Le Guin's struggle against the typecasting which routinely inhibits fantastic female artists.

In contrast to Le Guin, positioned as the polite good witch of the west, the science fiction critical establishment assigned to Russ the role of the unsubtle bad witch of the east. This binary opposition between positive and negative—the same tactic which manifests itself as high school "good girls" and "bad girls" —as well as the Madonna Whore Complex—is a categorization used to disempower women. Designating some of Russ's work as "controversial" figured in the decision to give her the Science Fiction Research Association Pilgrim Award in 1988, before Le Guin received it in 1989. According to 1988 Pilgrim Award committee chair Carol Stevens, the committee designated Le Guin as the "safe" candidate and Russ as the "unsafe" candidate. (For reasons beyond the purview of this essay, the committee chose to give the award to the "unsafe" candidate first).[14]

During the 1980s it was so easy to demonize Russ, a Jewish lesbian from the Bronx, and elevate the more conventional Le Guin to iconic science fiction status. (Remember that in the early 1990s Hillary Clinton had to present herself as a cookie baker; a "female man" definitely does not bake cookies.) As I mentioned, Le Guin has pointed out Americans' penchant for being afraid of dragons. I cannot recall any scholar who has posited that the different receptions accorded Le Guin's and Russ's early work can be attributed to the fact that Americans are afraid of class. Le Guin is the child of eminent scholars; Russ is the child of the working class. Russ, unlike Le Guin, did not walk the hegemonic walk or talk the hegemonic talk. The late Grace Paley, who paved the way for respecting the Bronx-born Jewish feminist literary voice, is a mainstream writer who is Russ's literary sister. Russ and Paley inhabit

---

[14] Carol Stevens gave me permission to include this information.

different cultural and class planes than Le Guin. Americans' fear of class should not silence stating this truth.

Nowadays a fictitious version of Russ, a Bronx-born Jew, would not qualify as being sufficiently different to be one of the ultra multicultural characters who populate Slattery's and Gibson's post 9/11 science fiction worlds. Presently, in the face of this extreme multiculturalism depiction, Le Guin and Russ, two white women, are not so different from each other. Now Le Guin's authorial voice in *Changing Planes* signals that she wishes to join with Russ in powerful feminist science fiction sisterhood. And, as a sign of this connection, in addition to noting the relationship between *Changing Planes* and the imaginary world stories of Swift, Borges, and Calvino, it is important to recognize that this text also repeats the form of Russ's *Extra(ordinary) People*, a collection of five stories about different imagined worlds. Le Guin seems to acknowledge this connection at the conclusion of *Changing Planes*. Readers learn that Sita Dulip, who, as I have explained, comes from central casting as a woman men don't see, is, in fact, an extra(ordinary) woman: "I was grateful to be back on my plane.... I found a flight to a beautiful, peaceful sane Los Engeles and went there" ("Confusions of Uni" 246). When the rain in Spain falls mainly in the plain, Dulip very plainly will not need an umbrella.

"Los Engeles" acts as a Rosetta Stone which reveals at the last minute that Dulip inhabits a plane which is not our own. We can't go back to the time pre-9/11. We, the denizens of a plane which includes an ugly, chaotic, mad mad mad mad science fiction world Los Angeles, can't go forth to "Los Engeles." Los Engeles is much more akin to the plane of flying winged people than to our plain ordinary City of Angels. The start of the first story in *Changing Planes* emphasizes the differences that seemingly similar words can convey: "the poles, the Poles, a lama, a llama" (Le Guin "Sita Dulip's Method" 1). Because Dulip of Los Engeles does not live *here,* she literally is an extra(ordinary) woman men don't see. Too bad that women cannot change planes, travel to her plane. It just might be better for us *there.*

Dulip never mentions that men live in her plane. Perhaps she inhabits a separatist feminist utopia where—unlike the many places Le Guin describes which biologically fused people and animals inhabit—women protagonists do not resemble slobbering walruses. In *Changing Planes*, Le Guin talks of many things—vegetables and kings included. The author of the gender crashing sentence "The king was pregnant," the author of the class crashing sentence "Everybody is a member of the royal family," the author whose plant/person protagonist announces "I'm corn, myself" ("Porridge on Islac" 14), can most certainly imagine a Cincinnati which differs from the Cincinnati we know. In *Changing Planes*, it would be perfectly sensible for Sita Dulip to have been born in a cabbage patch. We can never know for sure.

When readers first encounter Dulip, she explains that she "met a man from the Candensian plane which is very much like ours, only more of it consists of Toronto" ("Sita Dulip's Method" 6). In retrospect, we know that the Candensian plane is not at all "ours"; someone situated in the Candensian plane logically cannot think that they are in our Toronto anymore. As a final tie to the emphasis upon connection and combining in *Changing Planes*, I want to point out the affinity existing between two extraordinary women: Le Guin and her contemporary who hails from our own real Montreal. Le Guin shares more in common with Ita Aber, an artist who creates Jewish-themed needlework (a field even smaller and more esoteric than feminist science fiction) than with her male colleagues such as DeLillo, Foer, Gibson, Slattery, and Updike. Art historian Cassandra Langer indicates why this is so:

> Her skilled hands hold the power to draw the borders, boundaries, and raw edges that separate us, transforming them into works that hold us together.... By blurring the boundaries between abstraction and representation ... she deals with threads that twist the truth of our differences, merging them into designs and patterns carefully crafted to heal the inner fabric of our souls—all of which we have in common, rather than what drives us apart. Aber's attempt to mend our fragmented world ... is the highest form of artistic creativity (Langer exhibition brochure).

Le Guin's pen and paper (or computer), like Aber's needle and thread, transform separation into adhesion. Through representational abstraction, they tell the truth about how differences can be woven together to form a tapestry of human commonality. However, the preponderance of women's artistic attempts to mend the world, now called the highest form of artistic creativity, were until recently maligned and marginalized.

Women's needle art, quilts, for example, and feminist science fiction were both respectively routinely excluded from museums and the precincts of serious literature. These artistic expressions changed planes; once graded as "inferior," they are now given the "respected" seal of approval.

Le Guin and Aber, two women of a similar certain age, resist the temporal reality of joining the group of elderly women men don't see. They demand that we must look at them and their work head on. Le Guin, like Aber,

... has lived each moment to the fullest and she is adept at rekindling the flame of her imagination. She has the wisdom to know that physical aging does not diminish our optimism—our zest for life.... At an age when most people are ready for the rocking chair, Aber's desire is to touch, to taste to feel, to smell, and to envision art and life to their fullest measure. At the age of seventy-five, she is a hands-on artist who is not disembodied or distanced from her creativity (Langer exhibition brochure).

Regardless of our age, gender, or political leanings, we can all mend our differences by engaging with the once marginalized creative expressions these extra(ordinary) artists give us.

Aber, like Le Guin, artistically explores 9/11: her 9/11 quilt is exhibited in New York's World Trade Center Museum. And, as unlikely as it may seem, one of her handmade creations is self-consciously akin to feminist science fiction. Aber constructs her art out of feminine detritus: "artless materials: clothes, bags, ties, artificial flowers ... beads, and fish scales" (Langer exhibition brochure). One of her art works incorporates the metal tags the *Empire* kosher chicken company places on its poultry to certify that the product meets rabbinical standards. The title Aber gives this work is "The Empire Strikes Back." I read this feminist art work's science fiction title as a seal of approval for science fiction. A message in Aber's medium which now mainly and plainly falls in our own plane—and, by George, they've almost finally got it: feminist science fiction is kosher.

Works Cited

1. Aldiss, Brian and David Wingrove. *Trillion Year Spree: The History of Science Fiction*. London: Gollancz, 1986.
2. Barr, Marleen S. "'The Females Do the Fathering': James Tiptree's Male Matriarchs and Adult Human Gametes." *Science Fiction Studies*. 13 (1986), 42-49.
3. —. "Textism—An Emancipation Proclamation." *PMLA*. 119(2004), 429-441.
4. Bear, Elizabeth. "Of Woman Born." *Washington Post*. August 19, 2007. BWO2.
5. Belkin, Lisa. "The Feminine Critique." *New York Times*. November 1, 2007. G1-G2.

6. Calvino, Italo. *Invisible Cities*. New York: Harcourt Brace Jovanovich, 1974.

7. Dinesen, Isak. "The Blank Page." *Last Tales*. New York: Random House, 1957.

8. DeLillo, Don. *Falling Man*. New York: Scribner, 2007.

9. Dowd, Maureen. *Bushworld: Enter At Your Own Risk*. New York: G. P. Putnam's Sons, 2004.

10. Editorial. "Dread of Flying." *New York Times*. August 27, 2007. A16.

11. *Fahrenheit 9/11*. 2004. Lions Gate Films. Directed by Michael Moore. Written by Michael Moore.

12. Faludi, Susan. *The Terror Dream: Fear and Fantasy in Post-9/11 America*. New York: Metropolitan Books, 2007.

13. Foer, Jonathan Safran. *Extremely Loud & Incredibly Close*. Boston: Houghton Mifflin, 2005.

14. *The Flying Nun*. 1967-1970. ABC. Screen Gems Television. Directed by Jon C. Andersen. Written by Arthur Alsberg and Albert Beich. With Sally Field, Marge Redmond, and Madeleine Sherwood.

15. Gibson, William. *Pattern Recognition*. New York: G. P. Putnam's Sons, 2003.

16. —. *Spook Country*. New York: G. P. Putnam's Sons, 2007.

17. Gore, Al. *The Assault on Reason*. New York: Penguin Press, 2007.

18. Gubar, Susan. "'The Blank Page' and the Issues of Female Creativity." *Critical Inquiry* 8 (Winter 1981) 243-263.

19. Haraway, Donna. "A Cyborg Manifesto: Science, Technology, and Socialist-Feminism in the Late Twentieth Century." In *Simians, Cyborgs and Women: The Reinvention of Nature*. New York: Routledge, 1991, 149-181.

20. Hermes, Will. "The Tentacles of Foreigners." *Village Voice*. August 8-14, 2007, 58.

21. *Ita [Aber] in Her Time: 60 Years of Creativity*. New York. Yeshiva University Museum. June 24, 2007-October 14, 2007.

22. *It's A Mad, Mad, Mad, Mad World*. 1963. United Artists. Directed by Stanley Kramer. Written by William Rose and Tania Rose. With Spencer Tracy, Ethel Merman, and Milton Berle.

23. Itzkoff, Dave. "Spirits in the Material World." *New York Times Book Review*. August, 26, 2007, 12.

24. Kingston, Maxine Hong. *The Woman Warrior: Memoirs of a Girlhood Among Ghosts*. New York: Knopf, 1976.

25. Kurutz, Steven. "Not Buying It." *New York Times*. June 21, 2007, F1.

26. Langer, Cassandra. "Quiet Treasures: The Art of Ita Aber." *Ita In Her Time: 60 Years of Creativity*, exhibition brochure.

27. Le Guin, Ursula. *A Fisherman of the Inland Sea: Science Fiction Stories*. New York: HarperPrism, 1994.

28. —. "Another Story, or A Fisherman of the Inland Sea." *A Fisherman of the Inland Sea: Science Fiction Stories*. New York: HarperPrism, 1994.

29. —. *The Birthday of the World And Other Stories*. New York: HarperCollins, 2002.

30. —. *Changing Planes*. New York: Harcourt, 2003.

31. —. "Coming of Age in Karhide." In *New Legends*, ed. by Greg Bear and Martin Greenberg. New York: Random House, 1995.

32. —. *The Dispossessed: An Ambiguous Utopia*. New York: HarperPrism, 1974.

33. —. "Is Gender Necessary? Redux." 1987. In *The Language of the Night: Essays On Fantasy and Science Fiction*, ed. by Susan Wood. London: The Women's Press, 1989.

34. —. *The Left Hand of Darkness*. New York: Ace, 1969.

35. —. "The Matter of Seggri." *Crank*. 3 (Spring 1994).

36. —. "Mountain Ways." *Asimov's Science Fiction*. (August 1996).

37. —. "Saved By a Squirt." *The Guardian*. February 10, 2007.

38. —. "She Unnames Them." *Buffalo Gals and Other Animal Presences*. New York: New American Library, 1988.

39. —. "Solitude." *Magazine of Fantasy and Science Fiction*. 87 (December 1994).

40. —. "Sur." *The Compass Rose*. New York: Harper & Row, 1982.

41. —. *The Telling*. New York: Harcourt, 2000.

42. —. "Why Are Americans Afraid of Dragons?" *PNLA Quarterly*. 38 (Winter 1974), 14-18.

43. —. *The Word For World is Forest*. New York: Berkley, 1976.

44. Lessing, Doris. *The Cleft*. New York: HarperCollins, 2007.

45. Lessing, Doris. *Shikasta*: re, colonised planet 5: personal, psychological, historical documents relating to visit by Johor (George Sherban) emissary (grade 9) 87th of the period of the last days. New York: Knopf, 1979.

46. Olsen, Tillie. *Silences*. New York: Dell, 1978.

47. Rich, Frank. "The Clear Blue Sky." *New York Times Book Review*. May 27, 2007, 1, 8-9.

48. Rosenbloom, Stephanie. "Mommy Is Truly Dearest." *New York Times*. June 28, 2007. G1, G6.

49. Roth, Philip. *The Breast*. New York: Holt, Rinehart and Winston, 1972.

50. —. *The Plot Against America*. Boston: Houghton Mifflin, 2004.

51. Russ, Joanna. "Amor Vincit Foeminam: The Battle of the Sexes in Science Fiction." *Science Fiction Studies*. 7 (March 1980), 2-15.

52. —. *Extra(Ordinary) People*. New York: St. Martin's Press, 1984.

53. —. *The Female Man*. 1975. London: Women's Press, 1985.

54. —. "When It Changed." 1972. *Again, Dangerous Visions*. Book 1, ed. by Harlan Ellison. London: Pan, 1977. 271-79.

55. Sargent, Pamela. *The Shore of Women*. New York: Crown, 1986.

56. Scholes, Robert. "The Good Witch of the West." *Hollins Critic*. 11 (1974), 1-12.

57. Slattery, Brian Francis. *Spaceman Blues: A Love Story*. New York: Tor Books, 2007.

58. Slonczewski, Joan. *A Door into Ocean*. New York: Arbor House, 1986.

59. Solomon, Deborah. "Back From the Future." *New York Times Magazine*. August 19, 2007. 13.

60. Stevens, Carol. Email sent to Marleen S. Barr. December 6, 2007.

61. Tiptree, James, Jr. "Houston, Houston, Do You Read?" *Star Songs of An Old Primate*. New York: Ballantine, 1978.

62. —. "The Screwfly Solution." *Star Songs of An Old Primate*. New York: Ballantine, 1978.

63. —. "The Women Men Don't See." In *Warm Worlds and Otherwise*, ed. by Robert Silverberg. New York: Ballantine, 1975, 131-164.

64. Updike, John. *Couples*. New York: Knopf, 1968.

65. —. *Terrorist*. New York: Knopf, 2006.

Marleen S. Barr teaches in the Communication and Media Department of Fordham University. Her books include *Feminist Fabulation: Space/Postmodern Fiction*, *Genre Fission: A New Discourse Practice for Cultural Studies* and the humorous feminist academic novel *Oy Pioneer!* Barr has recently co-edited *Reading Science Fiction* with James Gunn and Matthew Candelaria.

A Wave in My Mind

Warren G. Rochelle

University of Mary Washington

I have written Ursula K. Le Guin more than one fan letter. I have even sent her copies of my dissertation on her fiction, then the dissertation-turned-into-a-book[1] (with the corrections she made), and most recently, my first and second novels. I finally met Ursula K. Le Guin in, of all places, Las Vegas,[2] in the Imperial Palace Hotel and Casino, in a brightly lit room, with yellow walls, a dark-colored patterned carpet, and chairs and tables in a configuration easily recognizable to anyone who has ever attended an academic conference. Pitchers of water and glasses littered the cloth-draped table where Le Guin sat; tall coffee urns and coffee paraphernalia occupied another table by the door. The talk was over, and the audience had divided into lines facing the guest authors, stacks of books in our hands. I brought more than we were supposed to, including a copy of *The Dispossessed* that I had had for a very long time—so long that the baroque cover was barely held together by tape. When my turn came, and she had finished signing all my books, I leaned over and took her hands and told her what I had been longing to do in person for years: "You changed my life."

I know: it's corny; it's a cliché. It just happens to be true. Reading Ursula K. Le Guin's fiction did change my life, and not just as a reader and a fan of science fiction and fantasy, but also as a writer, as a scholar and as a teacher. Her influence was and is profound and lasting. But, reading, writing, studying, and teaching are not discrete activities. They all connect; they overlap and blur together, and become part of a greater whole. These are recursive, not linear endeavors. They leap back; they spiral forward; one becomes the hinge for the other. But, for the sake of this essay, I want to consider each verb separately.

Reading logically comes first in this journey, and it is the reading of a particular journey that I find myself returning to, Shevek's, in *The Dispossessed*. *The Dispossessed* is not the only one of Le Guin's novels or stories with which I have fallen in love, and which I re-read on a regular basis: *A Wizard of Earthsea,* as I think about it, is probably the first of Le Guin's fiction I read, when I was a school librarian in North

---

[1] My dissertation, *Communities of the Heart: The Rhetoric of Myth in the Fiction of Ursula K. Le Guin,* was published by Liverpool University Press in 2001.

[2] Le Guin was one of the literary guests of honor at the Science Fiction Research Association 2005 annual conference, which met in Las Vegas, Nevada, that year.

Carolina, and in South America, back in the late 1970s and 1980s,[3] buying recommended books from various lists. There are passages in *Wizard* that still make me word-drunk, as when Ged tries to explain to Yarrow, Vetch's sister, something of the nature of power in their world:

> My name and yours, and the true name of the sun, or a spring of water, or an unborn child, all are syllables of the great word that is very slowly spoken by the shining of the stars. There is no other power. There is no other name. (164)

I come back often to *The Left Hand of Darkness,* certainly one of the most written about of Le Guin's novels, for its groundbreaking explorations of gender. Like *The Dispossessed,* it is a love story, and it is a story about story, about myth, and the nature of truth, and the truth in myth. As Genly Ai, one of *Left Hand's* two narrators, explains in the opening of his report as First Mobile on Gethen to the Stabiles on Ollul, "Truth is a matter of the imagination. The soundest fact may fail or prevail in the style of its telling" (1). And how many times, for that same reason, have I read, and taught, "Omelas"? "Unchosen Love," a story from later in Le Guin's career,[4] haunts me: the passion—awkward, painful, unchosen, overwhelming, drowning—of the love between Suord and Hadri, two men. I read it first somewhere in the middle of my own (albeit late) coming out process, and felt a fire of recognition. But, for brevity's sake, and because if I had to make a list of my most-loved and most-read books, *The Dispossessed* would be among the first, it is this novel's influence on me as a reader I want to consider.

It was in this book, in the story of this particular man, that Ursula K. Le Guin began to change my life, because with this story, I began to better understand my self—my sexuality, who I was, who I was becoming, who I am. As Le Guin argues in "Prophets and Mirrors: Science Fiction as a Way of Seeing," "The story—from *Rumplestiltskin* to *War and Peace*—is one of the basic tools invented by the human mind, for the purpose of gaining understanding" (112). When I read *The Dispossessed,* I fell in love. I fell in love with Shevek; I fell in love with the beauty of the novel's language, with its utopian ideas of human freedom; I fell in love with dusty, dry Anarres, where it does not matter who or how you

---

[3] A brief personal time line seems in order: UNC-Chapel Hill, BA, 1977; Columbia University, MS in Library Service, 1978; 1978-89, school librarian in North Carolina and in South America; 1989-98, MFA and PhD, UNC Greensboro, plus a one-year post-doc teaching fellowship; 1998-present, college and university teaching, Limestone College and the University of Mary Washington.

love. As I think about it, this examination of how reading and studying Le Guin changed my life *is* a love story.

Shevek is not an easy man to love, even as he is a man who attracts love, and who loves both passionately and intensely. His partner, Takver, and his friend, Bedap, and several others can attest to that, as ones who run up against the "uncompromising gentleness" and "[formidable] strength of Shevek's personality, unchecked by any self-consciousness or consideration of self-defense"[5] (Le Guin, *Dispossessed* 302). I met Shevek when I was young, in my late twenties or early thirties, I don't recall exactly, and I have gotten to know him well over the years, returning again and again to Anarres, to his double quests for his people and for himself, seeking his doubled public and private grails, and each time, his delight and fervor for his work. The poetry of his physics resonates, even though I was the high school kid who went to his guidance counselor to be sure it was OK *not* to take physics or chemistry before heading down the road to Carolina.[6] As Shevek puts it, "[Work is] my duty, it's my joy, it's the purpose of my whole life" (103). What greater joy could there be to love the work one is called to do, and to know that this work, the work that defines a person, is that of the "Creative Spirit," the divine madness of Plato?

I love Shevek for it and for showing it to me, so that when the Creative Spirit comes to me—mostly when I am writing—it is welcomed; it is wanted. It is as it was for Shevek when the numbers and equations came: "The delicate concentric mobiles hanging at different levels overhead moved with the introverted precision, silence, mystery of the organs of the body or the processes of the reasoning mind.... Gradually the sunlight entered, shifted across the papers on the table, across his hands on the papers, and filled the room with radiance. And he worked" (164).

I love Shevek for the same intense joy that he brought to those whom he loved and for doing what I could not do easily or without guilt or without pain and denial when I first met Shevek, admitting he loved a man. He and Bedap, his childhood friend, meet again three years after Shevek has gone on to Abbenay: "They had never written these three years. Their friendship was a boyhood one, past. Yet love was there:

[4] "Unchosen Love" first appeared in *Amazing Stories* (Fall 1994; vol. 69, no. 2), and then was published in the collection, *The Birthday of the World and Other Stories* (New York: HarperCollins, 2002).

[5] "Uncompromising gentleness" is a paraphrased version of a description of Shevek when he confronts Sabul's hypocrisy (*The Dispossessed* 102).

[6] *The Dispossessed,* like *The Lord of the Rings* trilogy, the *Chronicles of Narnia, A Wrinkle in Time,* and a few others, is a book I find myself re-reading at least once a year.

flamed up as from shaken coal" (142). They talk and talk and remember, and then, back in Shevek's room, number 46, they begin the conversation of what will eventually become Shevek's lifework outside physics, the renewal of the Odonian revolution; and they renew their friendship. This is a friendship that will sustain (and sometimes aggravate) Shevek for the rest of his life, reminding him of his humanity, that he must work against his "self-righteous[ness]" and his "damned pure conscience" (148). Yet, they can give each other this: "In the night one of them cried out aloud, dreaming. The other reached out his arm sleepily, muttering reassurance, and the blind warm weight of his touch outweighed all fear" (150-151).

Love is love is love. For a short time they partner, the sex a "reassertion of trust," a metaphor for the love of their friendship as men; it does not become a permanent part of their relationship; rather their fierce arguments, the engagement of their minds, the widening of Shevek's "hard puritanical conscience," are what matters. It is his friendship with Bedap that brings Shevek to Takver, his partner, who helps him see what it is he wants: "the bond. The real one. Body and mind and all the years of life. Nothing else. Nothing less" (158).

But two men loved—continued to love each other. It was there; someone wrote it; I read it. That mattered, too. I began to recognize myself. Loving someone of the same sex is accepted as so normal on Anarres that such love almost goes without commentary. One's sexuality just is. Today, in 2008, Anarresti acceptance of homosexuality and bisexuality as normal may not seem revolutionary to some. Twenty or thirty years ago, it was. American acceptance, on the other hand, is still a work-in-progress. My UNC Greensboro students, some years after my initial reading of the novel, didn't get it—to one earnest young man it was disgusting. For me, it was liberating.

I fell in love with Shevek's words—rather the beauty of Le Guin's language in this novel—and I fall in love with *The Dispossessed*'s language over and over, each time I read the book. This passage—when Shevek find Takver outside their mountain shelter, on a hiking tour Bedap organized—never ceases to amaze me:

> He found her on the steep slope, sitting among the delicate bushes of moonthorn that grew like knots of lace over the mountainsides, its stiff, fragile branches silvery in the twilight. In a gap between eastern peaks a colorless luminosity of the sky ¹ heralded moonrise. The stream was noisy in the silence of the high, bare hills. There was no wind, no cloud. The air above the mountains was like amethyst, hard, clear, profound. (156)

And, later, after Shevek and Takver have moved in together, Le Guin continues the weaving of their relationship with a silver thread: "Their naked arms and breasts were moonlit ... Shevek touched her silver arm with his silver hand, marveling at the warmth of the touch in that cool light" (166). I have never stopped wishing I had written those sentences, that I had woven that beautiful silver thread of words and moonlight.

But Anarres is not beautiful, it seems to Shevek, after his first glimpse of Urras, soon after his arrival, as he looks out the window of his university rooms:

> ... the land fell away to a broad valley. All of it was farmed, for the innumerable patches of green that colored it were rectangular. Even where the green faded into blue distance, the dark lines of lanes, hedgerows, or trees could still be made out, network as fine as the nervous system of a living body.... It was the most beautiful view Shevek had ever seen.... Compared to this, every scene Anarres could offer, even the Plain of Abbenay and the gorges of Ne Theras, was meager: barren, arid, and inchoate. (57-58)

I still love Anarres, though, no matter how meager or barren or hostile, because there, the promise born of the Odonian utopian impulse, has been kept, as Shevek explains in his speech to the Strikers in Nio Esseia, the capital of A-Io, on Urras:

> I am here because you see in me the promise, the promise we made two hundred years ago in this city—the promise kept. We have kept it, on Anarres. We have nothing but our freedom. We have nothing to give you but your own freedom. We have no law but the single principle of mutual aid between individuals. We have no government but the single principle of free association.... If it is Anarres you want, if it is the future you seek, then I tell you that you must come to it with empty hands.... You cannot buy the Revolution. You cannot make the Revolution. You can only be the Revolution. It is in your spirit or it is nowhere. (261-262)

Clearly the preferred way is that of Anarres, where, with the lushness of Urras removed, there is only the beauty of human beings. Yet despite the sound of her ax being ground for Anarres and Odonianism, Le Guin acknowledges the ambiguity and imperfection of being human, that we live in a world colored in shades of grey, and no choice comes without a price. Good and evil do co-exist, often in the same person, the same place. As Keng, the Terran Ambassador to Urras, tells Shevek:

> To me and to all my fellow Terrans who have seen the planet, Urras is the kindliest, most various, most beautiful of all the inhabited worlds. It is the world that comes as close as any could to Paradise.... I know it's full of evils, full of human injustice, greed, folly, waste. But it is also full of good, of beauty, of vitality, achievement. It is what a world should be! It is *alive,* tremendously alive—alive, despite all its evils, with hope. Is that not true? (303)

I want Urras to be like Anarres, to be a society that opposes power for the sake of power, and is built on mutual solidarity and responsibility and community. More to the point, I want Earth—Terra—to be that way. I am not a revolutionary, as much as I would like to be. Even knocking on doors for politics is not something I am comfortable doing. But, as Shevek ultimately changes his world with his theories and equations, I know that what changes I might effect will come in what I write and in what I teach about what I have read and studied. I want the hope of Anarres to be possible. I want what the "tall, soft-eyed girl" at Shevek's going-away party[7] says to be true: "Love is the true condition of human life" (53). Le Guin has shown me this can be part of what I write, what I teach, and that it can be part of my own life.

I wish I had written *The Dispossessed.* And when I have sat down to write, I can feel its weight—and the weight of Le Guin's fiction in general—in my own words and in my ideas. From Le Guin's words, her stories, her universes, there is a flow-through of ideas into my words, my stories, my universes. That "[the] story ... is one of the basic tools invented by the human mind, for the purpose of gaining understanding" has become part of my fictional credo. For Nick Gevers, in his review of my first novel, *The Wild Boy* (Golden Gryphon Press, 2001) to say my "literary craft recalls Le Guin" was indeed high praise. When looking at *The Wild Boy,* and my second novel, *Harvest of Changelings,*[8] and my third one, *The Golden Boy,*[9] what do I find as evidence of Le Guin's

[7] The party is given by Shevek's friends at Northsetting Institute, before he leaves for advanced studies in Abbenay. The "tall, soft-eyed girl" is probably Takver, but this is never made explicit.

[8] *Harvest of Changelings* was published in May 2007, also by Golden Gryphon Press.

[9] *The Golden Boy* is, as of yet, unpublished. As of this writing, it is being considered for publication by Golden Gryphon Press.

influence—or is that what I am looking for? Is it rather a synergy—the working together of her ideas, as I have absorbed them over the years, with mine to create something larger—and would my story itself be the larger, the greater of either individual effect?

What I find first in *The Wild Boy* is something I only discovered some years after the book's initial writing, which was as my MFA thesis for UNC Greensboro, back in 1991. Six years later, after a forced incubation, thanks to my doctoral coursework and dissertation,[10] I printed out *The Wild Boy* manuscript, took a deep breath, erased all the files, and then proceeded to re-enter the novel, re-reading, revising, rethinking, and reimagining it as I went. Graduate school for my doctorate had proved to be a time of intense self-examination and exploration that paralleled my academic exploration—therapy, introspection, experimentation. Eventually this brought me to a confrontation with self, with my sexuality. This process was well underway when I was reworking *The Wild Boy*. The story as a "tool for human understanding" proved to be my own, for understanding my self, for finally hearing the story I had been telling myself for years.

So what I find now in *The Wild Boy,* even as it is a tale of alien conquest, of humans bred as if they were animals for an alien project, of societal dysfunction and failure, is a love story between two males, albeit one is human, the other one of the alien conquerors, the Lindauzi. This is a tortured and complicated relationship—obviously!—and one of denial, rejection, betrayal, immense pain and grief, and eventual acceptance of a life bond that is finally seen as something far greater than either the human or the alien. While this relationship is played out over several years, in physical action, the real work, or lack of it, is interior. Shevek and Takver are not tortured, but their life bond is, ultimately, greater than the two of them and it is complicated and brings pain and grief, and much of the work both must do is interior. I had not even realized in 1991 just what sort of love story I was writing or how I had disguised it from myself, or that I had identified with the role the homosexual is often given in our society: alien, Other. I even missed the irony of making my ursine alien in *The Wild Boy* a double alien. Six years later, reading, and by then, studying a LOT of Le Guin, I realized how much of what I drew from her work and the freedom it gave me to imagine such a story, had become part of my new understanding of myself; and the power of story, especially one's own story, as it emerged, was transfigured into fiction in *The Wild Boy.*

[10] My dissertation, *Communities of the Heart: The Rhetoric of Myth in the Fiction of Ursula K. Le Guin,* after revision, was published by Liverpool University Press in February 2001. *The Wild Boy* was published the same year, in September.

Most noticeably, Le Guin's heroes, or rather protagonists, are often Outsiders, more specifically Outsider/Observers, something like anthropologists, as were her parents, particularly her father. Shevek finds himself an Outsider in his own culture and as the traveler from utopia, in another culture. In "Unchosen Love," when Suord takes him home to Meruo, Hadri becomes an Outsider: the one unlike the others both physically and temperamentally. Ged, as the country boy from Gont, is an Outsider on Roke as a result; on Gont, by his magical abilities. So I now find I have cast my own protagonists as Outsiders and almost by necessity, Observers. When he is captured by the aliens, Caleb, the title character in *The Wild Boy*, is placed in stark contrast to the tame humans. The aliens, as invaders and conquerors, by definition, are Outsiders. *Harvest*, while about many things, is a tale of the Other, the Outsider. Each of the four child-protagonists is an Outsider, marked as different. Malachi is half-fairy, and the other three are changelings, humans who have been changed by their fairy DNA. Hazel is marked by her extraordinary intelligence, and Russell and Jeff, both learning disabled, by their different intelligences. Russell and Jeff are also marked because one is physically abused, the other sexually. That (again found on re-reading) Russell and Jeff are gay, and as adolescents, just beginning to know what this means, seems to be perhaps the least remarkable difference—just not to them. By making them Outsiders, as Le Guin does, I find my characters gain a perspective on and understanding of their worlds that others don't have—that extra distance that lets one see connections and meanings invisible if one is too close.

Another key feature of Le Guin's fiction is her utopian impulse, an attempt at social critique and commentary, often through the thought experiment, the "what if" question. What if a society was a functioning egalitarian anarchy—without laws, without a government? How would it work, how would the trains run on time? How would partnerships— marriages, if you will—function when the only thing binding the people involved together is a personal promise in a society where the community is privileged over the individual, over the partners? Exploring these questions, Le Guin both uses and works against the traditional conventions of the utopian myth: the traveler, the isolated society juxtaposed against the writer's and/or the reader's society, the traveler's expositional exploration of utopia, the choice to stay or go, the acceptance or rejection of utopia. Shevek leaves Anarres, a utopia that is not paradisial. Reversing the generic conventions, he is first a traveler from utopia. Yet both Urras and Anarres could be seen as utopia or dystopia, depending on whose perspective is used. And eventually, Shevek returns to Anarres, from a utopia that is truly dystopian.

Le Guin uses a similar plot structure in *Always Coming Home:* Stone Telling leaves the valley, utopia, to travel to dystopia, the home of her father's people. There is far less ambiguity here: the country of the Dayao, the Condors, is a failed and collapsing patriarchy of oppression and exploitation; the valley, whatever its problems, is clearly the right choice. In both novels, the narrative is circular—there and back again, as the travelers, Shevek and Stone Telling, make the generically necessary choice of utopia, as flawed and as human as Le Guin's utopias are. In *The Dispossessed* there is the additional There and Back arc of time: Shevek growing up and coming of age, and the novel's present, Shevek's quest, involving his journey to Urras and his time there, working on his temporal theory, ending the isolation of his people, and renewing their revolution.

I found myself using a similar narrative structure of There and Back Again with time in *The Wild Boy.* The novel's present is, as it was for Shevek, the quest of the title character, Caleb, the wild boy, to find his missing father. The alternate plot, set in the past, is the story of Ilox, Caleb's father, growing up and coming of age and dealing with the truth of the alien society of the Lindauzi, which bred him. These aliens attempt to reorder and create a planned society for both humans and aliens—but this society fails. The Lindauzi are a dysfunctional species on a grand scale. Reviewers, seeing humans being bred as if they were dogs in an alien society, called the story a plea for animal rights. Well, not on purpose. I do want my stories to say *something,* to make a thematic point, to have metaphoric, even mythic weight. The influence of Le Guin's utopian impulse is powerful and profound, yet as with Shevek, the greater power of this impulse for me comes in the characters, their choices, the truths they must learn about themselves if they are to be themselves.

I haven't written a utopian novel. My third novel, *The Golden Boy,*[11] still an unpublished manuscript, is a dystopic coming out story. Even more so than in *The Wild Boy* I deliberately echoed the narrative structure of *The Dispossessed*: the novel's past is the story of Gavin's, the main character, coming of age; the present, his quest for survival as his society disintegrates around him. Gavin is part-fairy in an alternate skewed version of our own world, where the United States is not the land of the free, but is rather the Columbian Empire, an oppressive monarchy. In the Empire, Gavin, a hybrid, is proscribed; the very act that created him is illegal. He has hidden all his life. To compound his problems, he is also attracted to his own gender, not uncommon for fairies. And

---

[11] The original premise of the novel was this: fairies are fairies.

like many oppressive states, the Empire does not discriminate in its persecution of minorities, of Others: being gay—a term not invented in this world—is illegal, too.

Gavin learns powerful truths about love and his body—and as Le Guin has done with Shevek, idea is embodied in character (Rochelle, *Communities* 76). As Isidri in "Another Story, or A Fisherman of the Inland Sea," tells Hideo, "Love has a right to be spoken. And you have a right to know that somebody loves you. That somebody has loved you, could love you. We all need to know that. Maybe it's what we need most" (161).[12] He must learn this to become fully human, as he must learn what Rakam learns in "A Woman's Liberation": "It is in our bodies that we lose or begin our freedom, in our bodies that we accept or end our slavery" (208).[13] And letting such truths become part of my fiction, and knowing that it is OK for this to be so, is just one of my lessons and legacies from Ursula K. Le Guin. Challenging the "unquestioned assumptions," as Le Guin discusses in her essay of the same name,[14] has become/is becoming—as such challenges tend to be works-in-progress—part of the stories I want to tell, and am trying to tell.

For these challenges I am finding the best mode for me, as for Le Guin, is science fiction and fantasy, especially fantasy. In her essay, "The Child and the Shadow," Le Guin argues that "fantasy is the natural, the appropriate language for the recounting of the spiritual journey and the struggle of good and evil in the soul" (64).[15] She also argues, in an often-cited essay, "Myth and Archetype in Science Fiction," that science fiction "is the mythology of the modern world—or one of its mythologies," and that myth "is an expression of one of the several ways the human being, body/psyche, perceives, understands, and relates to the world" (69). True, as she explains, science fiction is a "highly intellectual art form, and mythology is a nonintellectual mode of apprehension," but science fiction—and I would add fantasy—"does use the mythmaking faculty to apprehend the world we live in" (69-70). Not that "the presence of

[12] "Another Story or A Fisherman of the Inland Sea" is a story in *A Fisherman of the Inland Sea: Science Fiction Stories* (New York: HarperCollins, 1994).

[13] "A Woman's Liberation" is a story in *Four Ways to Forgiveness* (New York: HarperCollins, 1995).

[14] "Unquestioned Assumptions" is included in Le Guin's essay collection, *The Wave in the Mind* (Boston: Shambhala, 2004). She discusses "four common varieties of the Unquestioned Assumption" and "[explores] a fifth one in more detail" (241). The four common varieties are: "We're all men; We are all White; We're all straight; [and] We're all Christian;" the fifth one, "we're all young."

[15] Both essays are in the collection, *Language of the Night: Essays on Fantasy and Science Fiction*, revised edition (New York: HarperCollins, 1989).

mythic material" is enough. True myth, Le Guin argues, is one of the connections between "idea and value, sensation with intuition, cortex with cerebellum ... the conscious and the unconscious" (73)—between the rational and the irrational. Or, to put this another way: to write about a quest, whether it is Shevek's double quest for a public and personal grail, or Ged's in *A Wizard of Earthsea,* to undo the release of an evil shadow, is at once to write about a particular quest and to write of the reader's quest and of the quest all humans must take, the choices all humans must make in how to live their lives. To write about a father is to write about my father and to write about fathers. This recognition is mythmaking, as Le Guin argues:

> Writers who draw not upon the words and thoughts of others but upon their own thoughts and their own deep being will inevitably hit upon common material.... "Yes, of course!" says I, the reader recognizing myself, my dreams, my nightmares. The characters, figures, images, motifs, plots, events of the story may be obvious parallels, even seemingly reproductions of the material of myth and legend. There will be—openly in fantasy, covertly in naturalism—dragons, heroes, quests, objects of power, and so forth. (75)

Yes. This is part of the stories I want to tell, as it is part of the stories Le Guin has told and continues to tell.

Have I achieved mythmaking as Le Guin has done, even as she questions the myth's original premises, its original characters and structures, as she does in *Tehanu* and *The Other Wind?* I don't know. Good and evil, yes, that is the great theme of fantasy, and an examination of this struggle is part of what motivated my second novel, *Harvest of Changelings.* Its original premise, that all fairy tales are true, is recognition of the power and force of these tales, and the myths from which they came. I draw from Celtic mythology, fairy lore, the ghost stories of North Carolina, from the mythos of my childhood, my own family narrative, and from the idea that story and story telling is essential to being human. To touch the mythic, to write it—my own reimagining and revisioning—is my personal quest. That I aspire to do so is perhaps one of Le Guin's most profound influences on my creative work.

As Le Guin's influence has overlapped from my reading to my creative writing, it has quite naturally permeated my other work. To understand and explore the connections between science fiction and myth, and Le Guin's own mythmaking in particular, is, and has been, a central feature of my scholarship. In *Communities of the Heart: The Rhetoric of Myth in the Fiction of Ursula K. Le Guin,* I examined two specific myths, the Hero and the Quest, or the Monomyth, and the Myth of Utopia. As the title indicates, I looked at how Le Guin has used each myth rhetorically. She has reimagined and reinterpreted both myths, and she has honored the truth of each myth. *The Dispossessed* is about both, the Monomyth and Utopia.[16] Shevek is on a personal and a public quest: to find the general temporal formula, his intellectual equals, to bring his isolated people back into the greater human community, and to force his people to remember who they are, children of a revolution that must be renewed to remain true. The grails of his quest are doubled as is his quest; the conventions of utopia are inverted and questioned, as Shevek travels *from* a utopia that is anything but perfect and far short of the traditional earthly paradise.

The first three *Earthsea* novels, the original trilogy, can also be read as an extended quest and as the biography of the protagonist, Ged, the Archmage. The Hero is male, and such markers of tradition, in Campbellian theory, as the unusual circumstances of his childhood, a wise old man mentor, an animal guide, confrontation with a goddess, are all easily discerned. His quests are public; they become part of the mythos of the archipelago. He fights dragons and evil spirits; he goes into the realm of the dead. Yet, Ged is a dark-skinned man. The bad guys in his universe, the barbarian Kargs, are white. The assumptions of the default white, Western reader are challenged and questioned; readers are forced to see just what their automatic defaults are, and why they are exclusionary and can lead to injustice. In *Tehanu,* as Le Guin explains in her long essay, *Earthsea Revisioned,* the Monomyth is turned on its head. Ged has lost his power; Tenar, a woman who refused power to be a farmer's wife and mother, is the narrator, the Hero, if you will. There are dragons, but they prove to be allies. Brave deeds are done, but many are small and private and will never become part of any mythos, save that of Ged and Tenar. The feminine is as privileged as the masculine.

Nevertheless, in whatever version, the inherent truths of each myth do not change: each life is called to the adventure of being human; each society is called to freedom, to improve. And the energy, the power of the mythic, even as it is reimagined and reinterpreted and retold—as it must be for each generation, each people, each person—has become

[16] For the sake of brevity, I will focus on just *The Dispossessed* and *Earthsea* here, but *Always Coming Home,* Le Guin's second utopian novel, is equally—if not more so—rhetorical than *The Dispossessed,* and again, she is playing with the conventions of the genre, such as having two travelers, two narrators, not the traditional one. Both are feminist utopias, with *Always Coming Home* a more realized and deeper exploration of feminist utopian thinking and philosophy.

part of the energy of my scholarly work. Here, pay attention to this, see what she is doing, this is why it is important. Read these stories as stories, and listen to what they are telling you, listen to the author's argument, listen.

So I tell my students when I teach Le Guin. I have used her work in several classes. As a utopian parable, "The Ones Who Walk Away from Omelas," a frequently anthologized story, is ideal for teaching argument in a first-year composition class, which is how I used it in English 102[17] at UNC Greensboro, as a graduate student and as a post-doctoral teaching fellow. It is a disturbing story but disturbing students is what teachers should do: by asking them to identify and question their assumptions, to *see* the water they swim in. From the beginning I have included Le Guin on the required reading list for the science fiction literature I teach at the University of Mary Washington (UMW). Partly, of course, because I enjoy rereading and discussing her work. And because, for those students who are not as familiar with the genre, I want to expose them to what is considered best in the field, to at least some of those writers who have led the field, influenced many, many others, broken barriers, written seminal works. Le Guin fits all of these categories. *The Dispossessed* has proven to be a highly teachable work of utopian fiction, a subgenre of science fiction I consider essential for understanding the genre as a whole. And, as does so much science fiction, it makes the students think: about feminism, about power, about equality, gender, sexuality. As Le Guin explains in her recent essay, "A War Without End":

> Even the novels *The Dispossessed* and *Always Coming Home*, in which I worked out more methodically than usual certain variations on the uses of power, which I preferred to those that obtain in our world—even those are as much efforts to subvert as to display the ideal of an attainable social plan which would end injustice and inequality once and for all…. To me the most important thing is not to offer any specific hope of betterment but, by offering an imagined but persuasive alternative reality, to dislodge my mind and so the reader's mind, from the lazy, timorous habit of thinking the way we live now is the only way people can live…. Fantasy and science fiction in their very conception offer alternatives to the reader's present, actual world

[17] Like many schools, UNC Greensboro has a two-course sequence in first-year composition. When I was there, 101 primarily covered the foundational skills for college writing; 102, argumentation and research. Using "Omelas" in this context is, of course, hardly original.

.... The imaginative fiction I admire presents alternatives to the status quo which not only question the ubiquity and necessity of extant institutions, but enlarge the field of social possibility and moral understanding. (218, 219-220)

And once readers begin to think, to consider these alternatives to their "present, actual world," the "field of social possibility and moral understanding," that world—our world—can be changed.

The Left Hand of Darkness is also frequently on my SF reading list. Like *The Dispossessed,* this novel forces students to question their assumptions about gender, about masculinity and femininity, and just what shapes our lives and how. Teaching this novel also lets me make plain the idea of science fiction as a modern myth, as the novel is as much about storytelling and myth as it is about gender. That our ideas of gender are often social constructs can be disturbing, as are such questions as what influences us most, who we are as men or women, or where we are, in a desert, in the ice. What does it mean to say, "Truth is as matter of the imagination"? Both novels help make students realize what I consider essential to understanding modern science fiction: that it is often social commentary and critique, explicitly so, or not. As Le Guin has said, "all fiction has ethical, political, and social weight" (quoted in Rochelle, *Communities* 1).[18]

For my UMW fantasy literature course, I often pair *Wizard* and *Tehanu.* The students, alas, generally find *Tehanu* slow, to use one of their kinder adjectives. So be it. But what I want them to learn, and strive for, with various degrees of success, is to see a handful of things about fantasy. Contemporary fantasy clearly owes a great deal to Tolkien and Lewis, especially Tolkien, as Le Guin acknowledges more than once. But the genre is more than Tolkien and C.S. Lewis, and it is much more than the ubiquitous Tolkien clones set in pseudo-medieval worlds. Fantasy, like science fiction, has the potential to show the reader his or her own world in a different light, from a different perspective, with different metaphors. Assumptions can and are often questioned. The Monomyth is true, but to remain so, it must be reimagined and retold. The Hero does have a thousand faces, and some of them are female faces, some are dark-skinned, some are gay, some are old, and some do not carry swords. Pairing these novels helps students to see these things, despite their lack of appreciation for *Tehanu.*

---

[18] Here, obviously, I am citing my own use of this quote, in *Communities of the Heart.* I have looked and looked for the original source in Le Guin's work and cannot find it. If anyone out there knows, please, let me know.

On this point, the title of my UMW senior seminar on Le Guin: The Rhetorical Fiction of Ursula K. Le Guin, seems to say it all. I tell my students that every essay has to have a *So what?* The writer has to make a point, and restating the thesis is not making a point. So, here and now, after this journey, so what?

Yes, Le Guin is "one of the most important speculative writers of the twentieth and twenty-first centuries" and her thought experiments have indeed "[challenged] many of our culture's most comfortable preconceived notions about gender, heterosexuality, monogamy, patriarchy, progress, organized religion, and capitalism" (Levy, Lindow 349). But, there are other "most important speculative fiction" writers whose thought experiments have challenged our preconceived notions. And Le Guin is not the only writer who has influenced me as a reader, a writer, a scholar, and a teacher. She is not the only writer that I could say has changed my life, how I see the world, how I make sense of the world. My literary pantheon, in no particular order, and from different times in my life, would include Tolkien, Lewis, L'Engle, Alexander, Susan Cooper, Julian May, Robert Heinlein, Neil Gaiman.... And lest you think I am so one-sided as to read only science fiction and fantasy, or only fiction: Faulkner, John McPhee, William Least Heat Moon, Annie Dillard, Ricky Bragg.... I read a lot; I always have.

I am also not so one-sided as to read Le Guin's work with rose-colored glasses. There are flaws. The sounds of those grinding axes can become louder than the story; she does cross into polemic. *Always Coming Home* is an example of this. But to delineate flaws is not my purpose here.

I wrote my dissertation on Le Guin. I have published several essays on Le Guin, one recently in a special Le Guin issue of *Extrapolation* (Winter 2006). There are people who describe me as a Le Guin scholar; I have described myself that way. I hear Le Guinian echoes in my fiction; critics have confirmed I am not just hearing what I want to hear. By reading her work, I have been better able to articulate my own purpose in writing, determine my own story to tell. By reading her work, by studying it, I have recognized myself. By reading her work, I have begun to understand the power of story, that, "Having the real though limited power to put established institutions into question, imaginative literature has also the responsibility of power. The storyteller is the truthteller" (Le Guin, "A War Without End" 219). I want to be able to do this, in my fiction (and, yes, in my criticism). The story comes first, but it must tell the truth, even, as Le Guin says in the introduction to *The Left Hand of Darkness,* while the story lies: "I talk about the gods, I an atheist. But I am an artist too, and therefore a liar. Distrust everything I say. I am telling the truth" (153).

Le Guin lies; she tells the truth. She insists her readers look, into a mirror, into themselves, into their world, into the water they swim in, and she does so in beautiful, lyrical prose. She gives her readers characters with whom they will fall in love, characters who are human and fallible, in whom they—we—I—can recognize myself. Reading Le Guin can, as Virginia Woolf says in a letter to Vita Sackville-West, make one "crammed with ideas, and visions, and so on," which "can't [be] dislodged, for lack of the right rhythm." But, "a sight, an emotion, creates this wave in the mind," that, "as it breaks and tumbles in the mind, makes words to fit it"—a story, a place, a character, a vision (Epigraph, *The Wave in the Mind* vii). What am I trying to say, here, in my conclusion? That Le Guin is a wave in my mind? Yes. That reading and studying her work has been part of what made my words fit? Yes. That, as I said in the beginning of this essay, reading Ursula K. Le Guin's fiction changed my life, and not just as a reader and a fan of science fiction and fantasy, but also as a writer, as a scholar and as a teacher? Yes. Her influence is profound and lasting?

Yes, again.

I am still in love.

Works Cited

1. Le Guin, Ursula K. *The Birthday of the World and Other Stories.* New York: HarperCollins, 2002.
2. —. "The Child and the Shadow." *The Language of the Night: Essays on Fantasy and Science Fiction.* Ed. Susan Wood, Revised Edition. New York: HarperCollins, 1992. 54-67.
3. —. *The Dispossessed.* New York: Harper & Row, 1974.
4. —. *Earthsea Revisioned.* Cambridge, MA: Children's Literature New England, 1993.
5. —. *A Fisherman of the Inland Sea: Science Fiction Stories.* New York: HarperCollins, 1994.
6. —. "Introduction to *The Left Hand of Darkness.*" *The Language of the Night: Essays on Fantasy and Science Fiction.* Ed. Susan Wood, Revised Edition. New York: HarperCollins, 1992. 150-154.
7. —. *The Left Hand of Darkness.* New York: Walker, 1969.
8. —. "Myth and Archetype in Science Fiction." *The Language of the Night: Essays on Fantasy and Science Fiction.* Ed. Susan Wood, Revised Edition. New York: HarperCollins, 1992. 68-77.

9. —. "Prophets and Mirrors: Science Fiction as a Way of Seeing."
    Living Light: A Christian Education Review 7 (Fall 1970): 111-
    121.
10. —. "Unquestioned Assumptions." *The Wave in the Mind: Talks
    and Essays on the Writer, the Reader, and the Imagination.*
    Boston: Shambhala, 2004. 240-249.
11. —. "A War without End." *The Wave in the Mind: Talks and
    Essays on the Writer, the Reader, and the Imagination.* Boston:
    Shambhala, 2004. 211-222.
12. —. *A Wizard of Earthsea.* New York: Bantam Books, 1968.
13. Levy, Michael, and Sandra J. Lindow. "Moving Towards Marriage:
    A Polygamous, Polyandrous Selection of Le Guin Criticism."
    Extrapolation 47.3 (Winter 2006): 349-350.
14. Rochelle, Warren. *Communities of the Heart: The Rhetoric of
    Myth in the Fiction of Ursula K. Le Guin.* Liverpool, UK: Liv-
    erpool University Press, 2001.
15. —. *The Golden Boy.* Unpublished novel, 2006.
16. —. *Harvest of Changelings.* Urbana, IL: Golden Gryphon Press,
    2007.
17. —. *The Wild Boy.* Urbana, IL: Golden Gryphon Press, 2001.

Warren Rochelle is an Associate Professor of English at the University of Mary Washinton, where he teaches classes in creative writing, science fiction and fantasy, and the teaching of writing. In addition to various articles and reviews on science fiction and fantasy, he is the author of *Communities of the Heart: The Rhetoric of Myth in the Fiction of Ursula K. Le Guin* (Liverpool UP, 2001). Golden Gryphon published his two novels, *The Wild Boy* (2001) and *Harvest of Changelings* (2007). He is presently at work on the sequel to *Harvest, The Called.*

Review of *The New Utopian Politics of Ursula K. Le Guin's* The Dispossessed

Mike Cadden
Missouri Western State University

The New Utopian Politics of Ursula K. Le Guin's The Dispossessed.
Laurence Davis and Peter Stillman, Eds. Lexington Books, 2005. 324
pp. ISBN: 13: 9780739110867

Laurence Davis' introduction points out that this is the "first ever collection of original essays devoted to Le Guin's novel" *The Dispossessed.* Even more specific, it is also the first ever collection of essays on the utopian politics in that one novel. One would think that 324 pages on this one aspect of this one novel by this one Le Guin might get a little thin; but I was happily surprised. It's worth noting that a reader of this text might not read all sixteen essays back-to-back in a relatively short time, but even in doing that I found the essays distinct from one another. Yes, one runs into the "problem" of reading the same passages cited again and again, but those citations don't support the same arguments, which allows the reader to see the versatility of the novel. Davis and Stillman must have seen, and rightly, that this one novel could sustain such a weighty and sustained treatment without being reduced to a few points. In fact, this alone argues well Plaw's observation on the two-hundred eighty-fourth page of this book that *The Dispossessed* isn't didactic at all but persuasive and pluralistic—a point well understood, I think, by this point in the book, assuming the reader has gotten to Plaw's point after first reading the previous fifteen essays in the book, as I had (slave to linearity that I am). Back in the introduction, Davis promises this outcome when he writes that "the editors of this volume ... do not pretend to offer a final, definitive analysis of the politics of *The Dispossessed.*" The book offers and celebrates ambiguity and balance.

In fact the book's controlling idea is balance. Although there are few essays that privilege Annares over Urras as the better place, most of these essayists don't assume that the ambiguous utopia named is necessarily one of the planets in particular. This collection, from its structural layout to the individual essays' contents, is a study of balance that recognizes the unproblematic ambiguity of the novel. All of the essays in the collection come to terms with Le Guin's demand through the novel that the two planets, through the character of Shevek, are in dialogue with each other. The fact that a character has to come from one of the two places, necessarily, has somehow lead other readers to conclude that this planet of origin is the endorsed planet, missing the point, of course, that Shevek's forebears came from Urras, who themselves came from Hain (as that story goes). There are no easy disassociations for characters in this or any Le Guin novel.

The structure of the book is almost compulsively balanced. A few essays get dangerously close to an either/or position, but the book mostly pursues political ideas that in some way acknowledge the ambiguity of the novel and its balanced structure. The book starts with an introduction by Davis in which he explains the contribution of the essays individually and the book as a whole in its offering a focus on "the radical political ramifications of the novel," which have been "woefully under explored" (ix). The book is then set up in four sections. The first and last are titled "Open–Ended Utopian Politics," each of which has two essays. The middle four sections ("Post–Consumerist Politics," "Anarchist Politics," "Temporal Politics," and "Revolutionary Politics," respectively) each has three essays. To balance out the collection by offering a parallel to the introduction, there is a "response" by Ursula K. Le Guin. The book is the Heya–if from *Always Coming Home*, perfectly hinged. What is most impressive is that, with the possible exception of the "Revolutionary Politics" section, the essays are clearly related to those headings and each other, making the sections somehow inevitable. This, I think, is testimony to good editing.

The first essay of the collection gives us a glimpse of a foundational assumption of all of the other essays. Davis' claim that despite the need for utopia to be static, we have in *The Dispossessed* a *dynamic* utopia. This claim for dynamism is seen in the subsequent essays' demand for balanced comparison rather than debate, and a balanced comparison that doesn't lead to simple answers, for balance isn't a problem to be solved. Simon Stow follows Davis with the assertion that the journey between worlds creates a comparative method of analysis and, unlike other utopias, uses two worlds rather than just the one fictional world to examine utopia and, as a result, provides us with a method for critical reflection (43). Douglas Spencer directly calls dualism into question, and points out that Shevek's experience in the two worlds regarding austerity (Anarres) and excess (Urras) show us a model for achieving grace through restraint (105). Dan Sabia considers the balance between individual needs and societal needs in the utopic vision of the novel: "between altruism and selfishness lies a proper or enlightened sense of self-interest, the kind of human motive that, just perhaps, can serve as the basis for reconciling individual and community" (120). Winter Elliott also considers the balance of individual and society and observes that the "book is not ultimately as interested in which world has the best, or even better, political system as it is in Shevek's role within these worlds" (150). Mark Tunick claims in his essay that "the political solution may be a dialectical mediation between conflicting ideals" (137). *"The Dispossessed* rejects one-sided and simplistic ideals that can lead only to hypocrisy" (142). For Ellen Rigsby, the issue of balance is between cyclical and linear time, considering them alongside the balance of the different functions of sequence and simultaneity—key terms of the physics of the book. "Willful human acts create linear time out of cyclical time" (171) and either alone is a trap. Jennifer Rodgers shows that in Shevek there is a balance between the "the personal journey toward fulfillment with the community journey toward utopia, uniting the two through understanding of time that is linear and cyclical, as well as moral, ethical, and social" (181). Tony Burns balances Shevek's constructivism and objectivism. Everett Hamner examines the use of walls regarding their dual function of providing freedom *from* something as well as *for* something (222). Bülent Somay claims that Le Guin is "heterodox" in her approach to utopianism and that "Le Guin's expression 'ambiguous utopia,' then, was some kind of oxymoron, ascribing 'two-ness' to something monolithic" (235). "Resolving conflict," Somay says, "by allowing one side to win absolute victory over the other can only end up in the destruction of both" (239). The claim for ambiguity, dynamism, and balance is rounded out in the last section with Claire Curtis positing that "capturing the nature of that ambiguity is essential for understanding the framework for a skeptical utopia" (265). Avery Plaw insists in the volume's last essay that the balanced presentation in the novel regarding what each society offers that the other does not is vital in our understanding the novel (291).

Ursula Le Guin's "A Response, by Ansible, from Tau Ceti" concludes the commentary and serves as a ready–made first book review packaged with the book. In this response she expresses relief that the essays in this collection "are not about an idea of the book. They are about the book" (306). A book is never reducible to one idea, nor a character to an author's position, Le Guin argues, so when Tony Burns says that he assumes "that the political beliefs expressed by Shevek in *The Dispossessed* are also those of Le Guin, and that they reflect a commitment on her part to some form of anarchism" (197), we can probably envision Le Guin's response. Le Guin goes on to qualify herself on the function of criticism: "If fiction is how it says what it says, then useful criticism is what shows you how fiction says what it says" (306). I agree that this collection achieves that through a careful examination of the novel's structure. This text would be useful in a course on literary criticism for just that reason, though one won't find an essay here that finds fault with the novel, which is something worth pointing out.

Le Guin complains that "a good many of the writers of this volume treat *The Dispossessed* as if it stood alone in my work. This ahistorical approach seems odd, since the book has been around so long, and it isn't an anomaly among my other works" (307). If one approaches the volume with the expectation that Le Guin, rather than this one book, is the ultimate subject, then it would be odd not to find many references to her other work, but I think this isn't Davis and Stillman's mission. The cover of the book might understandably give one the impression that Le Guin is the subject, though the marketing department at Lexington Books likely decided to make Le Guin's name so prominent and *The Dispossessed* so much less so in order to reach a wider audience. The book is not about Le Guin's work generally but about how this one novel says what it says about utopia and the politics of utopia, and that is more than enough.

Mike Cadden is Professor of English and Chair of the Department of English, Foreign Languages and Journalism at Missouri Western State University. He is the author of *Ursula K. Le Guin Beyond Genre: Fiction for Children and Adults* (Routledge, 2005)